**FIGHTING FOR
TOTAL PERSON UNIONISM**

THE WORKING CLASS IN AMERICAN HISTORY

Editorial Advisors
James R. Barrett, Julie Greene, William P. Jones,
Alice Kessler-Harris, and Nelson Lichtenstein

A list of books in the series appears at the end of this book.

Fighting for Total Person Unionism

Harold Gibbons, Ernest Calloway, and Working-Class Citizenship

Robert Bussel

UNIVERSITY OF ILLINOIS PRESS
URBANA, CHICAGO, AND SPRINGFIELD

© 2015 by the Board of Trustees
of the University of Illinois
All rights reserved

1 2 3 4 5 C P 5 4 3 2 1
♾ This book is printed on acid-free paper.

Library of Congress Cataloging-in-Publication Data
Bussel, Robert
Fighting for total person unionism : Harold Gibbons, Ernest Calloway,
and working-class citizenship / Robert Bussel.
    pages   cm. — (The working class in American history)
Includes bibliographical references and index.
ISBN 978-0-252-03949-2 (hardcover : alk. paper) —
ISBN 978-0-252-08104-0 (pbk. : alk. paper) —
ISBN 978-0-252-09760-7 (e-book)
1. Gibbons, Harold J. 2. Calloway, Ernest. 3. International Brotherhood
of Teamsters, Chauffeurs, Stablemen, and Helpers of America. 4. Labor
leaders—United States—Biography. 5. Working class—United States—
History. 6. Equality—United States—History. 7. Labor movement—
United States—History. I. Title.
HD6508.5.B87   2015
331.88092'273—dc23   2015005245
[B]

CONTENTS

Acknowledgments   vii
Introduction   1
1. Coming Up the Hard Way   9
2. "Apostles of a New Order"   16
3. Able and Militant Fighters for Workers   26
4. "A Bunch of Fellows Who Have Taken the Declaration of Independence Seriously"   39
5. "The Most Powerful Union in America"   55
6. "Those Fellows Back There Actually Hate You"   71
7. "The Other Sixteen Hours"   85
8. "A Hell of a Whipping"   102
9. "A Planned Social Revolution"   121
10. "A Trade Union Oriented War on the Slums"   141
11. "Fuck Him, He Wasn't With Us"   160
Epilogue   179
Notes   185
Bibliography   221
Index   237

Illustrations follow page 120

ACKNOWLEDGMENTS

To paraphrase the words of the old Beatles' song, I got by on this project with a lot of help from my friends, both old and new. A stellar supporting cast played an integral role in making this book possible, and I am deeply grateful for the assistance that many people offered during my years of work on this project.

Archivists are among the best friends that historians can have, and I was blessed from the outset to work with some of the best in the business. At Southern Illinois University Edwardsville (SIUE), where the Harold Gibbons Collection is located, Steve Kerber and Amanda Bahr-Evola functioned as savvy guides and generous hosts, responded patiently to my numerous requests, and expressed continuing interest in the progress of my work. Across the Mississippi River at the University of Missouri-St. Louis (UMSL), Kenn Thomas shared his compilation of Ernest Calloway's writings and helped me appreciate Calloway's seminal role in both Teamsters Local 688 and the black freedom struggle in St. Louis. Kenn's colleagues Susan Beatty, Linda Belford, and William Fischetti welcomed me during my many visits and facilitated my exploration of Calloway's papers and other relevant collections. I am also indebted to Jennifer Roberts at SIUE and Nancy McIlvaney at UMSL for creating the digital photographs that appear in the book.

Two other archivists provided valuable assistance during the latter stages of my research. Tom Connors helped me find significant documents at the Teamsters Archives housed at George Washington University. At the National Archives in Washington, Kate Mollan combed the records of the McClellan Committee's investigation of labor corruption prior to my visit, enabling me to discover pertinent materials quickly and efficiently. Closer to home, Tom Stave, head of the document center at the University of Oregon's Knight Library, directed me to important sources that were vital to my research.

Twenty-five people agreed to be interviewed for this project, and I am grateful for their willingness to discuss their relationships with Harold Gibbons and Ernest Calloway. I am especially indebted to Patrick Gibbons, Larry Gibbons, and Elizabeth Vasquez for sharing memories about their father. Regrettably, Charles Oldham, Jerry Tucker, and Margaret Bush Wilson died before this project was completed. Each offered many valuable insights, along with stirring examples of their personal courage and commitment to the cause of social justice.

At the University of Oregon, I have benefited from strong collegial support. Marcus Widenor, my colleague at the Labor Education and Research Center, gave the manuscript a thoughtful reading and repeatedly allowed me to tap his extensive knowledge of labor history. Dan Tichenor, senior fellow at the Wayne Morse Center for Law and Politics, and Jill Harrison, a professor in the Sociology Department, organized gatherings of teachers and students that provided me with useful feedback. I am also grateful to senior vice-provosts Russell Tomlin and Doug Blandy for encouraging me to take time from my administrative duties and complete this project.

Several fellow historians graciously assisted me in important ways. Robert Korstad enhanced my understanding of Ernest Calloway's involvement in Operation Dixie and the critical R.J. Reynolds campaign. Clarence Lang sent me copies of materials he compiled during his impressive research on the black freedom struggle in St. Louis, and David Witwer shared useful documents from his path-breaking study of the Teamsters Union.

Portions of the book have previously appeared in other publications. Parts of Chapter 7 are taken from my essay "Worker-Citizens at the Community Bargaining Table: The St. Louis Teamsters' Community Stewards' Program in the 1950s," which appeared in *Life and Labor in the New New South*, edited by Robert H. Zieger, University Press of Florida, 2012. Chapter 10, titled "A Trade Union Oriented War on the Slums," includes material first published in an article by the same name in *Labor History*, Vol. 44, No. 1, 2003, 49–67. I appreciate being granted permission to draw on this work and thank Meredith Babb, director of the University Press of Florida, and Craig Phelan, editor of *Labor History*, for their cooperation.

Rosemary Feurer and an anonymous reader for the University of Illinois Press offered numerous suggestions that have found their way into this book. Laurie Matheson, editor-in-chief at the University of Illinois Press, has displayed professionalism, patience, and support throughout the entire review and publication process. I deeply appreciate the many kindnesses that she has extended since I first submitted the manuscript. I am also deeply grateful to Tracy Petersen for her skilled copyediting and Linnea Dwyer for capably indexing the book.

Three historians, all of whom I count as trusted friends, read the penultimate version of the completed manuscript. For nearly twenty-five years, Nick Salvatore has both championed and critiqued my work, and once again I have benefited from his inimitable version of tough love. Joe McCartin offered equal portions of sage advice and strong encouragement. A model of engaged scholarship and thoughtful activism, he sets a standard that both challenges and inspires me. I am especially grateful to the late Robert Zieger, who read the manuscript just months before his untimely death. In addition to being an exemplary scholar and activist, Bob was a loyal and generous friend whose memory I hope this work will honor.

Bruce Smith has been my best friend and sounding board for more than forty years. His loyalty, comradeship, and lively intelligence have sustained me during this project and throughout the course of my life and career.

I owe my most profound debts to my family. My brother, David Bussel, recently completed his undergraduate degree in history at age 61. His work ethic, perseverance, and passion for history reinforced my commitment to keep working and get things right. My aunt and cousin, Fay and Michael Marker, provided warm hospitality during my many visits to St. Louis. They introduced me to the rich cultural and culinary delights of their adopted city and were always willing to listen to the latest news of my archival discoveries. Next time I'm in town, Auntie, the toasted raviolis and Ted Drewes frozen custards are on me!

My daughters, Lily and Ayla, came of age during the writing of this book. Their energy, enthusiasm, and adventurous spirits are infectious, along with their well-honed senses of humor that have provided much needed comic relief at critical times.

My wife, Jewel Nelson, reminds me of the selfless star athlete whose example inspires other players to elevate their games. For the last thirty years, her unwavering faith, honesty, and love have lifted and challenged me. This book is a small expression of my gratitude for her indispensable place in my life.

I dedicate this book to my parents, Beatrice Shefsky Bussel and Norman Bussel. Regrettably, my mother died just as I began this project. However, her profound belief in fair play, her intense curiosity about people, and her passion for storytelling continue to influence my work and shape my life. My father, who completed his first book at age eighty-five, instilled in me a deep reverence for the power of words and an obligation to use them wisely. Equally important, through both word and deed, he has taught me that the old-school values of loyalty, sacrifice, and integrity never go out of style.

Finally, I want to acknowledge my many friends and colleagues who carry on the quest of helping workers to realize their potential as citizens. I hope this book may offer them inspiration and insight as they continue to fight the good fight on behalf of working people.

FIGHTING FOR
TOTAL PERSON UNIONISM

INTRODUCTION

In its December 12, 1955, issue, *Life* magazine devoted considerable space to the recent merger between the American Federation of Labor (AFL) and the Congress of Industrial Organizations (CIO). Highlighting the union movement's "new respectability and affluence," the article featured pictures of prominent labor leaders, including International Brotherhood of Teamsters president Dave Beck working at his walnut desk in "the $5 million temple that [the] Teamsters built." *Life* elaborated on this theme of labor's legitimacy and maturation by describing the emergence of "a new kind of unionist[s] for labor's new role." One of the unionists it depicted was Earle Brown, the chief shop steward at Butler Brothers, a St. Louis, MO, warehousing firm represented by Teamsters Local 688. Photo panels captured Brown in three distinct settings—workplace, community, and church—and the captions explained his activities in each venue. "By day, Earle Brown airs problem with boss. By night, Brown oversees teen dance. On Sunday, Brown attends Lutheran service." The article concluded by noting that Brown "supervises . . . a half dozen civic betterment projects which his union is helping sponsor."[1]

Although the *Life* article did not say so directly, Earle Brown conducted his community activities under the auspices of Teamsters Local 688's "community stewards" program. This nationally acclaimed effort was the brainchild of two remarkable men, Harold Gibbons and Ernest Calloway, whose careers form the basis of this study. Through the vehicle of the community stewards program, which captured the imagination of workers like Earle Brown and the attention of St. Louis's power brokers, Gibbons and Calloway sought to develop "new kinds of unionists" whose workplace and civic lives were seamlessly integrated. Addressing the needs of the worker as a "total person," they looked beyond the shop floor and attempted to influence political decisions "affect[ing] the common economic, social, and civic well-being" of the union member.[2]

My interest in the community stewards program began with a gift I received over thirty years ago: a 1978 book on the Teamsters Union written by journalist Steven Brill. Appearing just three years after the unsolved disappearance of former Teamsters' president Jimmy Hoffa, *The Teamsters* chronicled the union's troubled history through a series of individual portraits. The final chapter examined the career of Harold Gibbons, a former socialist, prominent labor intellectual, and close Hoffa associate. Lamenting Gibbons's reluctance to oppose corruption in the union and use his considerable talents to lead it in a more positive direction, Brill presented his career as an allegory for the Teamsters' failure to become "the nation's largest, most powerful voice for real economic justice."[3]

Although I was intrigued by Brill's suggestion that Harold Gibbons might have led the American union movement to a different destiny, I was more impressed by his references to the community stewards program that Gibbons launched within Teamsters Local 688, the unit he had headed since the early 1940s. Based in St. Louis, this occupationally and racially diverse union of 10,000 members became a model of labor progressivism that gained national and even international recognition. During the postwar period, the U.S. State Department often sent foreign dignitaries to St. Louis to tour Local 688, and a prominent sociologist wrote a book about the activities of its members. At the time I first read *The Teamsters* and learned about Local 688, I was involved in developing community support for a nationwide boycott of the J.P. Stevens Company conducted by the Amalgamated Clothing and Textile Workers Union. Having personally witnessed the integral role that community involvement could play in turning a labor-management struggle into a broader fight for social justice, I found the community stewards' concept fascinating and resolved to learn more about this effort at a subsequent date.

That "subsequent date" came two decades later. After ten years on the Amalgamated's staff, I entered a graduate program in history, wrote a book about a prominent socialist and CIO activist, and went on to work with unions as a university-based labor educator. In the late 1990s, while considering a subject for a second book, I recalled Harold Gibbons and Local 688's community stewards program. This memory came at a time of renewed efforts by unions to establish closer connections with other social groups and made me to wonder if the community stewards' initiative might have contemporary relevance.

My initial inspection of Harold Gibbons's papers at Southern Illinois University Edwardsville (SIUE) exceeded my expectations. I uncovered extensive materials not only on the community stewards program but also information documenting other innovative Teamsters' activities in St. Louis. Just as I determined that there was sufficient source material and historical significance to warrant a biography of Harold Gibbons, a suggestion from Steve Kerber, the head archivist at SIUE, led me in an unanticipated direction. Steve mentioned that the papers of Ernest Calloway, who had also worked for the St. Louis Teamsters, were located across the river from Edwardsville at the University of Missouri in St. Louis. He thought I might find them helpful in supplementing my initial exploration of Gibbons's career.

My review of the Calloway collection revealed what one observer has described as a life worthy of a "fat Latin novel."[4] The son of a Kentucky coal miner, Calloway helped form the red caps' union in the 1930s, wrote prolifically as a labor journalist and public intellectual, refused to serve in a segregated military during World War II, and studied political economy at Ruskin College in London. After coming to St. Louis in 1950 at the behest of Harold Gibbons, he became one of the city's most prominent African American leaders and played a vital role in advancing the cause of racial justice. During the two decades of his political partnership with Gibbons, Calloway provided critical intellectual and strategic support for his colleague's ambition to help Local 688's members integrate the identities of worker and citizen. As I discovered the intertwined personal and ideological sources of their shared social vision, I decided that only a dual biography could capture the richness of their individual careers and the multiple dimensions of their quest to promote working-class citizenship and total person unionism in post–World War II St. Louis.

Although Gibbons was Irish and Calloway African American and each came of age in an America rigidly segregated along racial lines, they shared many formative experiences. The first half of the book alternates between Gibbons's and Calloway's individual stories in tracing how their parallel yet common experiences—hardscrabble upbringings in company-dominated coal towns, ambitions circumscribed by the boundaries of race and class, socialization in the politics of the non-communist left, participation in the inspirational labor revolts of the 1930s—ignited their mutual commitment to uplift the working class. Indeed, a burning desire to cast off the stigmas of racial and class inferiority animated Gibbons's and Calloway's determination to demonstrate that workers, both black and white, possessed the capacity to become engaged and effective citizens.

Gibbons's and Calloway's paths initially crossed in Chicago during the late 1930s, where they honed their political skills, assumed positions of labor leadership, and began formulating their ideas for the uses of working-class power. From their roots in the industrial union movement and the political left, Gibbons and Calloway gravitated to unlikely venues for launching their experiment in working-class citizenship: the Teamsters Union and the city of St. Louis. The Teamsters held an unabashedly narrow conception of the appropriate mission of trade unionism, while St. Louis's political culture was dominated by ward bosses, a parochial business elite, and a fragmented political structure resistant to reform. Through the experience of Gibbons and Calloway, we gain fresh insights into the Teamsters, one of the United States' most influential post–World War II labor organizations, and St. Louis, an important yet understudied American city.

Until recently, the Teamsters suffered from superficial and sensational treatment by researchers rather than thoughtful analysis that placed the union and its members in a social or historical context. With some exceptions, St. Louis also has received insufficient attention from historians, in spite of its strategic geographic location, vibrant union and civil rights movements, and well-publicized struggles to sustain itself as a viable city. Gibbons's and Calloway's continuing commitments to counteract St. Louis's post–World War II decline enhance our understanding of the fate of the post-industrial city and the impact of grassroots efforts to rekindle the promise of urban life.

As I came to know my characters better, I began to realize they were leading me toward a more nuanced account of the post-World War II union movement that departed from the dominant declension narrative developed in recent years. During the immediate postwar period, business interests and their allies launched a multi-pronged ideological and political counteroffensive aimed at containing labor's New Deal and wartime gains. After this effort succeeded in slowing labor's momentum, anti-union forces pursued even more aggressive efforts to thwart new organizing, curtail the union movement's political influence, and undermine its social legitimacy. Along with the machinations of labor's opponents, scholars also cite the union movement's own contributions to its decline, especially the CIO's expulsion of communist-influenced unions that removed from public life those leaders and activists best equipped to offer effective resistance. Following the ouster of the communists and diminished prospects for reviving New Deal liberalism, most labor leaders adopted a more defensive stance, eschewing rank-and-file mobilization, muting their advocacy of structural economic change, and failing to recognize the transformative potential of the emerging black freedom struggle.

The St. Louis experience of Harold Gibbons and Ernest Calloway offers a different twist on this declension story, especially regarding labor's reaction to the corporate counterattack of the postwar years. Although Gibbons and Calloway well understood the altered political terrain in which they were operating, they continued to regard themselves as the "new men of power" that sociologist C. Wright Mills described in his classic 1948 study of labor leadership. Determined to play offense in response to the "empire striking back," they aggressively used collective bargaining to limit managerial prerogatives and elevate the low-wage workers they represented. Yet in spite of their successes, they worried that newly affluent Teamsters might grow complacent and relinquish any sense of obligation to workers outside their immediate orbit. Seeking to counter this potential for parochialism and social isolation, Gibbons and Calloway developed an unusually sophisticated strategy offering workers an alternative venue in which to exercise their power: the neighborhoods where they spent their non-workplace hours. In its conceptual boldness and ambition, this strategy surpassed the labor liberalism of most postwar unions, including the United Auto Workers, whom most observers have regarded as the avatar of socially engaged unionism.

Through the community stewards program, Gibbons and Calloway tackled one of the most vexing historical challenges faced by the American union movement. Within the confines of the shop floor, workers often readily acted on the basis of mutual interest and class solidarity. In their homes and neighborhoods, however, this sense of class unity frequently splintered. Workers tended to make important social and political decisions on the basis of their racial, ethnic, or religious identities rather than as citizens concerned with broader community interests.

To address this divided consciousness, Gibbons and Calloway offered a vision of engaged citizenship that treated workers as "total persons" with both economic and social needs. Without a strong municipal infrastructure that provided vital public services and regulated the behavior of private interests, they argued that the enhanced social and economic standing of the working class remained precarious. More explicitly, they sought to create a community bargaining table where empowered worker-citizens negotiated with St. Louis's economic and political elites to ensure an equitable distribution of social resources.

Drawing on their shop-floor expertise, Local 688's community stewards mounted a series of highly visible campaigns to improve the quality of life in St. Louis. These efforts, which included ballot initiatives, legal action, and direct worker engagement with city officials, demanded that municipal government assume direct responsibility for the social health of the community. In contrast to most union leaders, including many labor liberals, Gibbons and Calloway did not shrink from taking on fights that challenged racial disparities in the distribution of social resources, especially in the controversial arenas of housing and education. With Calloway at the helm of the resurgent local National Association for the Advancement of Colored People (NAACP) chapter, he and Gibbons created an interracial alliance that defeated a 1957 attempt by St. Louis's business elite to amend the city charter and dilute working-class and African American political power. However, just as the community stewards were poised to expand the community bargaining table and seek greater structural change in St. Louis and its suburbs, Harold Gibbons ascended to national Teamsters leadership as a top aide to Jimmy Hoffa. Along with Calloway and other Local 688 leaders, he became preoccupied with resisting corruption charges that accompanied his rise to power in the union, leaving the initial promise of the community stewards program unfulfilled.

Returning to their advocacy of working-class citizenship and total person unionism, Gibbons and Calloway distinguished themselves from another key plot line in labor's postwar declension story: the union movement's isolation from social movements that arose during the 1960s. They became vocal critics of the union movement's cautious support for the civil rights movement, its reluctance to condemn the Vietnam War, and its inattention to the decline of America's cities. Their revised political strategy focused especially on the urgent need for urban revitalization. Believing that the fates of labor and city were inextricably linked, Gibbons and Calloway attempted to reverse the forces of racial polarization, disinvestment, and suburban flight that had accelerated St. Louis's deterioration. In response, they articulated a bold plan to shape the emerging post-industrial city through civic partnerships that would oversee economic development and permit local citizens and community groups to shape urban policy.

After failing to gain support for this joint approach from wary business leaders, Ernest Calloway, with strong support from Harold Gibbons, spearheaded a new initiative to advance total person unionism: a "trade union oriented war on the slums." Reflecting Calloway's biting critique of the War on Poverty, this effort connected the political savvy and institutional resources of Local 688's worker-citizens with grassroots forces seeking to dismantle the structural racial inequities that remained pervasive in St. Louis. These efforts culminated with Gibbons helping to settle a volatile 1969 public housing tenants' strike in St. Louis and Local 688's assuming administration of the city's public housing program. Both events represented an unusual display of union power and legitimacy at a time when most of the labor movement had been unable to tap into the insurgent spirit of the period.

Gibbons and Calloway's unabashed support for black aspirations and new social movements triggered a strong counterreaction from a sizable segment of the union's white members that revealed familiar fissures in working-class consciousness. Rather than embracing the working-class citizenship favored by Gibbons and Calloway, these white members now identified themselves as taxpayers, homeowners, and consumers whose sense of stability and security were threatened by African American demands for a fairer distribution of social resources. Moreover, they complained that Gibbons and Calloway's devotion to their trade union oriented war on the slums had led them to neglect worsening conditions on the shop floor. With the emergence of a vocal rank-and-file insurgency that excoriated Gibbons for failing to meet basic trade union obligations, he and Calloway faced an even more powerful challenge to their conception of total person unionism. In response, they created new opportunities for Local 688's members to act as effective citizens.

Before these initiatives fully materialized, Gibbons was deposed in a palace coup led by Local 688 staff members who had never fully supported his social vision, terminating the political experiment he and Ernest Calloway had launched two decades earlier. However, the collaboration between these coal miners' sons not only altered St. Louis's social and political landscape but also suggested the broader potential of their quest, in Calloway's words, to "inject the trade union apparatus into the mainstream of public life."[5]

Parallel to their shared political odyssey, Harold Gibbons and Ernest Calloway functioned independently as leaders and strategists, most notably during Gibbons's tenure as a national Teamsters official and Calloway's role as an influential figure in St. Louis's civil rights movement. The latter part of the book assesses the meaning and significance of these experiences, which saw Gibbons and Calloway wrestling with the perennial challenges facing leaders of social movements at defining historical moments.

Throughout his years as a Teamsters' leader and his close association with Jimmy Hoffa, Harold Gibbons could not shake a question repeatedly posed by the press, liberal allies, and much of the labor community: had he made a Faustian bargain in his rise to power? Critics asked this question more frequently following a widely publicized Senate investigation of union corruption in the late 1950s. Before a national audience, Gibbons defended questionable tactics he used to capture a top regional leadership position. Subsequently, he acquiesced in condoning Jimmy Hoffa's entangling alliances with organized crime and his increasingly authoritarian rule. However, following a well-publicized break with Hoffa in 1963, he looked to reassert the democratic commitments that had characterized his leadership during his CIO years. Unfortunately, his efforts to change the national union's culture and use Teamster power to extend total person unionism proved largely unavailing, as did his plans to seek the union presidency on a reform ticket after Hoffa's fall from power. Besides his respected work in St. Louis, Gibbons's greatest success in regaining liberal trust and restoring his reputation stemmed from his emergence as an outspoken critic of the Vietnam War. Ironically, his renewed credibility on the left led directly to the coup that ousted him, derailing new opportunities to introduce total person unionism to a wider audience.

Ernest Calloway fared better than Gibbons during the initial phases of his solo career. As leader of St. Louis's NAACP in the 1950s, he adapted trade union principles to the civil rights struggle, focusing on work and employment issues and moving the chapter toward more self-conscious political participation. Calloway went on to catalyze what he dubbed the "black political renaissance" in St. Louis, managing campaigns that led to the election of the first African Americans to important city and statewide offices. A crowning achievement in this string of successes came in 1962, when his wife, Deverne, became the first black woman elected to the Missouri legislature.

Like Harold Gibbons, Calloway later found himself increasingly estranged from the movement he had galvanized. As the barriers of de jure segregation began to fall, Calloway advocated moving from protest to politics, arguing that the political circumstances in St. Louis permitted a "planned social revolution" to occur. However, he ran afoul of a new generation of black freedom activists who rejected his pragmatic, union-influenced strategy in favor of a more racially oriented, direct action approach. Calloway's decisive defeat during a 1968 run for Congress by William Clay, a younger civil rights leader who had become his political nemesis, ended his leadership role in St. Louis's black community. During the last years of his active public life, Calloway turned to journalism and teaching, remaining an astute observer of black politics and a trenchant critic of labor who prophetically anticipated the forces behind its accelerating decline.

Whenever possible, I have attempted to explain how private considerations influenced the course of Gibbons and Calloway's public lives. However, limited evidence has complicated this customary biographer's task. Gibbons left behind virtually no record of reflection on either his public or private life. Calloway, who often wrote about his past political experiences, largely ruminated on their historical or social implications, keeping his innermost thoughts and details of his personal life to himself. Indeed, it was only through a passing reference in an FBI file and a slip of paper in an archival file that I discovered Calloway's first marriage, an event unbeknown to even his closest friends and acquaintances. Interviews with family members in Gibbons's case and associates of Calloway have helped fill in some of the gaps, along with a brief but revealing set of letters Calloway exchanged with his second wife in the late 1940s.

For all their similarities and common experiences, Gibbons and Calloway were quite different personalities. Gibbons had a legendary reputation as a womanizer, reveled in his friendships with celebrities, and relished the perquisites of power. Calloway was far more low-key and abstemious, comfortable in the security of his book-lined study where he crunched numbers and penned his polemics. In spite of these differences, these longtime political partners shared one unshakable bond. In his will Gibbons stipulated that he wanted Calloway to deliver his eulogy at a secular memorial service. Leaving no doubt about how he wished to be remembered, he supplied Calloway with a title for his remarks: "Gibbons: Concerned Citizen."[6]

The fervent quest of Harold Gibbons and Ernest Calloway to claim the identity of "citizen" for themselves and the workers they represented provides the basic frame of my story. It is a story that I believe has enormous relevance not only for their times but also for our own.

CHAPTER 1

Coming Up the Hard Way

In reminiscing about their childhoods as coal miners' sons, neither Harold Gibbons nor Ernest Calloway could conjure up warm memories of their youths. Gibbons characterized his "early boyhood days" as the "bleakest of my life." Calloway recalled working alongside his father in "the dark, deep, dreary bowels" of a coal mine and chafing at the stifling boundaries of a "contained company town." His sense of constraint was accentuated by the rigid barriers of racial segregation. "As Negroes," Calloway later explained, "we had a fixed place in that world. There were many things beyond our reach and we lived our lives of quiet frustration and survived on small expectations." Although Harold Gibbons did not suffer the stigma of race, he shared Calloway's frustrations, understanding all too well the sources from which they sprang. Indeed, the two men held much in common, with their coal mining origins creating a visceral personal bond that cemented their subsequent political partnership.[1]

* * *

Harold Joseph Gibbons was born April 10, 1910, in Archibald Patch, PA, a coal mining camp in the town of Taylor situated in the state's northeastern region. He was the youngest of twenty-three children sired by his father, Patrick Thomas Gibbons, who emigrated from Ireland to the United States in the early 1880s, and spread his progeny between two wives. The elder Gibbons was in his sixties when Harold was born, and his mother, Bridget Mulhern, was his father's second wife. Ernest Calloway was born a year earlier on January 1, 1909, in Heberton, WV, a tiny town in Fayette County located in the state's southeastern corner. Calloway's father, also named Ernest, was forty-two years old at the time of his birth, and his mother, Mary Hayes, was a fifteen-year-old orphan whom his father had married following the death of his first wife. In 1913, when Ernest was four, the family, which later grew to include a brother and sister, moved to Jenkins, KY, a newly created coal mining town in the Cumberland region's Big Sandy Valley.[2]

Both Gibbons and Calloway's fathers were coal miners, and their experiences reflected the influential role the coal industry played in shaping post-Civil War America. In the anthracite region of northeastern Pennsylvania where Patrick Gibbons mined coal, he joined other Irish and English immigrants who were among the first workers recruited to extract the hard substance prized for its long-burning capacity and affordability. Most anthracite miners lived in small towns known as "patches," which were tightly controlled by coal companies. In contrast to the bituminous coal mined by Ernest Calloway's father in West Virginia and Kentucky, anthracite veins were not nearly as level, and this irregular, unpredictable alignment beneath the earth's surface made anthracite mining more challenging and dangerous. The Glen Alden Coal Company, which owned the Archibald mine where Patrick Gibbons was employed, saw twenty-eight of its miners die in accidents between 1924 and 1927 as a result of roof collapses and explosions. In many coal patches this sense of danger was symbolized by the existence of "widow's rows," groups of homes where the wives of fallen miners struggled to subsist following the deaths of their husbands.[3]

Employed in a chaotic industry subject to fluctuating demand, overproduction, and price volatility, anthracite miners often suffered from unsteady employment and frequently failed to earn incomes sufficient to support a basic standard of living. They also had a more differentiated set of job assignments than their counterparts in bituminous mining, leading to persistent conflict over the determination of wages and frequent accusations of favoritism and discrimination. As a result, according to historian Perry Blatz, "militancy never lay far beneath the surface," and since the mid-nineteenth century, an unrelenting atmosphere of antipathy between anthracite miners and coal operators led to decades of bitter disputes.[4]

Ernest Calloway's paternal grandfather and great grandfather had been slaves in Bedford County, VA, located in the state's southwestern section where tobacco plantations cultivated the crop for one of the nation's largest regional markets. Calloway's father, whom he referred to as "Big Ernest," was born six years after the Civil War. When mining companies began to develop the rich Appalachian coal reserves, they found an insufficient labor force among West Virginia's mountaineers and turned to importing African Americans from adjacent states. This recruitment strategy led to the doubling of the black population in Fayette County, WV, the area where the senior Calloway had settled. By 1910, African American migrants comprised nearly 25 percent of the region's coal miners.[5]

Seeking to sustain the farms they had acquired following the Civil War, many of these migrants became "miner-farmers," journeying back to Virginia to maintain their land even as they sought improved wages in the emerging Appalachian coal industry. Mining not only offered better pay but also promised less closely monitored work, a benefit that was doubtless welcomed by those who had worked as slave laborers in antebellum Virginia. Moreover, the rigid segregation reinforced by the enactment of Jim Crow laws elsewhere in the post-Civil War south was less prevalent in West Virginia, where African Americans found greater opportunities in employment and more freedom to participate in civic and political affairs. As one union organizer observed, the opportunity to exercise "true American citizenship," a concept that powerfully shaped Harold Gibbons and Ernest Calloway's ambitions for the union movement, became an important factor influencing black migration to West Virginia along with the material improvements offered by work in the coal fields.[6]

West Virginia, however, was no nirvana for black coal miners. Company towns were more pervasive in West Virginia than elsewhere, and miners found virtually all aspects of their lives rigidly monitored by their employers. West Virginia's mines were among the most dangerous in the nation, and mine operators disregarded both safety and child labor laws with impunity. In both West Virginia and Pennsylvania, the United Mine Workers of America (UMWA), founded in 1890, sought to organize miners, drawing on their shared experience of danger and exploitation to forge solidarity among the different ethnic and racial groups that comprised the coal industry's labor force. Following what came to be known as the "Great Strike" of 1902, anthracite miners benefited from President Theodore Roosevelt's unprecedented intervention, an action alerting coal operators that they could no longer count on automatic federal support for their implacable opposition to unionism. By the time of Harold Gibbons's birth, Pennsylvania anthracite miners were highly organized and had gained a grudging respect from the coal operators for their tenacity and militancy.[7]

Miners in West Virginia were slower to organize than their Pennsylvania counterparts. They lacked the influential presence of class-conscious British, Irish, and Welsh miners who had applied their deep union experience and political acumen to launch organizing in the Pennsylvania coal fields. It also took time for UMWA organizers to recognize that miners in West Virginia had different priorities from miners in Pennsylvania, where the union had built its greatest strength. For West Virginia miners, their most significant demands were gaining union recognition and abolishing the utilization of private guards by mine operators. Accomplishing these goals would loosen the tight grip that the operators exercised over company towns and enable miners to exercise their full rights as citizens. Aided by the UMWA's growing recognition of these priorities, West Virginia miners began actively organizing during the first decade of the twentieth century. Although coal operators used a "judicious mixture" of different racial and ethnic groups in an attempt to undermine miner solidarity, the UMWA was able to achieve some level of interracial cooperation. Black miners, especially those from Virginia who were familiar with the Knights of Labor's organizing efforts in the late nineteenth century, proved particularly receptive to the union's message.[8]

Shortly before Ernest Calloway was born, West Virginia coal miners engaged in fierce battles with mine owners and private guards recruited from the infamous

Baldwin-Felts agency during the Paint Creek and Cabin Creek strikes in 1912 and 1913. These strikes were the precursor of the virtual class war that would characterize coal labor relations in West Virginia for the next two decades. The brutality of the Baldwin-Felts guards provoked violent retaliation from the miners. Big Ernest Calloway, who his son later described as an "ex-farmer, ex-gambler, ex-gun toting unionist, and refugee from a West Virginia posse of mine guards," had apparently been a strong union man and was wounded by Baldwin-Felts operatives during these clashes. Seeking a more stable environment in which to raise his new family, in 1913, Big Ernest led a group of five African American families to seek work in the new mines that the Rockefeller-owned Consolidation Coal Company was opening in eastern Kentucky.[9]

Jenkins, the town where the Calloways settled, had been created in 1911 by Consolidation Coal, which had bought over 100,000 acres of land in eastern Kentucky to develop for coal production. Named after a company director and well-financed by Consolidation, Jenkins had greater amenities than company towns dominated by smaller firms, at least for white miners. Without a trace of irony, the Jenkins Area Jaycees confirmed Consolidation's dominance of the town in a 1973 account of its history: "It has been said that the company brought the citizens of Jenkins into the world since they owned the only hospital, and it also escorted them out of this town since it owned the only funeral home."[10]

Ernest Calloway's father quickly distinguished himself as a leading civic figure in Jenkins, helping establish the town's first black church and school and serving as a liaison among the blacks, Poles, Hungarians, and Italians who populated Consolidation Coal's labor force. He promptly employed these diplomatic skills, smoothing relations with mountain clans who resented newcomers and for a time attempted to force their departure. Big Ernest's status and his claims on citizenship and respectability were reinforced by a photograph that showed him hoisting the American flag at an outdoor event in Jenkins. He also continued to display his union loyalties, becoming the first secretary of the UMWA local in Jenkins and ensuring that miners were credited properly for their output. The elder Calloway eventually became a subcontractor, employing his own crew, and lived in the Cumberland Valley until his death in 1957. A group of "old mountaineers and coal miners" reportedly carried him to his grave, "affirming the esteem in which he was held by his fellow workers and neighbors."[11]

Harold Gibbons's memories of growing up in a coal mining patch mirrored those of Ernest Calloway. The Gibbons home on Williams Street in Archibald Patch was located close to the mine, and he recalled ". . . hardly a day went by without an ambulance racing to the mine past the front of our house." Unionism was a "matter of course" in this environment. Several of Gibbons's brothers were union committeemen, and he described his father as a "union guy." "If you scabbed," Gibbons remembered, "it was never forgotten" in the close knit, intensely pro-union community in which he was raised.[12]

Buoyed by an expanding economy, corporate efforts to stabilize production, and the emergence of a strong union presence, the anthracite industry enjoyed a "golden age" in the first two decades of the twentieth century that brought improved wages and working conditions to Pennsylvania miners. This prosperity faded, however, after demand for coal declined sharply following World War I. Harold Gibbons might have been thinking about this period when he recalled his father being out of work for long intervals during strikes. One story that he often repeated to interviewers was his memory of subsisting on potatoes during occasions when his father and brothers were withholding their labor: "Almost all we had to eat was potatoes . . . they were the main course at breakfast, lunch, and dinner." These stark memories of deprivation remained with Gibbons, fueling his subsequent determination to improve the quality of working-class lives.[13]

Patrick Gibbons died of work-related lung cancer when Harold was twelve. "That taught me that a labor union is the only protection a working man has," Gibbons told an interviewer. Elaborating on this theme, he explained to a *New York Herald Tribune* reporter in 1964, "I'm a union man because I came up the hard way." An early 1950s article on Gibbons in a Toledo, OH, Teamsters publication characterized the Pennsylvania coal patch where he was raised as a place where "the coal barons had hearts as black as their product and considered a miner's life cheaper than his tools."[14]

This language underscored the outrage Gibbons felt toward the coal companies that had dominated his upbringing and consistently manifested their contempt for working-class lives. This powerful "sense of kind," as Calloway once described the consciousness of miners, was marked by the unwavering belief that the union was the one institution capable of averting their descent into total desperation. "Unquestionably," Calloway observed in his first published article in 1934, for miners and their families, "the Union is the only road to freedom." And, as he told members of the red caps' union whom he organized three years later, it was also "the only avenue of escape from the ravishing scourge of poverty."[15]

Coal miners have received extensive attention from historians, who have highlighted their attachments to self-reliance and collective action, their persistent efforts to forge interethnic and interracial solidarity, and their fervent embrace of the UMWA as a kind of "secular church." Harold Gibbons and Ernest Calloway paid homage to this rich legacy, expressing pride in their fathers' coal mining roots and abiding union loyalties. Yet their recollections of growing up in coal mining patches were tinged with neither romance nor nostalgia. In addition to recurring images of poverty and deprivation, Gibbons was scarred by the experience of being one of two Irish Catholic families in a community dominated by Protestants. "They let us know we were different," he recalled. One especially searing memory of this difference was an occasion when young Harold was not invited to a Christmas church gathering attended by most of the town's children.

He vividly remembered peering into a window where he could see other youngsters receiving presents while he remained empty-handed.[16]

Echoing Gibbons's reference to the bleakness of his upbringing, Ernest Calloway's memories were equally unromantic. African Americans in Jenkins attended overcrowded and underfunded schools. Housing in Jenkins was segregated and inferior to that inhabited by whites. For all of his father's success within the union and his standing in the community, the younger Calloway could not escape the realization that law, custom, and ideology in Jenkins were all designed to uphold white privilege and supremacy.[17]

For bright, ambitious youths like Calloway and Gibbons, the coal patch, ethnic and racial intolerance, and corporate domination converged in consigning them to what Calloway described as a "small, restricted, insignificant place" in the social order. These hidden and not so hidden injuries of class and racial oppression were the catalysts for Calloway and Gibbons's subsequent efforts to craft a "total person unionism" that would attempt to serve not only the economic but also the social and psychological needs of workers. Their deep commitments to a unionism that fostered interracial and interethnic solidarity were also formed as a result of their personal experiences with discrimination and their exposure to the UMWA, a union that had an admirable if imperfect record of attempting to organize across racial and ethnic lines.[18]

Describing miners and their offspring as "the forgotten children of American corporate feudalism," Calloway was repelled not only by the economic exploitation he witnessed but also by the miners' total dependency on the operators that left them unable to act as effective citizens. In his view the mine operators' exercised "autocratic power" and dominated almost every aspect of social, economic, and political life in a mining community, including the authority to "regulate your morals, restrict your politics, judge your innocence or guilt and tell you where to be buried." Calloway and Gibbons's subsequent commitments to boosting working-class confidence and encouraging civic participation were animated by their revulsion against this unchecked corporate power and its corrosive effects on both personal aspiration and effective citizenship. And in Calloway's case, his observation of the close nexus between economic power and political influence led to a lifelong fascination with the workings of power elites and an eventual role as a muckraking public intellectual eager to expose their machinations.[19]

Like many working-class youth of their generation, neither Harold Gibbons nor Ernest Calloway completed high school. Following his father's death, Gibbons felt compelled to help support his family. Fiercely protective of her youngest child, his mother refused to allow him to enter the coal mines that had claimed her husband's life. Nonetheless, economic necessity forced Gibbons to leave high school after his freshman year, lie about his age, and obtain work as a short-order cook at a Scranton hotel, where he put in twelve-hour days and seven-day weeks. In spite of this onerous schedule, he took night classes, attesting to his desire to obtain an education and rise above his circumstances.[20]

Attempting to curb his restlessness, Ernest Calloway's parents sent him to live with an aunt in Lynchburg, VA, where he would be afforded greater opportunities than those offered in Jenkins' constricted social environment. Calloway completed his junior year and played on Dunbar High School's state championship basketball team, but his rebelliousness remained unabated. As he recounted, several of his teachers and a Young Men's Christian Association (YMCA) secretary predicted that "the patterns of [his] life would be wholly negative, unproductive, and without purpose." Yet like Harold Gibbons, Ernest Calloway's intellectual aspirations were not completely extinguished. He recalled that when he was fifteen, a librarian introduced him to the "wonderful world of books," thereby opening "new possibilities" that he had not previously imagined and helping him discover his gift for self-expression.[21]

Calloway's restlessness was not easily assuaged, however, even by a glimpse of the wider world that he obtained in Lynchburg. During the summer of 1925, he ran away for eight months and lived in Harlem, where he found a job as a bus boy on the Harlem River Day Line. "For a young callow lad of 16 who had spent most of his years in a contained company town in the Kentucky Cumberlands, that summer in Harlem in 1925 was an enveloping experience," he wrote forty-five years later. Yet Calloway lamented that his sojourn in Harlem was "shallow," marked more by his adolescent interest in glitter and nightlife rather than exploring the rich milieu that writers, artists, and activists were creating during the peak of the Harlem Renaissance. Nonetheless, through this brief exposure to the world of art, music, and politics, Calloway found a tantalizing glimpse of the possibilities available in a cosmopolitan urban setting. Upon learning that his mother was critically ill (she would die a year later), Calloway returned to Jenkins in 1926. Reflecting a new sense of self-confidence and bravado, he briefly "convinced the powers-that-be that I could teach school," but this employment ended once his lack of training was exposed. Following this escapade, Calloway reluctantly entered the mines and spent the next three years digging coal alongside his father.[22]

As they approached their young adulthood, with Harold Gibbons preparing meals in a Scranton hotel and Ernest Calloway digging coal in a Kentucky mine, both had ample reason to be discouraged. Their educational opportunities were stymied and their career options limited, while the institutions they might have counted on to improve their fortunes—unions, schools, government—seemed incapable of providing assistance or support. Yet the nation and even the coal patches where Gibbons and Calloway had been raised were soon to be transformed by the social maelstrom unleashed by the collapse of the American economy in 1929 and the onset of the Great Depression. Under these circumstances, they each migrated to new venues, found influential mentors, and began their swift rises to positions of authority in the union movement.

CHAPTER 2

"Apostles of a New Order"

Before they first met in Chicago in the summer of 1937, the education of Harold Gibbons and Ernest Calloway continued on parallel tracks. Amid the profound social dislocation of the Great Depression, each experienced epiphanies that they subsequently credited with bolstering their determination to lift up the working class. At a University of Wisconsin labor school, Harold Gibbons "came away . . . with the conviction that if I had any talent, any energies, any brains, I'm gonna devote [them] to the have-nots and not the haves." During a riveting dream in the mountains of Mexico, Ernest Calloway ". . . discovered that one must believe in the essential oneness of people and be willing to fight for that belief." These revelations were accompanied by other pivotal experiences that boosted the self confidence and social awareness of the two coal mining refugees and gave them a budding sense of purpose and direction.[1]

* * *

Chicago was a geographic and socio-cultural crossroads where the forces of industrialization, immigration, and internal migration converged to create a constantly churning social milieu. The city was home to some of the nation's most visible and powerful corporations and featured a diverse working class comprised of European immigrants and African Americans who had fled the Jim Crow south to take jobs vacated by white workers during World War I. Imbued with what historian John Lyons has described as a "labor ethos," Chicago epitomized the American union movement's quest to fashion strategies that would enable it to moderate the exploitative practices of corporate capitalism. Moreover, the city spawned a multi-dimensional Progressivism, featuring an extensive settlement house movement, a vibrant Women's Trade Union League chapter, and one of the country's strongest urban labor bodies, the Chicago Federation of Labor (CFL). These overlapping circles of reform and radicalism made Chicago a political cornucopia for young men like Harold Gibbons and Ernest Calloway following their escape from the constricted world of their coal patch youths.[2]

In 1929, along with his mother and a sister, nineteen-year-old Harold Gibbons left his cook's job in Pennsylvania and went to Chicago, where he had several brothers who served as police officers. Gibbons briefly worked in construction before finding employment as a shipping clerk at a warehouse. He was laid off in 1932, however, and joined the ranks of the unemployed. Fortunately, Gibbons encountered three leading figures deeply rooted in Chicago labor and reform circles who saw his potential and played influential roles in helping him gain his footing.[3]

Two of Chicago's most prominent women activists became trusted lifetime mentors for Gibbons. Appointed the first industrial secretary of the national Young Women's Christian Association (YWCA) in 1918, Annetta Dieckmann held a similar position in the organization's Chicago branch when Harold Gibbons met her in the early 1930s. Dieckmann was steeped in the Chicago progressive tradition of middle-class women who engaged in investigation, agitation, and organizing to improve working conditions for women, immigrants, and blacks. Gibbons's other female booster, Lillian Herstein, led early efforts to organize teachers' unions and served as the sole woman on the Chicago Federation of Labor's executive board for a quarter century. Herstein also was a pioneer in workers' education and became a strong proponent of independent political action for the union movement as evidenced by her lifelong opposition to machine politics in Chicago. Both Herstein and Dieckmann doted on the young man they called "Hal," whose boyish good looks and earnestness proved attractive to his older female mentors. Herstein referred to Gibbons as "one of my boys," while Dieckmann expressed her disappointment when Gibbons could not deliver a scheduled speech at which she had prepared to introduce him as "Local Boy Makes Good." She wrote, "I am lonesome for the sight of you," attesting to the strong affection she felt for her young protégé.[4]

In the summer of 1932, Gibbons won a contest that financed his attendance at a summer school sponsored by the University of Wisconsin's School for Workers. This six-week program aimed at preparing workers for union leadership and civic participation and prompted Gibbons to reconsider his social attitudes and career options. Recounting his experience more than forty years later, Gibbons recalled, "I was going to be an engineer, and I was going to be a rich guy" until, as he told Ernest Calloway, his fellow students "locked him in a dorm room and talked socialism to him until he was finally converted." More soberly, he described his exposure to "socialist kids" whose description of "a society divided between those who own and those who work" gave him a framework in which to make sense of his own experience. Attesting to the program's impact on his development, Gibbons became president of the Wisconsin summer school's alumni association. After his arrival in St. Louis, he retained this connection by sending many members of Local 688 to Wisconsin for an orientation in trade unionism.[5]

At Wisconsin, Gibbons met Paul Douglas, a third prominent mentor who influenced his thinking and promoted his career. Later a United States senator from Illinois, Douglas was teaching economics at the University of Chicago when Gibbons encountered him. A strong advocate of government investment in the economy and enhanced regulation of the market, Douglas was also a staunch anti-communist who supported the growth of vigorous voluntary associations to protect citizens from both corporate and governmental overreaching. Even as the New Deal increasingly brought radicals under its umbrella, Douglas continued to embrace independent political action, although by the end of the decade, both he and Lillian Herstein aligned themselves with Franklin Roosevelt and the liberal wing of the Democratic Party.[6]

In addition to introducing Gibbons to the concepts of a strong union movement, independent political action, and the importance of education for effective citizenship, Dieckmann, Herstein, and Douglas helped him obtain employment and continue his learning. Through their intercession, he began teaching at the YWCA and the University of Chicago settlement house, and Douglas helped him gain admission to the University of Chicago so that he could take night courses. A greater opportunity emerged in 1933, when the Federal Emergency Relief Administration established forty centers across the country to train teachers to conduct workers' education classes. Through Lillian Herstein's connections, Gibbons obtained a job as an adult educator under the new program.[7]

Herstein, who consulted with Eleanor Roosevelt in creating the program and helped train teachers in Chicago, brought an expansive vision of workers education to the project: "Workers education should concern itself, let us grant, with those who are willing to be apostles of a new order." With Herstein's encouragement, Gibbons thrived as a workers' educator. His duties included teaching public speaking and writing textbooks on economics and the union movement. With the encouragement of Herstein and Maynard Krueger, a University of Chicago teacher and a leading Socialist who also helped train teachers for the WPA program, Gibbons organized his colleagues into American Federation of Teachers (AFT) Local 346. In September 1934, he was elected as the local union's first president. The union, which described its mission as "education for democracy, democracy for education," captured well the spirit of the times and Gibbons's new sense of social commitment. He also became the secretary of the Chicago Labor College, an independent workers education program backed by unions and the Socialist Party, and gained recognition for his passion and inspiring speaking style.[8]

Although there is little public record of Gibbons's political views from this period, the text of a 1934 speech he gave before a "youth week" conference offered an important glimpse into his emerging thought. Lamenting the existence of "thousands of youth whose home life has been smashed by 5 years of depression," Gibbons voiced the profound anxiety that he and other working-class youth were feeling: "They have been forced to take to the road, living in the best places the government has provided, flop-houses and transient camps." With a lack of jobs, limited access to education, and the impossibility of marrying and raising a family, the American Dream spiraled out of reach for Gibbons and his contemporaries. He also denounced the New Deal's failure to solve these problems, which he declared needed to be attacked "in a more fundamental manner." Gibbons concluded his remarks to his young audience with a passionate plea for socialism and the establishment of a moral economy: "We want a system where the means of production will be socially owned and controlled for the benefit of all instead of a few, a system for use instead of profit. We want a system that will put human values above material things, a system which will regiment things, not people."[9]

At one level Gibbons's assertions reflected the Socialist Party's standard critique of the early New Deal. Yet several themes emerged in his speech that would guide Gibbons's thinking about the role of unions and establishing a firm connection between work and citizenship. Socialism offered Gibbons a framework to develop a moral critique of capitalism ("it gave me a picture of the nature of the society we lived in," he later recalled), which he retained even as he and other radicals acknowledged the resiliency of the market system and refocused their efforts toward recasting America as a social democracy. Perhaps the most important sentiment expressed in his 1934 youth week speech, however, was the raw anger Gibbons displayed over the deprivation, insecurity, and social rejection he had experienced throughout his youth and early adulthood. His outrage that the dreams of workers were being deferred or denied, both materially and spiritually, fueled his efforts to create circumstances in which working-class people would have an "opportunity to enjoy a life of peace and security" and gain respect as first-class citizens.[10]

Gibbons subsequently downplayed any official association with the Socialist Party, although he apparently remained a member between 1932 and 1939, frequently attended and addressed Socialist-sponsored gatherings, and benefited from his party connections in gaining employment with the fledgling Congress of Industrial Organizations (CIO). "I was probably too much of a pragmatist to stay too long in the Party," Gibbons told a would-be biographer. "I was too busy doing things, meeting immediate needs." In part, this disclaimer was an effort to counter charges that he was a communist, an accusation frequently hurled at Gibbons throughout his early career. Yet Gibbons often told interviewers about his early socialist connections, suggesting that he retained an enduring pride in this youthful affiliation. Although his formal involvement with the Socialist Party was brief, it played a vital role in establishing his commitment to independent political action, a strong role for unions as principled critics of capitalism's shortcomings, and the need to prepare workers to assume the responsibilities of active citizenship.[11]

By 1935, twenty-five-year-old Harold Gibbons had come a considerable distance from his coal patch origins. Gaining growing recognition and respect in Chicago labor and political circles, he angled to assume greater responsibility with the rise of the industrial union movement. For both Gibbons and his future collaborator Ernest Calloway, the industrial union upsurge provided them with exciting opportunities to use their talents and become part of a movement powerful enough to transform working-class lives.

* * *

Ernest Calloway's journey to Chicago proved much more circuitous than that of Harold Gibbons. From 1926 to 1930, he worked in Kentucky coal mines, but his restlessness persisted. He found himself "bored" with the monotony of the work and "got mixed up with the usual drinking-gambling bouts plus certain troubles with women." With the UMWA unable to make inroads against staunchly antiunion Kentucky coal operators, Calloway bemoaned the long hours, low pay, and hard labor he experienced and was blacklisted when he began to engage in union activity. As he did four years earlier when he was sixteen, Calloway took to the road in 1930, joining thousands of other Americans searching for a way to survive hard times.[12]

Recalling his travels five decades later, Calloway described his four years of wandering as "raw survival and hungry years." "I had aimlessly wandered around the country ... hitchhiking ... hoboing ... freight cars ... gambling ... bootlegging ... odd jobs ... flop houses ... park benches ... panhandling ... soup kitchens ... hard ... cynical ... rootless and constantly on the move without a purpose and in search of nothing." Yet in an interview he gave to a Works Progress Administration (WPA) writer in 1937, Calloway suggested his experience was not totally devoid of direction or purpose. While in California, he had become involved in organizing the unemployed, assisted Upton Sinclair's End Poverty in California campaign, and wrote articles for the *California Eagle*, one of the country's oldest African-American newspapers. Like many who were on the road during this period, Calloway saw how extreme adversity could evoke expressions of sympathy and solidarity as well as uglier emotions. He recalled being picked up by a white police officer in West Virginia who took him to jail, gave him a key to his cell, and brought him food. In California, however, when he asked for a drink of water at a gas station, he was unceremoniously told: "Nigger, I wouldn't give you a damned thing." Calloway reported walking ten miles after this encounter and no longer feeling thirsty.[13]

In the autumn of 1933, Calloway had an experience that he credited with rescuing from his ennui and propelling him toward a life of meaning and purpose. In a 1981 article entitled "To Sleep, Perchance to Dream," Calloway recounted wandering in the Mexican mountains near the Pacific Ocean, not sleeping for nearly forty-eight hours, and fearing that he might die. In a haunting dream (or perhaps a hallucination) he saw an apparition of a breathtakingly beautiful female body that was suddenly consumed by worms. Convinced he had seen the "mirror of evil," Calloway was repulsed by his "own drab rudderless non-caring existence . . . devoid of any pretense of nobility and spiritual design." Awakening from this nightmare, he described his epiphany: "I was 24 years old and it was the day I became a man. It was the day I really opened my eyes to the world around me. It was the day life and living in the heart of the Depression took on a new meaning. It was the day I became inquisitive . . . It was the day my revolt began." Shortly thereafter, he decided to return to his "sturdy roots" in Kentucky, arriving back in Jenkins by Christmas Eve 1933.[14]

Calloway's life clearly assumed a new sense of direction and commitment following his mystical experience in the Mexican mountains. His revelation convinced him that some form of intense soul-searching and personal transformation was essential in preparing oppressed people to overcome their alienation, discover a sense of purpose, and conceive of themselves as social beings. As he wrote just a month after his retelling of the mountain episode in a piece examining the plight of poor blacks in St. Louis: ". . . the pursuit of self-hood or self-awareness becomes the first step towards achieving the strong vantage point from which to conduct the never-ending struggle against group inequality, uneven circumstances, and the conquest of our own fears and low self-esteem." Having grown up in a culture that systematically denigrated his humanity, Calloway began to embrace an organizing style that rallied workers, both black and white, not only around their economic interests but also on the basis of their broader personal and emotional needs.[15]

On his return to Kentucky, the twenty-five-year-old Calloway quickly attempted to act on his newfound sense of purpose. His initial foray was prompted by an all too familiar event that haunted African Americans throughout the early 1930s. As Calloway recounted in a 1973 interview, "a friend of mine was lynched in 1933. They tied him to the back of an automobile, dragged him up the mountain, poured gasoline on him, and set him on fire. Later I went to see the remains. It took me many years to forget the smell." Reflecting further on this devastating memory, Calloway recalled: "I grew up hating white people. Later I found hatred a waste of time. What you have to deal with are institutions, laws, customs. I have spent 50 years working hatred out of my system." This conscious effort to curb raw emotion and rely on coolheaded strategic responses to the systemic forces upholding racial oppression became a hallmark of Calloway's political approach. Over time, this impulse congealed into a disciplined pragmatism that suited his cerebral temperament and his growing embrace of trade unionism as the most appropriate vehicle for advancing African American aspirations.[16]

After his friend's lynching, Calloway attempted to organize an NAACP chapter that would enable the community to resist this kind of unconscionable violence. He later complained of being thwarted by local African American community leaders: "I came into contact with too many petty Negro politicians who were afraid to bring pressure to bear where it would be effective." Nonetheless, this abortive effort generated an invitation to write a piece on conditions in the coal fields for *Opportunity*, the official journal of the National Urban League. Although the magazine rejected his first effort, an article about marijuana use, it encouraged him to make another submission. This article, "The Negro in the Kentucky Coal Fields," appeared in March 1934 and was followed two months later by an essay on labor in the South. These pieces articulated Calloway's views on race relations, the union movement, and the status of the working class at a time when the passage of the National Industrial Recovery Act's (NIRA) right to organize provision had encouraged renewed working-class militancy.[17]

Although the opportunity for organizing in the south seemed propitious, Calloway expressed serious reservations about the ability of workers and unions to capitalize. He denounced the craft-oriented AFL's "incompetence" in its approach to organizing unskilled workers and described the UMWA as "eager" but handicapped by unqualified leadership. Workers, too, shared some of the blame. Reflecting his insistence on the need for personal transformation as a prerequisite for social involvement, Calloway lamented that the Kentucky miner "has never been weaned from the suckling breast of the operator, and manhood suddenly having been forced upon him by outside influences, he reminds one of a lad caught smoking a cigarette for the first time by his father, who stands undecided whether to declare his independence or take his punishment and go back to the so-called protective arms of his parent."[18]

Calloway conceded that in other instances white workers had been "busy as bees" in availing themselves of NIRA-inspired opportunities to organize. In contrast, African Americans were either "indifferent" or content to act as "Stepin Fetchits" or "Uncle Toms," thereby undermining the "really industrious Southern Negro." At this early stage of his political thinking, Calloway offered a host of competing perspectives: a firm belief that unionism was the best "means of fighting industrial despotism," doubts about the ability and commitment of union leadership, skepticism about the militancy of workers, and in the case of African Americans, a concern that they lacked the necessary discipline and self-confidence to function as effective unionists. Having been raised in an environment where coal companies dominated almost all aspects of workers' lives, Calloway feared that the shackles of patron-client relations would not easily be broken. His qualms soon yielded to greater hope and confidence, as he became exposed to a broader set of political influences, and the Committee for Industrial Organization (later the Congress of Industrial Organizations or CIO) moved forcefully to direct working-class militancy.[19]

Calloway's contact with the Urban League and especially Lester Granger, the official spearheading the League's effort to educate African American workers about unions, proved serendipitous. Granger concluded that in spite of the union movement's previous indifference and hostility to blacks, the extreme circumstances of the Depression suggested ". . . the day is gone when unorganized workers can protect themselves." In contrast to Calloway's harsh assessment of black workers, Granger described them as "discouraged" and "embittered" by the hostility of white unionists but by no means hopelessly apathetic. By forming workers' councils in cities throughout the country, he sought to change these attitudes by educating black workers about the benefits of unions and aligning the Urban League with the nascent industrial union movement. Impressed by Calloway's writing and hoping to encourage African Americans to aspire to leadership in the union movement, Granger and the editor of *Opportunity* helped the young miner win a scholarship to Brookwood Labor College in September 1934.[20]

Located north of New York City, Brookwood had been founded by missionaries associated with the pacifist Fellowship of Reconciliation in 1921. Brookwood aimed, in the words of one workers' education advocate, "to make workers understand the labor movement and . . . surround them with an atmosphere and influence which will create loyalty to the labor movement and to the working class." During the 1920s when the American union movement sharply declined in the face of intense corporate and political opposition, Brookwood remained committed to aggressive organizing, urged the union movement to reach out to African American workers, and prepared rank-and-file activists to help advance this agenda within their unions. These commitments gained momentum with the re-emergence of working-class militancy in the early 1930s and the more welcoming labor policies of the New Deal.[21]

Prior to his matriculation at Brookwood, Ernest Calloway described himself as a "provincial" and a "black hillbilly" with no fixed ideological views. Although his self-deprecation exaggerated his lack of sophistication, like Harold Gibbons, the former miner was captivated by his studies at a labor school and remembered it as a transformative experience. "For me," Calloway declared, "every class was an adventure in ideas." His all-star cast of teachers included the prominent labor economist and historian David Saposs, who especially influenced the young ex-miner. In addition to being a longtime Brookwood faculty member, Saposs had previously worked on the famed industrial economist John R. Commons's history of labor in the United States, wrote an influential book on left-wing unionism, and served as a union's education director. Saposs offered Calloway an example of how to function as both a union activist and a public intellectual capable of displaying institutional loyalty while also functioning as a thoughtful social critic.[22]

The influence of Brookwood on Calloway's thinking was evident in a November 1936 article he wrote for *Opportunity* titled "The CIO and Negro Labor." Echoing David Saposs's pragmatism and his dismissal of "unrealistic labor," Calloway chided the Knights of Labor for their "swampy mysticism" and inclusion of non-workers in their ranks, rebuked the Industrial Workers of the World for "being devoid of trade union realism," and excoriated the Communist Party's Trade Union Unity League for its "suicidal course of revolutionary dualism."

Curiously, he neglected to credit any of these organizations for their outreach to African Americans, their advocacy of industrial unionism, or their ability to craft effective appeals to the unskilled. The essay drew extensively on Marxist terminology, referring self-consciously to "the laws of dynamic social forces" and "the contradictions of capitalism," while advising its audience not to be too "panacea conscious" in believing that industrial unionism unaccompanied by strong "independent political action" could generate fundamental social change. These reflections contained elements that were to become staples in Calloway's thought: a focus on the economic forces that shaped political and social decision-making, an attachment to the pragmatic sensibilities associated with trade unionism and collective bargaining, a strong belief in independent political action for labor (a term not fully defined), and a pungent polemical style that delighted in deflating the arguments of those with whom he disagreed.[23]

After completing his year-long stint at Brookwood, Calloway looked to use his new knowledge in service of the working class. In 1936, he returned to the familiar turf of Lynchburg, VA, where he sought to organize unemployed WPA workers under the auspices of the Socialist Party's Workers Alliance of America. Although Calloway spent nearly a year organizing the unemployed and conducting classes in Virginia, he longed to become part of the dramatic organizing efforts that the newly formed CIO was mounting in auto and steel. Lester Granger, who had been cultivating ties with the new organization, recommended that the Steel Workers Organizing Committee (SWOC) hire Calloway and Henry Lee Moon, a black journalist and union activist. According to Calloway, Granger later informed him that "certain individuals in the National Negro Congress sabotaged the move to take me on as an organizer." In 1936, supporting its Popular Front strategy of broad outreach, the Communist Party (CP) had launched the National Negro Congress to unite disparate African American organizations into a working alliance that as one of its priorities sought to forge closer ties between blacks and unions. "Apparently," Calloway concluded in commenting on his rejected application to be a SWOC organizer, "my anti-Stalinist stance in unionism had become a liability."[24]

The exact origins of Calloway's anti-Stalinism are not entirely clear, but certainly, his antipathy towards the CP was stoked during his time at Brookwood. Although Brookwood had a distinctly leftist bent, many of its instructors had soured on communism, especially following Joseph Stalin's ascension to leadership of the Soviet Union. It was an encounter with Communist Party leader Earl Browder at Brookwood that seems to have made the most powerful impression on the young activist. At the time of Browder's visit in 1935, official CP policy favored establishment of an autonomous "Negro Republic" in the southern United States. Calloway recalled asking Browder if this proposal was tantamount to "superimposing a Russian ethnic approach on the U.S." He reported that Browder responded dismissively, calling Calloway "naïve" and insisting that

African Americans had a distinctive culture and language as evidenced by their speaking in a "Negro dialect."[25]

Following this encounter Calloway recalled "for weeks, I was kidded by fellow students of the sudden discovery that I had been speaking a foreign tongue." Although Calloway celebrated the distinctive contributions of blacks in shaping American culture, his familiarity with interracial cooperation in the UMWA and his own determined struggle to gain recognition as a full-fledged citizen precluded his support for any schemes based on racial separatism. His question to Browder also reflected his distaste for a "made in Moscow" prescription for addressing racial oppression in America and his belief that a separatist approach would simply isolate and marginalize African Americans in constricted racial enclaves. Moreover, Calloway denounced the proposed Negro Republic as an ill-conceived "propaganda vehicle" that the CP later discarded once it failed to generate black support.[26]

At Brookwood, Calloway had encountered former Communist intellectuals such as Bertram Wolfe and Will Herberg, both of whom were affiliated with the sectarian splinter group led by Jay Lovestone. Lovestone was a former American Communist Party leader who had broken with Joseph Stalin in 1929 and been expelled from the CP. Lovestone's belief that capitalism's deep roots in American political culture demanded a patient, measured approach clashed with Stalin's eagerness to launch a frontal assault on capitalist hegemony. His strategy acknowledging "American exceptionalism" clearly appealed to Ernest Calloway, who had no illusions about the revolutionary consciousness of American workers and knew from his experience in coal towns and the segregated south that overcoming "corporate feudalism" would be no easy feat. However, Lovestone's heresy made him an archenemy of the party establishment. Therefore, it is plausible that the CP-inspired National Negro Congress, which was working to cultivate ties with the CIO, sought to torpedo Calloway's candidacy for a position with SWOC on learning about his association with Lovestone's faction.[27]

With his entry into the CIO stymied, Calloway's own anti-communism hardened, drawing him more closely into Lovestone's orbit. In the spring of 1937, he headed to Detroit, where Lovestone angled to undercut CP influence within the fledgling United Auto Workers. Assigned to assist in this effort, Calloway made a stopover in Chicago, a fateful move that led to his initial encounter with Harold Gibbons and indelibly shaped his subsequent career.[28]

CHAPTER 3

Able and Militant Fighters for Workers

Ernest Calloway arrived in Chicago on the morning of May 30, 1937. Later that day, during an infamous event that came to be known as the Memorial Day Massacre, police attacked workers and their supporters who were picketing the Republic Steel plant in south Chicago, resulting in ten deaths and dozens of injuries. Amid the string of impressive victories the CIO had been compiling, the violence at Republic Steel represented a grim reminder that the advance of industrial unionism was by no means inevitable or assured. As Calloway recalled several years later, it was a "befitting anti-union welcome to one who had witnessed many of the bloody struggles to establish unionism and industrial democracy in that citadel of captive coal anti-unionism, Harlan County, Kentucky."[1]

Nonetheless, the Memorial Day Massacre represented a temporary setback for the industrial union movement, and Chicago quickly provided Calloway with his first opportunity to exercise leadership in a union setting. Although Harold Gibbons left Chicago not long after Calloway's arrival and they did not join forces until thirteen years later, their time in the Windy City led them to the shared experience of industrial union organizing and reinforced their faith in the potential of working-class mobilization. On a more visceral level, their stints in Chicago affirmed their growing sense of personal vitality and efficacy. As the novelist Richard Wright observed, ". . . there is an open and raw beauty about that city that either seems to kill or endow one with the spirit of life." In the case of Harold Gibbons and Ernest Calloway, their experiences in Chicago clearly suggested that the "spirit of life" had triumphed.[2]

* * *

During the time that Ernest Calloway had completed his wandering, matriculated at Brookwood, and searched for a niche in the union movement, Harold Gibbons had been busy solidifying his place within Chicago's labor community. By 1935, Gibbons's union, AFT Local 346, represented nearly 1,000 adult education teachers employed by the WPA. Although some AFT leaders resisted organizing

WPA teachers because they feared their lack of credentials would lower professional standards, most welcomed the energy and enthusiasm that these new recruits brought to the union. At the AFT's 1936 convention, the union officially committed itself to organizing the approximately 36,000 adult education teachers now employed by the WPA.[3]

Harold Gibbons spoke forcefully at the convention in support of this initiative, arguing that the union should assign a full-time official to lead this effort and provide sufficient resources to ensure its success. He also aggressively challenged delegates who advised caution in aligning the AFT with the CIO and supporting its industrial union insurgency, asking several times if they "fear[ed] to face the situation." Gibbons's brashness was apparently well-received by the convention delegates, who elected the twenty-six-year-old to a vice-presidential position and tapped him to lead the union's organization of adult education teachers. Following his election Gibbons began leaving Chicago periodically and gained national exposure in his efforts to recruit new members.[4]

Although the AFT organized nearly fifty WPA local teachers' unions between 1934 and 1939, Gibbons's status was neither certain nor secure. The newly formed WPA locals proved difficult to integrate into the broader culture of the AFT, because the concerns of non-credentialed adult education instructors differed from those of the professionally trained public school teachers that constituted the union's membership base. Moreover, the WPA locals often brimmed with sectarian controversy. Many of their members were young activists who had been radicalized by the Depression and were affiliated with left-wing groups that entered union politics in an attempt to gain leadership and translate revolutionary theory into practice. In Chicago, Harold Gibbons reported that in Local 346, he had to contend with active Socialist, Communist, Trotskyist, and Lovestoneite caucuses. By the summer of 1936, factional strife raged within Local 346, which according to the "Progressive Group" that Gibbons was associated with, "agitated our ranks and colored its internal life."[5]

Harold Gibbons's lifelong opposition to communism, a sentiment he shared with Ernest Calloway, appears to have congealed during this factional dispute. According to a June 25, 1936, document on an upcoming election of Local 346 officers prepared by the Progressive Group, Gibbons's faction had attempted to negotiate with its communist opponents but was met with "insolence" and a "blank refusal" to bargain. After a verbal agreement was finally reached to end hostilities, the communist caucus subsequently reneged. A specific sticking point was the unwillingness of the opposition to allow Gibbons a seat on the union's executive board, even though he had helped organize Local 346 and was "one of its most able and active members." Gibbons's caucus described this act as "an example of the most lightminded vindictiveness."[6]

Although there is no public record of Gibbons's reaction to these events, his direct experience with sectarian infighting appears to have soured him on the

CP. His subsequent references to what he regarded as the CP's lack of allegiance to democratic values and procedures perhaps most influenced his antipathy. Reflecting on the development of his political loyalties during the 1930s, Gibbons asserted that "the Socialist Party was advocating a democratic socialism as opposed to the totalitarianism of Communism." He consistently argued that "the only effective antidote to communism is a vigorous democracy which in its application can insure the highest possible degree of economic security and human justice." Although Gibbons's own political views continued to reflect a socialist sensibility, he regarded the CP as a disruptive, illegitimate force that he opposed without hesitation or compunction throughout his career. Indeed, Gibbons displayed a zest for sectarian conflict that matched if not exceeded the zeal of his communist opponents. Also, by designating a commitment to democratic values and practices as the chief distinction between his brand of unionism and that of the CP, he established a clear standard that he would strive to meet, at least during his early union career, and by which his own leadership would subsequently be judged.[7]

The Chicago phase of Gibbons's career took a decisive turn in the spring of 1937. The Roosevelt administration reduced the WPA adult education program's budget as part of a broader retrenchment in government spending, prompting the layoff of many of its teachers. At the same time, the CIO's early victories in the rubber, steel, and auto industries propelled organizing at workplaces throughout Chicago. In March, a strike among the city's taxi drivers spontaneously erupted. Inspired by deteriorating conditions and the contagion of organizing sweeping the city, "even the more individualistic drivers," according to historian Barbara Newell, "discovered the positive aspects of worker solidarity that were being preached elsewhere in the industrial community." The strike became a local cause célèbre, especially after management employed scabs in an effort to break the strike.[8]

Harold Gibbons was friendly with the taxi drivers' attorney and volunteered to help edit their strike bulletin. When the organizer who was assisting the strikers left for another assignment, Gibbons assumed coordination of the effort. Moving from the more genteel world of teacher unionism into a full-blown industrial conflict energized the young organizer, who recalled that "hundreds of guys were jailed and we moved the strike headquarters to a different place each night in an attempt to avoid harassment." Gibbons also sent a fiery message to cab company management about the strikers' determination: "Management needs to realize that they are dealing with MEN WITH GUTS who know what they want and will stick it out till they get it." Gibbons's effort to channel working-class anger and assure cabbies that they possessed the capacity to deal with their bosses on equal terms became central themes in his emerging approach to mobilizing workers.[9]

After the strike ended successfully in April 1937, Gibbons's prestige soared and led to his involvement in helping other Chicago workers organize under the banner of the CIO. His activities angered Chicago Federation of Labor president

John Fitzpatrick, who had remained loyal to the AFL despite his long record of support for industrial unionism. Fitzpatrick, who was close to Gibbons's mentor, Lillian Herstein, and had befriended the young organizer, apparently felt betrayed by his deepening CIO loyalties. After consulting with AFL president William Green, Fitzpatrick expelled Gibbons's AFT local in May 1937 after what press accounts called a "stormy" meeting. Local 346 was later reinstated, but the agreement barred Harold Gibbons from returning to the CFL. There is no record of Gibbons's reaction to his expulsion, but he did not appear to be overly disturbed by Fitzpatrick's actions. Given the declining membership of Local 346, his unsettling experience with factionalism, and budget cuts at the WPA, Gibbons's future prospects in the AFT had dimmed. Moreover, following the heady experience of the taxi strike, he readily grasped the potential of industrial unionism, the power of direct action, and the opportunity to exercise leadership on a larger stage.[10]

Under the direction of Frank Rosenblum, a Socialist and Chicago-based vice-president of the Amalgamated Clothing Workers, Gibbons began working with the Midwest region of the CIO and later as an organizer for the newly formed Textile Workers Organizing Committee (TWOC). He encountered an electric environment of spontaneous outbreaks of worker militancy, recalling that "we used to send a crew out just to walk the streets and find the sit-down strikes that were taking place in restaurants, factories, and anywhere else." Capitalizing on this militancy, Gibbons aided department store, laundry, and warehouse workers in Chicago and throughout Illinois and Indiana as a regional CIO organizer.[11]

Gibbons wasted no time becoming embroiled in the rough and tumble of mass mobilization and direct action. Assisting what a Champaign, IL, newspaper described as "girl pickets" who were attempting to organize the laundry where they worked, Gibbons was arrested by local police, an experience that occurred repeatedly during his years with the CIO. Leading a strike at a South Bend, IN, garment factory during the summer of 1937, the twenty-seven-year-old Gibbons demonstrated his quick adaptation to the arena of bare-knuckled labor conflict. He was arrested several times on the picket line and faced a variety of charges, including violating a court order and inciting to riot, in part because of allegations he had "slugged" a worker attempting to break the strike. Returning to the picket line after one of his arrests, Gibbons exhorted the mostly female group of strikers to keep scabs from entering the plant, reportedly declaring, ". . . we are going to fight it out on the picket line; that is better than in the courts." The hostile encounters with police and the courts left Gibbons with an enduring distrust of governmental authority. As he later told a journalist in recounting his CIO experience, "We were outlaws. If you could have seen the way the cops treated us in those days, you'd understand a little more about why we became so cynical and disgusted about law and the establishment."[12]

These attitudes hardened during Gibbons's experience with the Textile Workers Organizing Committee, which he joined in 1938 for a two-year stint. TWOC's effort to organize the southern textile industry was spearheaded by Sidney Hillman, one of America's most respected labor leaders who, along with John L. Lewis, had orchestrated the CIO's 1935 break with the AFL. Hillman developed a sophisticated carrot and stick approach to gain union recognition from southern textile manufacturers. The carrot was Hillman's promise of "responsible unionism" that could benefit employers by helping stabilize an often chaotic industry. The stick was TWOC's potential to wage selective strikes and the threat that the new National Labor Relations Board would intervene to punish managerial wrongdoing. However, most southern textile employers rejected Hillman's inducement of the stabilizing benefits of collective bargaining and remained adamantly opposed to unionization.[13]

Gibbons ran afoul of Hillman's carefully calibrated strategy, gaining a reputation within TWOC as a "hellraiser" and "agitator." A 1939 strike he led at the Louisville Textile Company resulted in imagery that TWOC had studiously attempted to avoid in organizing within a "genteel" social milieu. In Gibbons's memory, "hundreds of women workers would lie down in the slush and mud to keep the scabs out and there would be hair-pulling sessions among the women when scabs would attempt to cross the lines." When the company finally agreed to settle, it was on the condition that Gibbons be transferred. Gibbons's zeal for direct action rankled TWOC leaders, who claimed he "had far too many strikes to be a good negotiator." His aggression especially irked Sidney Hillman, who Gibbons recalled, "fired me four times because I wasn't satisfied with recognition—I wanted to fight for union shop contracts."[14]

Gibbons's clashes with Hillman and others in the TWOC hierarchy both disturbed and inspired the young organizer. In a 1957 interview, Gibbons explained that he had first assumed leadership of the distribution workers union in St. Louis "to prove to Hillman that I could administer an outfit and accept responsibility, that I wasn't just another dime a dozen labor leader." Beyond the personal dimensions of Gibbons's differences with Hillman lay distinct visions of labor strategy and leadership. At this stage of his career, Gibbons rejected the posture of industrial statesmanship and responsible unionism espoused by Hillman. His memories of the feudal relations practiced in company towns and his encounters with the police and courts as a CIO organizer made him much less willing than Hillman to place his faith in what Steve Fraser has described as the "social potential" of the administrative state. Instead, Gibbons's profound distrust of authority, whether corporate or governmental, impelled him to use working-class power as a blunt instrument capable of wringing concessions from employers and the political forces that supported them. In the coal fields, among WPA teachers in Chicago, and among industrial workers throughout the Midwest and upper South, Gibbons had encountered a working class full of fighting spirit. At this point in his career, he was prepared to ride these waves of militancy as far as they could take him.[15]

Toward the end of his two-year stint with TWOC, Gibbons met the woman who shortly thereafter became his wife. Like most socialists and others on the political left, he feared that Franklin Roosevelt's arms sales and loans to the Allies reflected a policy that viewed war as the only means by which economic prosperity could be sustained. At a 1939 anti-war rally on the University of Louisville campus, Gibbons encountered Anne Culter, an art history major from a well-to-do family that traced its roots back to colonial times. As a young idealist growing up in a conservative political environment, Culter was instantly attracted to the tall, handsome, and articulate labor organizer, who was one of the first bona fide leftists she had encountered in Louisville. They married several months later and had three children, two sons and a daughter, over the course of the next decade.[16]

By 1940, the thirty-year-old Harold Gibbons had become a husband and father, a committed unionist, and, as a worker who encountered him during his TWOC days recalled three decades later, "an able and militant fighter for workers." His vision of unionism and his political philosophy had come into sharper focus: a resolute anti-communism that nonetheless continued to view economic and political relations through a socialist lens, skepticism toward excessive reliance on the administrative apparatus of the state, a strong commitment to direct action by workers, and a clear realization of the challenges involved in organizing. Although his reputation in TWOC had been checkered, not even his harshest detractors questioned Gibbons's talent and determination. When an offer came in 1941 to lead a group of warehouse workers in St. Louis who had unionized several years earlier, he readily accepted and began a thirty-year association in which he and his union would re-cast the political and social landscape of the Gateway City.

* * *

Soon after his arrival in Chicago, Ernest Calloway met two men who played instrumental roles in shaping his career. Through a contact working on a WPA research project that helped launch Horace Cayton and St. Clair Drake's famed urban study *Black Metropolis*, he encountered Willard Townsend and John Yancey. Townsend and Yancey were leading an effort to organize the nation's red caps, a mostly African American group of workers who handled passengers' baggage at the nation's railroad terminals. Calloway quickly embraced their campaign and abandoned his mission to help Jay Lovestone undercut communist influence in Detroit auto factories. To support himself, Calloway obtained employment with the Chicago WPA worker education program and joined the adult education teachers' union, where he first met Harold Gibbons. The "tall, lanky, aggressive young organizer" immediately made a strong impression on the Brookwood College graduate that lingered long after Gibbons left Chicago to work for the CIO.[17]

Red caps had emerged in the late nineteenth century to help railroad passengers transport their baggage while boarding or disembarking from trains. Their name derived from the action of a porter in New York who tied a strip of red flannel around his cap to be recognized. Although most red caps were African American, there was a smattering of whites and Asians, mostly Japanese, within their ranks. Many of the black red caps were well-educated, with one local union estimating that seventy-two of its ninety members had attended college, including two who were doctors. Indeed, Willard Townsend, who became president of the red caps union and served on the executive board of the CIO, had attended the University of Toronto and the Royal College of Sciences in Canada.[18]

Given the limited job opportunities available even for educated African Americans in a racially segmented labor market, red capping carried considerable prestige and security. Nonetheless, the red caps' working conditions deteriorated with the onset of the Depression. Faced with declining ridership, many railroads decided to forego paying wages and instead forced red caps to rely solely on tips. Employers also shifted to smaller crews and the use of more temporary workers, actions that eroded any sense of job security. As Calloway tartly observed, railroad management now considered red caps to be "independent concessionaires" or "privileged trespassers," and their workplace had become a "competitive gratuity jungle [where] every man was out for himself." This reduction of proud, educated black men to the status of servants outraged Calloway, who saw the railroads' disregard for their workers' well-being as akin to the "corporate feudalism" he had encountered in the coal fields.[19]

Angered by their worsening conditions and diminished status, red caps began to organize in the mid-1930s, but they faced a thicket of obstacles. Local red cap unions had sprung up in different stations and gained federal charters with the AFL but concluded that the federation was unwilling to devote sufficient resources to help create an effective national organization. The fledgling red caps union also had to resist efforts by the AFL-affiliated Brotherhood of Railway and Steamship Clerks (BRSC) to assert jurisdiction, a claim it particularly resented because the BRSC was only willing to organize African Americans on a segregated basis. However, the most challenging hurdle the red caps faced was the unwillingness of railroad management to recognize them as employees, which left them without legal status and outside the protections of labor law. Consequently, as Calloway later explained, "... red caps for the most part were confined to a peculiar no man's land; they were not employees of the company for which they labored daily, and they were covered by the jurisdiction of a union they could not join."[20]

Just prior to Calloway's arrival in Chicago, the disparate local red cap unions formed the International Brotherhood of Red Caps (later to become the United Transport Service Employees of America or UTSEA). Initially, the union's membership was interracial, but this promising show of unity was short-lived. Many white red caps expressed doubt that railroad management would ever negotiate with a union headed by African Americans and returned to the BRSC, which persisted in its refusal to organize on an interracial basis.[21]

As whites departed, the union decided to break with the AFL. This was the situation that Calloway encountered when he first met Willard Townsend in the summer of 1937, and he sensed an opportunity to play a far more significant role than he would have been permitted as one of Jay Lovestone's minions in Detroit. Calloway gained quick acceptance from red cap leaders who recognized the former miner's strategic acumen. In turn, he discovered ingredients for social change and labor militancy that had eluded him in the Kentucky coal fields and Virginia. In the more welcoming, cosmopolitan culture of Chicago, he found a sophisticated group of black workers willing to take risks, bold leaders committed to helping them secure justice, and a progressive activist network he could tap for both intellectual stimulation and political support. The opportunity to demonstrate that "colored men" could successfully "run things" also appealed to Calloway, who was eager to help black workers gain not only economic justice but also a sense of personal efficacy and social respect.[22]

Calloway moved to help the red caps develop an effective organization and formulate a strategy for gaining union recognition. Among his immediate objectives was gaining a commitment for a union newspaper that would inform the membership about the union's activities and create a greater sense of unity among the red caps' disparate local units. Launched in the fall of 1937, *Bags and Baggage* was the first publication over which Calloway had substantial editorial authority. Under his direction the paper sought to educate the red caps about "the history, theory, and practice of unions" and gain acceptance for labor's role as a force for social change. The result was a lively publication that included poems, cartoons, book reviews, and commentary, along with numerous stories and photographs spotlighting rank-and-file activity in both the workplace and the community. Commenting on Calloway's desire to nurture pride in the economic, cultural, and political achievements of African American unionists, Horace Cayton praised *Bags and Baggage* as "the best example of Workers Education in a Negro trade union or at least a union where Negroes predominate."[23]

Although the red caps had withdrawn from the AFL, Calloway realized they needed to develop ties with progressive elements in the union movement and cultivate broader social relationships. Drawing on his Brookwood connections, Calloway convinced labor and political leaders to join an advisory board for the red caps. One of the board's members was Harold Gibbons's benefactor, Paul Douglas. Douglas, who Calloway would later describe as a "dear friend," introduced the red caps to Leon Despres, a lawyer who had once been an NLRB trial examiner and a Socialist Party member. In contrast to Harold Gibbons's use of direct action as a primary tactic, Calloway and the red caps relied on government intervention to legitimize their representational claims. Leon Despres helped the union devise its "March Forward to Legality" strategy, which aimed to convince the Interstate Commerce Commission (ICC) that the red caps were bona fide employees entitled to protection under the Railway Labor Act (RLA). As a result of these efforts, the ICC ruled in the red caps' favor in September 1938, allowing the new union to file for representation elections and negotiate directly with railroad management.[24]

In an October 15, 1938, *Chicago Defender* article, Calloway hailed the ICC ruling "as a new landmark in the development of Race labor in America" and took justifiable pride in the integral role he had played in helping the red caps gain legal status. Yet his assertion a year later that the union had shifted its emphasis from legal efforts to ensure workers' rights toward a focus on organizing, bargaining, and representational activities was overstated. Gaining union recognition did not translate directly into bargaining strength, and the red caps were forced to rely on the minimum wage provisions of the newly enacted Fair Labor Standards Act (FLSA) to raise pay for their members. Railroad management also sought to circumvent the FLSA standards by arguing that tips should be counted as wages, thereby reducing its salary liability and lowering the red caps' overall pay. The Wage and Hour Division of the Department of Labor ruled in the union's favor, but the Supreme Court later overturned this ruling. Although Calloway publicly hailed the union's success in making railroad management "look on their red caps in a new light," he was too much the student of power relations not to appreciate the perils of excessive reliance on the state and the persistent problems presented by the union's limited ability to wrest concessions from employers at the bargaining table.[25]

During his early years with the UTSEA, Ernest Calloway also began to articulate a concept of working-class citizenship. Describing the union as a "miniature government" in the workplace, he declared that this new entity was buttressed by a "24 hour police force" that operated to ensure railroad management would respect its contractual obligations. The imagery of workplace constitutionalism was a staple among many New Deal era advocates of industrial democracy, suggesting that the shop floor would no longer be a setting where employers had predominant decision-making authority. For Calloway, industrial citizenship also had other implications. In the workplace it meant that red caps could not solely rely on the intercession of their leaders if they were to exercise their new citizenship status effectively. Instead, they had to continually educate themselves and their fellow workers about the responsibilities of union membership, actively assist their leaders in contract enforcement, and prepare for direct action to preserve their burgeoning economic security. Moreover, Calloway encouraged the red caps to use the new skills and confidence they had gained as unionists and apply this acumen to the broader struggle for civil rights and social equality in their communities.[26]

Accompanying these thoughts on working-class citizenship, Calloway began to elaborate his views on the relationship between work, family, and community that had begun to animate his thinking about an appropriate social role for the newly powerful union movement. In a January 1940 piece in *Bags and Baggage* titled "Women, the Home, and the Union," he asserted that the "home and family of its membership should be the real organization units of the Brotherhood. In the struggle for security the working red cap plays one part and the family plays [the] other part," with both settings being "equally important." Dismissing what he called the "old-fashioned" view that the union is an "exclusively man's world," he argued that the UTSEA's women's auxiliary was integral to the union's success and called for red cap wives to become more involved in politics, consumer movements, and support for trade unionism. Indeed, his future wife became the national director of the UTSEA's women's auxiliaries in 1942, further attesting to the importance he assigned this activity.[27]

At one level Calloway was affirming the role that most women's auxiliaries played within the labor movement. By serving as "union wives," most auxiliaries reinforced women's traditional roles as managers and keepers of the home, albeit with greater resources to make the domestic realm more comfortable and secure. At the same time, Calloway was eager to have both black men and women understand that while the union enhanced the security of home and family, this security did not exist in isolation from the surrounding community. Given the pervasiveness of racism in both their workplaces and communities, he realized that African Americans were more likely than white workers to grasp the integral connection between these spheres. Although Calloway was not advocating a major shift in gender roles, he began to glimpse the possibilities of a strategy that acknowledged the vital relationship between work and family matters and capitalized on women's untapped potential to act as effective political citizens.[28]

By the early 1940s, Calloway had few regrets about his having remained in Chicago rather than completing his intended journey to Detroit. From his solid perch as education director for the UTSEA, he began to enter the realm of cultural and political affairs in Chicago, developing relationships that sharpened his political vision, enhancing his appreciation of the city as an arena where working-class citizenship could be effectively exercised, and reaching a larger audience as a confident and assertive public voice.

Like Harold Gibbons several years earlier, Calloway became part of a progressive political network that he later described as "an interlocking directorate in the field of social action . . . that set much of the social action tone of the city at the time." Calloway worked with numerous labor-liberal-church alliances, serving as a director of the Institute on Racial Minorities and an executive board member of Labor's Council for Community Action. He also was a member of the People's Forum, a program sponsored by a Chicago community center directed by *Black*

Metropolis co-author Horace Cayton. The People's Forum discussed a wide range of domestic and foreign issues affecting African Americans and sought to give "community members sociological knowledge for understanding local issues."[29]

The young activists with whom Calloway worked experimented with new social protest tactics and drew on the industrial union movement's expanding power to develop a broader labor-community alliance capable of moving Chicago politics in a more progressive direction. In 1944, he served as vice-chairman of the American Commonwealth Party, a Socialist-inspired effort in Chicago to create "a mass political party of the left . . . to solve the problems of poverty, unemployment, and wars. . . ." This approach, however, risked confining Calloway to the political margins in a city dominated by a powerful Democratic Party machine. Although the machine had made some efforts to accommodate African American interests, it remained largely under the control of white ethnic ward leaders whose relations with blacks resembled those of patron and client. Many African Americans in Chicago had switched their allegiance from the Republican to the Democratic Party during the New Deal, but at least half hesitated to make the shift, continuing to doubt the Democrats' commitment to an aggressive assault on discriminatory practices.[30]

The subservient relations embedded in machine politics reminded Calloway of the feudal relations in coal towns that he found so abhorrent. In 1940, he became involved in an effort to install a "new indigenous Negro Democratic party leadership" that would provide "black voters [with] representation and empowerment as well as favors from the Democratic Party." Supporting the insurgent candidacy of UTSEA president Willard Townsend, Calloway and his allies aimed to unseat Arthur Mitchell, the ward's African American congressman, who was widely regarded as beholden to the Democratic Party machine's white overlords. Running on an "anti-bossism" platform, Townsend's insurgency failed due to low name recognition and his lack of electoral experience. In spite of this defeat, Calloway remained committed to pursuing greater African American political independence and more fully appreciated the challenges involved in taking on entrenched political power.[31]

In addition to his political and community work, Calloway also found another public platform through his frequent writings for the *Chicago Defender*, one of the nation's most popular black newspapers. Although most of his contributions consisted of articles reporting on the progress of the red caps, Calloway occasionally wrote longer, reflective commentaries on contemporary social issues. A piece on "Negro Labor" that appeared in July 1942 offered important insights into his evolving social and political thought.

Calloway hailed the CIO's commitment to organizing African American workers (indeed, UTSEA had affiliated with the CIO in 1942) as integral to creating a "functional industrial democracy" and proudly listed the names of several dozen blacks who had become union leaders. In addition to building strong unions that would provide a powerful social example of interracial cooperation, Calloway also urged African American union leaders to use their growing power and prestige to help establish an assertive political presence at the community level. Yet Calloway cautioned African American unionists to eschew a "narrow racializing of all important issues" and urged them to resist the tendency "to think too much with our skins instead of our minds. . . ." In de-emphasizing direct appeals to racial pride, Calloway faced the persistent challenge of convincing his fellow African Americans that the lens of class was more strategically useful and politically relevant than the lens of race. This approach, which he maintained throughout his career, was not always an easy sell to a people who in such a color conscious society could not help, in Calloway's terms, continuing to "think with their skins."[32]

Nonetheless, Calloway remained attuned to the richness of African American culture and reveled in becoming part of Bronzeville, the name that black Chicagoans proudly used to describe their vibrant south side community. Having been too young and immature to appreciate the offerings of the Harlem Renaissance when he was a teenager, he immersed himself in Chicago's Black Renaissance, the clustering of writers, poets, artists, and scholars that made Chicago a political and cultural mecca for African Americans. Calloway also began to appreciate the city as both a social organism and an ecological system whose interrelated parts (housing, schools, infrastructure, political and cultural institutions) merged to create a fertile social environment that could serve as a vehicle for personal development and an incubator for fulfilling the promise of American democracy. And whenever Calloway despaired about the fate of the city, he would remind himself of the constricted life he had escaped from, telling one interviewer, "I had too tough a time in the coal fields not to enjoy being an urban resident." This deep attachment to the city and profound belief in its vital social role powerfully shaped Calloway's strategic prescriptions for both the civil rights and the union movements, especially after he arrived in St. Louis and became committed to changing that city's political culture.[33]

Calloway's immersion in Bronzeville's rich cultural milieu drew him to Martha Briggs Sutton, a features writer for the *Chicago Defender* whose pen name was Diana Briggs. Sutton was the daughter of a veteran educator who had held administrative positions at black colleges throughout the southern United States. A graduate of Fisk University and a "gifted soprano," Sutton had also studied in Europe. She reportedly "thrilled" Chicago audiences in the late 1930s and directed a music program at Barber-Scotia College in North Carolina before returning to Chicago and assuming her post with the *Defender*. The couple was married on January 21, 1942, by Archibald Carey, Jr., a prominent black Chicago minister and civic leader who would later take on the city's political machine. A *Defender* notice on the wedding showed a dapper, relaxed Calloway smiling warmly at his bride. His marriage to such an accomplished member of Chicago's black cultural elite in a ceremony performed by one of the city's most respected clerics underscored the completeness of Calloway's transition from "black hillbilly" to urban sophisticate. Chicago, in Richard's Wright's words, had fully "endowed him with the spirit of life" in just a few short years. The security of his status, however, would be tested seriously as America went to war, the red caps faced new challenges, and Calloway renewed his search for meaning and purpose as his old restlessness re-emerged.[34]

CHAPTER 4

"A Bunch of Fellows Who Have Taken the Declaration of Independence Seriously"

For liberals and radicals in the union movement, the United States' entry into World War II posed a host of complex challenges: balancing support for the fight against fascism with continuing skepticism about the democratic commitments and ultimate aims of America's political leaders, determining the extent to which trade union militancy should be moderated in accommodating the war effort, and assessing how new political arrangements that offered labor enhanced authority could be used to enact a broader working-class agenda.

These calculations occupied Harold Gibbons and Ernest Calloway throughout the war years, and their responses placed each of them outside the social consensus embraced by most Americans, the union movement, and the political left. Nonetheless, in St. Louis, Harold Gibbons gained credibility as a union leader and discovered a group of workers with whom he could begin to implement his emerging vision of total person unionism. At the same time, Ernest Calloway's odyssey took a more dramatic turn with his refusal to serve in a Jim Crow military. This act, along with the experience of personal tragedy, led Calloway away from his secure perch in Chicago. Before he arrived in St. Louis and joined Harold Gibbons in 1950, Calloway's wanderlust re-emerged, transporting him to new arenas where he attempted to regain his footing, clarify his thinking, and affirm his dual identity as an activist and a public intellectual.

* * *

At the behest of a vice president of the United Retail, Wholesale, and Department Store Employees of America (URWDSEA) whom he apparently had known in Chicago, and URWDSEA president Samuel Wolchok, Harold Gibbons arrived in St. Louis in 1941 to assume leadership of the city's warehouse workers. Benefitting from its strategic location on the Mississippi River, St. Louis boasted a diversified economy rooted in industries such as auto assembly and auto parts, light manufacturing, beer brewing, agricultural processing, and warehousing.

These industries were overseen by a self-conscious local business and civic elite that in Ernest Calloway's words sought "to limit outside investment and the development of heavy industry." Operating within a broader regional economy dominated by independent and single plant operations, business leaders felt particular pressure to keep wages low to offset larger competitors who could extract savings through economies of scale. By the 1930s, however, industrial unions forcefully challenged this strategy, led by the United Electrical Workers (UE) and their charismatic leader William Sentner. Sit-down strikes at Emerson Electric in 1936 and Chevrolet's Fisher Body plant in 1937 were among the most visible uprisings, with clothing and steel workers joining the fray along with the warehouse workers Harold Gibbons was summoned to lead.[1]

St. Louis's strategic geographic location made warehousing and distribution an integral part of both the local and regional economy. As unskilled and semi-skilled workers without representation, the area's many warehousing and distribution employees suffered at the hands of their employers. Wages were low, overtime irregularly paid, and layoffs imposed with little regard for seniority. In addition to these grievances, the indignity of frequent arbitrary treatment outraged warehouse workers. As longtime union activist Elzie "Red" Smith recalled, after a co-worker's friend had died in an accident, the worker requested permission to attend his friend's funeral. According to Smith, the worker was told by his supervisor: "You can't take off work, this is the heavy season.... You can do me more good that you can him. He's dead."[2]

Although St. Louis warehouse and distribution workers received some assistance from other CIO unions, they largely organized on their own. The workers' aggressive tactics, which included a sit-down strike protesting the firing of a union activist and picketing the homes of nonunion workers to persuade them to join the union, convinced several major employers to capitulate without putting up much resistance. The picket sign of a local union of J.C. Penney warehouse workers underscored the union's success in raising the workers' standard of living: "Now Making Dollars Where Pennies from Before." Another sign attested to the democratic aspirations of the workers and their belief that the union was upholding traditional American values: "Organized Labor is Freedom's Protector." Staking their claims as workers and citizens, St. Louis warehouse and distribution employees flocked to the CIO, prompting the national organization to seek a permanent home for them within a specific union.[3]

Jurisdiction was a continual issue for warehouse and distribution workers with multiple AFL and CIO unions vying to represent them. After the national CIO ordered the St. Louis warehouse locals to join its retail and distribution affiliate in 1938, the fiercely independent workers reluctantly complied. In return, they extracted a commitment from union president Samuel Wolchok to establish a warehouse division and provide them with additional resources to help them continue organizing their jurisdiction. However, by the time Harold Gibbons arrived in St. Louis in 1941, local unions complained that Wolchok had not honored his pledges and viewed their national leaders with disdain.[4]

Although the St. Louis warehousemen had a reputation for unruliness that Wolchok was eager to curb, Harold Gibbons responded positively to their militancy. He found a core of workers from gritty backgrounds among the leadership of the warehousemen, including some from mining families. The coal miner's son quickly bonded with them, appreciating their instinctive sense of solidarity and faith in unionism as a means of democratizing workplace relations. Gibbons's immediate tasks were to turn a weak advisory council into a strong, centrally organized body, combine individual local unions into coordinated industry-wide units, and reinvigorate organizing campaigns. His efforts were well-received by the supposedly ungovernable warehousemen, who in a December 1941 newsletter expressed their confidence in his leadership: "Since 'Hal' came to St. Louis a few short months ago, the membership has learned to depend on him to furnish a clear realistic program of action in any crisis which may arise."[5]

One initial crisis that Gibbons used as a rallying point was a jurisdictional conflict that erupted late in 1941 when the International Longshoremen's and Warehousemen's Union (ILWU) came to St. Louis and attempted to organize workers at Rice-Stix, a major wholesaler and apparel manufacturer with a national distribution network. Having secured their position on the west coast, ILWU leaders were eager to extend their jurisdiction to other parts of the country. Prior to Gibbons's arrival, St. Louis warehousemen, especially those involved in distribution occupations, had resisted suggestions from the CIO that they affiliate with the ILWU, citing "certain ideological issues" that would undercut their efforts in "convincing the public that our people were in accord with the sentiment prevailing [in] the great *Middle* West." Presumably, these "ideological issues" referred to the strong communist presence within the ILWU's ranks that was condoned by union president Harry Bridges, himself a suspected but publicly unacknowledged Communist Party member.[6]

Harold Gibbons attacked Bridges and the ILWU on several fronts. Besides denouncing them as communists, he charged that the ILWU leader was acting without CIO authorization and establishing dual unionism in St. Louis that would "result in chaos and disorder in the labor movement." To deter the ILWU incursion, Gibbons urged the St. Louis warehousemen to amalgamate their disparate locals, pool their resources, and rededicate themselves to aggressive organizing. The successful repulsion of Harry Bridges's "invasion" of St. Louis firmly established Gibbons's leadership of the St. Louis distribution workers and acquired a mythic status in the union. This episode revealed several tactics that would become hallmarks of Gibbons's union leadership: a bare-knuckled approach to matters of jurisdiction, a shrewd ability to rally the rank and file by portraying opponents as meddling outsiders, and an unabashed willingness to level charges of communist affiliation as a political weapon.[7]

By 1942 Gibbons had succeeded in merging all St. Louis warehouse locals into a joint council, reflecting what became an enduring commitment to centralized administration as an essential feature of successful unionism. Membership increased from 1,900 to 4,100 during his first two years as the union's director, and at the bargaining table, the union made impressive strides. In August 1942, the three largest wholesalers in St. Louis granted workers substantial pay raises, and the union convinced employers to eliminate a separate pay classification for African American workers. For unskilled and semi-skilled workers who until recently had been grossly underpaid and for black workers languishing in segregated pay scales, these gains attested to the power of solidarity and the leadership ability of the union's new director.[8]

In St. Louis, Gibbons also found a group of workers who shared his qualms about becoming mired in an entangling alliance with the administrative state and were eager to defend their improved standard of living. Once the United States entered World War II after the Japanese attack on Pearl Harbor, most of the union movement agreed to support the war effort and refrain from striking for the duration of the conflict. The no-strike pledge reflected both the deep patriotism felt by most unionists and a pragmatic calculation that support for the war effort would pay significant dividends. The Roosevelt administration's establishment of a National War Labor Board (NWLB) to oversee labor-management relations and the prospect of increasing union membership through a modified version of the union shop known as "maintenance of membership" also offered powerful incentives for most unions to cooperate with the president.[9]

Throughout the war Harold Gibbons and the workers he represented repeatedly criticized the union movement's bargain with the Roosevelt administration. "Maintenance of membership is a sorry substitute for the union shop and was an outright concession to the employer," the union charged in an April 26, 1944, editorial in its official publication, *Midwest Labor World*. Showing contempt for the wartime labor relations apparatus and affirming his faith in working-class militancy, Gibbons breathed socialist and syndicalist fire: "It is our job to wrest control of the agencies of government so that we instead of the employers will enjoy the benefits we rightly deserve as producers of the wealth of the world."[10]

Gibbons coupled his disdain for wartime cooperation between labor, management, and government with continuing advocacy of independent political action. He favored formation of a labor party and only grudgingly supported his old antagonist Sidney Hillman's formation of the CIO Political Action Committee (PAC) in an effort to revive labor liberalism. Following the 1944 election, he continued to press for independent political action, declaring, "we gave our support too early and too cheaply." He also insisted that workers must be prepared to step in and "run industries" that management might abandon if they failed to turn a profit.[11]

These positions placed Gibbons well outside the consensus that guided union strategy during World War II. His denunciations of the wartime labor relations regime, insistence on the need for direct action, and attacks on communists led some in the St. Louis labor community to charge that he was a member of the Socialist Workers Party (SWP). The SWP was a Trotskyist sect that was unalterably opposed to Joseph Stalin's leadership of Soviet Union, distrusted the intentions of the Allies while critically supporting the war against fascism, and refused to renounce strikes as a working-class weapon. The available evidence suggests that Gibbons had no formal relationship with the SWP, although he was clearly acquainted with some of its leaders, attended SWP gatherings, and occasionally contributed to its efforts. The close correspondence between his pronouncements and the SWP's positions does suggest, however, that he was significantly influenced by the party's views, even if he resisted formal affiliation.[12]

In spite of his fiery advocacy of working-class militancy, Harold Gibbons exercised restraint throughout the war, recognizing that engaging in protracted strikes and acting in isolation carried serious risks. His union only conducted two brief strikes and continued to use both NLRB and NWLB procedures in adjudicating labor disputes. The union's experience with these boards during its wartime effort to organize Famous-Barr, however, reinforced Gibbons's grave reservations about the limits of New Deal and World War II industrial jurisprudence. Famous-Barr, which became a longtime nemesis for Harold Gibbons and his union, was St. Louis's most prestigious department store. It was owned by the May Company, one of the nation's leading department store chains whose corporate headquarters were based in St. Louis. Gibbons and the URWDSEA were convinced that if they could successfully organize Famous-Barr, they would have the momentum and leverage needed to bring thousands of other department store workers in St. Louis under their jurisdiction and establish the retail workers as the city's preeminent labor organization.

In 1942, the union began its effort to organize the company it dubbed the "gilded sweatshop." In response, Famous-Barr unleashed a full repertoire of tactics designed to discourage unionization, resulting in the union's defeat in representation elections held in 1944 and 1945. One store manager's assertion during an NLRB hearing that "it took me a long time to get the Wagner Act through my head" illustrated for Gibbons the hazards of relying on labor law and strengthened his determination to return to direct action once wartime restrictions were lifted.[13]

Gibbons's wartime restraint did not, however, extend to the Communist Party (CP). The CP had a visible and active presence in the St. Louis industrial union movement, largely through the success of the United Electrical Workers (UE) and their dynamic leader, William Sentner, who in contrast to many CP unionists openly acknowledged his party membership. As the largest union in St. Louis, the UE played a significant role in the local CIO Industrial Union Council (IUC) and spearheaded an imaginative campaign to create a Missouri Valley Authority to oversee flood control and economic development along the Missouri River. However, with CP policy dictating a subordination of trade union militancy in deference to the besieged Soviet Union, the UE faced growing criticism within the council. Fresh from his tussle with Harry Bridges and influenced by the Trotskyist critique of the CP's wartime stances, Harold Gibbons assumed a prominent role in seeking to negate its influence.[14]

Gibbons's wrath against the CP grew exponentially during the URWDSEA's April 1944 strike against mail order giant Montgomery Ward. Montgomery Ward's chair, Sewell Avery, was an arch-conservative opponent of the New Deal who had defied the NWLB's directives to bargain. The union's leadership dispatched Gibbons to see if he could convince the ILWU, which represented workers at some of the company's warehouses, to support the strike. The ILWU's CP-leaning leadership, however, rejected his request. For Gibbons, the ILWU's refusal to support the job action against Montgomery Ward, which was the sole wartime strike authorized by the CIO's leadership, hardened his resolve to expunge communist influence from the ranks of labor. He led efforts to defeat CP-backed candidates seeking leadership of the St. Louis IUC, and in 1946 succeeded in denying the council presidency to a strong Sentner ally.[15]

On one level Gibbons's aggressive actions represented a continuation of his deep-seated antipathy toward the CP. Yet the CP's actions during World War II introduced a sharper edge to his critique of communism. Gibbons prized a militant working class and an independent union movement that were free from domination or undue influence by either political parties or the state. Repeatedly, in his view, the CP had abandoned these cherished principles and betrayed the interests of the working class. Regarding Communist-led unions as subservient to outside forces, he believed that the CP had forfeited its claim to be accepted as a legitimate participant in the labor movement.[16]

Gibbons was now prepared not only to attack Communists but also non-Communist labor leaders who "worked with the termites of the Stalin Party." This harsh sectarian indictment overlooked the fact that the Communists had generally performed well as union leaders, often enjoyed solid rank-and-file support, and in William Sentner's case, had built broadly based labor-community alliances to advance a visionary social agenda. Moreover, Gibbons's no-holds-barred approach to fighting the CP was at times indistinguishable from the tactics of anti-union forces who used red-baiting to discredit all shades of left-liberal politics. Although his anti-Communist campaign attracted support from his own membership and some other unions, Gibbons's belligerence torpedoed the possibility for a larger, more vibrant alliance of left-liberal forces in St. Louis. These early battles over Communism and wartime labor policy were the precursors of increasingly contentious relations between Gibbons and other segments of the labor community that intensified as his union sought to expand its influence after the war.[17]

Gibbons's zeal in fighting communism did not, however, deflect him from taking advantage of wartime opportunities to begin developing his vision of total person unionism. In March 1944, the URWDSEA in St. Louis approved a resolution authorizing the union to create a health care program for its members. Beginning with eight employers who funded the program by contributing a percentage of their gross payroll, the Labor Health Institute (LHI) opened in November 1945. LHI provided fully paid medical care for eligible members, served their families for a nominal fee, emphasized preventive care, and quickly expanded to include low-cost dental care and other services. Employers, both in St. Louis and elsewhere within the union's jurisdiction, consented to these arrangements for several reasons. They had the resources to fund them given their wartime profits, were able to deduct health care contributions from their tax liability, and believed that they could create a more stable, productive workforce by providing quality medical care. As a St. Louis candy company executive under contract with the union observed, "We're in it for selfish as well as humanitarian reasons; healthy workers are efficient workers."[18]

For Harold Gibbons, the Labor Health Institute had multiple meanings. Attributing his father's death to mine operators' disregard for the health and safety of their employees, he had a deep personal commitment to ensuring that his members receive quality medical care. He also knew, as a 1954 report on the program explained, that the low-wage workers he represented "usually obtain only a fraction of the services which LHI provides routinely. Without such a plan, they would become dependent on public assistance or charity if they incurred substantial expenses for medical care."[19]

In contrast to many unions whose health plans were managed by private insurers, Local 688 was actively involved in the development and management of LHI. Gibbons and other union leaders were doubtless pleased when two respected evaluators praised LHI's facilities for their "emphasis on the comfort and convenience of people coming to a medical center." For Harold Gibbons, this praise affirmed LHI's status as a symbol of working-class achievement, demonstrating the union's ability to administer an essential service and provide low-wage workers with a level of medical care approximating that offered by the nation's most respected health care facilities. LHI also attested to Gibbons's managerial and leadership capabilities, allowing him to transcend his reputation as a hotheaded young militant who lacked the judgment required to lead workers effectively.[20]

LHI epitomized Gibbons's belief in the integral connection between workers and their communities. As a 1950 LHI report explained, "A human being is part of his environment and is healthy only when he synchronizes his life with his surroundings. The Institute believes that health is not an individual but a community problem because the health of each individual affects the health of his neighbor." This view of health contained several important implications for the kind of unionism that Gibbons intended to develop in St. Louis. He insisted that the security and well-being of his members did not exist in a vacuum; the quality of their lives was directly affected by the entire social ecology of the city. Synchronizing individuals with their surroundings, as LHI advocated, required workers to exercise their roles as citizens to create a healthy community reinforced by strong structural supports needed to maintain their personal well-being.[21]

Besides his early initiatives on health care, Harold Gibbons also moved decisively during the war years to advance racial justice in St. Louis, leading the CIO Industrial Union Council's committee on racial discrimination and gaining a national award recognizing his work. His strong civil rights advocacy took political courage in St. Louis, which in spite of its reputation for promoting gradual racial progress, maintained segregated schools, public accommodations, and housing. The city did have a vibrant network of civil rights organizations, including a strong Urban League chapter, an aggressive local March on Washington Movement, and women from the NAACP who led wartime sit-ins seeking to desegregate downtown department store restaurants. The labor movement, however, with the exception of the UE and a few other CIO unions, was slow to champion the cause of black workers in a community where many of its white members held racist views and were determined to protect their prerogatives.[22]

With a 10 to 15 percent African American membership in his union, Gibbons sought to set an example within his own ranks, pursuing a multi-pronged approach to persuade his members that discrimination and intolerance were unacceptable. The union sought to negotiate non-discrimination clauses in its contracts and succeeded in abolishing racially based pay differentials. Under Gibbons's leadership the union also insisted on holding integrated recreational programs and social events. He recruited African Americans, Jews, and Asians for his staff, including Yuki Kato, a woman of Japanese descent who had been interned during the war. When African American cab drivers could not find another union in St. Louis to represent them, Gibbons came to their aid. The aggressiveness of these efforts to address racial injustice distinguished Harold Gibbons's leadership from most other CIO leaders, who were often reluctant (the UE being a notable exception) to take action that matched their lofty rhetoric on racial matters.[23]

Reflecting on the union's achievements under his leadership at a 1946 conference, Harold Gibbons articulated the profound psychological dimension that lay at the core of his philosophy of unionism: "This was a job of building that was not done by college professors, smart lawyers, or high salaried executives, but by little people. Common ordinary people. The men and women of the shops. I emphasize this because all too often, we of the working class have far too great an inferiority complex. Far too many of us fail to realize our powers, our abilities, our potentialities. Far too often we lack the confidence to plan as we should to tackle the jobs that have to be done."[24]

This deeply personal imperative to overcome the stigma of working-class inferiority fueled the intensity of Harold Gibbons's ambitions and commitments. Following World War II, he would move even more aggressively to provide "the men and women of the shops" with expanded opportunities to realize their "powers, abilities, and potentialities" and demonstrate their capacity to be full-fledged civic participants.

* * *

While Gibbons was establishing himself as a union leader in St. Louis, Ernest Calloway faced a wrenching dilemma prior to the United States' official entry into the Second World War. As Franklin Roosevelt's defense mobilization accelerated following Adolf Hitler's advances in Europe, the president gained congressional approval for the nation's first peacetime military draft in September 1940. While the legislation was being considered, civil rights organizations, political leaders, and the black press successfully lobbied to have nondiscrimination language included in the new law. Yet to the dismay of African Americans, President Roosevelt did not press to desegregate the military. Even though blacks were well aware of Hitler's pernicious racial views, they readily grasped the hypocrisy of serving in a Jim Crow Army and openly questioned whether they should support the war effort if the United States were to become directly involved.[25]

In December 1940, Ernest Calloway became one of the first African Americans to seek conscientious objector status solely on the basis of racial discrimination. In responding to a questionnaire he had received from Selective Service, he outlined his rationale for refusing to serve: "I have lived all my young life in an environment of state-imposed racial segregation, bigotry, and second-class citizenship, but in dying for my country, it must be as a free and equal American." In a subsequent statement before his Chicago draft board, Calloway elaborated on the reasons for his non-cooperation. Resisting what he regarded as an illegitimate demand, Calloway asked, "How can I in good conscience respect the claims of a state that continually violates and disregards the moral contract upon which our constitutional and democratic government is established?" He concluded by posing a direct challenge to the draft board that reflected widespread sentiment among many African Americans: "If the state wishes to preserve democracy and morality in the world, then it should begin at home. . . . The gesture to make America 'the land of the free and the home of the brave' would be a genuine effort to improve the morally delinquent character of the country and would demonstrate a purity of motive that could be respected in the conduct of war."[26]

Calloway's bold action, which he knew subjected him to imprisonment, reflected a long African American tradition of demanding that America honor its constitutional principles and democratic ideals by tearing down the walls of segregation. As sociologist St. Clair Drake, who along with Calloway helped form a group called Conscientious Objectors Against Jim Crow, declared, ". . . Segregated camps are un-American institutions . . . We don't have any martyr complex; we're just a bunch of fellows who have taken the Declaration of Independence seriously. . . ." Calloway's eloquence attracted national attention. NAACP national secretary Walter White lauded his statement of noncompliance as "one of the most moving, intelligent, and well-written enunciations of principle I have seen in a long time." In a January 18, 1941, editorial, the *Chicago Defender* asserted that Calloway's "view is shared by many in the race who are perhaps too timid to register their sentiments with similar vigor and effectiveness."[27]

The momentum behind the Chicago-based resistance to a segregated military faded, however, after the Japanese attacked Pearl Harbor, and the United States entered the war. Although most African Americans remained conflicted about serving in a Jim Crow military, they quickly embraced the notion of the "Double V," believing that their support for achieving victory over fascism would be rewarded by victory at home with the recognition that a truly democratic society could no longer tolerate segregation. Meanwhile, Calloway's test case became submerged within the Selective Service bureaucracy, dragging on for the next eighteen months away from public view. By the summer of 1943, the Chicago draft board declared him physically unfit due to a malformed elbow. His case never reached an appeals board, where he had hoped to press his argument for conscientious objection on racial grounds. The board's decision suggested its reluctance to make Calloway's case a cause célèbre and invite further criticism of a segregated military.[28]

Although Calloway emerged from the draft board fracas with enhanced personal integrity and political prestige, he received a mixed reaction from the leadership of the UTSEA. Union president Willard Townsend worried that his action might tarnish the union's image. Townsend's ambivalence foreshadowed a growing tension in his relationship with Calloway, who apparently came to resent ghostwriting the union president's *Chicago Defender* column and being consigned to a subordinate role in the organization.[29]

Calloway took pride in the red caps becoming a more firmly established union and exulted when workers chose the UTSEA over the Brotherhood of Railway and Steamship Clerks (BRSC) in numerous representation elections. These elections were "a great day for the step-children of American democracy," he wrote in October 1941. Several months earlier, he hailed the UTSEA's call for a national strike after the railroads rejected its wage demands as evidence that "our union is entering upon [a period] of growth and stature where trade union statesmanship will play a major role in meeting the problems of our membership."[30]

At the same time, Calloway's elation was tempered by his knowledge that the UTSEA faced an uncertain future. As early as 1940, he observed that structural changes in the railroad industry, most notably corporate mergers and technological advances, had sharply reduced employment, a trend that was likely to continue. The railroads also struck back at the red caps by instituting a per-bag fee at terminals. This step radically altered the passenger-red cap relationship, leading to declining tips and a reduced passenger willingness to use the red caps' services. As a shrewd observer of economic and industrial trends, Calloway had to wonder if the UTSEA possessed the potential to accommodate his talents and ambitions.

Although he operated less visibly than Harold Gibbons did in Chicago, Ernest Calloway was involved with similar issues during World War II and appears to have shared Gibbons's perspective on what constituted appropriate labor strategy during wartime. He assisted efforts in Chicago to support A. Philip Randolph's March on Washington Movement and was part of a broad community effort demanding that the Chicago Rapid Transit Company hire blacks for skilled positions. Calloway also threw himself into CIO activity. He helped draft the 1942 convention resolution that established the CIO Committee to Abolish Racial Discrimination and participated in the Chicago Industrial Union Council, where he joined the council's non-communist wing that sought to thwart the Communist Party's wartime initiatives. Like Harold Gibbons, Calloway's opposition to the CP intensified during the war. Years later, he charged the Communists with "going slow" on issues of racial justice after the Soviet Union was attacked and not fully supporting A. Philip Randolph's March on Washington Movement. He also cited the CP's inaction during the Montgomery Ward strike as another reason for his antipathy.[31]

Calloway was especially moved by his encounter with Angelo Herndon, a CP southern organizer who had gained international attention in the 1930s after he was jailed in Georgia for alleged "insurrectionary" activities. Herndon later became disillusioned with the CP and left its ranks. According to Calloway, he found Herndon in "virtual hiding" in Chicago and was angered by what he viewed as the party's abandonment of its former revered martyr. Although there is no record of Calloway's taking public stands against the CP during this period, the evidence suggests that his attitude hardened and prompted him to oppose the party even more aggressively following the war.[32]

In 1944, Calloway joined the editorial staff of the *CIO News*, the house organ of the industrial union federation, and began to split his time between Chicago and the CIO headquarters in Washington. This move was in part prompted by the UTSEA's April 1943 decision to cease publishing *Bags and Baggage* due to financial constraints. Calloway's byline did not frequently appear during the years he wrote for the *CIO News*, and in some cases he simply reported on CIO events such as conferences and convention proceedings. Yet several of the pieces bearing his name were more analytical, reflecting the CIO's need to convey positive images of interracial cooperation and cross-class unity. However, these articles lacked the pungent rhetoric and sharp analysis of his previous writing for African American publications. For a man who had already established his credentials as a public intellectual and political activist, Calloway may well have found writing under institutional constraints an inadequate use of his talents.[33]

In October 1946, Calloway experienced a serious personal loss. His wife, Martha, died after a "long illness" that had forced her to abandon her musical career and later to relinquish her role in leading the UTSEA's women's auxiliary. The impact of Martha Sutton's death on Calloway is impossible to calculate. Although he subsequently wrote about his years in Chicago and other aspects of his personal life, he never alluded to his marriage or Sutton's death in the many personal stories and reminiscences he authored. Indeed, Calloway's friends and acquaintances in St. Louis appear not to have known about his relationship with Martha Sutton. Perhaps the memories were too painful to recall, conjuring images of the new life he had fashioned in Chicago, the personal satisfaction he had found, and their precipitous collapse. Whatever the case, Calloway quickly found solace in a new relationship after the war when he met Deverne Lee, who was working as a secretary in the UTSEA's Chicago office.[34]

A native of Memphis, Lee was the daughter of a railroad worker, who she recalled "had a lot of mean things happen to him because he was black." Determined to rise above her circumstances, she attended LeMoyne College in Memphis, where a professor got her interested in helping organize southern tenant farmers, and she began to appreciate more fully the harshly enforced political economy that supported white supremacy. After briefly teaching in Georgia, Lee left the south in disgust over the indignities of segregation and found her way to Philadelphia, where she obtained employment with an African American judge. Displaying a growing rebellious streak, Lee worked for the Red Cross in India during World War II and became actively involved in protesting the maintenance of segregated facilities for black G.I.s.[35]

After the war Lee settled in Chicago, supporting herself by doing clerical work at the UTSEA headquarters there. Her memory of her first encounter with Ernest Calloway offered important insights into the character of their relationship. Lee was repelled when she observed the disarray of Calloway's office: "His desk looked like several hurricanes had passed through. I took it upon myself to straighten out this man's desk." In response, Calloway ". . . wanted to know who the hell had come in there and messed up his office." From this initial clash a close personal and political partnership blossomed that endured for over forty years. A witty, tough-minded, and independent woman, Deverne Lee combined deep respect for her husband with a no-nonsense candor that helped sharpen his political thinking and focus his activism.[36]

Lee and Calloway married in 1948. A year later, Calloway won a British Trades Union Congress scholarship funding a year's study at Ruskin College in Oxford, England. If Brookwood Labor College had provided Calloway with his "undergraduate education," Ruskin offered him the chance to pursue what amounted to "graduate studies." Ruskin had been founded at the turn of the century to provide opportunities for workers denied access to the country's higher education system. The Ruskin scholarship afforded Calloway exposure to some of Britain's finest scholars and granted him time to assimilate the tumultuous changes in his personal life. He had also chosen an auspicious occasion to be in England. With strong working-class and trade union support, the British Labour Party had gained its first outright parliamentary majority four years earlier. As a result, Calloway's time in England gave him the opportunity to observe social democracy in action, witness a union movement's role in shaping public policy, and refine his own ideas about appropriate strategies for labor in the United States.[37]

In letters to Deverne, Calloway described a daily routine that he obviously found quite pleasurable: attending evening talks by the famed British historian and labor intellectual G.D.H. Cole, hearing members of Parliament debate social issues at the Oxford Labor Club, and relaxing with classmates and teachers over tea or beers at local pubs. He quickly won notice for his "bright ties and socks," which contrasted with the "plain and dull" haberdashery of the British. As a thirty-nine-year-old man and a trade union veteran, he also enjoyed a peer relationship with many of his instructors, most notably Ben Roberts. Eight years younger than Calloway, Roberts had won a trade union scholarship to study at the London School of Economics and went on to become one of Britain's most prominent industrial relations scholars. Roberts became Calloway's tutor and supervised his studies during his time at Ruskin.[38]

The weekly tutorial lay at the foundation of the Oxford experience. After writing a lengthy essay each week, students discussed their work with their tutor, a process that according to Calloway was regarded as the "great ogre in the lives of Oxford students." However, he found his tutorials with Ben Roberts to be respectful, lively exchanges about the relative merits of British and American unionism. Calloway used the tutorial, along with articles he wrote, talks he delivered, and contacts with English and European unionists, to identify the most important challenges facing the American union movement and clarify his own career options.[39]

Calloway found much to admire in the British union movement: a deep sense of class loyalty and the presence of "fighting traditions," a strong commitment to workers' education, and a "cohesive political philosophy" grounded in institutions such as cooperatives and the Labour Party. In an October 1948 tutorial essay, Calloway warmly greeted labor's "new potential function in a cooperative, democratic socialist economy" where unions "are accepted into full partnership and their role and functions are positive with definite responsibilities for the well-being and maintenance of the economy." Yet as much as he longed to see American unions play a comparable role, Calloway characterized the post-World War II state's attitude toward labor as one of "hostile toleration." He also noted that efforts to "weaken the collective bargaining process and uproot the whole structure of free unionism" were well underway in the United States.[40]

Recognizing the dimming political prospects for extending the welfare state in America, Calloway conceded that the American union movement would need to rely heavily on the collective bargaining process to "serve the immediate needs of its members" and ensure "the basic security of the individual," without which "there can be no such thing as the common good or the general welfare." However, if bargaining power were to be translated into political power, Calloway asserted that American unions would do well to emulate their European counterparts. In contrast to political organizations in Britain and Europe that were "knitted together ... by a common social perspective with a consciousness of class," he lamented that "we have no such political animal in America." As he told one British audience, the "basic modern political philosophy of U.S. unionism has been reduced to the vacuous phrase of defeat your enemies and reward your friends," an approach he disparaged as lacking "social vision." Yet for all his railing about the inadequacy of American labor's political approach, Calloway was vague on his prescription for change. He hinted at the need for independent political action but remained silent on the propriety of creating a labor party and offered no specific proposals on how American unions could transcend the constraints of the two-party system.[41]

Calloway did, however, provide some suggestions about how the union movement in America could develop a social vision commensurate with its newfound economic influence. Not surprisingly, he identified racial exclusion as one of labor's greatest challenges. "This is truly the one test of a revitalized labor movement," Calloway declared, "and U.S. labor must meet this challenge honestly and fearlessly." In addition to leading the fight for racial justice, Calloway urged American unions to explore the possibilities of encouraging engaged working-class citizenship beyond the confines of the shop floor, insisting that labor "must now think in terms of the total community and the contribution it can make in establishing an equitable social order."[42]

During his time at Ruskin, Calloway also grappled with the recurring restlessness he seemed unable to overcome. Expressing her weariness with his vagabondage, Deverne issued a blunt challenge to her husband in a July 1949 letter: "Ask yourself if you are willing to come to terms with the American values, or if on the other hand you prefer to float through life dreaming of the 'new world.' . . . Ask yourself if you are going to be willing to assume the role of a husband and a provider—rather than one of a starry-eyed philosopher." Noting that he had not spoken about his future plans, she also urged him to break with the UTSEA: "I only hope you return with some plan to stand on your own feet rather than lounge perpetually in the shade of some person's or some organization's shimmering halo."[43]

Calloway acknowledged his wife's criticism, although he remained noncommittal on his next career move. During a Christmas holiday break in late 1948 and early 1949 that he spent in Paris, he wrote: "From now on all of my years must be productive, and perhaps it is symbolic that Paris, the world center of self-expression, is the beginning point for the next period of my life." Nonetheless, even with his wife's directive that he choose a more settled and remunerative career outside the UTSEA and his own pledge to be more focused, Calloway remained unsure about how to proceed. In September 1949, shortly after his return to the United States, he learned that his application for a Fulbright Scholarship to study workers' education programs in Britain had been approved. However, later that fall, he opted for another assignment: working for the CIO's Operation Dixie organizing drive and joining the UTSEA's effort to supplant the Food, Tobacco, Agricultural, and Allied Workers Union (FTA) as a representative of southern workers.[44]

The context for this effort was the onset of the Cold War, which shattered the uneasy truce that CIO president Philip Murray had brokered with the federation's Communist-influenced affiliates. The FTA, which had a sizable CP contingent, had long been at odds with the CIO leadership. When the union's leaders initially refused to sign Taft-Hartley affidavits denying CP membership, Murray and CIO organizing director Allan Haywood sought to oust them. One of the FTA's most visible strongholds was Local 22, which represented R.J. Reynolds workers in Winston-Salem. The FTA, with strong CP support, had built a vibrant local union among the approximately 12,000 workers employed at Reynolds by encouraging interracial cooperation, cultivating rank-and-file leadership, and empowering workers to press for racial justice in both the community and political arenas. Nevertheless, when Murray and Haywood asked the UTSEA to spearhead the CIO's anti-FTA effort, union president Willard Townsend eagerly accepted their invitation. In addition to being a staunch anti-communist, Townsend recognized that expanding the union's jurisdiction into tobacco and fertilizer products perhaps offered the UTSEA its best chance at survival. By 1947, as Calloway had anticipated, the union's ranks had dwindled to less than 7,000 members. If the UTSEA could not find a new group of workers to represent, its future appeared increasingly bleak.[45]

Years later, Calloway claimed he had accepted the initial CIO assignment because he felt "almost smothered in the rarefied intellectual atmosphere of Oxford," and ". . . wanted to return to the U.S. and the harsh human terrain of southern organizing." Yet he had given no indication of feeling "smothered" in any of his contemporaneous reflections on his time at Ruskin and had applied for continuing study in England through the Fulbright Scholarship. Instead, it appears that other factors influenced his decision. One reason may have been his residual loyalty to UTSEA secretary-treasurer John Yancey, who pleaded with Calloway to maintain his ties with the union in spite of his rift with Willard Townsend.[46]

Also, Calloway's antipathy toward Communism had intensified during his time in England. While in France, he had met "refugee socialists from behind the 'iron curtain'" and was disturbed by their accounts of oppression under Stalinism. In England, he had witnessed a struggle between Communist and anti-Communist forces within the British Trade Union Congress (TUC) that paralleled similar clashes within the CIO and concluded that the TUC could not "permit its democratically determined policy to be disrupted at the behest of an outside party." Given these events, the opportunity to hasten the CP's demise appears to have influenced Calloway's decision more than a desire to reconnect with the working class after the genteel repose of Oxford.[47]

Calloway actively red-baited the FTA, charging in a radio statement that it was a "weak little communist clique" and "a little bunch of communist carpetbaggers" that had left the workers "at the mercy of the tobacco barons" while focusing its attentions on Henry Wallace's presidential campaign. His argument fell on deaf ears. In the March 8, 1950, election at the Reynolds plant in Winston-Salem, the UTSEA was outpolled nearly 6 to 1 by the FTA and 2 to 1 by the AFL's Tobacco Workers, while a plurality of workers narrowly favored "no union." In a subsequent runoff election, the FTA lost by a slim margin. In a lengthy post-mortem addressed to Willard Townsend, Calloway outlined his serious reservations about CIO strategy and described bitter personal clashes with CIO leaders that led to his being declared persona non grata within the campaign's organizing staff.[48]

Calloway had rebelled against the direction of veteran CIO leaders who he charged were too inflexible to develop a strategy that recognized the "complex issues involved and the relationship of the company to the community." Reflecting his growing belief in a unionism that attempted to address the needs of the worker as a total person, Calloway averred "that there were far too many reasons why the ordinary person voted for a union aside from the narrow trade union consideration." In fact, he acknowledged the FTA's deep roots in Winston-Salem's African American community and its attempt to create the kind of working-class citizenship that Calloway himself believed was essential to a socially visionary unionism. In contrast, he concluded that the CIO's real intention in Winston-Salem was to "put up a 'token' campaign as a nuisance value in the elimination of the FTA from the scene" rather than mount a genuine effort to obtain a UTSEA victory.[49]

In the aftermath of losing their representation rights at Local 22, the FTA's experiment in "civil rights unionism" disintegrated, and white power brokers reasserted their dominance over Winston-Salem's economic and community affairs. Ever the strategist, Calloway crafted an elaborate proposal outlining how the UTSEA could become "a dominant force in the [fertilizer] industry in North Carolina." However, the UTSEA lacked the resources to implement his strategy, and Calloway became increasingly disenchanted with the CIO, which had begun to curtail its southern organizing drive. A few months later, when his old Chicago acquaintance Harold Gibbons offered him the opportunity to come to St. Louis, Calloway accepted his invitation. At age forty-one, he was now prepared to focus his energies and draw on the resources of a dynamic union where he could test his assumptions about the potential of collective bargaining, working-class citizenship, and the pursuit of racial justice.[50]

CHAPTER 5

"The Most Powerful Union in America"

As Ernest Calloway prepared to return to the United States, Harold Gibbons made a momentous decision that transformed the course of his labor career. In January 1949, he opted to merge his newly independent union with the International Brotherhood of Teamsters (IBT). Gibbons's alignment with an AFL union known for its unabashed pragmatism and strong-arm methods stirred disbelief and anger in both local and national labor circles. According to labor journalist John Herling, some of Gibbons's friends were shocked into "speechless rage." When asked his opinion of Gibbons, Allan Haywood, the national CIO's organizing director, retorted, "Gibbons double-crossed and betrayed me once and I don't want to talk about him."[1]

Undaunted by the controversy stirred by his action, Gibbons moved quickly to exploit the benefits provided by his new affiliation. In his old acquaintance Ernest Calloway, he found another "CIO man" ready to defect to the AFL. Simultaneously, aided by prominent labor educators and scholars, Gibbons undertook an intensive assessment of his members' attitudes and their willingness to embrace his conception of a unionism that in Calloway's words "view[ed] the . . . member within the frame of his total environment—economic, social, cultural, and political."[2] The results provided important insights that would prompt Gibbons and Calloway to develop new strategies for cementing member attachment to the union and boosting its standing as an advocate for working-class interests in the community.

* * *

In the five years that elapsed between the end of World War II and Ernest Calloway's arrival in St. Louis, Harold Gibbons began to expand the boundaries of his union's participation in civic affairs. To assist him in his ambitious undertakings, he assembled a talented and diverse staff. The staff included warehousemen like Lou Berra and Pete Saffo, Italians from the St. Louis neighborhood known as the Hill, who were veterans of the union's earliest organizing drives and ranked among its most respected local leaders. Richard Kavner, a tough URWDSEA organizer from New York who became one of Gibbons's closest allies, came to St. Louis following World War II and relished picket line confrontations with both management and the police. Several gifted former Washington University students, including Joseph Ames and Marvin Rich, worked in the union's political and research departments. Bernice Fisher was one of the few female staff representatives. A former University of Chicago divinity student with whom Ernest Calloway was acquainted, Fisher had helped to establish the Congress of Racial Equality (CORE) and joined the union's staff because she admired Harold Gibbons's commitment to racial justice. Two African Americans, Arthur Johnson and Arthur Chapin, also served as union representatives; each subsequently entered government careers working on civil rights matters. This impressive group exemplified Gibbons's egalitarian sensibilities and demonstrated his willingness to draw on both shop floor and social movement experience to craft his vision of socially engaged unionism.[3]

With the no-strike pledge rescinded following the end of World War II, St. Louis warehouse and distribution workers enthusiastically joined the strike wave that engulfed the nation. This return to direct action underscored Gibbons's commitment to use working-class power not only to extract concessions from individual employers but also to convey that wartime restraint had not softened the union's ability to wage effective strikes. In the spring of 1946, a six-week strike at Shapleigh Hardware, a local employer with whom the union had a history of contentious relations, resulted in a contract in which the company agreed to fund Labor Health Institute (LHI) coverage for its workers. Shapleigh's capitulation bolstered the union's new health insurance program and signaled to other employers that workers regarded LHI's high quality, low-cost medical care as a fundamental obligation that they would fight to uphold.[4]

Several months later, a strike occurred at International Shoe's St. Louis warehouses protesting the discharges of twenty-four union members. In sympathy, both AFL and CIO unions refused to cross the warehouse workers' picket lines, leading to the idling of 18,000 shoe workers in three adjacent states who depended on the materials stockpiled at the struck St. Louis locations. This strike, which resulted in a settlement favorable to the union, angered corporate leaders, who saw a vital regional industry hobbled and expressed concern over labor's ability to exercise unbridled collective power. In several other instances, distribution workers struck to gain recognition at St. Louis warehouses rather than risk having their organizing efforts become entangled in the labor board's increasingly tortuous procedures. Moreover, Gibbons did not confine the union's activity strictly to immediate workplace matters. In another bold assertion of its resolve to protect workers' wartime gains, the union shut down all of its St. Louis shops for several hours on August 23, 1946, and 5,000 members marched through the city to protest the removal of wartime price controls. Harold Gibbons's multiple uses of the strike reflected a shared impulse of postwar labor liberals that Nelson Lichtenstein has described as "an organic amalgamation of strike action, organizing activity, and political mobilization." This strategy of linking working-class mobilization with broader political goals, which Gibbons and Calloway clearly endorsed, aimed at positioning the union movement to be an integral player in shaping postwar economic and social decision-making.[5]

According to figures that Calloway compiled for a tenth anniversary report for the union, St. Louis warehouse and distribution workers struck thirty-two times between the end of World War II and the summer of 1951, with just under half of these strikes aimed at securing union recognition for newly organized workers. These organizing drives, mostly involving small warehousing and distribution units, were largely successful, with five of the seven recognition strikes in 1947 resulting in union contracts. Capitalizing on the strategic place warehousing and distribution occupied in the chain of production, Gibbons found his faith in direct action reaffirmed after years of chafing under the constraints of the no-strike pledge.[6]

The passage of the Taft-Hartley Act over President Harry Truman's veto in June 1947, however, marked the culmination of a decade-long political backlash against the New Deal's support for union organization and collective bargaining. Many provisions of Taft-Hartley posed minimal obstacles to Harold Gibbons's mode of operation. However, the new law's ban on secondary boycotts and its granting employers additional latitude during union organizing drives were immediately consequential, as Gibbons discovered in a bitter recognition strike he and the union conducted against the J.H. Grady Company in 1948.[7]

Grady's 120 mostly female workers made a variety of balls used in sporting activities at a north St. Louis plant. Although the company was profitable, wages had remained stagnant, and workers complained of intense managerial harassment once they began to organize. Eager to expand their jurisdiction into the light manufacturing occupations that constituted a significant segment of the St. Louis economy, the warehouse workers offered to help the Grady workers organize. Ninety percent of the workers quickly signed authorization cards favoring union representation, but Grady's management rebuffed Gibbons's request for recognition. Buoyed by the passage of Taft-Hartley and a similar Missouri law that restricted striking and picketing, the company launched a fierce campaign to dissuade workers from supporting the union and raised numerous procedural issues in an effort to delay an NLRB election. Frustrated by these tactics, Gibbons led Grady workers on strike in June 1948, using the direct action formula that had proved so successful in gaining union recognition from other St. Louis employers.[8]

Clashes between strikers, scabs, and police resulted in nearly 100 arrests and the beating of union organizer Richard Kavner. More damaging to the workers' cause was the limited ability of union members to display solidarity by refusing to handle Grady's products lest they violate Taft-Hartley's restrictions on secondary boycotts. The union's attempt to have the NLRB designate the walkout as a strike over unfair labor practices, which would have granted workers the right to regain their jobs, was rejected by the board's new general counsel, a conservative St. Louis lawyer named Robert Denham, in spite of Gibbons's journeying to Washington and making a personal plea. As Washington University student Harry Ball observed in his 1950 case history of the union, in contrast to the union's customary use of raw power and solidarity to achieve its objectives, ". . . the fight in this stage was a legal battle being fought on a distant stage where none of the workers could watch."[9]

After a thirteen-month strike that cost the union over $100,000 in legal fees, Harold Gibbons reluctantly conceded defeat. For a union that "defined itself as an organization of conflict" committed to direct action and the practice of solidarity, the Grady strike signified a tectonic shift in the political landscape in which Gibbons and Calloway now were operating. Although Gibbons did not eschew the strike or other forms of direct action, he understood that subsequent uses of working-class power would become both economic and ideological battlegrounds in which employers could now draw on new resources to bolster their resistance. As he bluntly told his members in 1949, "The honeymoon of the last seven years is over. The gravy train has come to an end." In the wake of Taft-Hartley's passage and the failure of the Grady strike, Gibbons began an intensive re-evaluation of union strategy in the months prior to Calloway's arrival in St. Louis in the spring of 1950.[10]

The decision in January 1949 to merge his union with the Teamsters represented Harold Gibbons's boldest response to the changed circumstances he and the warehouse workers now faced. This move was preceded by the union's disaffiliation from the national Retail, Wholesale, and Department Store Union (the URWDSEA became the RWDSU following the addition of local unions from Canada) a year earlier in January 1948. Gibbons and his St. Louis locals had long been at odds with RWDSU president Samuel Wolchok, and Gibbons had joined a group of dissidents that called itself the "Committee for a Decent, Democratic Trade Union in the RWDSU." Although Gibbons was angered by what he regarded as Wolchok's coddling of the union's CP-dominated New York locals, he was especially dissatisfied with the national union's tepid commitment to organizing. As several of his fellow dissidents declared in formal charges they filed against Wolchok in October 1947, "Our union has become notorious in the CIO for the degree with which it has applied itself to the consideration of internal politics to the exclusion of organizational work. . . . Our organization has bungled its opportunity and stunted its growth." While Gibbons and his fellow critics may have overstated Samuel Wolchok's culpability, they clearly were embarrassed by the union's low standing within the CIO and its inability to fulfill its initial promise.[11]

In an effort to discredit one of his most prominent opponents, Wolchok attempted to convince St. Louis warehouse union leader Lou Berra to turn against Gibbons by offering him a position of greater influence in return for his support. He dispatched New York representative Richard Kavner to make the offer, which backfired when Berra rejected Wolchok's proposition as a thinly disguised attempt at bribery. Kavner resigned from the union after Wolchok demanded he sign a loyalty oath; this act of defiance endeared him to Harold Gibbons and cemented what was to become a long and loyal relationship. Increasingly desperate to derail his opposition, Wolchok fired Gibbons and one of his closest allies, Pete Saffo, from their union posts in December 1947. These actions, preceded two months earlier by an internal committee's rejection of the dissidents' charges against Wolchok, led Gibbons and his members to disaffiliate from the RWDSU in January 1948. They realized, however, that remaining an independent, locally based unit was not a viable long-term option. The resolution supporting withdrawal directed Gibbons to seek affiliation with another union, a task he conscientiously pursued over the next year.[12]

Gibbons explored merging with several other unions, including the Textile Workers, Machinists, and Auto Workers. He also considered a proposal to join the Building Service Employees Union and establish a warehouse division under its aegis. The decision to merge with the Teamsters, then, was not without due diligence on the part of Gibbons and other leaders within his inner circle and was overwhelmingly approved by the union's stewards' council in January 1949.[13]

At first glance the socialist-inspired politics and rank-and-file-oriented unionism espoused by Harold Gibbons seemed an odd match for the Teamsters, an organization with a markedly different trade union culture. With a membership rooted in delivery occupations that were economically marginal and fiercely competitive, the Teamsters often found it beneficial to enter into collusive arrangements with employers. These arrangements were frequently lubricated by bribery or extortion, along with sweetheart deals that granted employers special treatment in return for union recognition. Their roots in transportation led the Teamsters into organizing related industries, including warehousing and distribution, where other unions also made jurisdictional claims, often leading to bitter disputes in these highly competitive arenas. Although Gibbons was no stranger to jurisdictional disputes and picket line violence, he clearly shunned the kinds of relationships that Teamsters often cultivated with employers, which contradicted his instinctive class consciousness and his conception of trade union morality.[14]

Using strikes and secondary boycott techniques, along with creating joint councils of local unions that could engage in coordinated activity, the Teamsters became an organizing juggernaut that dramatically improved conditions and living standards for workers long abused by their employers. Teamsters' membership had tripled between 1933 and 1941, increasing more than any union in either the AFL or the CIO. By the time that the St. Louis warehouse and distribution workers merged with the Teamsters, IBT membership had passed one million, and under the leadership of aggressive leaders such as Dave Beck and Jimmy Hoffa, appeared poised for even greater expansion.[15]

In spite of their willingness to organize on an industrial basis, the Teamsters fully reflected the social and political orientation of the AFL that Gibbons had long disdained. Their forays into political action were narrowly focused on the union's immediate self-interest, with Beck and Hoffa flaunting their embrace of business values. On the critical issue of racial justice, the Teamsters had been more supportive of African American workers than most AFL unions, but their commitment fell well short of Harold Gibbons's exacting standards. In a union comprised of numerous regional fiefdoms where internal discipline and obedience to authority were regarded as the highest virtues, there was little room in most Teamsters locals for the kind of member participation and civic involvement that was central to Gibbons's concept of unionism. In Ernest Calloway's formulation, most Teamster leaders were inclined to view workers as economic rather than social beings. Given these profound differences, why did Harold Gibbons elect to affiliate with a union whose practices seemed so antithetical to his core beliefs?[16]

In spite of his obvious differences with the Teamsters, Gibbons shared one fundamental affinity with his new partner: a clear recognition that amassing economic power was essential to fulfill his ambitions. As he explained in a January 27, 1949, letter to his membership justifying the merger, "The Teamsters is the most powerful union in America." Gibbons also observed that in spite of Taft-Hartley and an unwelcoming political climate, the Teamsters remained committed to aggressive organizing and cited their ability to "cover[s] the country so thoroughly that there is no place where an employer planning to become a 'runaway' might hide." Here, then, was a union with the ambition and capacity to realize the unmet potential of the RWDSU and match the achievements of other industrial unions by organizing warehouse and distribution workers on a massive scale.[17]

There was another factor that influenced Gibbons's decision to merge with the Teamsters. Chartered in 1941, the same year Gibbons arrived in St. Louis, Teamsters Local 688 had begun to organize many of the smaller warehousing and supply facilities not under the umbrella of the RWDSU, which had focused its attention on larger firms. At the time of the merger, Local 688 had approximately 2,500 members as compared with the distribution workers' 6,000. Although the two unions had largely avoided the jurisdictional clashes that had surfaced elsewhere, they tangled in 1947 when Gibbons attempted to help a group of dissident Teamster truck drivers disaffiliate. According to FBI reports, he was quietly assisted in this task by Farrell Dobbs and Vincent Dunne, Minneapolis Trotskyists whom Teamsters president Daniel Tobin had suppressed with Jimmy Hoffa's assistance. This direct jurisdictional conflict and the presence of Dobbs and Dunne doubtless raised concerns among the Teamsters and accelerated merger discussions. As a January 27, 1949, *New York Times* story reported, there was "talk in labor circles that the Teamsters had served notice on Mr. Gibbons to turn over the CIO local or face raids." Dave Beck, the Teamsters' west coast leader who led the negotiations with Gibbons, was notorious for encroaching on the jurisdiction of other unions, so it is quite possible that Gibbons's decision to merge with the Teamsters reflected a pragmatic response to this credible threat to raid his membership.[18]

Although negotiated under some measure of duress, the terms of the final merger agreement were quite favorable to Gibbons. The new union, which retained the name Teamsters Local 688, had a membership of nearly 9,000 and was now one of the largest local unions in Missouri. The warehouse workers also gained assurances that strong support for new organizing initiatives would be forthcoming. Gibbons assumed leadership of the new union after agreeing to provide almost $80,000 in severance pay to the incumbent Local 688 president and several other staff members, an arrangement that subsequently drew scrutiny from a Congressional committee investigating labor corruption.[19]

Although the stewards' council of the warehouse workers approved the merger with only seven dissenting votes out of 300, Gibbons's action was greeted with disbelief and shock by many of his friends and colleagues. Oscar Ehrhardt, the St. Louis CIO Industrial Union Council leader long at odds with Gibbons, complained that the decision to merge was rubberstamped by the union's stewards' council and not submitted to a membership vote. Others disparaged the merger as the "biggest labor raid in the city's history." For his part, Gibbons either dismissed these concerns or described them as exaggerated. However, his bolting to the Teamsters and the AFL further alienated him from much of the union movement in St. Louis, leaving a lingering distrust that complicated subsequent prospects for united labor action.[20]

Shortly after the merger, it became apparent that Gibbons's decision to merge with the Teamsters had thrust him into a far more complicated and ambiguous moral universe than he had previously inhabited as a union leader. In the spring of 1949, the Teamsters, Retail Clerks, and Building Service Employees launched an ambitious joint effort to organize 15,000 department store employees in St. Louis, including the union's old antagonist Famous-Barr. The campaign reflected the shared Keynesianism of New Deal labor liberals with its declared goal to increase the low wages of these workers, which they described as a "drag on consuming power in the community." A "Department Store Organizing Council" was created in St. Louis under the direction of Gibbons and Richard Kavner and reported initial progress, obtaining close to 1,000 union authorization cards. Here was the type of coordinated, well-financed effort that Gibbons had been unable to mount during his years with the RWDSU and which seemed to confirm the wisdom of his decision to join the Teamsters' ranks.[21]

The department store campaign abruptly shifted, however, when Dave Beck directed Gibbons and Local 688 to sever their ties with the Retail Clerks in retaliation for a jurisdictional dispute raging between the two unions on the west coast. Beck then ordered Gibbons to raid the Retail Clerks membership in St. Louis grocery stores, an effort that fizzled and was condemned by other unions and the local news media. Moreover, Gibbons acted without receiving authorization from Local 688's stewards' council, the body through which all major policy decisions were typically approved. John Nedich, a chief steward from Brown Shoe, also noted the warehouse workers' longstanding opposition to engaging in jurisdictional disputes and demanded an explanation from Gibbons. Gibbons responded that "the obligations of the international were paramount and that the international had ordered the 'raid' as part of a nation-wide struggle with the retail clerks centering on the west coast."[22]

The raid on the clerks led Bernice Fisher, the union's sole female organizer, to resign. Her moral compass would not allow her to condone raiding another union, an act she viewed as antithetical to the venerable principle of solidarity and a distraction from the fundamental task of creating working-class citizenship. Acknowledging the kinds of compromises he would now be compelled to make, Gibbons explained to his old mentor, Annetta Dieckmann, "that he had no practical alternative" but to comply with Beck's directives. Nonetheless, by sidestepping democratic procedures and jettisoning solidarity during the raid on the Retail Clerks, Gibbons had violated some of the values most cherished within the organizational culture of St. Louis's warehouse workers. To be sure, labor leadership was of necessity a complex enterprise that required balancing a host of imperatives: self-interest and solidarity, democracy and discipline, power and morality. Whether or not Harold Gibbons had embraced a Faustian bargain in becoming a Teamster, as Bernice Fisher implied, became a charge his critics frequently leveled as he sought to reconcile the lofty aspirations of total person unionism with his new obligations as an increasingly visible leader within the IBT hierarchy.[23]

Concurrent with the warehouse workers' merger with the Teamsters, Harold Gibbons took the unusual step of engaging outside consultants to assess the union's success in transmitting its social vision to its members. This assessment had three components. In 1949, Gibbons tapped Arnold Rose, a respected Washington University sociologist who had worked on Gunnar Myrdal's pioneering study of race relations, to conduct an extensive survey of his membership. As Gibbons explained, "I want to know where we must concentrate education when a section of the membership shows poor trade union attitudes." This was partially a reference to racial attitudes but also alluded to Gibbons's concern that with union success at the bargaining table, too many members had become "mere recipients of benefits without realizing that they are under an obligation to cooperate with their organization." The union's task was to make these "wage conscious workers" more "union conscious" and help them develop the "group moral convictions needed to achieve continued progress."[24]

Along with Arnold Rose's study on member attitudes toward the union, Gibbons enticed Dieckmann to undertake the "St. Louis Labor Education Project." The project had two principal goals: "to educate the great mass of new unionists in ideals and loyalties of real unionism" and "to educate [labor] for democratic non-discriminatory attitudes within its own ranks." The project represented an unusual attempt to go beyond the CIO's rhetorical commitment to racial egalitarianism by attempting to dismantle racial barriers at the shop-floor level. According to Gibbons, he not only wanted to assess the effectiveness of "anti-prejudice" efforts the union had undertaken but also wanted "help in devising new techniques to better meet the interracial problem in our union." These anti-prejudice efforts assumed an even greater urgency following the merger with the Teamsters, creating a union in which African Americans comprised nearly 20 percent of the total membership. The final evaluative component Gibbons authorized was a history of the union by Harry Ball, Jr., a student of Arnold Rose's at Washington University, who was granted full access to union records, staff, and members. Published in 1950, Ball's account offered some penetrating insights into the union's internal culture and the implications of its merger with the Teamsters.[25]

As part of her work on the St. Louis Labor Education Project, Dieckmann advised Local 688's Committee on Democratic Rights on strategies to remove racial barriers lingering in the shops. The union focused special attention on placing blacks in retail sales positions, reasoning that breaking the color line in visible public spaces would represent a powerful symbol of racial equality in the workplace. Although some members of the Committee on Democratic Rights reported that "management is indifferent and the rank-and-file of the union is hostile," committee leaders sought to enforce seniority rights for black workers and collaborated with the St. Louis Urban League to increase the pool of qualified recruits. For his part, Gibbons expressed impatience with the slow pace of change and told Dieckmann that rank-and-file hostility to upgrading black workers could be overcome "if necessary by disciplinary measures."[26]

Given Gibbons's belief, which he shared with Ernest Calloway, that the pursuit of racial justice was the foremost moral test for both the nation and the postwar union movement, he and other union leaders were disappointed in Arnold Rose's finding that ". . . the mores of the community rather than the policies of the Union so largely determine the attitudes of the rank and file membership." Rose discovered that the union's racial egalitarianism had made some white members more willing to respect their African American co-workers' rights on the job, but most remained committed to maintaining racial separation in social and community affairs. As he observed in *Union Solidarity*, his 1952 book based on interviews of Local 688 members, "social learning developed in one context is not necessarily transferred to other comparable contexts, at least when external social pressures work against that transfer." In St. Louis, a city where the notorious racist and anti-Semite Gerald L.K. Smith had actively recruited among the white working class and where a 1949 effort to integrate a public swimming pool provoked fierce white resistance, "external social pressures" were clearly quite operative. Rose's sobering conclusion, which contradicted Gibbons's earlier pronouncements of the union's success in changing the racial views of its members, suggested that convincing workers to transfer their union-inspired "social learning" from the shop floor to the community would be a much more strenuous challenge than he had anticipated.[27]

Gibbons's commitment to the pursuit of racial justice, however, did not extend to addressing gender concerns. Approximately one-third of the union's membership was female, with most located in clerical and sales positions. Arnold Rose did find that nearly half of those surveyed, whether male or female, approved of women serving as stewards as long as they were "capable," and even higher percentages favored having women on staff. Indeed, of the union's thirty chief stewards pictured in the 1951 anniversary report edited by Ernest Calloway, seven were female, so women were certainly represented at middle echelons of leadership and as members of union committees.

Annetta Dieckmann, who had deep commitments to women's rights, repeatedly pressed Gibbons and other Local 688 leaders about the reluctance of female members to participate actively in the union. Observing a young female worker make a motion at a union meeting, Dieckmann remarked, "Women speak so seldom in the stewards' meeting that this was worth noting." Yet when informed of Arnold Rose's finding that few women under age thirty participated in union affairs, Gibbons appeared unconcerned. Dieckmann expressed frustration at her protégé's indifference to the union's female members but had no success in persuading Gibbons, who fully accepted traditional cultural assumptions regarding women's roles, to cultivate them as activists and leaders. At this point Gibbons's conception of working-class citizenship remained a masculine affair with women serving largely in auxiliary or secondary roles.[28]

Several other revelations from Rose's study and Dieckmann's educational activities spotlighted the challenges Gibbons and Calloway would face in gaining member support for total person unionism and sustaining the sense of organizational attachment they had witnessed within the mine workers and the CIO. Rose uncovered a phenomenon also cited by several other scholars of post–World War II unionism: the tendency of workers to maintain loyalty to both union and company and to see no contradiction in parceling out their affections. Accompanying this sense of dual loyalty, Rose found that "antagonism toward employers as such, or a class struggle mentality, is very minor in this union." This finding provoked a spirited debate between Gibbons and Richard Kavner, the hard-nosed RWDSU transplant from New York, on the implications of Rose's discovery. In Kavner's view this dual loyalty threatened to blur the class consciousness needed to spur direct action and ensure that justice prevailed on the shop floor.[29]

Gibbons took a more flexible view, contending that unceasing class antagonism was "untenable as a base for a large union" and noted "points in the administration of a union where a concept of 'fairness' is utilized." His interpretation reflected an awareness of other gaps Arnold Rose had found between leaders and the rank and file in Local 688, including workers' balking at the union "telling" them how to vote, the belief by a quarter of those surveyed that the union staff was too "radical," and the view that "lately the union has been trying to regiment thinking according to European class ideas." These views reflected the multiple influences shaping workers' attitudes in St. Louis—ethnicity, religion, small-town rural agrarianism, an entrepreneurial, customer relations oriented work culture—that clashed with Gibbons and Calloway's cosmopolitan conception of working-class citizenship. Richard Kavner's question about what might replace class antagonism as the foundation for reinforcing member loyalty, solidarity, and willingness to engage in direct action was not immediately addressed by Gibbons. However, he and Calloway moved to develop a moral equivalent of class conflict that looked to community and political affairs as the arena in which to take the concept of "fairness" and infuse it with broader political meaning.[30]

The final source for Gibbons's re-examination of union culture and operation was the master's thesis of Harry Ball, the Washington University sociology student who had also worked on Arnold Rose's study. Although a strong admirer of the union, Ball voiced concern that in the wake of Taft-Hartley and the merger with the Teamsters, the union's commitments to member involvement might be subsumed by the growing professionalization of labor-management relations and the shift to more centralized union structures. Increasingly, Ball observed, "workers are governed by a set of rules decided on at a top level and about which they must learn after the rules have been completely established." Under the Teamster's aegis, he feared that the union was beginning to resemble a "machine" and workers might come to "feel just as lost in their union as they felt in their industry before the era of unionization."[31]

Reflecting his post-Taft-Hartley conviction that considerations of power were paramount, Gibbons conceded that "some loss of democracy is inevitable with the enormous growth in size" but insisted that "this loss of democracy ... is more than compensated for by an increase in strength." In reviewing Ball's conclusions and attempting to calm Gibbons's concern that his commitment to democracy was being questioned, Annetta Dieckmann argued for the legitimacy of both perspectives. Noting that the newly merged union now had nearly 9,000 members and 122 separate negotiations in progress, she lamented, "The size and complexity of this union is appalling to one whose concern is for democratic participation and education." Yet Dieckmann, who observed the union up close for nearly two years, was impressed by its efforts encouraging members to exercise the kind of creativity she associated with active working-class citizenship. As she explained after attending the union's citywide conference in January 1950 (this was an annual gathering where the union established its goals for the coming year), "This annual conference is thrilling—and exhausting. The hotel was too hot, the meetings too long. But what a boost to one's faith in democracy."[32]

Indeed, the warehouse workers under Harold Gibbons's leadership had vigorously attempted to establish a participatory union culture that sought to instill in its members a clear sense of institutional obligation and loyalty. In 1947 and early 1948, the union had experimented with what it called "crew meetings," gatherings of twenty-five members in each shop that aimed at "bringing the rank and file closer to the union." Although this experiment proved too demanding of staff time to sustain, it signified the union's continuing effort to reduce the distance that was surfacing in many unions between professional staff and the rank and file. The union also maintained an active group of committees (education, political action, publications, organizing, recreation) in addition to the Committee on the Democratic Rights of Members that Dieckmann had advised; these committees were encouraged to analyze issues and develop recommendations for action. Yet in a February 1950 letter to Harry Ball, Dieckmann acknowledged his qualms about the future of participatory democracy in Local 688, as the union faced increasing pressures to align its policies with the mores of Teamsters' culture. Describing the reconstituted Local 688 as "highly volatile, flexible, [and] dynamic," she expressed concern over the long-range implications of Harold Gibbons's decision: "Whether it [Local 688] will continue to be so or whether it will become a typical Teamsters Union Local is another story."[33]

* * *

As Harry Ball, Annetta Dieckmann, and Arnold Rose concluded their work with Local 688, Ernest Calloway arrived in St. Louis in the spring of 1950. After a conversation with Harold Gibbons in a Chicago bar, he accepted his old acquaintance's request to come to St. Louis for three months and help the union establish a research department. This initial assignment blossomed into a working partnership between the two former socialists that lasted for over two decades. Presumably, Calloway relished the opportunity to work for a union whose resources matched its ambitions. He was also attracted by the promise that he would be granted the political authority and intellectual freedom to act as union strategist, civil rights leader, and public intellectual. In Harold Gibbons, he found a union leader who continued to think in a socialist idiom, remained committed to pursuing racial justice, and was determined to explore the possibilities of independent political action. And in St. Louis, his traditional wanderlust was replaced by a firm sense of purpose and the opportunity to play a substantive role in shaping the visionary social unionism he had long favored.[34]

With Calloway's arrival Harold Gibbons found what one former staffer called his "intellectual in residence," and another observer described as his "house utopian." Over the years Calloway wore numerous hats, including administrative assistant to Gibbons (1951), research director for Joint Council 13 (1955), director of organizing for Joint Council 13 (1958), and during the last decade of his career, associate research director for the Central Conference of Teamsters. Beyond these official roles, Gibbons drew heavily on Calloway's skills as a publicist, his insights into organizational structure and administration, and his acumen as a strategist. Most importantly, Gibbons relied on Calloway for ideological and political advice on nearly all of his major initiatives. As Mike Ryan, the union's education director in the 1960s, recalled, "Calloway's sphere of influence was immense." Calloway quickly established his credibility within Local 688, editing a stylish publication celebrating the distribution workers' tenth anniversary and advising a union committee that prepared a report on school integration in St. Louis. In recognition of his acceptance, he soon earned the affectionate nickname of "Cab" from his colleagues. This nickname represented both a reference to the famed African American entertainer, Cab Calloway, and good-natured ribbing about his use of taxis because he lacked a driver's license.[35]

Margaret Bush Wilson, a prominent St. Louis lawyer and civil rights leader who knew both men, remembered each member of the newly formed political partnership as a formidable presence and personality. Gibbons was tall (over 6 feet), "almost stately looking," "extremely articulate," and "not at all the caricature of a trade union boss kind of person." In contrast, Calloway was short (about 5'6" tall), looked more "South American or Cuban" than African American, "had a very appealing speaking voice," and impressed her as both "articulate" and "wise." Others recalled Gibbons as a man who was "strikingly good looking," "tastefully dressed," had a "commanding" physical presence, and possessed "enormous energy" that enabled him to function effectively on minimal sleep. Friends and colleagues of Calloway cited his "very, very impish sense of humor," "astute and perceptive" social and political analysis, and the fact that he was both "well read" and "self taught." This contrasting yet complementary duo now prepared to transform the social and political landscape of their adopted city, taking on what Calloway later described as a "bland, conservative community [reluctant] to accept new, exciting ideas."[36]

Establishing the Teamsters as a political presence in St. Louis and a recognized spokesperson for working-class interests became a high initial priority for Gibbons and Calloway. Although they both sensed the dimming prospects for establishing a labor party, they were determined to position Local 688 as a political force independent from the machine politics that dominated civic affairs in St. Louis. By the late 1940s, Democrats were on the verge of eclipsing Republican influence in the city, continuing to ride the waves of changing political loyalties unleashed by the New Deal. Nonetheless, both political parties in St. Louis remained electorally competitive in the immediate post World War II period.

Although St. Louis's political machine was not as centralized as its counterparts in other cities, ward-based organizations rooted in ethnic loyalties and personal relationships exercised considerable authority. One prominent faction, led by Morris Shenker, a controversial lawyer who defended St. Louis mobsters and later represented Jimmy Hoffa, Edward "Jellyroll" Hogan, a former Irish gangster turned AFL union official and state legislator, and Thomas Callanan, whose brother, Lawrence, headed the politically powerful Steamfitters Union, was perhaps the most recognizable symbol of the city's postwar machine politics. The narrow parochialism they associated with machine politics especially repelled Gibbons and Calloway. Both regarded St. Louis's machine politicians as unresponsive to demands for racial justice and too cozy with the city's corporate and civic elites to conceive of local government as an equalizing institution capable of promoting a fair distribution of resources and maintaining decent living standards for the working class.[37]

Yet when the union movement attempted to exert its influence more overtly in the 1930s and 1940s by running its own mayoral candidates in CIO strongholds such as Akron and Detroit, white working-class voters rejected these efforts. In Detroit, the racial liberalism of UAW candidates discomfited many white workers seeking to preserve their new status as well-paid union members and homeowners while in other instances, the electorate seemed reluctant to grant expanded political power to unions. As Thomas Sugrue has observed regarding Detroit's working-class voters, they "failed to see the relationship between their lives in the plant and their lives in the community." Gibbons and Calloway explicitly attempted to bridge this divide several years later but began more modestly in their initial efforts to define a political role for the union in St. Louis. For Gibbons, the first step was to establish a more independent labor presence within the constraints of the two-party system. As Local 688's political education committee explained, "It is absolutely essential that we have candidates who are not 'lesser evils' but men and women who can command our respect and wholehearted support. Our endorsement must never be regarded as the automatic right of those who give lip service to liberalism."[38]

An opportunity to send this message emerged in 1948. Rejecting a union proposal that he seek elective office, Gibbons nonetheless declared his "wish that we had a Political Action Committee that would think in terms of running a Trade Unionist for office." In the fall of 1948, Gibbons's wish became a reality with the campaign of Robert Pentland, a J.C. Penney's worker and chair of the union's political action committee, for a Missouri state senate seat from a south St. Louis District.[39]

The senate district was represented by a Republican who was regarded as pro-labor by the St. Louis CIO. In spite of receiving no support from other unions, the press, or community groups, Gibbons and the RWDSU were determined to run their own candidate and elect a stronger legislative voice to promote their agenda at the state level. In a predominately white working-class district where Gerald L.K. Smith's Christian Nationalists had considerable support, Pentland made no attempt to hide his support for racial justice. Drawing on its 500 members who lived in the district and dozens of volunteers, the union mounted an intensive grassroots effort on Pentland's behalf. Buoyed by this outpouring of union activity and Democratic presidential candidate Harry Truman's coattails, he won a narrow victory that was wholly unanticipated.[40]

Pentland decisively moved to advance the union's agenda on racial justice, seeking passage of fair employment practice legislation and urging Missouri's governor to call a special session to consider opening the state's higher education institutions to African Americans. In addition to demonstrating the union's political efficacy and underscoring its refusal to conform to the conventions of St. Louis machine politics, Robert Pentland's election was yet another assertion of working-class achievement and potential that was essential to Gibbons and Calloway's conception of unionism. By electing a coal miner's son and rank-and-file warehouse worker to the state legislature, they underscored their belief that the skills and confidence workers gained from their union roles on the shop floor could be transferred into the corridors of political and social decision-making. At the same time, however, they angered other St. Louis unions for their go-it-alone approach to politics, reinforcing the perception that they were only willing to practice solidarity on their own terms.[41]

Recalling Arnold Rose's finding that the union's support for racial equity on the shop floor had not substantially altered members' attitudes regarding civil rights in the community, Gibbons and Calloway also accelerated their efforts to transform race relations in St. Louis. Anticipating the Supreme Court's 1954 decision striking down segregated schools, they requested that Local 688's Committee on the Democratic Rights of Members prepare a report on "Planning for an Integrated School System in St. Louis." Developed with Calloway's consultation and released in December 1951, the report proposed that the city take steps to "prepare for the inevitable change with a minimum of disturbance and tension." The committee offered numerous ideas to foster better race relations in education, including interracial recreational and sporting activities, gradual integration of teaching staffs, and requiring high school students to take a class in human relations. The plan received considerable public attention, brought the "subject of public school desegregation to a 'community-conscious discussion' level," and helped build support for initiatives being undertaken by the city's Board of Education. When a February 28, 1952, letter to the editor of the *St. Louis Post-Dispatch* criticized the report, Gibbons vigorously defended the union's stance, arguing that its "citizen-members" were obligated to help bridge the "gulf between the spirit and practices of American democracy . . . before it is too late." This impassioned defense reinforced many of the assumptions guiding Gibbons and Calloway's emerging efforts to "view the union member within the frame of his total environment." These efforts would embody several crucial concepts: extending shop-floor expertise into the arena of community engagement, crafting a union role in shaping the direction of urban policy, and pursuing racial justice as an affirmation of the union movement's fundamental commitment to equality and democracy.[42]

Armed with enhanced resources from his affiliation with the Teamsters, basking in the national attention he was beginning to receive as an innovative union leader, and with Ernest Calloway at his side to provide intellectual and strategic support, Harold Gibbons prepared to expand total person unionism into new arenas. However, his entry into the universe of Teamsters unionism produced some unanticipated challenges and opportunities that simultaneously elevated his ambitions, altered his approach to labor leadership, and placed his career on a new trajectory.

CHAPTER 6

"Those Fellows Back There Actually Hate You"

Harry Ball's description of the St. Louis warehouse and distribution union as an "organization of conflict" remained an apt characterization following its merger with Local 688 and the beginning of Harold Gibbons and Ernest Calloway's collaboration in the early 1950s. In some instances this conflict assumed familiar forms, most notably in a protracted 1953 construction drivers' strike that disrupted the St. Louis economy and riveted community attention. Gibbons and Calloway's determination to expand the boundaries of collective bargaining also triggered some unforeseen consequences. Along with other segments of the Teamsters, Local 688 became the target of a series of investigations that persisted throughout the 1950s. At the root of this enhanced scrutiny was the union's bold assertion of economic power and its continuing forays into social engineering, actions that aroused fears among St. Louis's business and civic elite about Harold Gibbons's ultimate ambitions. As one employer told a *St. Louis Globe-Democrat* reporter, "In this age when everybody is chasing a dollar, it makes you suspicious when you come across somebody like Gibbons, who doesn't have the same interests. If the guy isn't interested in money, what does he want?"[1]

The concerted political backlash against Gibbons, Calloway, and Local 688 gathered force following a dramatic confrontation between the union and St. Louis's criminal underworld. In defending his position, Gibbons became closely aligned with controversial Teamsters leader Jimmy Hoffa, prompting new concerns about his loyalty to the values and commitments that had previously defined his career.

* * *

Although organized crime never reached the level of influence in St. Louis that it achieved in cities such as New York, Chicago, or Detroit, gangsters had carved out a significant presence dating back to the Prohibition era. At least five gangs mostly run by mobsters of Irish or Italian descent vied for control of bootlegging and gambling operations during the 1920s, and conflicts between rival factions of

American and foreign-born Italians led to nearly forty killings at the peak of this internecine warfare. With the repeal of Prohibition in 1933, these criminal gangs shifted their attention to unions. In fiercely competitive, locally based industries such as jukeboxes, pinball, and slot machines, mob elements provided muscle to assist favored employers and help unions gain recognition over their rivals. These collusive arrangements positioned the mob to profit handsomely from enterprises with a continuous cash flow that were susceptible to skimming before income could be reported and taxed.[2]

The opportunity to trade bribes and payoffs for labor peace led St. Louis's mob to the construction industry, where it exercised powerful influence within the Laborers and Steamfitters Unions. Largely untouched by these elements in the warehousing industry, Harold Gibbons possessed a visceral distaste for the sweetheart deals proffered by mob connected unions. However, in the orbit of the St. Louis Teamsters, several local unions representing truck drivers had strong connections to mobsters. In late 1952, these elements directly confronted Gibbons when emissaries of Frank "Buster" Wortman, a mobster who oversaw gambling, bookmaking, and other criminal enterprises in southern Illinois and part of St. Louis, approached him and demanded that he place several of their associates on his payroll. Wortman, who already exercised influence within several Teamsters' locals, was seeking to expand his operations and saw Gibbons as an impediment to his plans.[3]

Wortman was a notorious career criminal whom the *St. Louis Post-Dispatch* described as an "East Side agent for the Chicago Capone syndicate." A member of Steamfitters Local 562, Wortman had a history of shaking down union leaders and businessmen, along with a reputation for violence if his demands went unheeded. Although Gibbons rejected Wortman's ultimatum to accept mobsters on his payroll, he was clearly frightened when he received death threats for his refusal to comply.[4]

One of Gibbons's first moves was to apply for a gun permit. The St. Louis police department denied his application and rejected his request for protection against Wortman's threats, no doubt reluctant to aid a labor leader who had earned what one observer described as its "top-level enmity." Gibbons also reported receiving little support from others he approached about his dilemma, including a *St. Louis Post-Dispatch* editor and a St. Louis police board member. Almost all accounts, however, including FBI reports and interviews with union staff present at the time, concurred that Gibbons's life was in danger. His fears were likely accentuated by the murders of two local Laborers Union officials earlier in 1952, reportedly by associates of John Vitale, the reputed head of the "Italian syndicate" in St. Louis.[5]

Rebuffed by St. Louis officialdom, Gibbons turned to Jimmy Hoffa for help, apparently at the suggestion of Richard Kavner. Hoffa, a rising star within the Teamsters who had developed a widespread reputation for his aggressiveness, had considerable experience dealing with mob elements in Detroit, using these relationships to support Teamsters' organizing in the face of fierce jurisdictional battles with other unions. The Detroit Teamster outlined Gibbons's options succinctly: he could accede to Buster Wortman's demands but be beholden to him, directly confront Wortman and his henchman, or accept help from the international union in ousting Wortman's cronies from the trucking locals.[6]

Harold Gibbons chose the latter option. With the approval of Teamsters president Dave Beck, Thomas Flynn, a special representative from the international union, came to St. Louis in March 1953. Accompanied by Hoffa, Flynn quickly obtained resignations from the officers of the trucking local through which Wortman had leaned on Gibbons, placing it under trusteeship. At the same time Gibbons convened a meeting of Local 688's shop stewards, announced his intention to "clean up" the mob-infested locals, and received approval to shut down St. Louis warehouses if employers attempted to negotiate with gangsters and circumvent the union. Shortly thereafter, Hoffa imported bodyguards to protect Gibbons, underscoring the international union's resolve to enforce its decision. Indeed, angry members of Local 600 rushed the stage to get at Hoffa during one union meeting, resulting in an extended melee. At Local 682, a dissident seeking to enter a meeting suffered a serious beating, an incident that underscored Gibbons's willingness to use muscle to establish his authority.[7]

In a later interview, Gibbons asserted that Hoffa had obtained approval from the Chicago and Detroit mobs to help stage what turned out to be a largely bloodless coup to rid the union of Wortman's influence. According to Hoffa, he negotiated a non-aggression pact with Wortman, using the imprimatur of the Detroit mob to persuade the St. Louis mobster to leave Gibbons alone. Whatever the case, this event marked the beginning of Harold Gibbons's close relationship with Hoffa and his rapid rise to power within the Teamsters' hierarchy.[8]

Gibbons's relationship with the volatile Detroit Teamster became the object of intense speculation, leading labor leaders and media observers to puzzle over the unlikely alliance between the former CIO socialist and the consummate business unionist. For Hoffa, there were clear benefits in assisting Gibbons. Rescuing the St. Louis Teamsters from the grasp of Buster Wortman enabled him and Teamsters president Dave Beck to advance their strategy of consolidating local unions into area conferences that could coordinate organizing efforts and establish uniform bargaining standards. Moreover, gaining an ally of Gibbons's caliber and reputation supported Hoffa's ultimate ambition of succeeding Beck as Teamsters' president.

Although the relationship with Hoffa paid obvious dividends for Harold Gibbons, it was rooted in a deeper bond than simple self-preservation or careerism. Gibbons and Hoffa had the shared experience of impoverishment and losing their fathers as youths, a powerful antipathy for established authority, and a fierce desire to succeed in a society that consistently denigrated working-class aspirations. Both men were determined to amass working-class power and use it to command economic, social, and personal respect. Although Gibbons's sense of voluntarism and his disdain for convention were not as extreme as Hoffa's, he nonetheless admired his new ally's ferocious commitment to working-class self-reliance and avoiding dependence on the uncertain loyalties of outsiders.

Gibbons's alliance with Jimmy Hoffa also marked his full passage into a moral and political universe far different from the milieu of socialism and industrial unionism in which he had been reared. Signs of this transition emerged soon after the expulsion of Buster Wortman's forces in the person of Barney Baker, an imposing brawler who had served as an enforcer for criminal gangs in New York and Florida. Baker provided muscle in strike situations, established relations with leading local gangsters, and reinforced the message that Gibbons's well-being and authority should not be challenged.[9]

Although there is no evidence that Gibbons engaged in personal acts of corruption (indeed, FBI informants, employers, and other observers consistently commented on his personal integrity), his deepening alliance with Hoffa compelled him to accommodate the role of organized crime within the Teamsters. Gibbons acquiesced in Barney Baker's activities and tolerated the presence of mob figures in and around the union in St. Louis. Concrete drivers Local 682, which later came under Gibbons's authority, retained close mob connections. Gibbons also rubbed elbows with Morris Shenker, a political power broker in St. Louis who won renown as a lawyer for organized crime and later as Jimmy Hoffa's attorney. Shenker, who accessed Teamsters pension funds to help finance his ownership of a Las Vegas casino, played an integral role in brokering other Las Vegas investments with Hoffa and mob-connected elements.[10]

Gibbons attempted to keep these relationships at arm's length by sequestering most of his St. Louis locals, especially 688, which remained a showcase for his social commitments. He also avoided direct involvement with the Central States Pension Fund, which under Jimmy Hoffa's direction became a lender of choice for organized crime. However, Gibbons never spoke out publicly against Teamsters with mob connections, accepting their presence as an unavoidable reality and a necessary price to be paid for his ascension to power. In contrast to Hoffa, who flaunted his relationships with mob figures and profited from them personally, Gibbons's moral calculus led him to a more passive form of accommodation that he could personally justify but which permanently tainted his public image as an exemplar of progressive unionism.[11]

What especially rankled Gibbons in the aftermath of the Buster Wortman episode was the minimal social recognition he and the union received for what they regarded as a "cleanup" of mob elements within the Teamsters' ranks. Although labor journalist Victor Riesel praised him in his nationally syndicated column as a "local crusader" against organized crime, Gibbons found reaction in St. Louis far more muted. In his view, official authority in St. Louis had displayed indifference to his plight, confirming that when it came to the rights of workers and unions, it was unwilling to provide the basic protection it afforded other citizens and social institutions. As a result, Gibbons had been forced to act alone, with Jimmy Hoffa and the international union being his only allies. After the expulsion of Wortman's forces in 1953 and the subsequent intensification of political attacks on him and Local 688, Gibbons, like Hoffa, increasingly began to embrace the image of the outlaw and anti-hero. This image served dual purposes. It enabled Gibbons to rally strong internal support while signaling that the union would not be constrained by the parameters of "mature labor relations" that were emerging between powerful unions and employers in the mass production and distribution industries.[12]

Gibbons's accentuated sense of belligerence and disdain for respectability soon manifested itself in a controversial 1953 strike waged by Local 682, which represented truck drivers who transported concrete and building materials to construction sites. Eager to win the loyalty of the new members under his authority, and reflecting Teamster determination to eliminate disparities between St. Louis workers and those in comparable cities, Gibbons aggressively pressed the union's cause. Four employer associations settled with the Teamsters, but one hold-out, the concrete and ready mixers association, resisted Local 682's demands. As the strike dragged on and attracted widespread criticism, Ernest Calloway began to play a prominent role in formulating how the issues of the strike would be framed for public consumption.[13]

According to Calloway, management had been "evading their responsibility as employers" by treating drivers as independent contractors and not paying for basic protections such as workers compensation, overtime, and social security. From his days with the red caps, Calloway well understood the plight of workers who lacked employee status. Calloway's influence could also be seen in the union's accusation that a group of the larger employers in the association were prolonging the strike to drive smaller competitors out of business. This charge reflected the Teamsters' eagerness to portray themselves as victims of dark forces that colluded to curb their exercise of working-class power. Angling to attract public support, the employers' association argued that the union's demands would inflate construction costs, a potent allegation in a city with ambitious plans for downtown development.[14]

With thousands of workers idled by the strike which commenced on May 19, 1953, $75 million in construction projects on hold, and economic losses estimated by some observers as reaching $100 million, the walkout quickly became politicized. Recently elected St. Louis mayor Raymond Tucker, an engineer with a strong technocratic bent who abhorred the raw emotions unleashed by the strike, declared that neither side had the "moral right" to act "as if the society and the community around them has no part or interest in their struggle." He proposed that the combatants allow a panel of arbitrators to settle the dispute.

Gibbons and the union accepted Tucker's offer but only on the condition that management open its books and allow public scrutiny of its claim that it lacked the ability to meet the union's wage demands. The employer association balked at this proposal, with its attorney asserting that these records were "sacred" and would not be exposed under any circumstances.[15]

Neither side budged from its position. Along with its refusal to heed the mayor's request, the union rejected a circuit court grand jury's recommendation that it accept arbitration. A small group of women whose non-striking husbands had been thrown out of work by the walkout met with the mayor and gained considerable publicity from a sympathetic local press with their plea that the parties resolve their differences. As the strike dragged on, Dave Beck sent his top aide, Thomas Flynn, back to St. Louis to help restart negotiations. A week after Flynn's arrival, a settlement was reached on August 12, 1953, that met most of Local 682's demands, including substantial wage increases, additional payments for owner-operators, and implicit acknowledgment of their employee status. During the concluding round of negotiations, Jimmy Hoffa joined Flynn at the bargaining table to finalize the agreement, after some employers balked at having Harold Gibbons sign on behalf of the union. Indeed, Gibbons was present for neither the final bargaining sessions nor the photo ops that showed Raymond Tucker shaking hands with Hoffa and Flynn following the settlement. Commenting on these developments, Hoffa reportedly observed to his new ally that: ". . . there are some men in Detroit who dislike me—but those fellows back there actually hate you!" Hoffa's observation accurately reflected growing anxiety among St. Louis's business and civic elite that Harold Gibbons's use of economic power threatened their control over the local economy and their plans for urban revitalization.[16]

Although the cement drivers' strike sent shock waves through the St. Louis establishment and discomfited other labor leaders, it elevated Gibbons's standing within the Teamsters and set the tone for the broader economic strategy he and Calloway were preparing to pursue. Gibbons's approach as an uncompromising negotiator who thrived on conflict, which had marginalized him within the Textile Workers Organizing Committee, was greeted far more favorably by his Teamster superiors and had an immediate impact on the trajectory of his career. His rapid rise was remarkable, especially as a CIO expatriate in a union steeped in the culture and practice of the AFL. In quick succession he became director of the union's national warehousing division and secretary-treasurer of the recently established Central States Conference, the Midwestern regional structure that became Jimmy Hoffa's power base. Within St. Louis, the union's engagement with Raymond Tucker was but the first in a series of spirited confrontations with the St. Louis mayor over whose vision would shape the direction of the emerging post-industrial city. And for Gibbons and Calloway, the strike affirmed the potential of their political partnership in seeking to implement total person unionism on a wider basis.[17]

In the collective bargaining arena, Gibbons, with Calloway's intellectual and strategic input, began to construct the economic foundation central to total person unionism. Although acknowledging its achievements, historians have become increasingly critical of the post-World War II collective bargaining regime. Unions had hoped that employers would support an expanded welfare state to relieve them of shouldering the full cost of health care and pensions. Instead, many employers were content to accept the creation of private, collectively bargained "welfare states" rather than assume the larger responsibilities they associated with the extension of social democracy. Although collective bargaining markedly improved the standard of living for workers represented by powerful unions, it offered limited assistance to their non-union brethren and workers of color, who frequently lay outside the reach of union contracts or legal protection by the state. This "truncated universalism" has been seen by some historians as a "strategic error" that dampened the prospects for politicized bargaining and broader working-class solidarity while enabling critics to portray the union movement as a special interest indifferent to the needs of workers outside its ranks. Years later, Harold Gibbons and Ernest Calloway acknowledged the merits of these criticisms. However, in the heady days of the 1950s, they possessed a profound faith in the transformational power of collective bargaining, and they elaborated on this belief in several illustrative documents.[18]

In the wake of Taft-Hartley's passage and the election of Dwight Eisenhower in 1952, Gibbons and Calloway bemoaned the growing reluctance of some labor leaders to take aggressive action in support of organizing and bargaining for fear of legal repercussions. Outlining strategy for the national warehouse division, Gibbons, with encouragement from Calloway, urged a return to the risk-taking spirit they had been weaned on in the 1930s: "The labor movement was built by people who were so profoundly moved by the justice of the cause that they were willing to take 'chances' in order to build a better America." Seeking to extend New Deal Keynesianism into the post-World War II era, justify public policies aimed at sustaining a high wage economy, and counter employer arguments about the growing importance of foreign trade, the warehouse division statement asserted that American wage earners were "the only effective peace-time market for the sale of industrial products." Therefore, Gibbons and Calloway insisted, collective bargaining had a powerful patriotic purpose: "The future prosperity of the Americans cannot be achieved unless the employers of America today accept the principle of an expanding purchasing power which can only result from substantial increases in the real wages of American workers."[19]

In addition to its patriotic and egalitarian social purposes, Gibbons and Calloway viewed collective bargaining not only as a vehicle for the demonstration of working-class power but also an outlet for the expression of working-class ingenuity. In 1956, at Gibbons's behest, Calloway elaborated on this view in a pamphlet titled "The Nature and Structure of the Collective Bargaining Agreement." This widely distributed document revealed the deeper meanings they attached to this basic trade union function. In the foreword, Gibbons argued that for "the worker on the job, it [collective bargaining] can be his passport to human dignity and functional freedom." Calloway spent considerable time establishing the broader historical significance of collective bargaining, describing it "as much a part of the democratic fabric as universal manhood suffrage and the right of free speech." To underscore this point, the cover of the document juxtaposed the first page of the famous 1806 trial of boot and shoe workers for "a conspiracy to raise their wages" with the first page of a union contract covering Central States cartage carriers. This juxtaposition highlighted Calloway and Gibbons's awareness that the labor movement's legitimacy had not come easily and underscored their belief that collective bargaining ranked as a profound working-class achievement deserving of social recognition.[20]

Throughout the early 1950s, Gibbons and Calloway used the St. Louis Teamsters' expanding economic power to translate their lofty expectations for collective bargaining into agreements that would provide economic security for their members and affirm their status as industrial citizens. Like other powerful unions whose industries were substantially organized, they attempted to negotiate contracts that would reinforce managerial respect for labor's legitimacy in an increasingly hostile political climate. Acting on the recommendations of several committees that Calloway had advised, Local 688 began seeking long-term agreements that included provisions to enhance worker security and legitimate expressions of working-class solidarity. Security needs were addressed through guaranteed annual employment (2,000 hours a year excluding overtime) for workers with a certain level of seniority, employer-paid health care and pensions, and an employer-financed welfare plan that would initially provide life insurance and later be used to fund recreational programs for members and their families. The ability to engage in direct action, which employers had attempted to circumscribe via Taft-Hartley and negotiated limitations, was preserved by contract language permitting the union the right to strike over grievances and to refuse to handle the goods ("hot cargo") produced by a struck employer.[21]

These provisions were not accepted by all of Local 688's employers. However, by the end of 1953, Local 688 had won five-year agreements in twenty-two of its contracts. The guaranteed annual employment clause covered nearly 3,000 workers, and at Brown Shoe, the union gained company approval to make up the difference between what workers compensation would pay in the event of injury and a worker's regular wage. The wall of security that Gibbons and Calloway were determined to construct for their members had certainly become higher and sturdier in a relatively short period, and they proudly noted that the unskilled warehouse workers they represented were now earning almost as much as their semi-skilled and skilled counterparts. Forty percent of the agreements they negotiated by the end of 1953 permitted workers to refuse to handle hot cargo, and half of the contracts contained the right to strike over grievances. The right-to-strike clauses reflected Gibbons and Calloway's distaste for compulsory arbitration, which in their view was guided more by "legalism" than considerations of justice. The hot cargo clause preserved a prerogative essential to Local 688's culture as an "organization of conflict" and alerted employers that even in the face of political backlash, the union could still practice acts of solidarity and coordinated action.[22]

Besides these achievements on behalf of their membership base in warehousing and distribution, Gibbons and Calloway used collective bargaining to elevate some of St. Louis's most marginal workers—the city's taxi drivers. Gibbons had long been committed to improving conditions for taxi drivers and had organized African American cabbies in St. Louis after World War II. Prior to his joining the Teamsters, the union's Joint Council 13 had declined to grant a charter to African American drivers. This policy changed dramatically under Gibbons. Early in 1949, the union negotiated a master agreement representing approximately 600 workers employed at the city's fourteen black-owned taxi companies and expanded their efforts after the merger with the Teamsters brought in Local 405, a unit of white drivers. By the 1950s, Gibbons began to accelerate the union's efforts to upgrade conditions for taxi drivers, spurred in part by a commitment from the international union to bring these workers under the Teamsters' banner.[23]

Taxi drivers were notoriously difficult to organize. They worked in a ruthlessly competitive industry, where costs for fuel, insurance, maintenance, and licenses kept companies on the margins and created considerable insecurity for both employees and drivers who owned and operated their own vehicles. In addition to their precarious economic status, cabbies inhabited a volatile social environment, where they often clashed with police, passengers, and employers who resisted their sporadic attempts to organize. Some cabbies became associated with criminal activity such as prostitution, drugs, and theft to supplement their meager incomes. Along with their numerous and persistent frustrations, drivers found solidarity elusive, with owner-operators often viewing themselves as small businessmen or entrepreneurs rather than workers willing to show solidarity with other cabbies who were employed by fleets or leased their vehicles from them. Although taxi drivers were capable of acting collectively, their strikes were often undisciplined and short-lived, leading Michael Quill, the leader of the Transport Workers Union in New York, to dub them the "limping proletariat."[24]

In a series of negotiations, many of them accompanied by violent strikes, Harold Gibbons, with assistance from Ernest Calloway, mobilized both black and white drivers to seek improved working conditions and greater economic security. In 1950, at a new cab company where all the taxis were company-owned, the union bargained the first paid vacations and Labor Health Institute (LHI) coverage for workers in the industry. Five years later, Calloway helped negotiate an agreement that brought drivers health and welfare coverage and contained provisions that provided owners with incentives to improve service, expand business, and stabilize their operations. Although the taxi industry never fully embraced Calloway's concept of the union as a stabilizing force, it made concessions that brought St. Louis cabbies a modicum of economic security and social respect.[25]

The union's relations with the St. Louis taxi industry remained quite contentious throughout the first half of the 1950s. The presence of Barney Baker as an organizer for taxi drivers accompanied an escalation in the union's tactics, which it claimed in a brief July 1953 walkout were provoked by police harassment. A December 1953 strike against Yellow Cab led to the indictments of Richard Kavner and 688 other staffers and members on extortion charges under the Hobbs Act. Business agent Herman Hendricks was jailed on contempt charges after refusing to answer questions about gunshots that had been fired during a 1954 strike when black workers at Allen Cab, apparently with managerial encouragement, voted to leave Local 688 and form an independent union. Gibbons himself was arrested in December 1953 at a Democratic Party dinner in St. Louis where his old Chicago mentor Paul Douglas was speaking, and was charged with pushing a cab into the Mississippi River during a bitter taxi strike. Although the charges against Gibbons, Kavner, and the others were eventually dismissed and Hendricks was released from custody, these well-publicized incidents reinforced the union's outlaw image in St. Louis. In addition to the aura of violence surrounding the union's taxi strikes, Local 405 emerged as an outpost of resistance to Gibbons, becoming a hotbed of intrigue marked by decertification efforts, wildcat strikes, and raids by other unions.[26]

Basking in their achievements at the bargaining table, Gibbons and Calloway could not help but notice cracks in the wall of security they were building for their members in St. Louis. Even as they were negotiating five-year contracts and generous social welfare benefits, employers in St. Louis began undercutting these agreements by moving warehousing facilities to other locations. Between 1952 and 1954 alone, a host of warehouses closed, including several owned by companies that were part of national chains. In 1954 at Rice-Stix, one of the major St. Louis warehouses organized shortly after Gibbons's arrival, the union was forced to defer scheduled wage increases to help the firm repel a hostile takeover by an outside anti-union firm. The consolidations and closings were in part prompted by changing managerial practices, including a shift toward greater direct buying and shipping that made warehousing less necessary for many retailers. These visible closings were well-covered by the local media, which intimated that the Teamsters' militant tactics and costly contracts were driving businesses out of St. Louis and devastating the city's economy.[27]

Local 688 disputed these claims, obtaining letters from employers citing other reasons for their departure (obsolete facilities, trends toward direct buying, limited available space in which to upgrade or expand) and noting it did not press to gain five-year deals from less well-off firms. Privately, Gibbons, Calloway, and other union leaders expressed fear that as collective bargaining raised costs for employers, they might begin to find automation more attractive, raising the possibility of a "push button warehouse" that could be operated by fewer workers. And as Local 688 leader John Naber observed at a February 1955 warehouse division meeting, national chains had indicated that they would not upgrade facilities in St. Louis due its high wage and benefits costs. Management's ability to restructure and relocate its warehousing and distribution operations revealed that in spite of the Teamsters' bargaining and organizing aggressiveness, it still held powerful cards to circumscribe union growth.[28]

The St. Louis Teamsters' aggressive bargaining, assertive political forays, and seemingly limitless ambitions triggered a powerful backlash in the early 1950s, a local microcosm of a broader counterattack against the IBT that was occurring in many parts of the country. In St. Louis, the move to derail Gibbons, Calloway, and Local 688 had its roots in a 1953 federal grand jury investigation that led to the indictment of sixteen construction union leaders. At the same time these indictments were issued, UE leader and old Gibbons nemesis William Sentner went on trial for subversion, an action aimed at completing the marginalization of a once powerful left-led union in St. Louis by discrediting its Communist-affiliated leadership. It was in this context that Gibbons and Local 688 became the target of a coordinated investigation by federal and local authorities during the summer and fall of 1953.[29]

Reflecting Ernest Calloway's conviction that conspiracy lurked behind corporate machinations against the union movement, Local 688 accused bankers, the Chamber of Commerce, and the press of launching a planned effort to "get" Harold Gibbons in retaliation for the union's success in "busting the low-wage barrier" in St. Louis. This suspicion of orchestrated plotting against Local 688 was by no means misplaced. In a June 1953 memo to FBI director J. Edgar Hoover, the FBI special agent in charge of the bureau's St. Louis office noted "It is possible that considerable pressure to have GIBBONS' activities investigated is being exerted by industrial leaders in St. Louis." Another communication from St. Louis to FBI headquarters in Washington alleged that Gibbons was now "in a condition to dominate and tie up completely trucking, transportation, and warehousing" in the city. The memo went on to observe that Gibbons is "very definitely radical in his thinking, and could easily cause considerable damage to the industries of our city." These complaints led assistant U.S. attorney general Warren Olney III to authorize a preliminary investigation of the St. Louis Teamsters in August 1953.[30]

Max Goldschein, a special assistant to the attorney general who had worked with Senate investigations into organized crime, led an aggressive federal probe into Local 688's financial affairs during the early months of 1954. The investigation drew on information provided by informants, local police, private detectives, and business leaders seeking to establish that LHI funds were being diverted inappropriately, and membership dues were being improperly spent as political contributions. According to the union, one of the sources for these allegations was a doctor who had been fired from the LHI staff and provided information to a St. Louis police sergeant. The sergeant, who reportedly showed the informant his membership card in Gerald L.K. Smith's Christian Nationalists, revealed his own special bias against Local 688, averring that Harold Gibbons "was personally responsible for the Fairgrounds Race Riot" that had occurred during efforts to integrate city swimming pools several years earlier.[31]

Some FBI officials in Washington questioned Goldschein's approach, observing that the "vast majority of information" he and local FBI officials had generated was "general," "non-specific," and "conjectural." While employers complained that Gibbons and Local 688 "dominated" the administration of LHI, Goldschein and his investigators found no evidence demonstrating the misuse of union funds. For his part, Goldschein was especially interested in Local 688's extensive political involvement and the "dollar volume of expenditures made for this purpose by the union." The political animus of the investigation was underscored by the grand jury's June 9, 1954, report. Frustrated by its inability to uncover indictable offenses, the grand jury lamented the influence of union political action funds, accused Local 688 of driving business out of St. Louis with its "excessive" demands, and complained about "the great concentration of power in a few men."[32]

The federal probe resulted in several direct brushes between Local 688 and the criminal justice system. In February 1954, Harold Gibbons was charged with contempt and briefly jailed after refusing to provide the grand jury with union financial records in response to a subpoena. Longtime union leaders Pete Saffo and Lou Berra also became targets of the grand jury investigation. Saffo spent forty-seven days in jail after refusing to answer questions about Local 688's purchase of holsters during its 1953 confrontation with the mob, and Berra was indicted on allegations that he had accepted kickbacks from a contractor doing work at the Labor Health Institute. On May 18, 1954, Gibbons and fellow union leader Edward Brown were indicted for filing false financial reports with the Department of Labor, because they "deliberately omitted" strike fund and political action expenditures from reports submitted in the previous three years. A federal judge later dismissed the charges on the grounds that it was impossible to determine in which jurisdiction (local or federal) the false reporting had actually occurred. Although Max Goldschein obtained a new indictment in November 1954, a judge again threw out the charges for similar reasons, prompting the Justice Department to close its investigation of Gibbons. The only charges that withstood legal scrutiny were those faced by Lou Berra, who was sentenced to a four-year prison term for falsifying his income tax return. Local 688 insisted that Berra was the victim of an anti-union vendetta, noting that the chief witness against him was a three-time felon and supported his ultimately unsuccessful appeal all the way to the U.S. Supreme Court.[33]

The legal offensive against Local 688 was accompanied by a political assault that especially outraged Harold Gibbons. Allegedly concocted by notorious anti-union operative Fred Bender, a virulently conservative local publication called *Spotlight News* launched a series of attacks on Gibbons coinciding with the grand jury investigations in the spring of 1954. Highlighting his associations with Trotskyists, *Spotlight News* accused Gibbons of being part of a "red front," blamed him for driving businesses out of St. Louis, and charged that he was "an absolute one-man dictator." Fully aware that in a red-baiting atmosphere, youthful political associations could destroy the career of even the most fiercely anti-communist unionist, Gibbons acquired a citation from the American Legion praising him for his opposition to the CP. After *Spotlight News* and other antagonists attempted to have his citation rescinded, Gibbons obtained letters of support from powerful political figures, including senators Paul Douglas and Stuart Symington. Although this strategy blunted the paper's attacks, it aligned Gibbons with forces that were actively seeking to extinguish virtually all forms of oppositional politics in their crusade against alleged communist penetration of American institutions. Gibbons's response to Fred Bender and *Spotlight News* underscored the kinds of personal and political compromises he increasingly felt compelled to make, illustrating his growing vulnerability as the Teamsters faced concerted efforts to undermine their legitimacy.[34]

Gibbons and Calloway mounted a multi-pronged counterattack aimed at rallying their membership and discrediting the forces arrayed against the union. Articulating themes that would become staple elements in Teamster rebuttals of their critics, they portrayed the union as an unwilling actor in an anti-union morality play that cast Gibbons as "the arch-criminal of St. Louis unionism" and made him "a new scapegoat for all of the economic and industrial ills of the St. Louis community." They also denounced the criminal justice system as an instrument for class oppression, describing Lou Berra's conviction for income tax evasion as evidence that there was "one law for the rich and another for the poor." The argument about "rigid dual standards" was repeated in justifying Gibbons's holding multiple positions of union authority, with the union observing that a business leader in a "parallel situation ... would be held in high public esteem and accepted without question as one of the pillars of the community."[35]

Gibbons and Calloway concluded that the attack on the union had to be seen as a refusal by local and national elites to accept organized labor's legitimacy as "an integral continuing part of the American community." In language that bore Calloway's stamp, he and Gibbons placed this refusal in a broader context, accusing their antagonists of undercutting the nation's efforts to promote democracy as an alternative to Soviet totalitarianism: "A great free-enterprising, industrial community which cannot afford a single set of standards in determining the value of both the business man and the union leader to the common well-being is one which is seeking to reject the basic assumptions of democracy and is headed in a dangerous direction." Gibbons and Calloway's assertion of their anti-communist credentials to establish their legitimacy fell flat, however, in the polarized political environment that was emerging with the onset of the Cold War. For St. Louis's power brokers, Local 688's exercise of working-class power was the primary social danger, with the union's militancy threatening not only their economic but also their political and civic hegemony.[36]

Grateful for the union's achievements on their behalf, most of Local 688's leaders and rank-and-file members accepted Gibbons and Calloway's view that the union was being persecuted not for actual wrongdoing but for its success in advancing working-class interests. As members of a union frequently embroiled in industrial and political conflict, Local 688's rank-and-file had long experienced hostility from St. Louis police, courts, political and business leaders, and the media. As a result, images of inquisition, lynching, and conspiracy during what Calloway later described as "the year of the wolfpack" resonated with Local 688 members, who embraced Gibbons and Calloway's portrayal of their union as a victim and remained loyal throughout the legal battles of 1954.[37]

Although he had few doubts about the loyalty of his members, Harold Gibbons began to think systematically about another line of defense for his embattled organization: developing a public relations program to improve its image. This new preoccupation reflected his growing ambition to play a more prominent national role in the IBT and his conclusion that the mainstream media were treating the Teamsters unfairly. Gibbons's interest in shaping the Teamsters' public image assumed several forms. He cultivated relationships with labor journalists Victor Riesel and Daniel Bell during the grand jury investigation that resulted in their writing articles sympathetic to Local 688. Consulting with a professional public relations firm in the spring of 1954, Gibbons began to contemplate additional moves, including persuading noted labor journalist Mary Heaton Vorse to write a piece on Local 688's accomplishments, hosting meetings with civic leaders to tell his side of the story, and publicly exposing corporate sponsorship for *Spotlight News'* smear campaign. Ultimately, Gibbons concluded that these moves were insufficient and decided that an effective public relations program for the union needed full-time professional direction.[38]

In 1955, Gibbons hired Jake McCarthy, a former publicist for the St. Louis archdiocese, to direct Local 688's public relation efforts. McCarthy quickly joined Ernest Calloway as part of the union's brain trust and became one of Gibbons's most trusted advisers. McCarthy's arrival coincided with one of Gibbons and Calloway's most ambitious initiatives to promote the exercise of working-class citizenship and the practice of total person unionism: Local 688's community stewards program. This highly visible attempt to improve the quality of life in St. Louis lifted Gibbons and Calloway to new levels of influence as they sought to create a "community bargaining table" that would establish the Teamsters as a dominant social force in the city's civic affairs.

CHAPTER 7

"The Other Sixteen Hours"

Early in the 1950s, an internal Teamsters Local 688 memo discussed what it called "the wide view and the narrow view" of the union movement's mission. "The narrow view," the memo observed, "would train stewards to do the job in the shop and nothing else. We believe there can be no excuse for the narrow view in these days. The union member is also a citizen and his interests as a citizen coincide with the interests of his fellow citizens." Local 688 leaders elaborated on this theme in their officers' report to the January 1952 City-Wide Shop Conference, an annual event at which the union set goals and priorities for the coming year: "And above all," they asserted [the union member] is willing to assume his or her responsibility in the maintenance of a democratic union and a democratic society."[1]

This "wide view" of member responsibility led Harold Gibbons and Ernest Calloway to establish a new program that mobilized Local 688 members to address issues affecting their lives during the "other sixteen hours" they spent off the job. The program, which featured the presence of "community stewards" located in St. Louis's neighborhoods, quickly aroused the interest of Local 688's members and threatened to alter the city's entrenched ward politics. Simultaneously, Ernest Calloway assumed a leadership role within the St. Louis NAACP and promoted a similar vision, creating new possibilities for the labor and civil rights movements to shape social policy in post-World War II St. Louis.

* * *

In spite of Local 688's economic and political successes, Gibbons and Calloway worried that these achievements rested on fragile foundations. Although the Teamsters had not been deterred by the post-World War II political counteroffensive against the union movement, Calloway observed that labor could no longer rely on "the apron strings of government a la FDR days." The prospect of sharply diminished support from the state prompted him to articulate an additional concern: "If the time comes when [government] protection is not forthcoming, then where is the necessary vitality among workers' organizations to resist?" With the continuing improvement of wages and benefits and the increasing centralization of collective bargaining, Calloway and Harold Gibbons feared that Local 688 members might become passive recipients of services rather than engaged unionists or active citizens. In response, they began to formulate a program of community involvement that would allow Local 688 members to develop their capacity to act as effective citizens.[2]

Although the political environment for unions had grown increasingly hostile, Gibbons and Calloway insisted that the labor movement now possessed the legitimacy to assert itself in the realm of community and civic affairs. As they explained at a 1953 Local 688 staff orientation, from "the early days of the American trade union movement [that] saw the entire community pitted against the union," with labor's new economic power, "many church, educational, and community leaders are seeing unions in a new light." The union movement was now poised, in Calloway's words, to take "its place as an integral part of the social and economic family." However, if unions were to assume greater responsibility for the health of the community, they needed to imbue their members with a broader social consciousness and offer them opportunities to play a more visible civic role. "Unions," Gibbons and Calloway explained, "must be more than dues collecting agencies or slot machines for wage increases. Members must be seen as total human beings and not as economic units only."[3]

In developing Local 688's community stewards program, Gibbons and Calloway sought to redefine the terms of labor's political involvement with the ultimate aim of making the union a potent force in shaping social and economic decision-making in St. Louis. According to political scientist Lana Stein, they undertook this work in a local political culture whose most salient characteristics were a "weak mayor, fragmented power, and ward factionalism." At the root of St. Louis's complicated politics was a post-Civil War "divorce" that separated the city of St. Louis from adjacent St. Louis County but left important elective city offices under state rather than city jurisdiction. In addition to creating positions with budgets and patronage opportunities not under the full authority of city officials, the divorce and St. Louis's adoption of home rule resulted in a decentralized governing structure that encouraged the exercise of political power at the ward level. After 1950, the Democratic Party dominated St. Louis politics, but serious divisions remained between the "mayor's group" (the business elite, the press, and the city's middle and upper middle class) and the "county group" (county office holders, aldermen, African Americans, unions, the working class, and the poor). Within this arrangement ward leaders and committeemen continued to wield considerable power on the basis of ethnic loyalty and access to patronage. In this uninviting soil Gibbons and Calloway began to cultivate the community stewards program, and their strategy reflected a keen awareness of St. Louis's distinctive political history.[4]

To blunt the power of ward leaders and gain recognition as an independent political force, Gibbons and Calloway realized they would have to convince Local 688 members that effective political action needed to occur year-round rather than just during the election season. Moreover, given the importance of the ward as the principal arena in which politics was practiced in St. Louis, the union had to establish its community program at the neighborhood level. As Gibbons explained in a January 1953 *New Republic* article, "the natural habitat of political action is in the wards and precincts, not in the union hall. The development of ward organizations is perhaps the most important task we face during the next few years." For men like Gibbons and Calloway, who resisted the paternalistic relationships that characterized ward politics, developing an alternative locus of power and authority at the neighborhood level was a high strategic priority.[5]

As the union movement grappled to understand the reasons for its members' increasing defection from labor-endorsed candidates, Gibbons attracted national attention as he elaborated on Local 688's emerging political strategy in several *New Republic* articles that appeared in the early 1950s. "At their present level of understanding," he observed, "most workers are much more concerned over the fact that their garbage is not collected in time rather than the pending Tidelands Oil giveaway." Over time, Gibbons contended, "as politics are brought down to earth, [and] made a part of the everyday life of the individual union member, greater political consciousness is developed. It is only one short step in the political awareness of the member from lower bus fares to lower taxes, from better trash collection to better labor legislation, from more street lights to more civil rights." Eventually, Gibbons and Calloway hoped that this enhanced political awareness would lead Local 688's members to support structural changes needed to improve their communities and press municipal government to fulfill these obligations.[6]

Most ambitiously, Gibbons and Calloway attempted to address one of the union movement's most enduring historical challenges, what scholars Ira Katznelson and Becky Nicolaides have respectively described as the "radical separation in people's consciousness . . . of the politics of work from the politics of community," and the tendency of those who were ". . . good unionists on the job [to] quickly shed these principles once they walked outside the factory gate." Workers who recognized the value of solidarity and mutual obligation on the shop floor often failed to apply these principles beyond the parameters of the workplace. Within the confines of the neighborhood or community, many unionists tended to define themselves in narrower ethnic, racial, or religious terms, or as taxpayers or homeowners based on their new collectively bargained affluence. By focusing their efforts on what they called "the other sixteen hours" that workers spent away from the shop floor, Local 688's community stewards attempted to bridge this historic divide by demonstrating that the split between the "politics of work" and the "politics of community" was neither intractable nor inevitable.[7]

Gibbons and Calloway were keenly aware that the collectively bargained security they had helped create for their members did not exist in a vacuum. Many of the maladies that afflicted postwar American cities had already surfaced in St. Louis and threatened its future viability. In the late 1940s, the *St. Louis Post-Dispatch* starkly described the city's choice as one of "Progress or Decay," noting that job and population losses had led to inadequate social spending, a moribund downtown, and especially harsh conditions for the city's growing African American population. Under these circumstances Gibbons and Calloway knew that the prospects for working-class advancement would remain limited in spite of their strong record of bargaining table achievements. Accordingly, they regarded the "politics of work" and "the politics of community" as intimately connected, and this awareness infused their effort to promote working-class citizenship with a powerful sense of urgency.[8]

The outline for a 1955 training course for Local 688 shop stewards elaborated on Gibbons and Calloway's evolving conception of working-class citizenship: "Workers are citizens first. While they pledge loyalty to their union because it has improved conditions in the shop, they and their union must necessarily broaden their horizons beyond the shop and into the community in which they live." By focusing on the union member as a "total person," the community stewards would help workers overcome the social fragmentation created by the bureaucratization of both private and public institutions (the conditions that intellectuals were increasingly describing as "mass society") by allowing them to apply their shop-floor expertise in their neighborhoods and communities.[9]

To create "worker-citizens," Gibbons, Calloway, and other Local 688 leaders appropriated the familiar apparatus of the shop floor and transplanted it to the community sphere. Officially launched in November 1951, their plan called for rank-and-file members in each of St. Louis's twenty-eight wards to be represented by community stewards. At least once a year, union leaders suspended regular shop meetings and encouraged members to attend community meetings in their wards. At these gatherings, workers discussed neighborhood and community issues and selected priorities for the union to address. Although these meetings often involved city officials, community stewards directed members to avoid discussion of party politics and instead focus on mobilizing to improve their neighborhoods. This directive anticipated the possibility that ward leaders might seek to co-opt the new effort and attempt to contain it within the familiar parameters of St. Louis's ward politics.[10]

Adapting elements of the formal grievance procedure used in Local 688 shops (the union even distributed copies of a "community grievance form"), the community stewards initially approached the ward's alderman seeking action on a specific concern. If a satisfactory resolution was not reached, the steward could then take the grievance to the appropriate city agency for redress. Subsequent options included bringing the unresolved grievance to the mayoral level, going to court, or attempting to rally public opinion. Underscoring the political dimensions of the program, the union offered one final step if the "grievance procedure" proved unavailing, declaring that the "ultimate recourse is the traditional weapon of democracy—our action at the polls." To reinforce this message of engagement and empowerment, Local 688 developed an eight-week training program covering issues such as leadership, politics, and advocacy skills to prepare community stewards for their new responsibilities as worker-citizens.[11]

The most powerful civic education for Local 688 members, however, resulted when community stewards launched specific campaigns that led to their direct engagement with the city's social and political establishment. The union's initial efforts involved issues that crossed racial and class lines and dealt with the quality of community life at a most basic level: the inadequate service provided by St. Louis's transit and sewer systems. Attendees at the union's first community meetings in late 1951 and early 1952, many of whom relied on buses and streetcars, complained loudly about rising fares and sub-standard service. In December 1951, twenty-two members of Local 688, among them Ernest Calloway, testified before the city's board of aldermen. A passionate plea from Thelma Lee Stone, a staff member at the union's Labor Health Institute, a resident of St. Louis's 25th ward, and one of eight women who testified, climaxed their appearance: "We have had enough of absentee landlords, of higher fares, of poor service," she declared. "We suggest that the transit system should be used by St. Louisans—by all of us. We ask that the city make plans to take over ownership." Stone's advocacy of public ownership underscored Gibbons and Calloway's belief that private transportation companies were ill-equipped to provide working-class citizens with the quality of service they deserved.[12]

Dissatisfied with the aldermen's lukewarm response to their demand for transportation improvements, Local 688 members sought voters' approval to create a public transit district that would encourage greater efficiency and better customer service. The community stewards convinced nearly 40,000 people to sign petitions supporting this initiative and helped formulate plans for the new entity, refusing to cede this authority to elected officials or bureaucrats. Although the city's CIO unions supported the plan, the AFL Central Trades and Labor Council believed that labor agreements with transit unions might not be honored under public ownership, thereby placing retiree pensions at risk. Voters also feared that increased taxes might be needed to subsidize a new public entity, and in January 1955, they rejected Local 688's plan for a consolidated transit district. Nonetheless, Local 688 and the community stewards had introduced the argument that public oversight would serve popular needs more efficiently than private management and demonstrated the union's commitment to grant citizens the opportunity to determine how public services could be administered most effectively.[13]

A year earlier, however, the community stewards experienced greater success with their campaign to create a metropolitan sewer district. This initiative stemmed from the persistent flooding and drainage problems that plagued St. Louis. Besides damage affecting personal residences, the lack of an adequate sewer system threatened public health. Open sewers emitted noxious odors that continually fouled the air and diminished the quality of life in both urban and suburban neighborhoods. In part, these problems existed because of the separation between the city and the county, which left nearly 100 municipalities that often duplicated services and were unable to take coordinated action. Driven by their distrust of unaccountable private power, Local 688 and the community stewards fought for public administration of this essential service. As Harold Gibbons bluntly recalled in a subsequent interview, "When a private company fucked up the sewerage system in the county, we went out and got all the signatures necessary and got a metropolitan sewer district." In February 1954, voters approved the union's proposal. As the "first successful attempt since the [1876] separation to adjust the governmental relations between St. Louis City and St. Louis County," the creation of the metropolitan sewer district marked an important victory for the community stewards in challenging the structural political barriers impeding efficient provision of vital public services.[14]

By the mid-1950s, Gibbons had become increasingly involved in national Teamsters affairs, and Calloway was beginning to establish himself as a leader of St. Louis's NAACP chapter. In 1955, although both retained their connection to the community stewards, they ceded day-to-day direction to Sidney Zagri, a talented Harvard-trained lawyer and former government investigator who led the program to some of its greatest successes. Remembered by Jake McCarthy as "Mr. Massive Retaliation" for his combativeness, Zagri became the community stewards' program's most visible spokesperson.[15]

Many of the issues Local 688 members brought to the attention of their community stewards dealt with matters of public safety and the quality of neighborhood life. By the mid-1950s, the union claimed to have successfully processed over 250 separate grievances with city agencies. These grievances involved problems such as dirty streets, cracked sidewalks, the lack of stop signs and traffic lights, and irregular trash collection. In these instances the community steward or program director simply contacted the appropriate city agency and requested that it take remedial action. Some observers noted that in conducting such intercessions, the Teamsters appeared to be challenging ward leaders by usurping their traditional roles. This perception heightened as the community stewards became increasingly assertive at the ward level.[16]

Under Zagri's leadership the community stewards also began to engage in a deeper form of civic participation that involved mobilizing members to investigate a grievance, develop a proposed solution, and create sufficient public pressure to compel a response. Taking on a social problem that had become a national preoccupation during the 1950s, Local 688 formed a committee on juvenile delinquency. Although the extent of juvenile delinquency was subject to exaggeration and even social hysteria, upwardly mobile working-class members of Local 688 expressed concern about teenage misbehavior. They had struggled hard to gain economic security and did not want their children to succumb to anti-social activity that would diminish the expanded opportunities now available to them.[17]

Community stewards Robert Weber, Floyd Glisper, and Vera Vinyard led Local 688's committee that helped formulate union policy on juvenile delinquency. To provide youths with greater opportunities for structured activity, the committee recommended that municipalities expand recreational programs for teenagers and urged schools to make their facilities available for after-hours activities. Many of the committee's recommendations were incorporated in a grand jury report on juvenile delinquency that had been commissioned by the St. Louis Circuit Court. In a September 1955 letter to the editor of the *St. Louis Globe-Democrat*, community steward Robert Weber justified the union's involvement in language that clearly demonstrated his self-awareness as a "worker-citizen." Referring to concerns about teenage drug abuse, he declared that "I think this 'Goof Ball' rage is a serious community problem. I think we as good and decent citizens should unite and wipe it out." Weber and other community stewards went on to work with a citizens committee that sought to secure funds for a supervised drag strip where youths could safely pursue their interest in car racing. The juvenile delinquency committee also established "Teamster Teentown," a program that offered entertainment for youths within a supervised setting. The committee's actions drew support from a local Parent Teacher Association (PTA) president, attesting to increasing social recognition of the community stewards' efforts.[18]

The community stewards program appears to have attracted a cross-section of the union's membership, establishing roots in many of St. Louis's neighborhoods. Although white migration to the suburbs was underway, Local 688 still had members of Irish, German, and Italian ancestry residing within St. Louis who became community stewards. Women also played a visible role in the community stewards program, even though the union made no special appeal to solicit their participation. As one union leader noted after the initial round of community meetings, "another surprise was the way in which women members who have never spoken before in the meetings took the floor repeatedly." Historically, women tended to place work and family affairs on a continuum rather than regarding them as separate social spheres, and the community stewards program offered them a vehicle to act on this awareness. Within Local 688, a significant segment of the union's female members endorsed Gibbons's observation that ". . . there is not much sense in winning higher wages and shorter hours unless the community is improved simultaneously so that workers [and their families] get fuller enjoyment out of higher wages and leisure."[19]

The experience of Vera Vinyard, a community steward in St. Louis's 22nd ward, illustrated the power of this understanding. Vinyard hosted the first home meeting of community stewards, appeared on local television to discuss the union's opposition to charter change, and became secretary of the community assembly Local 688 later formed to coordinate the community stewards' activities. Her husband and two daughters also participated actively in community stewards' events. Their involvement reflected Vinyard's apparent belief that her entire family had a stake in the union's efforts to make St. Louis a more "livable" city. By addressing issues of immediate interest to their members and showing how union power could be used to prompt change in the community, Gibbons and Calloway helped a diverse segment of Local 688's members to conceive of themselves as citizens who could speak authoritatively on matters affecting their lives outside the workplace.[20]

As their activities evolved, the community stewards began to raise basic questions about the quality of life in St. Louis. Their insistence that government ensure citizens a basic level of security and protection manifested itself most visibly around housing issues. One of St. Louis's largest challenges following World War II was the lack of decent, affordable housing. From the outset of the community stewards program, black members of Local 688 voiced concerns about substandard housing in their neighborhoods. As new public housing was erected in St. Louis during the 1950s, complaints also emerged about selection policies that favored white applicants while relegating African Americans to waiting lists.[21]

Exemplifying Local 688's longstanding commitment to racial egalitarianism, the community stewards aggressively engaged the problems posed by Local 688's African American members. In 1955, they mobilized 300 members to attend a ward meeting after a household fire killed four African American children, pressing for stricter enforcement of the city's housing code. Local 688 responded to concerns expressed by its members residing in public housing, forming a council to address issues such as crime, inadequate recreational facilities, and recurring rent increases. When police refused to patrol the Pruitt-Igoe housing project on the grounds that it was federal property, Local 688 obtained a ruling from the city requiring them to provide residents with protection. The union also convinced the city's schools superintendent to provide hot lunches for children in public housing whose nutritional needs were not being fully met at home.[22]

Gibbons and Calloway both recognized urban deterioration and flight to the suburbs as urgent problems that demanded a timely social response. As Sidney Zagri noted in a 1957 article entitled "Labor's Stake in Good Neighborhoods," many of Local 688's members lived in "twilight" neighborhoods suspended between conservation and decay. In response, Local 688's housing committee proposed eliminating high-rise complexes and providing greater access to shopping, recreation, and social services, along with stricter enforcement of city housing ordinances and making low interest loans available to residents for home improvements. The committee also recommended building new public housing for residents facing displacement by slum clearance initiatives. This agenda garnered support from other community groups, especially from faith-based organizations. The housing issue marked the community's stewards' emerging conception of what Sidney Zagri called the "community bargaining table," whereby citizens began to define and negotiate the terms of a social contract with public officials and other members of the city's power elite.[23]

Along with ward leaders who warily eyed the community stewards' increasing boldness, St. Louis Mayor Raymond Tucker experienced a series of uncomfortable encounters with Local 688's band of worker-citizens. A consummate technocrat who relied on the advice of professional staff, Tucker resented the community stewards' intrusion into city decision-making. In November 1955, a Tucker aide informed Sidney Zagri "that the method you have established constitutes a duplication of effort for the average citizen, yourselves, and city officials." The clash between Tucker's technocratic sensibilities and the union's determination to gain acceptance for the community bargaining table culminated in one of the community stewards' most dramatic public campaigns: a protracted struggle to induce the city to enforce its rat control ordinance.[24]

The dispute revolved around the decaying housing stock in St. Louis's inner core, which civic and political leaders planned to demolish to launch massive downtown redevelopment. With the prevalence of dilapidated housing and outdoor privies, rat infestation emerged as a significant public health hazard. This issue evoked widespread community anger when two-month-old Reginald Harrington was hospitalized in February 1955, suffering from life-threatening injuries caused by rat bites. Sixth ward community steward Floyd Glisper brought the issue to Local 688's attention, and the union quickly formed a committee to investigate. Comprised of community stewards and Local 688 members, most of whom were African American, the committee toured affected areas, photographed the conditions they observed, and interviewed residents and local officials. It found that in almost one-third of St. Louis's wards, the city had failed to enforce its rat control ordinance and estimated that during the past year 150 residents had suffered rat bites. Ernest Calloway, who accompanied the committee in conducting its initial survey, later quipped, "I believe the rats around here are paying protection money to the cats. The Grand Jury better look into it."[25]

The city's deputy health commissioner privately confirmed the accuracy of the community stewards' claims. Nonetheless, facing resistance from realtors and landlords and reluctant to invest resources in areas slated for demolition to pave the way for downtown development, city officials took minimal steps to control rat infestation. Although the community stewards orchestrated a series of public meetings, testified at hearings before the Board of Aldermen, and gained sympathetic media coverage, the Tucker administration remained unmoved. With the union charging that there was a "gentlemen's agreement" not to enforce the rat control ordinance, community stewards Rothchild Hall and Leoulie Adams filed a suit in March 1955 directing the city to meet its legal obligations. In August, a local judge concurred and issued an order directing the city to enforce the ordinance.²⁶

Appreciating the broader implications of the rat control campaign, Harold Gibbons strongly supported the community stewards' efforts. A testy exchange of letters between Gibbons and Raymond Tucker after the judge's decision highlighted sharply contrasting views of the social contract between city government and the citizens of St. Louis. Gibbons proclaimed that the judge's decision represented a "victory for social responsibility, [and] a frank recognition of the city's responsibility for a large segment of its population during a long transitional period from slums to land clearance and low-cost housing." In response, Tucker retorted that he would continue to be guided by the advice of his professional staff, declaring, "I attach great importance to the recommendations of disinterested experts in this or any other field." Convinced that the Teamsters were using the rat control issue for political purposes, Tucker defied the judge's ruling and took no action to enforce the rat control ordinance.²⁷

After more than a year of foot dragging, the city proposed revisions to the ordinance aimed at weakening enforcement procedures. Local 688 and the community stewards mobilized broad opposition to the city's proposal, gaining support from other unions, the NAACP, and the Metropolitan Church Federation. Spotlighting the class and racial implications embodied in the dispute, United Auto Workers Regional Director Russell Letner asserted that "the health of any person living in a slum area is as important as the health of any person fortunate enough to live in the most exclusive area." Letner also angrily rebuked the city's health commissioner for suggesting that unions had no business injecting themselves into the issue, which he described as one in which "community welfare" was at stake.²⁸

In March 1957, the St. Louis board of aldermen rejected the city's effort to weaken the rat control ordinance, unanimously approving a new arrangement ensuring that regular inspections would continue. Local 688 leaders proclaimed that the union had achieved a "clear cut victory on the rat control fight with the cooperation of the entire labor movement." Beyond rallying union support, the rat control controversy brought Local 688 and the community stewards enhanced prestige in St. Louis's African American community, as evidenced by supportive coverage in the black press. In a report to the community stewards, Local 688 leaders explained the broader implications of the union's work on rat control: "Although city officials termed rat control in the slums 'impracticable,' our union believed that human rights and the basic protection of government belonged to ALL people, regardless of their economic position in the community." The rat control campaign accomplished several vital objectives for the community stewards program. It educated participants about urban power relations and mobilized popular opinion around an issue of public health that enabled Local 688 to emerge as a staunch defender of the community's safety and well-being.²⁹

Another major initiative championed by the community stewards, creating new opportunities for higher education in St. Louis, illustrated their expansive view of appropriate subjects for the community bargaining table. Reflecting the social aspirations of a more confident and ambitious working class, the community stewards explored the possibility of establishing a free, four-year city college. The initial impetus for this idea came from Earle Brown, the community steward featured in the December 1955 *Life* magazine article on "new kinds of unionists." After a survey of Local 688 members found widespread interest in free higher education, the community stewards moved to mobilize public support. Although the free city college attracted interest from other unions and community groups, the initiative faltered when the city claimed it lacked authority to issue bonds to fund the project. Nonetheless, the campaign to establish free higher education affirmed the potential of establishing a community bargaining table where empowered working-class citizens could negotiate substantive improvements beneficial to the entire community.[30]

* * *

As the community stewards program gathered momentum, Ernest Calloway took his community activism more directly into the civil rights arena when he became president of the St. Louis NAACP in 1956. Although Calloway had earlier avoided the NAACP, he now found reasons for a rapprochement. With the increased entry of African Americans into union ranks during the New Deal and World War II, NAACP leaders regarded newly organized black workers as a fertile source of membership. After the war, the NAACP drew even closer to labor, connected by a shared anti-communism and the threat of a resurgent right-wing that sought to blunt the influence of both the civil rights and union movements. Sensing the organization's potential to collaborate more closely with Local 688 and the opportunity to build a movement powerful enough to dismantle racial barriers, Calloway and his wife Deverne became involved in the NAACP soon after their arrival in St. Louis. The Calloways quickly gained respect for their organizational skills, with Ernest leading the organization's membership drive in 1951 and becoming the chapter's first vice president a year later.[31]

A convergence of circumstances created the context for Calloway's assumption of the NAACP presidency. As he observed, a gradual process of desegregation had begun in St. Louis with the-post World War II integration of local educational institutions and the city's swimming pools. Moreover, the "human arithmetic" of the city was changing due to the continuing migration of African Americans, who by 1956 totaled 18 percent of the city's population. This new sense of political potential made the Congress of Racial Equality (CORE) and some elements of the NAACP eager to press for deeper concessions from the city's power brokers. Calloway lamented, however, what he described as "an in-grown fragmented conservative Negro community that had great difficulty raising its social and political sights" and "wallowed in the small doses of status and 'acceptance' flowing from the Accommodation" with white political and business leaders. For Calloway, this accommodation was symbolized by Jordan Chambers, an African American ward leader who gained prominence as a committeeman and political fixer. Having witnessed the corrosive effects of black political dependency in Chicago, Calloway was eager to capitalize on what he called "the possibilities for indigenous political development" free from manipulation by "outside influences."[32]

During the early 1950s the St. Louis NAACP was headed by Henry Winfield Wheeler, a longtime civil rights and union leader. Although Wheeler's activist credentials were impeccable, a younger group of NAACP members, including Calloway, had reservations regarding his cautious leadership. In October 1953, the branch's executive board sought to remove Wheeler from office over alleged misappropriation of funds, but the NAACP membership overruled the board's recommendation. By 1955, however, Wheeler prepared to run for the Missouri legislature, and the branch presidency became open. The younger, restive faction of the branch approached Calloway to seek the office. Wary of factionalism in the branch, Calloway nonetheless agreed to run. He saw the potential to make the NAACP a "mass organization" that could command sufficient respect to establish a bargaining relationship with St. Louis's white power structure. By expanding the NAACP's working-class membership and offering new opportunities for engaged citizenship, Calloway looked to reinforce the spirit of racial egalitarianism that the community stewards had begun to nurture.[33]

In November 1955, Calloway defeated his opponent, a lawyer named George Draper, in a campaign marred by a "stench of anti-union activities" encouraged by "outside influences [that] attempted to take advantage of Draper's candidacy to get Mr. Calloway." Although the *St. Louis Argus* editorial did not name these "outside influences," Calloway's position as a top official in St. Louis's most aggressive union and his professed desire to wage a "planned relentless campaign against the powerful economic citadels within our community" presumably prompted some white business and political leaders to oppose his election. Calloway's initial pronouncements on assuming office affirmed these trepidations. At his swearing-in ceremony on June 3, 1956, he outlined his plan for "a new offensive on the local civil rights front." Calloway observed that the rapid growth of the African American population in St. Louis meant that blacks now had opportunities to negotiate what he described as a "community partnership" with political and business leaders. However, if blacks in St. Louis were to seize this opportunity, they would need to escape from "the structural and psychological straight-jackets that keep the local NAACP branch from becoming a mass grass-roots organization in the full sense of the word." Although Calloway's fierce pragmatism would later distance him from the dominant spirit of the St. Louis civil rights movement, most of the NAACP membership accepted his analysis and welcomed the prospect that the branch could play a more dynamic social role.[34]

In a second important statement of his intentions, Calloway spelled out his strategy more explicitly. In a June 19, 1956, open letter to the chair of the Democratic Party's Central Committee and the president of the St. Louis Board of Aldermen, he acknowledged the NAACP's official nonpartisan status while noting that African Americans overwhelmingly tended to support Democrats. According to Calloway, African Americans were among "the most articulate segment of our voting population," and he estimated that seven out of every ten blacks voted their class interest in politics. Yet when it came to matters of civil rights, Calloway accused the Democrats of "moral dishonesty" and condemned the "social callousness of the aldermanic game of political pantomime" that led them to mute their support for racial equality. Although the city's top Democrats did not respond directly, the St. Louis Board of Aldermen passed an ordinance to promote fair practices in municipal employment, a sign that they recognized the growing black electoral power Calloway had referred to in his open letter.[35]

As Calloway knew from his trade union experience and the community stewards' efforts, the NAACP needed to demonstrate common purpose and tactical dexterity to persuade St. Louis's economic and political power brokers that it was in their interest to bargain with them. With a membership totaling less than 3 percent of the black community, the NAACP could not convincingly claim to represent community sentiment, and Calloway declared that his first task as president was to make the NAACP a mass organization. Calloway's strategy for accomplishing this task was to reach out to existing organizations such as churches, women's groups, and unions by establishing divisions based on social and occupational groupings. As he explained to a top NAACP official in a February 1956 letter, "The central idea of the technique or experiment is to 'fan-out' into the community on a series of concentrated group campaigns."[36]

Not surprisingly, Calloway focused particular attention on recruiting black trade unionists. Like Local 688's community stewards, he believed that they could apply their shop-floor expertise to help mobilize other workers and create the leverage needed to change racial politics in St. Louis. According to a 1954 St. Louis Urban League study, of the 60,000 African Americans working in the city, 30,000 were union members and constituted approximately 15 percent of all unionists in St. Louis. A general who worked alongside his troops, Calloway convinced 173 of Local 688's African American members to join, and his wife Deverne had similar success in recruiting members of women's social clubs to become NAACP members. By the end of 1956, the branch's membership had doubled, reaching 5,500 people. Although this number fell short of the 20,000 members Calloway believed were necessary to make the St. Louis NAACP a genuine mass organization, he had quickly rejuvenated the branch and expanded its working-class composition. As Margaret Bush Wilson recalled, he "ran the NAACP with a level of competence that I had not seen before. He learned this from the union." Other NAACP colleagues praised his "quiet, unassuming manner and a type of dignity" that marked his leadership, providing the organization with a sense of direction and purpose it had previously lacked.[37]

With these achievements under his belt, Calloway prepared to address what he described as "the foremost social and economic problem of our community, the tremendous income gap between white and Negro workers." His determined quest to secure better employment for African Americans in St. Louis reflected deeply felt personal and social imperatives. As he recounted in a 1965 talk to a group of job trainees, Calloway knew all too well the intense psychological damage that "restricted opportunity and limited expectations" had imposed on the "dreams and hopes and aspirations" of African Americans: "Like running the gauntlet in military fashion," he recalled, "I have gone through the whole Negro fixed employment process—shoe shine boy, paper boy, country club caddie, bus-boy, waiter, garbage collector, cook, ditch-digger, coal miner." Removing the barriers to skilled employment, then, not only meant reducing the 44 percent income disparity between white and black workers in St. Louis but also creating opportunities for African Americans to erode racial stereotypes and develop their "full human potential."[38]

Calloway also emphasized the connection between jobs and effective civic participation, arguing that access to skilled employment enhanced the prospects for African Americans to gain the "dignity and self-respect that makes for good functional citizenship." As a 1958 NAACP leaflet seeking to open skilled grocery employment to blacks declared, "Good Jobs + Equal Pay = Good Citizens," while "Poor Jobs + Small Pay = Slums, Disease, [and] Crime." For Calloway, the fight for skilled employment aimed not only to provide black St. Louisans with the economic security and confidence needed to exercise "functional citizenship," but also represented the key to ridding St. Louis of the racial and class inequities that threatened its future as a viable twentieth-century city. This recognition guided Calloway in formulating what he described as a "comprehensive" strategy to dismantle the foundations of employment apartheid in St. Louis.[39]

Repeating the technique he had employed with Democratic Party leaders, in May 1956 Calloway sent an open letter to "All Business Firms Drawing Trade from the Negro Community." Articulating a brand of civil rights Keynesianism, he argued that narrowing the wage gap between blacks and whites would boost African American purchasing power and reward cooperating employers with increased customer loyalty and higher profits. "Thus," Calloway observed with characteristic pragmatism, "it is just plain economic horse sense for business establishments drawing their trade from the Negro community to encourage and support the NAACP in a very practical way." In an explicit nod to early New Deal social policy, Calloway offered to award cooperating St. Louis businesses a "Freedom Seal" emblazoned with the slogan "Making St. Louis the First City of American Democracy." Although few businesses accepted his offer, Calloway served notice that under his leadership the branch would take a much more aggressive stance in demanding non-discriminatory employment policies.[40]

In the summer of 1956, while Calloway began to develop a "comprehensive ongoing black employment strategy" for the NAACP, he became involved in two significant campaigns to open African American access to jobs previously reserved for whites. The first effort, which tested Calloway's dual identities as labor official and civil rights leader, occurred at Coca Cola, where the NAACP, the Urban League, and Local 688 attempted to fashion a policy to make driver-salesman jobs available to African Americans. This type of labor-management-community tripartism was to become Calloway and Harold Gibbons's preferred methodology in using Teamster power to confront the structural foundations of racial inequality in St. Louis.

Wearing his civil rights hat, Calloway rejected a company proposal to employ black driver-salesmen in selected African American neighborhoods as "tokenism." Reflecting his trade union sensibilities, he resisted management's willingness to elevate blacks by violating seniority agreements. Instead, he insisted that blacks who aspired to become driver-salesmen should first gain expertise in servicing vending machines. As these workers upgraded their skills and accrued seniority, they would eventually be qualified to bid on job openings for driver-salesman routes. Calloway's proposal gained the approval of all parties and accomplished the difficult balancing act of opening skilled jobs to blacks, mollifying white concerns, and ensuring that African American workers would serve a racially integrated clientele.[41]

A more volatile employment dispute that involved both Calloway and Harold Gibbons occurred in August 1956 when the Teamsters, the St. Louis Human Rights Commission, and the NAACP reached an agreement with four white-owned taxicab companies to hire twenty black drivers. Faced with shortages of drivers and idle cabs, these companies indicated their willingness to work with the union and civil rights advocates to negotiate an orderly integration of the industry. On August 18, 1956, however, the day that black drivers were to begin working alongside their white counterparts, over 700 members of Teamsters Local 405, a taxi drivers local under the trusteeship of Harold Gibbons, staged a wildcat strike.

In subsequent testimony before a Senate committee investigating labor corruption, strike leader Donald Cortor charged that Gibbons had violated contractual procedure that allowed taxi companies to choose their drivers. Denouncing Gibbons's use of "high-handed tactics by forcing the firms to hire Negro drivers," Cortor claimed that he and other strikers did not oppose the presence of black cabbies but rather wanted more time to make the transition to an integrated workforce. Yet he also complained that "proportionately they [African Americans] had twice as many jobs in the cab industry [as] in any other particular type of work," suggesting that granting blacks jobs with white-owned cab companies represented an unacceptable incursion into an area of white privilege. Cortor also neglected to mention that black cab drivers had previously been restricted by what the *St. Louis Argus* described as a "gentlemen's agreement" that limited their access to taxi stands near the city's main train station and other lucrative sites.[42]

The *Argus* reported that "hate groups" in the white ethnic neighborhoods of south St. Louis attempted to stir opposition to the integration of the cab companies. At the same time, the wildcat strikers "discovered a more sympathetic metropolitan press and an issue that tended to make a villain of a union leader." Shifting their attention away from a strictly "anti-Negro stance," the strikers attempted to make Gibbons's "dictatorial" rule the fundamental issue and announced the formation of an independent union. To bolster their case, the insurgents portrayed the dispute as yet another example of Gibbons's subversive influence on St. Louis's public life. As strike leader Don Cortor declared, "Harold Gibbons has become too powerful and is a threat to the economy of the community." Cortor's charge gained some traction, especially among the city's white media establishment, when Gibbons and other union leaders sent "official Teamsters cars on[to] the street." Manned by some notorious local thugs and others with lengthy criminal records, the "official cars" kept the cabs operating but not without some incidents of violence directed against the wildcat strikers. In turn, the wildcatters received "complete police cooperation" from a department with a long history of picket line and strike-related clashes with Harold Gibbons dating back to his CIO days.[43]

Gibbons and Calloway held firm against the strike, with Gibbons asserting "we are not going to back up one inch on the policy of hiring Negro drivers." The union won praise from liberal church and civil rights organizations, along with strong editorial support from the *St. Louis Argus*. Faced with the union's determined refusal to retreat and condemnation from the religious and civil rights communities, the wildcat strikers ended their twelve-day walkout on August 30, 1956. Noting that it had not always agreed with Harold Gibbons, the *Argus* observed in an August 31, 1956, editorial that "through the years the [Teamsters] have exhibited a fairness in jobs policy in theory and practices. This philosophy," the editorial concluded, "has not jelled well with many of the powers that be in the community."[44]

The taxi strike held important implications for each of its principal actors. For Ernest Calloway, the successful integration of St. Louis's taxi industry, along with his earlier success at Coca Cola, boosted his credibility among African Americans. Harold Gibbons affirmed his willingness to challenge the St. Louis political establishment's gradualist approach to civil rights and reinforced the Teamsters' reputation as an outspoken advocate for racial justice. Prominent liberals, especially in the faith community, hailed the agreement as further evidence that St. Louis's "orderly progress toward fair employment for all citizens" held promise as a viable strategy.[45]

Yet Gibbons and Calloway's success in breaking the color line in St. Louis's taxi industry was not an unfettered triumph. Gibbons's tough stance with the strikers not only prompted the denunciation of St. Louis's top decision-makers but also fueled a growing backlash from Teamster units outside of Local 688 that feared the consolidation of his authority. The city's white-owned newspapers repeatedly questioned Gibbons's tactics. Because the first taxi company to admit black cabbies was owned by a mob-connected figure, the press wondered about the purity of Gibbons's motives, and the head of the St. Louis Crime Commission abjured the importation of the "jungle tactics of the New York waterfront." Also, strike leader Don Cortor's accusation that Gibbons was exercising unrestrained power over the "economy of the community" would soon be repeated by national political leaders increasingly concerned that St. Louis's example might be replicated elsewhere.[46]

However, a year after the taxicab strike, a much higher stakes contest awaited Gibbons, Calloway, Local 688, and the NAACP. Throughout 1957, the community stewards and the NAACP led the opposition to proposed changes in St. Louis's city charter. This epic confrontation rocked the city's political and economic establishment and attracted national attention as a demonstration of how Teamster power could stymie the ambitious modernization plans of urban elites. It also marked a distinct triumph for the working-class citizenship and interracial cooperation championed by Gibbons and Calloway and opened new possibilities to establish the community bargaining table as an accepted element in St. Louis politics.

CHAPTER 8

"A Hell of a Whipping"

The August 7, 1957, front page of the *St. Louis Post-Dispatch* featured a jubilant Harold Gibbons and other members of Local 688 celebrating the defeat of proposed changes in the city charter favored by St. Louis's major power brokers. Working closely with Ernest Calloway and the NAACP, Gibbons and the Teamsters had been instrumental in mobilizing opposition to charter revisions that would have diluted the union movement's political power and circumscribed the St. Louis civil rights movement's growing influence. Speaking on behalf of the anti-charter change coalition that Local 688 had helped assemble, the Teamster leader declared that "any future attempt to create a new city charter must be based upon a free exchange of ideas between big business and all the other groups in the city." In response, Mayor Raymond Tucker complained that the defeat of the charter raised the question of "whether the citizens of St. Louis or the Teamsters would run the city." The defeat of the charter reform initiative captured national attention, with a *Business Week* article declaring that St. Louis business leaders would have to deal with the "Problem of Gibbons" and suggesting they seek a "civil rapprochement" with labor regarding their economic development agenda. Local observers noted that the community stewards' successful leadership of the anti-charter fight had embarrassed not only the city's business and civic establishment but also threatened to challenge the political hegemony of St. Louis's powerful ward leaders. However, just as Gibbons and Calloway prepared to capitalize on this decisive triumph, their ambitious plans were thwarted by aggressive investigations of alleged union corruption in which the Teamsters became a primary target, and Local 688 faced sharp public scrutiny.[1]

* * *

Ostensibly a conflict over restructuring political governance, the 1957 charter revision fight ultimately became an epic debate over which social groups would shape post–World War II St. Louis's policies regarding urban revitalization. The debate stemmed from the activities of Civic Progress, a group of St. Louis's top business and community leaders who promoted an ambitious agenda aimed at attracting new investment, reviving the city's lagging economy, and averting accelerating urban decline. Created by his predecessor in 1952, Mayor Raymond Tucker enthusiastically embraced the new organization as a "civic conscience" and "benign father" that would function as an unselfish promoter of the public good. Equally important for Tucker, Civic Progress would offset the power of ward politicians and unions that existed for "the sole purpose of representing one particular segment of our community."[2]

The 1957 battle over charter change was preceded by clashes over two of Civic Progress's initial efforts to secure funding for civic improvements aimed at reducing urban blight and revitalizing St. Louis's downtown. Reflecting the education in socialist economics that they had received at Wisconsin and Brookwood, Gibbons and Calloway vehemently opposed Civic Progress's promotion of an earnings tax that targeted the gross income of wage earners but taxed the self-employed and corporations on net rather than gross income. As a keen analyst of St. Louis's political economy, Ernest Calloway became a leading spokesperson in rallying opposition to the earnings tax. Speaking in a September 1954 television address, he denounced the proposed tax as "class legislation" and accused proponents of political blackmail, charging that "we are given the choice of the earnings tax or a doomed ghost town." Instead, Calloway called for an equitable tax system based on ability to pay and advocated greater coordination between the city and the county to address the structural deficits (an antiquated tax system, duplication of services, ruinous competition between the city and the county) that he argued were the true sources of St. Louis's social and economic woes.[3]

The union also opposed the first of several bond issues favored by Civic Progress that aimed to clear slums and build new housing. Harold Gibbons charged that supporters had not fully identified the projects on which bond revenues would be spent. In language that reflected his determination to ensure working-class input into critical political and economic decisions, he proclaimed, "We have a right as citizens to know." Although the public approved the bond measure in 1953, Raymond Tucker acknowledged the growing power of Local 688 and the community stewards by seeking union support for Civic Progress's most ambitious initiative, a $100 million bond issue to fund slum clearance, highway construction, and riverfront development. After Tucker addressed a June 1955 community stewards meeting, Local 688 supported passage of the bond while simultaneously advocating structural reforms to address the city-county fragmentation it deemed most responsible for St. Louis's declining fortunes.[4]

However, following the bond issue's passage, Gibbons and Calloway began to have buyer's remorse over the lack of resources being directed to the city's neediest neighborhoods. In a direct slap at Civic Progress, community stewards' program director Sidney Zagri claimed in an August 1957 article that "our Civic Conscience should not be hemmed in by the prejudices of race or class." Disturbed that the redevelopment agenda of St. Louis's business and civic elites was reinforcing class and racial inequities, Gibbons and Calloway were more than ready to counterattack in 1957, when Raymond Tucker and Civic Progress proposed changes in the city charter aimed at curbing opposition to their plans for St. Louis's economic and political modernization.[5]

In the view of Tucker and Civic Progress, the most serious obstacle to their redevelopment agenda stemmed from the power of local ward leaders to stymie development plans through their use of zoning laws and "aldermanic courtesy." The latter practice gave city aldermen virtual carte blanche to veto development projects in their wards. They also resented roadblocks posed by Local 688's growing political capacity and its insistence on closely scrutinizing development proposals, along with increasing agitation by the African American community for a greater social voice. To dilute the power of aldermen and ward leaders and assure private investors that redevelopment projects would not be delayed by political obstruction, Tucker, Civic Progress leaders, and their supporters proposed to reduce the size of the Board of Aldermen by half while increasing the number of aldermen elected on an at-large basis. The mayor's office would also gain enhanced executive authority under the new charter. The clear intention of these changes was, as Tucker explained, to break the power of aldermen "under the tight control of selfish political interests and the officers of the Teamsters Union who seek control of city government without running for election." Clearly smarting from his earlier confrontations with Local 688 and the community stewards, Tucker portrayed the Teamsters as a special interest out for their own aggrandizement at the expense of civic betterment and the public good.[6]

With Gibbons and Calloway leading the charge, the Teamsters and the NAACP bitterly denounced the proposed charter revisions as a blatant attempt by St. Louis's power elite to reassert the prerogatives of both class and racial hegemony. Reflecting his preoccupation with the clandestine operation of corporate and political power, Calloway characterized the proposed charter changes as a "well-planned conspiracy" that was "not so much a new constitution for the city as it was a 'treaty of surrender' to the Chase banking interests of New York who were demanding this as a condition in making extensive investments in the St. Louis area." Although Calloway's description of a conspiracy may have been hyperbolic, he raised a legitimate concern: that the new charter's proposed political restructuring had been drafted in private by a "small group of hired specialists" at the behest of corporate interests. Calloway also feared that creating more at-large positions and increasing the size of wards would "contain the growing political influence of the Negro community by carving out a new political ghetto for the increasing Negro population." For Calloway, who had been prodding St. Louis's Democratic Party leaders to reward African American electoral support, the charter's attempt to create a legislative iron curtain circumscribing black political influence represented an insulting rebuff.[7]

With the community stewards playing an important role, Local 688 mobilized broad opposition to the changes proposed by the city's business, civic, and media elites. By creating more at-large seats, opponents argued, charter change would result in greater business domination of city politics by making candidates more reliant on corporate resources to run successfully citywide. Both the Teamsters and the NAACP regarded the charter's language on racial discrimination as unresponsive to rising African American demands for equal access to municipal employment. They gained support from other unions, some city aldermen, and small business owners who concluded that corporate interests would benefit at their expense. Anticipating higher taxes and fearing that the charter's support for slum clearance would prompt more African American settlement in their neighborhoods, many working-class whites also embraced the anti-charter campaign.[8]

Although this coalition was not ideologically cohesive, some of its members—the Teamsters, other unions, the NAACP—shared the view that the new charter threatened to rewrite the social contract in St. Louis on terms that would reduce their growing influence and grant the city's power elite a free hand to make critical economic and social decisions. For Gibbons and Calloway, the anti-charter campaign assumed an even deeper meaning. Throughout their careers they had sought to help low-wage, marginalized workers overcome their powerlessness and gain a place as equals on the shop floor and at the community bargaining table. In this context they saw the charter as a distinct threat to the working-class citizenship and political independence Local 688's community stewards had cultivated and that African Americans in St. Louis were beginning to assert under the aegis of the NAACP and Calloway's leadership.

Advised by the respected Fleishman-Hillard public relations firm, Civic Progress, Mayor Tucker, and most of St. Louis's major church and community organizations touted the civic and social benefits to be gained from charter reform. The local press took a harsher tone, directly attacking Local 688 and the NAACP in an effort to discredit the opposition. Claiming that the Teamsters and the NAACP feared creation of a new political system they could no longer dominate, the *St. Louis Globe-Democrat* charged in a June 24, 1957, article that "the NAACP was asked, and to their shame, acceded, to be a stalking horse for the Teamsters Union in their mad grab for power in St. Louis." The paper also drew on powerful racial and anti-Communist imagery. Spotlighting Ernest Calloway's Teamsters' connection and implying that he was being manipulated by white handlers, the *Globe-Democrat* observed, "The president of the group [NAACP] is a paid employee of the Teamsters Union. He was flanked by two other officers of the Teamsters Union, neither of them colored." Moreover, while "the best thinking colored people support the charter," the NAACP stood "side by side with the Communist Party" in its opposition.[9]

A less vitriolic but equally heartfelt criticism came from charter advocates who blamed the Teamsters for undermining the spirit of civic unity and non-partisan cooperation that they believed would be created by the new charter's structural political reforms. In a July 1957 debate with Sidney Zagri, Ada Sommer, a former League of Women Voters president and member of the freeholder board that had drafted the new charter, accused Local 688 of attempting to "foment class distinctions" and "pit one group against another on [an] economic, social, and geographical basis." Other critics cited corruption charges swirling around the Teamsters and the union's numerous brushes with the law during strikes in St. Louis. Depicting the Teamsters as a manipulator of the African American community, a power-hungry institution bent on dominating St. Louis politics, and an instigator of class warfare, charter proponents sought to undermine the goodwill Gibbons, Calloway, and Local 688 had earned through the activities of the community stewards.[10]

Although most of the *Globe-Democrat*'s charges amounted to red-baiting and racial fear mongering, the newspaper accurately identified a split among African Americans. Some leaders, especially middle-class professionals who valued their role as intermediaries between the black community and the city's white establishment, believed that supporting the new charter would enhance their influence with St. Louis's power brokers, with whom they felt a greater affinity than racially insensitive ward politicians and the working-class constituency represented by the Teamsters. Indeed, a cartoon in a St. Louis black newspaper portrayed African American committeeman Jordan Chambers and Local 688 community relations director Sidney Zagri as puppeteers pulling strings on Calloway and several other NAACP leaders who wore sheets labeled "NAACP Respectability." One of the cartoon's captions, "Be Sure Your Sheets *Don't* Slip," underscored the fears of St. Louis's black elite that charter opponents threatened to undermine the gradual progress achieved by the civil rights movement and violate the organization's commitment to non-partisanship. The NAACP's Youth Council also rebuked Calloway after it became known that he had printed literature asserting the branch's opposition to the charter before the membership took an official vote. Although the branch voted overwhelmingly to support Calloway's recommendation to oppose the charter, the clash with the Youth Council illustrated the volatility of the NAACP's internal politics and foreshadowed divisions between Calloway and a younger generation of civil rights activists that subsequently became more pronounced.[11]

Local 688 worked in conjunction with the NAACP, other unions, neighborhood associations, and small businesses in opposing charter change. One potent line of attack declared that the new charter would mean "Taxes, Taxes, Taxes, and More Taxes," a charge clearly aimed at convincing white workers and small business owners that expanded executive authority would allow the "heavy hand of the tax collector" to threaten their security and status. Contrasting elite interest in structural political change with the working-class desire for economic security and an equitable distribution of social resources, the Citizens Committee

Against the Charter asserted that the proposed revision "places more emphasis on balancing the ledger books than on taking care of human needs." The NAACP supplemented these potent class appeals with fervent pleas to uphold racial solidarity and embrace the spirit of the emerging civil rights movement. While "They Walked for Freedom in Montgomery," one NAACP leaflet asserted, "We Will Vote for Freedom in St. Louis." Along with the NAACP, Local 688 and the community stewards helped mobilize other St. Louis unions and worked tirelessly at the ward and precinct level to disseminate the anti-charter message.[12]

On August 6, 1957, the charter was defeated by a 3 to 2 margin that reflected sharp class and racial cleavages. Voters in only five of the city's twenty-eight wards, all encompassing middle or upper income sections of St. Louis, supported the measure. The city's African Americans followed the NAACP's lead in rejecting charter change by a 5 to 1 margin. To be sure, the white working-class vote that opposed charter change was partially animated by anti-tax sentiment, racial fear, and continuing loyalty to the ward system, in contrast to Local 688's concerns that the proposed changes would have seriously compromised the union's attempt to establish the community bargaining table and advance interracial politics. Largely ignored by Gibbons and Calloway in the heady days following the charter defeat, white working-class concerns over race and taxes reflected social divisions that emerged a decade later to challenge their conception of working-class citizenship. Still, many observers recognized the pivotal role the community stewards had played in mobilizing the anti-charter forces and upsetting the plans of St. Louis's power elite.[13]

In the aftermath of the charter vote, local journalists and political analysts concluded that the community stewards had embarrassed ward officials with their superior mobilization capabilities. Herbert Trask of the *Post-Dispatch* proclaimed that Local 688's success represented a striking development in St. Louis politics, observing that "this combination of forces creates a new power in St. Louis which must be reckoned with." Having witnessed the close Teamsters-NAACP cooperation during the charter fight, Washington University political scientist Robert Salisbury noted that the "militant and volatile character of the Teamsters and the increasing numbers and self-consciousness of blacks make possible" a political realignment in St. Louis. Elaborating on this theme, *Globe-Democrat* reporter John Hahn predicted that the union "could become the strongest pressure group in the city because they may well move into the position to deliver more votes on any given election day than anyone else."[14]

At the same time, an editorial in the *East St. Louis Journal* posed a question doubtless on the minds of many: "Is it [the community stewards program] a sincere effort to bring the average citizen into awareness of his government and his rights and powers to participate in that government for the sake of the citizen? Or is it a bid by Labor leaders to become political bosses?" Civic Progress leaders clearly believed the latter, lamenting that St. Louis aldermen were "only hearing from the Teamsters and not the business community" and bemoaning the "disintegration of the political parties" that was leaving a vacuum for the Teamsters and the NAACP to fill. According to public relations guru Alfred Fleishman, Civic Progress needed to create a social alternative "led by people who are not working for a labor-political organization but for the benefit of their own neighborhoods" if it were to develop a stronger base for political reform and urban redevelopment.[15]

Civic Progress's fears were not unjustified. Following the charter change victory, the community stewards prepared to capitalize by seeking new opportunities for the exercise of working-class citizenship. Pronouncing that the union now had "new status at the community bargaining table," Sidney Zagri boasted that the "community steward supplanted the role of the precinct captain" during the charter fight, creating a new locus of power that the business community needed to recognize. Along with Harold Gibbons, Zagri called on business to enter into a new social contract with labor in St. Louis. "How much more effective would the Business Community be in attracting new businesses into our dying downtown area," Zagri asked, "if the old bugaboo of high labor costs could be dispelled through a joint labor-management approach to the recruitment of industry?"[16]

In the months immediately following the charter fight, Local 688 flexed its enhanced political muscle on a variety of fronts. Gibbons demanded public hearings on city redevelopment plans to ensure that taxpayer dollars used to subsidize slum clearance would deliver genuine community benefits. Angered that the newly created sewer district had not consulted citizens before instituting fee hikes, the community stewards insisted that more "democratic procedures" be used in subsequent decision-making. Gibbons also continued to criticize St. Louis's "unjust" earnings tax, denouncing a Civic Progress–sponsored effort to increase the levy as a "new tax grab" that failed to make ability to pay a core principle of St. Louis's tax policy.[17]

Seizing on the momentum of the anti-charter fight, community stewards began to expand their efforts in the suburbs of St. Louis County, which they discovered "crawled with grievances." Their investigations found that many developers had included waivers in their contracts with homeowners that made them liable for street maintenance and found persistent sewer problems in the new subdivisions. "People are hopping mad at the real estate developers who give people out here a real trimming," one community steward concluded. Within the city of St. Louis, the community stewards began a promising effort to mobilize city residents to seek abatement of pollution from soap and chemical factories that emitted noxious fumes and were affecting public health. And, by the spring of 1958, union leaders announced plans to create a "community assembly" that would enable community stewards to adopt a citywide approach in dealing with quality of life issues. Over 200 people attended the assembly's inaugural meeting, which aimed to establish neighborhood organizations whose activities would be coordinated by the community stewards. All of these efforts—addressing the concerns of mostly white suburban homeowners, seeking to hold polluters responsible for community health, pressing for equitable taxation, and creating a citywide structure to coordinate working-class activism—sought to create new arenas for the exercise of working-class citizenship and expand the scope of negotiation at the community bargaining table.[18]

Following the charter campaign, Ernest Calloway joined Harold Gibbons and the community stewards in savoring their decisive victory. He especially relished meeting with Edwin Clark, the president of Southwestern Bell Telephone and a prominent Civic Progress leader, who subsequently confessed to him, "Mr. Calloway, there is one thing I would like to say now. You colored people gave us business leaders a hell of a whipping in that charter fight last August." Emboldened by this new sense of power and possibility, Calloway prepared to launch his planned assault on employment discrimination in St. Louis. Several weeks after the charter's defeat, he announced the formation of the NAACP's Job Opportunities Council (JOC), tapping Margaret Bush Wilson and Brotherhood of Sleeping Car Porters leader Theodore "Ted" McNeal, a longtime St. Louis civil rights leader and anti-discrimination activist, to join him in leading this new initiative.[19]

Although Calloway and the JOC had discussed taking on job discrimination in government contracts, manufacturing firms, and building trades' apprenticeship programs, they initially focused on softer targets: the local outlets of national grocery and retail chains. These businesses were highly visible in the black community and while they employed African Americans, they invariably consigned them to unskilled, low-paying positions. A & P was an especially egregious offender, employing only four of its full-time African American workers at jobs above the porter level. To create sufficient leverage to bring chain store management to the community bargaining table, Calloway launched "Freedom Lines" at A & P stores. The picketers distributed "customer concern" cards that read, "We want more than token employment of Negroes in your business. Signed 'a regular customer.'" In January 1958, after A & P received over 5,000 customer concern cards, it agreed to hire African Americans at jobs above the porter level and convinced the meat cutters union to take on its first black apprentice. Coming on the heels of the charter defeat, the NAACP's victory at A & P underscored the value of community mobilization, economic pressure, and the focused direct action that Calloway saw as essential to creating an atmosphere for negotiation.[20]

With the A & P agreement setting the standard, the JOC negotiated similar arrangements with local affiliates of National Tea and Kroger. According to Margaret Bush Wilson, Ted McNeal, Calloway, and she were a "pretty sophisticated and attractive team," and the "combination of the timing, the posture of the organizational structures behind each of us, and our demeanor" impressed employer representatives and convinced them to make concessions. Calloway continued to invoke civil rights Keynesianism in pressing employers to open better paying jobs to African Americans, arguing that Southwestern Bell Telephone, whose few black workers mostly held custodial positions, had "reduced purchasing power" for black consumers, thereby robbing the community of the economic stimulus provided by decent wages. During the summer of 1958, however, the JOC's promising efforts met more sophisticated resistance from Famous-Barr, St. Louis's flagship department store and Local 688's old nemesis.[21]

The St. Louis chapter of CORE had sought to open sales and clerical jobs at Famous-Barr to blacks, and with NAACP support, announced a mass demonstration to press its demands. In what Calloway later described as a "master stroke," Famous-Barr management instead offered to provide integrated seating at its tea rooms. This gesture appealed to black middle-class professionals who responded favorably to Famous-Barr's implicit acknowledgement of their social status and accused CORE and the NAACP of not consulting with the community before undertaking direct action. Faced with this split among black leaders and uncertain about their ability to sustain picket lines, CORE and NAACP leaders called off the demonstration. In a face-saving move, they settled for a deal that allowed black women elevator operators being replaced by automated technology to be hired for sales jobs.[22]

Although Calloway publicly endorsed the deal as a significant advance, he resented that middle-class black professionals had subverted the JOC's successful formula for toppling bastions of segregation. The setback at Famous-Barr contributed partially to his decision in the fall of 1958 not to seek re-election as NAACP president. Margaret Bush Wilson, who at Calloway's urging succeeded him as the branch's leader, recalled that a "decided faction in the local branch did not want Calloway to continue to do a leadership role." Wilson speculated that his opponents were uncomfortable with Calloway's "trade union connection," while Calloway cited pressure from unnamed sources over his prominent role in the charter fight. Clearly, Calloway's aggressive forays into politics and his attempts to turn the NAACP into a mass organization had alienated elements of the black middle class who valued their relationships with St. Louis's white power brokers and favored a more cautious approach to civil rights advancement. As a result, his efforts to create a civil rights community bargaining table faltered, and he looked to other arenas where he could guide the black community's political strategy.[23]

* * *

The afterglow of the charter change victory also proved short-lived for Harold Gibbons, who had closely aligned himself with Jimmy Hoffa and openly supported his benefactor's ambition to supplant Dave Beck as Teamsters president. Gibbons began to help Hoffa burnish his public image by coordinating a gala 1956 testimonial dinner in Detroit. Over 2,800 political and labor luminaries gathered to honor Hoffa, with the proceeds going to fund a children's home in Israel. The effort gained additional publicity when Hoffa, Gibbons, and an entourage of labor and business leaders journeyed to Israel to lay the cornerstone for the children's home and dramatize their solidarity with the Jewish state.[24]

Hoffa's ambitions were boosted when Dave Beck, who had succeeded longtime IBT president Daniel Tobin in 1952, suffered a rapid fall from grace amid growing public concern about union connections to organized crime and racketeering. In 1956, Robert Kennedy, chief counsel for the Senate Permanent Subcommittee on Investigations and brother of John F. Kennedy, the ambitious junior senator from Massachusetts, learned from informants that Beck had been involved in misusing union funds. Based on Kennedy's findings, in January 1957, the Senate created a Select Committee to investigate these charges. Chaired by John McClellan, a conservative Arkansas Democrat and longtime union foe, the proceedings became popularly known as the "McClellan Committee" and in some quarters as the "Senate Rackets Committee."[25]

Dave Beck appeared before the newly formed committee in March 1957. In an anxious and inept performance, he repeatedly invoked the Fifth Amendment, a strategy that backfired badly. Subsequently, the AFL-CIO expelled Beck from its executive council, citing federation policy barring its members from taking the Fifth Amendment before official inquiries. A few months later, with federal tax evasion charges looming, Beck announced his intention not to seek re-election as Teamsters president. Several observers attributed this decision to neither the indictment nor the McClellan Committee's revelations but rather to Jimmy Hoffa's studied refusal to defend the embattled Teamsters' president.[26]

Hoffa had some significant obstacles to overcome, however, in his ascension to the Teamsters presidency. His celebrated feud with Robert Kennedy began in March 1957 following his indictment on federal charges of attempting to bribe a McClellan Committee investigator. In a strong public show of support, Harold Gibbons appeared beside Hoffa during his arrest, underscoring his loyalty in the face of Kennedy and McClellan's growing determination to prevent the Detroit Teamster from succeeding Dave Beck. To Kennedy's considerable embarrassment, a jury acquitted Hoffa of the bribery charges. Undeterred, Kennedy and McClellan subpoenaed Hoffa to testify before the committee, and in August 1957, he made the first of thirteen separate appearances.

Hoffa did not repeat Beck's mistake of invoking the Fifth Amendment. However, he faced withering criticism over multiple allegations of wrongdoing. These allegations included both soliciting loans from and making loans to employers, steering insurance and pension management contracts to mob-connected figures, negotiating sweetheart deals with employers, and allowing men with criminal records and mob connections to serve as union officers and staff. Hoffa's unapologetic associations with notorious mob figures drew particular attention. He affirmed his support for Joey Glimco, a prominent Chicago mobster and head of a Teamsters taxi drivers' local who demonstrated callous disregard for his members and used his position to shake down employers. Hoffa's connections to another Chicago gangster and union leader, Paul "Red" Dorfman, whose son Allen managed the union's Central States Pension Fund, raised questions about mob elements gaining access to resources specifically designated for members' security and well-being. One of Hoffa's most disturbing relationships involved his alliance with New York hoodlum John Dioguardia, popularly known as "Johnny Dio." Dioguardia, who was suspected of arranging a 1956 acid attack that blinded labor journalist Victor Riesel, had used strong-arm tactics to help Hoffa solidify his political support among Teamsters locals in New York. Committee investigators also spotlighted how Hoffa had personally profited from his collusion with employers and the mob, asserting that he had betrayed the trust of rank-and-file Teamsters through these blatant and self-aggrandizing conflicts of interest.[27]

Shrugging off the committee's allegations, political and media criticism, opposition within the Teamsters, and threats of expulsion from the AFL-CIO, Hoffa handily won election as Teamsters president in September 1957, aided by Gibbons's deft management of his campaign. Nonetheless, he was unable to assume office after dissidents filed charges alleging election irregularities. To settle these charges, Hoffa reluctantly accepted a consent decree that allowed him to become Teamsters' president but also established a board of monitors to oversee his governance of the union. One immediate consequence of Hoffa's victory was the AFL-CIO's December 1957 decision to carry out its threat and expel the Teamsters. Although this eviction from the house of labor had little impact on the Teamsters' membership growth or bargaining power, it left the union politically isolated and sharply curtailed Gibbons and Calloway's ability to work with other labor liberals at the national level.[28]

Seeking greater professionalism in the union's operations and demonstrating sensitivity to the importance of public relations, Jimmy Hoffa tapped Harold Gibbons to serve as his executive assistant. The news media, which tended to portray most Teamster leaders as thugs or unimaginative unionists with limited social vision, struggled to make sense of Gibbons, an "intellectual Teamster" who had attended classes at Wisconsin, lectured at Harvard, and directed pioneering social programs in St. Louis. The titles of their articles—"Meet Hoffa's Gem Smooth Crown Prince," "Prince Hal at the Tavern," and "A Profile of Harold Gibbons: Hoffa's Left Hand"—reflected their fascination with the newly appointed top aide of the United States' most notorious labor leader. Several commentators followed a *Toledo Blade* writer's lead in describing Gibbons as "The Teamsters No. 1 Egghead," reveling in the apparent contrast between Gibbons's "brains" and Hoffa's "muscle."[29]

Journalist John Bartlow Martin grasped the exaggerated distinction behind this glib characterization. "To say this," he asserted, "is to underestimate both Hoffa's 'brains' and Gibbons' 'muscle.'" Others, especially in liberal publications such as *New Republic* and *The Nation*, speculated about the former CIO leader's ability to enlarge the political perspective of the new Teamsters president and move the union toward greater social involvement. In an October 7, 1957, column, however, veteran labor journalist Murray Kempton scornfully dismissed this notion: "To discuss Hal Gibbons' influence on Jimmy Hoffa," Kempton sneered, "is to discuss the influence of a dog on its master."[30] These conflicting views regarding Gibbons's potential impact on Hoffa and the Teamsters underscored the intense emotions the former socialist and CIO leader aroused among both his ardent detractors and cautious defenders.

Recognizing that the McClellan Committee's investigation had seriously damaged the union's public image, Harold Gibbons turned to Ernest Calloway for advice on mounting a counteroffensive. In a November 21, 1957, memo, Calloway offered a series of recommendations, acknowledging the presence of corruption within the union and signaling his distaste for its prevalence. Urging Gibbons to act with "boldness" and "imagination," Calloway proposed adoption of a "voluntary code" to govern the salaries of union officers and staff and the establishment of a blue ribbon national advisory commission on "ethical and democratic practices that would have the authority to consider internal methods, practices, and operations of the Teamster Union . . . and make corrective recommendations." Perhaps inspired by the United Auto Workers' creation of a similar oversight body and his own use of prominent outside allies during the red caps' early organizing, Calloway asserted that an ethical practices commission could be quite influential "in restoring public confidence" in the union.[31]

At the same time, Calloway described his idea as an "off-balance proposal" that would require "a certain amount of boldness to carry . . . out." Calloway's description recognized that Teamsters' leaders tended to regard outsiders suspiciously, viewing their intrusion as a threat to the primal sense of loyalty and solidarity that had enabled the union to keep its enemies at bay. Although Gibbons did move to implement Calloway's ideas regarding political action and public relations, he disregarded his colleague's recommendations to confront corruption directly. Instead, Gibbons's loyalty to Jimmy Hoffa and his rise to power within the Teamsters required what historian David Witwer has described as a "passive accommodation to corruption" that accepted the presence of mob elements within the union while attempting to circumscribe their influence.[32]

McClellan Committee investigators had already begun to scrutinize Gibbons's St. Louis operations in the spring of 1957. They intensified their probe following a hotly contested election that resulted in his assuming the presidency of Teamsters Joint Council 13, a regional body of Teamsters' locals totaling nearly 40,000 members. The controversy had its roots in Gibbons's hostile takeover of Joint Council 13 in 1953, when the international union had placed it under trusteeship. Gibbons waged what one observer described as a "ruthless campaign" to oust mob-connected locals and install new leadership in other dysfunctional Teamster units. However, his aggressiveness alienated the leaders of some prominent locals who resented their loss of autonomy. And as one observer noted, some old-line

Teamsters saw him as "that CIO Communist punk" whose commitment to racial justice and attachment to left-wing politics represented a form of unionism they abhorred. Indeed, in Local 682, the construction drivers' unit that became one of Gibbons's leading antagonists, he had been questioned about his "communistic leanings" shortly after the international union placed the local under trusteeship.[33]

Following Jimmy Hoffa's disputed election as Teamsters' president, the union's increasing use of trusteeships rankled local Teamsters across the country and came under scrutiny from Congressional investigators. This criticism prompted Gibbons and Hoffa to remove Joint Council 13's long-standing trusteeship and have the St. Louis Teamster seek election as president. A rival slate led by Elmer "Gene" Walla, head of construction drivers' Local 682, emerged to contest Gibbons's bid for the presidency. Walla's candidacy reflected opposition to the international union's relentless usurpation of local autonomy and a rejection of the aggressive militancy, social vision, and political ambition that were trademarks of Gibbons's leadership. Walla and his allies contended that "Gibbons has too many titles and cannot give full attention to all his duties," criticized a "lack of democratic action within the Teamster organization," and called for the joint council to be "directed by local officers." Further distinguishing himself from Gibbons, Walla called for "better relations between the union and employers, harmony between the political parties, improvement in relationship with the city administrator, and restoration of respect for the union by the public." Coming in the wake of the community stewards' growing ambitions and Gibbons's new national role, Walla's candidacy endangered Gibbons's personal ambitions and also threatened to inspire additional revolts against the still uncertain authority of the new Teamsters' president and his top lieutenant.[34]

The procedure surrounding the Joint Council 13 election quickly became mired in controversy and garnered extensive media coverage. Forsaking democratic procedures, Gibbons erected numerous roadblocks to deter his opponents. Apparently concerned that the balloting would be close, he announced his intention to allow delegates from a small carnival workers' local to vote even though their union had been in trusteeship and had not paid the per capita taxes required for eligibility. After Walla and his slate objected, Gibbons declared he would set aside the carnival workers' ballots and count them only if they proved determinative.[35]

Gibbons then delayed the election by several weeks while Harry Karsh, a business agent accused by the McClellan Committee of using strong-arm tactics to organize workers, recruited carnival workers from across the south to come to St. Louis to cast their ballots. Meanwhile, anti-union consultant Fred Bender, after conferring with a member of the opposition slate, disclosed to the *St. Louis Post-Dispatch* his use of Karsh as an informant during the grand jury investigation of Gibbons in 1953–1954. This disclosure represented a clear attempt to embarrass Gibbons on the eve of the election. When the election finally occurred on January 15, 1958, Gibbons initially lost by two votes but ultimately prevailed with a five-vote victory after he allowed the disputed ballots of the carnival workers to be counted. This action prompted the opposition slate to charge fraud, and the local press blasted Gibbons for his electoral tactics. Shortly after the vote, the McClellan Committee decided to review the conduct of the election and announced its intention to hold hearings on Gibbons's administration of Joint Council 13 following their probe.[36]

Throughout its investigatory work in St. Louis, the McClellan Committee had full cooperation from parties still smarting from their unsuccessful effort to prosecute Gibbons several years earlier. Eager for another opportunity to take Gibbons down, his local opponents welcomed renewed scrutiny of their archenemy. In a March 1957 letter, James W. Connor, operating director of the St. Louis Crime Commission, warned committee chair John McClellan that Gibbons's "calculated arrogance" and his skills as a "resourceful, dirty in-fighter" put him "on the road to becoming the committee's greatest antagonist." To blunt this anticipated counterattack, Connor offered the full support of local officials, including IRS agents, an empathetic federal judge, newspapers that were "anxious to topple Gibbons," a police intelligence unit, and the crime commission. Committee investigators took advantage of Connor's offer, supplementing local assistance with their own exhaustive probe into Gibbons's activities in Local 688, Joint Council 13, and his association with Jimmy Hoffa.[37]

In formulating their strategy for Gibbons's September 1958 appearance before the committee, John McClellan and Robert Kennedy knew that they could not accuse him of betrayals of membership trust such as pursuing collusive arrangements with employers or personally profiting from his union position. As committee investigator Irwin Langenbacher concluded in a November 1957 memo to Kennedy, "it is generally conceded in St. Louis that Harold J. Gibbons does not directly appropriate union funds to his use and will not accept bribes or any type of payoff." Unable to tar Gibbons with the brush they had used on Jimmy Hoffa, Kennedy and McClellan instead chose to depict his experience as a simple morality tale that demonstrated how the Teamsters' culture of corruption could tarnish even those who entered the union movement with the highest of aspirations. As McClellan explained after Gibbons had completed his testimony, ". . . if Mr. Gibbons started out his career dedicated solely to the betterment of the lot of the working man—as I am confident he did—somewhere along the line those ideals have disintegrated." Robert Kennedy reserved a special scorn for Gibbons, whom he described as a "bright, self-centered, arrogant man . . . with a cold, superior look." Kennedy seized on reports that Gibbons "indulges in wine, women, and song and charges the expenses thereof to the union." While keeping his family in a modest home, Gibbons lived "expensively and well," enabling him to "enjoy the finer things" with Teamster members footing the bill. Although Kennedy offered no examples of Gibbons using his position for personal gain, he eagerly drew attention to his expense account-supported hedonism in an effort to depict the coal miner's son as a hypocrite and narcissist whose comfort came at the expense of union members and even his own family.[38]

McClellan and Kennedy proceeded to lay out a detailed prosecutorial brief outlining Gibbons's alleged descent into corruption. Repeating the charge of the St. Louis federal grand jury several years earlier, they accused him of "buying" his way into the Teamsters by paying off their local leaders without gaining the approval of his membership. A parade of witnesses then attested to Gibbons's anti-social behavior: he had used notorious felons with long criminal records to provide muscle during strikes, provided legal counsel to those accused of violence or convicted of crimes, condoned the beating of Local 682 dissident James Ford, failed to distance the union from associations with organized crime, and acquiesced in allowing corrupt, mob-connected figures to retain positions of union leadership. Many Local 688 staff members and others closely associated with Gibbons refused to answer the committee's questions, as did several reputed St. Louis mobsters, reinforcing the impression that he was attempting to conceal his underworld associations. The testimony of Barney Baker, who clumsily attempted to deflect attention from his violent behavior and criminal activities, especially spotlighted the associations that in Kennedy and McClellan's view constituted a breach of trust between the Teamster leader and his members. Most tellingly for Kennedy, Gibbons's disputed election as Joint Council 13 president demonstrated that, while posing "as an advocate of democracy," he "was not averse to using the tactics of racketeers" to maintain his hold on power.[39]

For months, Gibbons prepared for his appearance before the committee, vowing to defend Teamster policy and "my beliefs, record, and fidelity to trust within the trade union movement." During his testimony on September 2 and 3, 1958, he rebutted each of McClellan and Kennedy's charges. He insisted that his merger with Local 688 and the severance arrangements with its former officers had been approved by the union's stewards council and were known to the membership, explained that the beating of James Ford occurred in the context of violent threats by Local 682's ousted leadership, and alleged that police and employer actions were largely responsible for provoking union violence during strikes. Much of Gibbons's testimony, however, had him on the defensive. His explanations—union leaders convicted of crimes deserved financial support and the continuing presumption of innocence throughout their appeals, he had wanted carnival workers' votes counted only to ensure their future participation in the joint council, and that "to his knowledge" he had never instructed Teamsters to take the Fifth Amendment—appeared strained and implausible. He seemed especially uncomfortable when queried about his dealings with Johnny Dio and repeatedly demurred when Senator Irving Ives pressed him to denounce Dio's activities. At the same time, Kennedy and McClellan gave Gibbons little credit for some of his most courageous actions: ousting mob elements and resisting the wildcat strike that ensued after he pressed for racial integration of St. Louis's taxi industry. As journalist Paul Jacobs observed, when strike leader Donald Cortor testified before the committee, Kennedy "was quick to lead the witness away from revealing his own racial bias." Gibbons might have had this incident in mind when he complained about Kennedy's behavior several years later: "One of the great talents that Bobby displayed when I was up there was to take the most decent act you ever performed in your life, give a slight twist, and dirty the whole thing up."[40]

Some of the most compelling moments in Gibbons's testimony occurred during his exchanges with Irving Ives, a liberal Republican businessman from New York and a strong union supporter. As the first dean of Cornell University's School of Industrial and Labor Relations and a strong supporter of collective bargaining, Ives struggled to comprehend Gibbons's continuing militancy and contentious relations with employers. He pleaded with him "to be a missionary in this business" and apply his "above average intelligence" and "considerable background in labor relations" toward pursuing more harmonious relations with management and keeping mob elements out of the union movement. Otherwise, Ives warned, "laws will be enacted which will be very tough on organized labor."[41]

While Irving Ives found Gibbons's militancy an atavistic reversion to class warfare, John McClellan portrayed him as a borderline sociopath whose contempt for law and authority threatened what the latter described as "the ancient verities and the spiritual values that are the very pillars of our republic." McClellan and Robert Kennedy also aimed to shred Gibbons's credibility by placing his misdeeds in a Cold War context: "The committee cannot help but feel that the Gibbons' interpretation of democracy is more applicable in a totalitarian society, where through fear and violence the incumbents inevitably remain in power." This charge had to have stung Gibbons, whose well-established distaste for communism had reflected his commitment to democratic principles that he now stood accused of violating.[42]

However, Gibbons's critics failed to appreciate that he had long resided in a parallel social universe where the managed industrial conflict championed by Irving Ives and the evenhanded administration of the law presumed by Robert Kennedy and John McClellan rarely existed. From his earliest days in the union movement, Gibbons had favored the raw exercise of working-class power over reliance on the regulatory apparatus of the state. After Taft-Hartley, he not only faced stiffer resistance from management but also was denied critical tools that limited the exercise of working-class solidarity on which he had previously relied. Driven by a visceral desire to elevate the working class, Gibbons remained unwilling to play by the rules outlined by Irving Ives and other proponents of mature labor relations. To Ives's astonishment, Gibbons bluntly declared that violence was "inevitable" in social conflict and especially in strike situations. Gibbons also justified the use of rough tactics and displays of working-class power by the nature of the industries he represented. "You have to understand also," he explained, "that we are operating in a very low-wage sweat industry, the warehousing field," where it took years to obtain the wages and benefits needed to provide workers with the personal security Gibbons deemed essential to support total person unionism. "These things are a little unique and the business community does not want it to spread too far," Gibbons averred, in accounting for the continuing conflict with St. Louis employers that occurred under his leadership.[43]

The media universally panned Gibbons's performance, with a September 15, 1958, *Time* magazine article offering a representative appraisal. Labeling Gibbons a "hard-boiled egghead," *Time* portrayed him as a "blood brother to the purple-jawed hoods and goons who have filed before the committee . . ." and doubted "that smooth-talking Harold Gibbons would ever field another invitation to lecture at Harvard." More hurtful to Gibbons, however, was the desertion of old liberal and socialist comrades. The Workers Defense League (WDL), an organization created by the Socialist Party in the 1930s to defend the rights of marginalized workers, asked Gibbons to resign from its board. Clearly angered, Gibbons complained to the WDL's national counsel that in spite of "his long record with the American labor movement and the Socialist labor movement," the League "left" him during the McClellan Committee's "reactionary attacks." Now isolated not only from most of the union movement but also from the liberal left, Gibbons lost something even more fundamental, what social critic Daniel Bell described as the popular sense of unionism as a "moral vocation" and the respect of "a middle-class public which . . . was tolerant of, if not sympathetic to, unionism." Regaining this moral standing would challenge Gibbons for the remainder of his career, with many on the liberal-left regarding him as a symbol of the union movement's squandered social legitimacy and lost promise.[44]

Gibbons's increasing preoccupation with defending the Teamsters against corruption charges had another telling consequence: the demise of the community stewards program. Gibbons's new role as Hoffa's executive assistant meant that his attention was increasingly diverted from St. Louis. The community stewards program also suffered when Gibbons tapped Sidney Zagri to coordinate the Teamsters' opposition to congressional passage of the proposed Landrum-Griffin Act. In January 1959, Gibbons conceded that preoccupation with the McClellan investigation, rising legal fees, and Zagri's departure had gutted the program. Although *Midwest Labor World* claimed that the effort had simply shifted from a local to a national focus, Gibbons and Calloway's hope that the community stewards might mobilize a broader political coalition, expand their activities into the suburbs, and gain further legitimacy for the community bargaining table no longer remained viable.[45]

In 1959, the changed circumstances under which Gibbons and Calloway were now operating became especially apparent. As Irving Ives had predicted, tough legislation to curb Teamsters' power appeared in the form of the Landrum-Griffin Act, a law that further enhanced the rights of individual union members to challenge their leaders and placed new restrictions on the exercise of worker solidarity. Regarding Landrum-Griffin as an existential threat, Gibbons convinced Hoffa that the Teamsters should launch an intensive campaign to defeat the proposed legislation. By the summer of 1959, the union's strategy congealed, with Gibbons, Calloway, and Sidney Zagri all playing prominent roles.[46]

Under Zagri's direction, the union met with more than 250 members of Congress in sessions where he, Gibbons, and other Teamsters outlined their opposition to Landrum-Griffin. Initially, many legislators expressed admiration for Gibbons and Zagri's meticulous preparation and powers of persuasion. However, Zagri's hard-nosed lobbying of wavering representatives alienated some politicians, who reportedly felt intimidated by his aggressive threats of political retribution. Although many of Gibbons and Zagri's tactics were legitimate albeit forceful (flooding congressional offices with mail and telegrams, organizing members to confront recalcitrant or fence-sitting congresspersons), the media described them as replicating in the political arena "the bullyboy methods that [the] Teamsters made famous in trade unionism." Most observers concluded that the union's tactics backfired, with the final legislation containing additional provisions inimical to labor's interests. The unsuccessful fight against Landrum-Griffin foreshadowed some of the problems Gibbons would encounter in attempting to create a national political program for the Teamsters, which became a union priority in the wake of the McClellan investigations.[47]

Gibbons also enlisted the aid of Ernest Calloway in pursuing another strategy to derail Landrum-Griffin. Calloway sought to rally support for an amendment proposed by New York Congressman Adam Clayton Powell to bar unions from practicing racial discrimination. This approach represented an explicit attempt to split the coalition of anti-labor southern Democrats and conservative northern and midwestern Republicans who favored the bill by creating a poison pill that segregationist southerners would be unwilling to swallow. Calloway drew on his NAACP and other civil rights contacts in attempting to create pressure to approve the Powell Amendment. However, in an August 4, 1959, strategy memo that acknowledged the Teamsters' diminished social standing, he advised against "open advocacy" of the union's role, fearing that public disclosure by a "hostile press" would taint the effort as an "improper use of [the] Civil Rights issue for [a] questionable purpose."[48]

Calloway's attempt to wage a stealth lobbying campaign for the Powell Amendment was quickly torpedoed by a leak to the news media. Just six days after Calloway penned his memo, Ted Poston, a veteran African American journalist, provided an extensive analysis of his plan in the *New York Post*. According to Poston, national NAACP leaders quietly urged their local affiliates to distance themselves from Calloway's outreach, which the journalist described as a Jimmy Hoffa-inspired effort to use the pretext of race to halt Landrum-Griffin. Uncomfortable with the aura of corruption surrounding the union and wary of the Teamsters' newfound commitment to civil rights, NAACP leaders balked at supporting an initiative that seemed to reflect political expediency rather than a sincere attempt to address racial injustice in the union movement.[49]

Frustrated by his inability to garner support for the Powell Amendment, Calloway angrily denounced his putative allies. In a letter to Adam Clayton Powell, he disdainfully noted the silence of the "professional civil righters" on the AFL-CIO staff and black leaders in AFL-CIO unions, charging that their antipathy toward the Teamsters deterred them from taking a strong stand against Jim Crow within the house of labor. Calloway also blasted liberals for supporting Landrum-Griffin, complaining, "Liberal Congressmen needing the support of anti-labor, anti-Negro dixiecrats to pass an anti-labor bill. What in the hell has happened to American liberalism?" Both liberals and the AFL-CIO, Calloway claimed, had demonstrated a lack of moral courage by their willingness to jettison a potential remedy for racial injustice in their zeal to undermine the Teamsters.[50]

The intrigue surrounding the Powell Amendment also revealed how in the wake of the McClellan hearings and attacks on Teamster morality, Calloway had begun to embrace an unabashed pragmatism as his guiding tactical and political philosophy. Rebutting charges that the Teamsters' interest in Powell's anti-discrimination bill was a simple reflection of political expediency, Calloway declared that the sturdiest foundation for an alliance between the civil rights and union movements rested not on shared moral or ethical commitments but rather on the basis of self-interest. "And in the final analysis," he asserted, "I have far more faith in the lasting qualities of a policy that is grounded in economic self-interest than in the 'wide, blue yonder' of morality or that elusive thing called 'social consciousness.'" However, this deterministic pragmatism failed to acknowledge the Teamsters' spotty record on combating racism within their own ranks and ran counter to the civil rights movement's crafting of sophisticated moral appeals to justify its demands.[51]

Several years earlier, Calloway had noted the irony of Teamster membership and economic power reaching their apex, while the union simultaneously faced concerted political assaults and widespread public opprobrium. As the 1950s drew to a close, Calloway and Gibbons confronted a similar conundrum, stymied by the machinations of powerful counterforces seeking to undermine the achievements of the community stewards program and the St. Louis NAACP. With their legitimacy damaged by the McClellan hearings and the emergence of new social movements that challenged labor liberalism, Calloway and Gibbons entered a period of recalculation in their quest to promote interracial politics, establish the community bargaining table, and advance the prospects for total person unionism.

A late 1930s demonstration of St. Louis warehouse workers who became the "working-class citizens" that Gibbons and Calloway cultivated during their two-decade-long political partnership. (Harold Gibbons Collection, Bowen Archives, Southern Illinois University at Edwardsville)

Gibbons (third from left in back row) shortly after arriving in St. Louis to take charge of the warehouse workers union. He quickly gained the confidence of the workers and set out to prove that he could both remain a firebrand and assume the responsibilities of leadership. (The State Historical Society of Missouri)

Workers outside the Labor Health Institute (LHI). LHI was one of Harold Gibbons's earliest forays into a unionism concerned with the needs of workers as total persons. (Harold Gibbons Collection, Bowen Archives, Southern Illinois University at Edwardsville)

A nattily attired Calloway (far right) posing with fellow students at Ruskin Labor College in London. (The State Historical Society of Missouri)

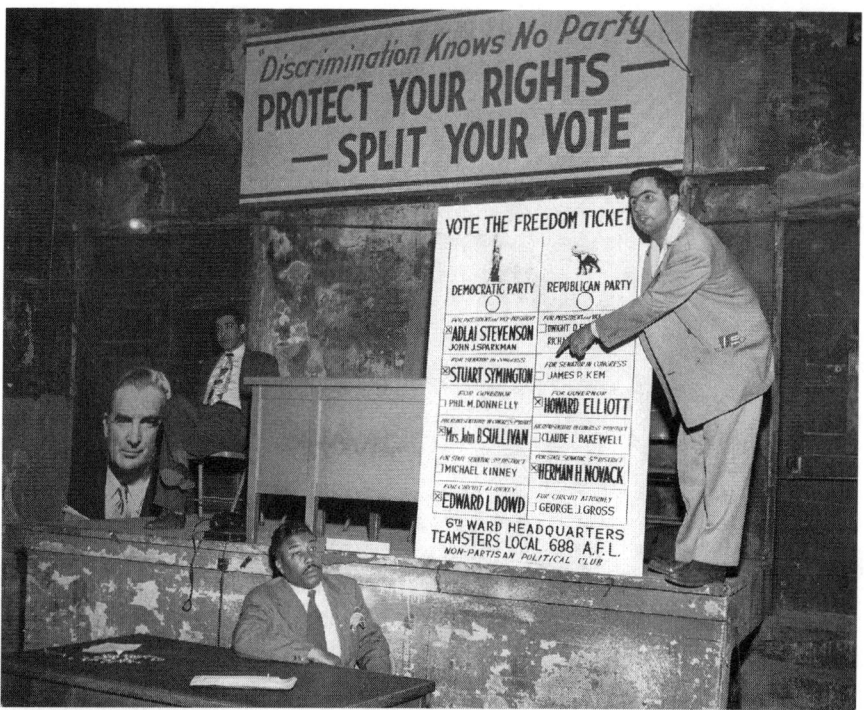

(above) Calloway (seated to left of table) looks on as an unidentified Local 688 member points to a poster that exemplified the union's commitment to political independence and ticket splitting during the 1952 elections. (The State Historical Society of Missouri)

(left) The community stewards' first significant campaign sought to improve transportation in the city of St. Louis. Robert Pentland, a J.C. Penney warehouse worker who also served as a Missouri state senator, poses with a fellow worker next to a sign tracing the campaign's progress in securing signatures to place the issue on the ballot. (The State Historical Society of Missouri)

Calloway conferring with Local 688's community stewards program director Sidney Zagri during the union's successful 1957 campaign against a new city charter that would have blunted African Americans' growing political influence in St. Louis. (The State Historical Society of Missouri)

Ernest and Deverne Calloway putting together the *New Citizen*, "an off-set, off-beat do-it-yourself community newspaper" that enabled them to advance their vision of the black freedom struggle in St. Louis during the early 1960s. (The State Historical Society of Missouri)

Gibbons conferring with Teamsters president Jimmy Hoffa at a union convention. Gibbons's alliance with Hoffa propelled him to the top levels of union leadership but also generated considerable controversy and tarnished his public image. (Harold Gibbons Collection, Bowen Archives, Southern Illinois University at Edwardsville)

Gibbons and Hoffa seated with Martin Luther King, Jr., at a service for Viola Liuzzo, the wife of a Teamsters business agent who was murdered while transporting civil rights demonstrators in Selma, Alabama, in 1965. (Harold Gibbons Collection, Bowen Archives, Southern Illinois University at Edwardsville)

Gibbons, flanked by members of the Hollywood Rat Pack. From left, Frank Sinatra, Dean Martin, and Sammy Davis, Jr., along with Johnny Carson, who emceed a 1965 Local 688 charity show in St. Louis. Gibbons relished his relationships with Hollywood celebrities who shared his love of the nightlife, flouted convention, and lived by their own set of rules. (Harold Gibbons Collection, Bowen Archives, Southern Illinois University at Edwardsville)

Calloway, Gibbons, and an unidentified person reviewing a photograph of St. Louis urban redevelopment plans. Urban revitalization that benefited the working class was a key issue that Gibbons and Calloway sought to negotiate over at the "community bargaining table." (The State Historical Society of Missouri)

Leroy Graham, an organizer for the Local 688-inspired Tandy Area Council (TAC), helps a picketer adjust her sign at a demonstration for clean air and water outside a U.S. Senate hearing in St. Louis. The union's commitment to a healthy environment helped align Local 688 with an emerging social movement that most of labor avoided or shunned. (Harold Gibbons Collection, Bowen Archives, Southern Illinois University at Edwardsville)

Gibbons lining up a tee shot while President Richard Nixon looks on. Gibbons was the lone dissenter against the Teamsters executive board's 1972 endorsement of Nixon, which prompted a chain of events that led to his ouster as head of Local 688. (Harold Gibbons Collection, Bowen Archives, Southern Illinois University at Edwardsville)

Ernest and Deverne Calloway opening presents at Calloway's retirement party as Harold Gibbons looks on. (The State Historical Society of Missouri)

CHAPTER 9

"A Planned Social Revolution"

On March 30, 1965, NBC newsman Chet Huntley reported on his daily radio program about an interview he had conducted with Teamsters' vice-president Harold Gibbons. According to Huntley, Gibbons had chided unions for their tendency to invest their pension fund holdings in profit-making enterprises. Instead, Gibbons argued that the union movement should direct its resources toward the revival of American cities by building housing, offering job training, and developing programs to combat crime and delinquency. Huntley concluded his commentary by praising the Teamsters' leader: "One therefore goes away from an evening with Harold Gibbons hoping that some of his ideas and ideals will yet prevail. His socialist days are over, of course, but there is still the predilection toward idealism. It's good to find it still around."[1]

As the nation entered the 1960s, the spirit of idealism cited by Chet Huntley had penetrated into America's political and cultural bloodstream. The freedom rides and sit-ins launched by the civil rights movement to challenge the evil of segregation generated calls for America to rediscover its moral compass and honor its constitutional commitments. In their 1962 founding manifesto, the Port Huron Statement, Students for a Democratic Society expressed "a yearning to believe that there is an alternative to the present, that something can be done to change circumstances in the schools, the workplaces, the bureaucracies [and] the government." Clearly, an expectant social mood had emerged, creating hope among labor liberals for new political alliances that might allow the uncompleted agenda of the New Deal to be fulfilled.[2]

For Harold Gibbons and Ernest Calloway, these currents of idealism offered new opportunities to implement their vision of total person unionism. As second-in-command at America's largest union, Gibbons now had access to a national audience. In St. Louis, Calloway had solidified his reputation as a gifted strategist and envisioned new possibilities for a community bargaining table where African Americans could sit as equals with the city's power brokers. Nonetheless, Gibbons and Calloway experienced a growing sense of marginalization as social ferment bubbled. After the McClellan Committee hearings, the Teamsters became a suspect institution, detaching them from both old allies and new insurgencies. Gibbons encountered an entrenched Teamster culture loath to expand its social vision, and Calloway faced a new generation of civil rights activists in St. Louis that challenged his leadership. By the mid-1960s, each found himself struggling to navigate the maelstrom of social change that threatened to relegate them to the political sidelines.

* * *

Shortly after the agreement creating the Board of Monitors that allowed Jimmy Hoffa to assume the Teamsters' presidency, a January 26, 1958, *St. Louis Globe-Democrat* article featured a picture of Harold Gibbons seated in his "plush headquarters office" with the U.S. Capitol visible in background. Clad in a well-tailored suit and exuding confidence, the coal miner's son from Archibald Patch had traveled full circle from his humble origins, reveling in his proximity to power and his enhanced capacity to promote his social vision. Gibbons outlined an ambitious set of goals for the new Teamsters' administration: increasing the union's membership from 1.4 million to 2 million in five years, creating a legislative and political action program to expand Teamster influence in Washington, and improving the union's public image through more visible participation in community affairs. To help him implement this agenda, Gibbons brought to Washington several of his old CIO comrades and imported some of his best talent from St. Louis, including Jake McCarthy and Sidney Zagri. There is no record of whether Gibbons offered Ernest Calloway a chance to join his brain trust in Washington. Presumably, Calloway wished to continue his civil rights activity in St. Louis, while also leaving Gibbons with a trusted ally to look after his home base.[3]

During his five-year tenure as Hoffa's executive assistant, Gibbons's ambitions repeatedly became entangled in charges of corruption that lingered following the McClellan investigation. These accusations intensified when Robert Kennedy became attorney general following his brother's election as president. In the spring of 1960, a federal grand jury indicted Gibbons, Zagri, and other officers of locals 688 and 405 for illegally using treasury funds to support federal candidates in the 1956 and 1958 elections. Gibbons claimed that the union had only solicited voluntary political contributions from its members, and a federal judge agreed, directing a verdict of acquittal. A year later, Local 405 officers did plead guilty to "technical" violations of Taft-Hartley provisions on political contributions, suggesting that Gibbons's approach to political fundraising skirted the edge of official legality. Still, the *St. Louis Globe-Democrat*, which had long been critical of Gibbons, was not far from the mark in characterizing the convening of the St. Louis grand jury as a "fishing expedition which borders on persecution." These episodes foreshadowed the relentless efforts of the Kennedy Justice Department to achieve its ultimate objective of ousting Hoffa from the Teamsters' presidency.[4]

Under Hoffa, it was Teamsters' policy to support virtually all union officials accused or convicted of corruption. This policy compelled Gibbons to defend notorious figures such as Chicago taxi drivers' president Joey Glimco, whose mob connections were public knowledge, and Raymond Cohen, a Philadelphia Teamster leader who had been convicted of misusing union funds and negotiating sweetheart deals with employers. Gibbons also actively opposed efforts that sought to restore rank-and-file governance at the local level, further eroding his credentials as a proponent of participatory democracy and working-class citizenship.[5]

According to B.J. Widick, a former Trotskyist and an astute labor analyst, Gibbons regarded Jimmy Hoffa as a "new John L. Lewis" whose mastery of power relations might be harnessed in support of a more ambitious social agenda. Nonetheless, he experienced continual frustration in his efforts to enlarge Hoffa's perspective. For Gibbons, labor's willingness to support the quest for racial justice remained his barometer of the movement's moral standing, and he pressed the Teamsters to assume a more active, visible role. As he explained in a July 1963 speech to the Western Conference of Teamsters, labor's inaction on race ". . . is a crime and a disgrace. The enemies of the Negro people today are the enemies of the labor movement. We should be out there carrying part of the burden of the American Negro fight."[6]

Gibbons did succeed in convincing Hoffa to compel southern locals to desegregate, a move that Ernest Calloway cited in defending the Teamsters' president's record on racial matters. Calloway also hailed the role that area-wide agreements played in eliminating pay differentials based on race, a point he made when he led a delegation of black Teamsters' business agents who met with Martin Luther King, Jr. In 1965, Gibbons persuaded Hoffa to contribute $25,000 to King's parent organization, the Southern Christian Leadership Conference, which Calloway recalled generated "tremendous opposition . . . among our southern white members." However, Hoffa rejected Gibbons's suggestion that he speak at the 1963 March on Washington and also refused to seek strong anti-discrimination language in trucking contracts, fearing that such actions posed unacceptable political risks. Although Gibbons could point to incremental progress in the union's overall approach to racial matters, he remained an isolated voice in the Teamsters' hierarchy on the issue that he regarded as essential to restoring the trade union movement's moral legitimacy.[7]

Hoffa also kept Gibbons on a short leash in other arenas where he had hoped to change Teamsters' culture. Gibbons looked to create a Teamsters' political apparatus involved not only in electoral activity but also in other civic matters where the energy of working-class citizenship could be used on a national scale to shape urban policy. These ambitions, however, collided with a union culture ill-suited to embrace such initiatives. Historically, Teamster political efforts had not been coordinated nationally and were largely defensive. As political attacks on the union mounted, Gibbons finally convinced Hoffa to launch a national program to ramp up Teamster political activity.

The new program, Democratic-Republican-Independent Voter Education (DRIVE), sought to move beyond the union's traditional approach of seeking to buy political influence through campaign contributions. Instead, Gibbons looked to involve Teamster members and their families directly in the political process by mobilizing them to exert pressure on their elected leaders, and tapped Sidney Zagri to become DRIVE's director under his guidance. Fearing that Gibbons might develop an independent power base within the union, Hoffa insisted that Zagri report directly to him. For his part, Gibbons apparently believed that Zagri's aggressive tactics had backfired during the fight over Landrum-Griffin, triggering adverse publicity that undercut his efforts to upgrade the union's image. The Gibbons-Zagri relationship became strained as a result, with Zagri assuming direct control of the union's political and legislative operations and Gibbons being relegated to a supporting role.[8]

To Gibbons's dismay, DRIVE's programmatic thrust did not depart significantly from the Teamsters' traditionally utilitarian approach to political action. For example, in the 1960 election, the union supported Richard Nixon over John F. Kennedy, compelling Gibbons to corral votes for a Republican with clear anti-union sympathies. DRIVE also made Landrum-Griffin a litmus test, focusing its efforts on ousting politicians who had supported the legislation regardless of their overall voting record on labor matters. This strategy achieved limited success, however. Ultimately, DRIVE never accumulated the level of funding Hoffa had sought nor articulated the broad social goals advocated by Gibbons. One of its major vehicles, luncheons for Teamster wives hosted by Hoffa's spouse, did generate greater women's interest in politics. However, these events were orchestrated affairs devoid of the commitment to working-class citizenship that had attracted women to the community stewards program in St. Louis. Although DRIVE represented an improvement over the union's previous political efforts, its achievements fell well short of Gibbons's ambitious goals.[9]

Perhaps not surprisingly, Gibbons's greatest achievements during his tenure as Hoffa's top aide came in the more familiar arenas of organizing and collective bargaining. Although the union did not reach the 2 million membership mark Gibbons had set as a goal, the Teamsters' ranks did swell to 1.75 million by the end of 1963, an impressive figure given the limited organizing success of most other private sector unions during this period. Gibbons played an active role in promoting organizing, helping establish an airline division that aimed to protect the union's base in trucking and railroads. He also spearheaded moves toward national agreements at grocery chain warehouses that paralleled Hoffa's most prized objective, the 1964 master freight agreement in trucking that substantially equalized wages for drivers across the country.[10]

To union audiences, Gibbons repeated a point often made by Hoffa in the wake of Landrum-Griffin's passage: "I don't know of any other answer there may possibly be to the kind of secondary boycott provision which is now the law of the land—excepting through the medium of area contracts and the national agreement." Unlike Hoffa, Gibbons not only acknowledged but also lamented veteran labor journalist Sam Romer's observation that "... the rise of the area conference ... marks the end of the local union as a significant factor in collective bargaining." Gibbons feared that centralization of bargaining threatened to turn local union leaders into passive observers with limited opportunities to bring the pulse of the shop floor to the increasingly distant location of the bargaining table. "What is left for local leaders during time of national agreements and centralization of power?" Gibbons wondered. "Can this leader escape the dangers of lethargy unless there is a strong thrust in new directions for the American labor movement?" As his dissatisfaction with Hoffa's leadership grew, this question troubled Gibbons, who chafed at the union's aloofness while social ferment continued to simmer.[11]

Although Gibbons and Hoffa shared a hotel suite in Washington and were often photographed in intimate poses (one *Life* magazine article showed Gibbons in his bathrobe and Hoffa preparing their breakfast), their relationship had long been stormy. One area of initial contention revolved around Gibbons's personal conduct. Frequently away from St. Louis and living apart from his wife, Gibbons engaged in unabashed womanizing, which he flaunted without reservation. Perhaps impelled by the extraordinary deprivation of his youth, he became widely known as a legendary bon vivant who loved hanging out in nightspots and hobnobbing with Hollywood celebrities. He was especially drawn to Frank Sinatra and a group of fellow entertainers the press dubbed the Rat Pack, whose public revelry, stylistic "cool," and disregard for convention appealed to Gibbons's status aspirations and personal proclivities. Bankrolled by his access to expense account funds, Gibbons's fondness for the nightlife fascinated and puzzled many of his acquaintances. Sidney Lens, a left-wing unionist and writer who knew Gibbons and shared his politics, spoke for many in describing him as a "man of many contradictions." Lens made this observation after recalling Gibbons fleeing a party to escape from a woman imploring him to take her away from her husband.[12]

Fiercely ascetic in his personal life, Jimmy Hoffa abhorred what he regarded as Gibbons's lack of discipline but tolerated his lieutenant's antics as a character flaw that did not undermine his overall effectiveness. However, as the "Get Hoffa" squad at the Justice Department intensified its activities, he became increasingly suspicious of his subordinate's loyalty, frequently subjecting Gibbons to verbal abuse. For a proud and ambitious man like Gibbons, Hoffa's paranoia, volatility, and demands for loyalty clearly grated. Commenting on the Hoffa-Gibbons relationship, warehouse division director Sam Baron noted, "Jimmy has to be Number One and Gibbons has to remember it."[13]

In 1962, Hoffa's outbursts reached new heights when he assaulted Sam Baron, whom he suspected of leaking information to the Justice Department. Under duress, Baron dropped charges he had filed against Hoffa. However, in a July 1962 *Life* magazine expose, he bitterly denounced Gibbons for backing Hoffa's account of the altercation and turning his back on his longtime friend. Repelled by Hoffa's behavior but reluctant to intervene, Gibbons's resentment finally exploded a year later following the assassination of John F. Kennedy in November 1963. With both Hoffa and Gibbons absent from the union's national headquarters in Washington, Gibbons's longtime colleague and friend Larry Steinberg had ordered the office's flag lowered to half-staff out of respect for the slain president. When he returned to the office, Gibbons approved Steinberg's action and joined him in drafting a letter of condolence to the Kennedy family. Several weeks later, Gibbons issued a front-page statement in the *Missouri Teamster* that acknowledged the assassination's deep wound to the American psyche: "This hideous crime will take its toll on every American citizen. The prayers of every trade unionist in the nation are with the Kennedy family at this time of deepest sorrow."[14]

These actions prompted an enraged tirade from Hoffa, whose unvarnished hatred for the Kennedys led him to order the flag raised, rescind the letter of condolence, and spew invective that the media quickly disseminated to a grieving public. For Gibbons, Hoffa's political tone deafness represented the final straw in their relationship, and he promptly resigned his post as executive assistant. Although Gibbons publicly denied reports of a rift and continued to perform assignments for Hoffa, he left the international union's payroll and returned to St. Louis. Shortly after Hoffa's outburst and Gibbons's departure, public reports surfaced citing growing discontent with Hoffa among his fellow executive board members, raising the possibility that a palace coup might occur.

Gibbons contemplated challenging Hoffa but ultimately decided not to oppose him. His hesitation stemmed from several factors, including his abiding sense of gratitude to his benefactor and the realization that he lacked sufficient internal support. In December 1963, an unnamed source poetically described Gibbons's dilemma to A.H. Raskin of the *New York Times*: "When Gibbons stops playing Hamlet and begins playing Iago, maybe we'll begin making progress toward getting Hoffa out." In the same article where this quote appeared, Raskin astutely summarized Gibbons's complicated status within the Teamsters: "Mr. Gibbons's handicap now is that he is such an unusual blend of egghead and bon vivant and that he comes out of the CIO. All these attributes make him something of an alien in the Teamsters hierarchy, accepted solely on the basis of his sponsorship by Mr. Hoffa."[15]

Attempting to put a positive spin on his break with Hoffa, Gibbons declared in the January 1964 edition of the *Missouri Teamster* that the national office was isolated from "the real pains and dreams of those who labor in the streets and shops of America" and claimed that he had "wanted for some time to return to [St. Louis]; to replenish the sense of urgency without which the trade union movement must stagnate." He now devoted more focused attention to St. Louis and pursued new initiatives to expand the reach of total person unionism.[16]

Throughout his tenure as Hoffa's executive assistant, Gibbons had maintained close contact with Local 688, which remained his social laboratory. In the late 1950s, he had launched what the head of the St. Louis Rabbinical Association described as a "noble experiment in health and recreational pioneering" with the establishment of Local 688's "Health and Medical Camp" in Pevely, MO, a small town thirty miles south of St. Louis. Eternally the coal miner's son whose impoverished upbringing remained a searing memory, Gibbons "sought to provide a dimension that is basically lacking in working-class life—the opportunity for a family-focused health and fitness program in a setting that provides fresh air, sunshine, and wholesome recreation as well." Insisting on the need to address the Teamster member's needs as a total person, Gibbons noted that "decent shop conditions were indispensable, but the worker and his family spent far more hours in his small apartment or low-cost home in neighborhoods that were often overcrowded and sometimes decaying." Marcus Albrecht, a young Teamster who became close to Gibbons and Calloway near the end of their careers, recalled Gibbons describing the camp as "a place where people could go and have the feeling they were at a country club." According to Albrecht, Pevely underscored Gibbons's insistence that the working class deserved ample off-the-job opportunities for a richer life and the chance to participate in leisure activities on an equivalent basis with their employers.[17]

Coinciding with the waning months of his tenure as Jimmy Hoffa's executive assistant, Gibbons became increasingly occupied with an even more ambitious attempt to create greater security for workers: the construction of senior citizens' housing in the Mill Creek Valley area of St. Louis. Mill Creek Valley was a blighted, largely African American neighborhood targeted for slum clearance in the late 1950s. Ernest Calloway and the St. Louis NAACP had eagerly endorsed the project, with Calloway describing it as "one of the most exciting municipal rehabilitation programs of any American city" because it promised to "slow down the stampede to the suburbs," and "revive the heart of our city." Several years later, however, a disappointed Calloway and most of the city's African American leaders regretted their support. The city had torn down over 450 acres of housing and built a new expressway on some of the vacated land. However, the promised commercial and residential redevelopment was slow to materialize, prompting some to describe the leveled area as "Hiroshima Flats." This debacle accentuated black St. Louisans' anger regarding the abject failure of urban revitalization initiatives to deliver promised benefits.[18]

It was in this context that Harold Gibbons proposed Council Plaza, an apartment complex for senior citizens to be built on undeveloped land in Mill Creek Valley. Council Plaza represented Gibbons's determination to demonstrate that the Teamsters could use pension fund holdings for broad social purposes and play an integral role in revitalizing the urban landscape. In a draft brochure for the project, Gibbons noted the limited reach of the truncated post-World War II welfare state, with Social Security and pension benefits falling short of enabling senior citizens to lead fulfilling, engaged lives. Reflecting his multidimensional view of working-class needs, he applied the concept of total person unionism to the circumstances of retirees: "Can a man retire on less than 50% of his former earnings and still satisfy all of the physiological, sociological, psychological, and economic requirements he needs to remain in the stream of life as an active, healthy citizen?" To answer this question affirmatively, Council Plaza would "offer [the] senior citizen a total program for satisfying and creative living at a cost within his reach." As Gibbons later observed, "It's not just brick and stone. We've created a way of living."[19]

By 1966, the first Council Plaza building was ready for habitation, and the second set of apartments opened for occupancy two years later. In contrast to most other union housing projects that restricted residency to their own members, Gibbons made Council Plaza available to unionists and community members outside the Teamsters' ranks. And although other unions took steps to instill a cooperative spirit within their housing projects, Gibbons went further. In keeping with his concept of transferring shop-floor expertise to the realm of community activity, Council Plaza managers developed a "buddy system" with "floor shop stewards" to provide security and a "good neighbor program" where elected delegates made rules for running the facility. For Gibbons, the successful completion of the Council Plaza complex represented yet another example of working-class efficacy in an arena where government had fallen short of meeting its social responsibility. As he declared in a March 1965 article, the nation's housing problem could not be solved by projects that have "no concern for the total person" and urged the union movement to fill the vacuum created by government inaction.[20]

However, amid all the favorable attention Council Plaza received, the project struggled to overcome the racial divide that Gibbons and Calloway remained committed to bridging. In September 1965, project administrator Arthur Klein acknowledged that out of 272 security deposits placed by prospective residents, only one had been received from an African American. In a meeting with African American leaders, Klein insisted "we are not apathetic as to the paucity of Negro applicants for residency at Council House." He suggested that several factors, among them an inability to afford the rent and inadequate publicity about the project, had deterred blacks from applying. Still, the nonparticipation of African American applicants demonstrated that Gibbons and Calloway's determined efforts to surmount racial barriers in St. Louis faced stubborn obstacles that would not be easily overcome.[21]

Even more worrisome, Local 688's rank-and-file members demonstrated growing signs of indifference to the edifices of total person unionism that were such a source of pride to Gibbons and Calloway. In the fall of 1964, Gibbons asked his old mentors, Annetta Dieckmann and Lillian Herstein, to serve as consultants in helping Local 688 re-establish an educational program. In a September 1964 report to Gibbons, Dieckmann and Herstein expressed concern that many of the union's members seemed detached from his social vision. Observing member reaction to Jimmy Hoffa's address at Local 688's 1964 annual citywide conference that defiantly underscored his narrow conception of labor's responsibilities, they wondered, "Did the enthusiastic response to President Hoffa's bitter closing speech indicate they did not recognize its negation of many of the brave resolutions passed or was it only the normal recognition of the leader of the organization?" Two months later, Dieckmann and Herstein questioned their protégé even more pointedly: "Your consultants need enlightenment as to why the many excellent and unusual features of this union fail to arouse the enthusiasm of all its members. Why is even the LHI controversial . . . Why is the camp not appreciated by everyone?"[22]

One answer to Dieckmann and Herstein's query came in a 1966 internal report on the health and medical camp. The report lamented the low use of the camp by Local 688's membership, estimating that only 5–10 percent of the rank-and-file had availed themselves of its offerings. In part, the report attributed this low usage to a working-class reluctance to pursue the "family oriented recreation" promoted by the camp and noted that the union's higher paid, middle-class members appeared more comfortable bringing their families to the facility. More troubling, however, was the refusal of white members to mingle socially with Local 688's black members in an off-the-job setting. As "one woman member" asserted: "I might have to go to church, work, ride to work with them and [send] my kids to school with 'em, [but] you or nobody else can tell me I'm going to eat with them, let alone swim in the same pool." The report concluded, "In short, a large number of our membership does not want voluntary social integration."[23]

Annetta Dieckmann and Lillian Herstein had presciently sensed a growing alienation among a segment of Local 688's rank-and-file members, who seemed to prefer Jimmy Hoffa's bombast to Gibbons's vision of working-class citizenship. These sentiments unveiled an inchoate but increasingly visible disgruntlement that spiked as the social turmoil of the 1960s unfolded. Indeed, as Gibbons began to contemplate ways to revive the participatory spirit of the community stewards program within Local 688, Ernest Calloway experienced his own challenges in seeking popular support for his strategy to advance the cause of racial justice in St. Louis.

* * *

Following the disappointing results of the campaign to end employment discrimination at Famous-Barr, Calloway had resigned from his post as St. Louis NAACP president. Now free from the organization's ban on participation in partisan politics, Calloway applied his strategic skills to the electoral arena. In 1959 and 1960, he managed two prominent campaigns that resulted in notable African American political breakthroughs. Determined to win greater influence over their children's education, black St. Louisans had long lamented their inability to place a black candidate on the city's school board. At the urging of key community leaders, Calloway agreed to manage the campaign of Reverend John Hicks, a respected minister and NAACP activist, for a school board seat. He organized a massive get-out-the-vote operation that enabled Hicks to win the June 1959 election with the second largest tally among all candidates in a crowded field.[24]

An even more impressive victory followed a year later when Calloway's close political ally, Ted McNeal, became the first black elected to the Missouri state senate. Even as north St. Louis's population had grown increasingly African American, Irish politicians had retained their control in this section of the city. With Calloway managing his campaign, McNeal won an overwhelming victory over Edward "Jelly Roll" Hogan, a longtime state senator who chaired the powerful Ways and Means committee. Along with other black candidates defeating Irish legislators and committeemen, McNeal's sweeping triumph signaled the demise of Irish political domination in north St. Louis. Indeed, Calloway and other black leaders had successfully "encouraged" John Dwyer, an Irish committeeman and major power broker who sought to remain politically relevant, to back McNeal's candidacy. Dwyer's decision to support McNeal affirmed Calloway's conviction that the city's white Democratic leadership was increasingly prepared to make pragmatic accommodations in acknowledgment of growing African American political power.[25]

Managing notable black electoral "firsts" boosted Calloway's reputation for political savvy in the African American community, with the *St. Louis Chronicle* describing him as "a whiz at tidy organization and political know-how." At the same time, his successes aroused concerns about his role as a political kingmaker. Asking in a March 1960 article if Calloway was "the Iron Fist in the Velvet Glove in Coming Political Campaign," a *Chronicle* writer claimed that ". . . many express fear at the Calloway political touch" and his "creeping tentacles." The article concluded with a familiar refrain, wondering "whether the Teamster worker is on his own—or has more powerful backing." Although Calloway did not respond directly to this charge, he quite likely resented the insinuation that he was a puppet doing Harold Gibbons's bidding. In fact, he had kept his role as Ted McNeal's campaign manager a virtual secret within Local 688 to keep questions about his purported manipulation by Gibbons from becoming a campaign issue.[26]

In December 1960, just a month after McNeal's election, Calloway returned to his journalistic roots, launching a weekly newspaper first called the *Citizen Crusader* and later the *New Citizen*, which he used to promote his strategic vision, deepen his connections within the black community, and affirm his political independence. Calloway later described the *New Citizen* as "an off-set, off-beat do it yourself community newspaper" that he and his wife Deverne produced each week at their kitchen table. Chiding other African American newspapers that "seek to create the dangerous image and illusion that all is well in our community, state, nation, and world during this critical period of our history," Calloway articulated a different mission for the *New Citizen*: to shake up "an in-grown, fragmented, conservative Negro community that [has] great difficulty raising its social and political sights." The paper provided Calloway with a platform to promote his belief that black St. Louisans were poised to obtain full functional citizenship if they were prepared to act with the requisite discipline, unity, and strategic focus.[27]

In numerous articles written throughout the early 1960s, Calloway elaborated on his belief that the moment for "a new dynamic political and community partnership between Negro and white citizens" was at hand. Noting that the black community had provided critical support for bond issues favored by St. Louis's white civic elite, Calloway declared that African Americans had transcended the constraints of race-based politics by repeatedly demonstrating their willingness to assume "an increasing share of responsibility for [the] well-being of the total community." Given these developments, Calloway insisted that black St. Louisans should not accept an externally determined "yardstick that measures consideration in terms of crumbs instead of a substantial portion of the loaf." Here he was implicitly criticizing longtime black committeeman Jordan Chambers for accepting the limited benefits of patronage rather than pressing white Democrats for a fuller commitment to pursue racial justice. Indeed, Calloway exulted in a 1960 interview that "we have forced Chambers to come around to running on issues," suggesting that ward paternalism was no longer an acceptable paradigm for African Americans beginning to taste the possibilities of exercising genuine political power.[28]

Calloway also implored black St. Louisans to look beyond obtaining their civil rights and pay closer attention to structural issues such as land use, industrial growth, zoning, and taxes. ". . . The problems of industrial land use and the rate of industrial development must be given as much sober and articulate attention as the agitational picket line or the protest mass meeting," Calloway insisted. This assertion reflected Calloway's growing concern that a preoccupation with direct action was deflecting attention from the real arenas where St. Louis's power elite determined the distribution of resources vital to the quest for social and economic equality.[29]

As he fought to convince the black community to establish a working partnership with key St. Louis decision makers, Calloway and his wife, Deverne, negotiated their own political arrangement with John Dwyer. As Deverne Calloway recounted, leading figures in the black community and the white Democratic Party establishment had urged her husband to seek electoral office. Implicitly acknowledging that holding public office might constrain his role as a social critic, Calloway opted to step aside in favor of his wife, who had compiled an admirable record of community service in the city's heavily African American 26th ward. In November 1962, with support from Dwyer and Ted McNeal, she became the first black woman elected to the Missouri legislature. At her request Joint Council 13 did not endorse her candidacy, a move illustrating both Calloways' sensitivity to the perception they were subservient to Teamster authority.[30]

Meanwhile, Ernest Calloway made personal progress in his bid to forge a civic partnership with the city's political and economic elite. He won praise (and an invitation for cocktails) from David Calhoun, a prominent local banker and founding member of Civic Progress, for *New Citizen*'s editorial support for a 1962 bond measure that had failed at the polls. Even his old foe Raymond Tucker hailed his work on the bond issue and solicited his advice on how to secure its subsequent passage. However, just as Calloway's cultivation of personal ties with city power brokers bolstered his belief in the possibilities of crafting a civic partnership between black and white leaders, he faced a formidable challenge in the political emergence of 26th ward alderman William Clay. Throughout the next decade Clay became Calloway's principal antagonist in a bitter contest over whose vision would guide the political strategy of African Americans in St. Louis.[31]

Handsome, charismatic, and ambitious, Clay burst onto St. Louis's political scene in the late 1950s. Two decades younger than Calloway, he had a long history of rebellion against racial injustice. Clay had first encountered Calloway during his work with the NAACP Youth Council when the latter was serving as branch president. Initially, Calloway had won respect from Clay and other youth council members for his heroic stand as a World War II draft resister and his leadership capabilities. However, Calloway was disturbed by the Youth Council's increasingly freewheeling approach and its zest for direct action, prompting him to rein it in. In March 1956, he rebuked the Youth Council for accepting proceeds from a concert by folk singer Pete Seeger. Seeger's alleged association with the Communist Party disturbed Calloway, who feared that the communist label might taint his efforts to make the NAACP a respected social force in St. Louis. Following Calloway's decision to red-bait the Youth Council to undermine its credibility, Clay and other young activists left the NAACP and joined the St. Louis Congress of Racial Equality (CORE) chapter. This incident launched a personal and political feud between the two men that profoundly affected Calloway's career.[32]

Although both Clay and Calloway identified politics as the most appropriate venue to advance the cause of racial justice in St. Louis, their tactical and ideological approaches differed sharply. Anticipating an argument made in a celebrated 1964 essay by civil rights strategist Bayard Rustin, Calloway insisted that the black freedom struggle make the transition "from protest to politics" and build an interracial, class-based movement. For Calloway, direct action tactics that made sense in the intransigent political cultures of Birmingham and Selma were less applicable to the "community mores" of St. Louis, whose white economic and political elite had demonstrated some willingness to accommodate the demands of the black freedom struggle. Under his leadership, Calloway claimed that a "planned social revolution" had been occurring in St. Louis and recoiled at the unruliness he increasingly associated with direct action.[33]

Clay retorted that while Calloway and his peers regarded "incremental success as a great achievement," he and his cohorts took an almost apocalyptic view, guided by the conviction that "we either get our rights, or we don't, and we're willing to challenge any and everything." In contrast to Calloway, Clay did not seek to build an interracial political coalition but rather used black electoral power to broker deals that left the basic structure of ward politics undisturbed. As political scientist Lana Stein observed, "Clay's immersion in ward politics and its political infighting... strengthened the prevailing political culture based on individualized rewards, factional loyalty, and other quid pro quo transactions." Yet as subsequent events revealed, Clay more astutely grasped the emotional and psychological mood of the black community in St. Louis. In the wake of the Mill Creek Valley debacle and the power elite's halfhearted attempts to address the structural inequities that perpetuated racial inequality, Clay successfully tapped these wellsprings of discontent to gain support for his strategy to obtain racial justice.[34]

These sharp tactical and ideological differences were exacerbated by a deep personal animosity that raged between the two men. In Calloway's view, Clay's overweening ego (he once dubbed his younger foe "Emperor Clay: The King of I Am") led him to betray former political allies in the black community, pursue alliances with regressive white South St. Louis machine politicians, and align himself with the Steamfitters Union, which was notorious for maintaining a rigidly segregated membership and supporting corrupt ward politics. Of course, Calloway himself had not remained aloof from pursuing rapprochements with white power brokers, among them former foes John Dwyer and Raymond Tucker. However, he regarded Clay as a rank opportunist whose unbridled ambition and lack of personal integrity made him an unreliable political actor.[35]

By 1962, the simmering conflict between Clay and Calloway spilled over into the tumultuous arena of union jurisdiction. Believing that "Calloway and the Teamsters were always interfering with my politics in the 26th ward," Clay retaliated by actively supporting unions that sought to raid Teamster bargaining units. Clay found especially fertile ground for his forays in a bitter jurisdictional dispute between the Teamsters and the Seafarers International Union. Seafarers' president Paul Hall detested Jimmy Hoffa and saw Teamster-represented taxi drivers as a discontented constituency poised to defect. This assessment accurately described the mood of many taxi drivers in St. Louis, who still remembered Harold Gibbons's suppression of their 1956 wildcat strike. In 1961, nearly 200 cabbies at one company narrowly voted to decertify Local 405 and go independent. Sensing an opening, the Seafarers moved to organize them under their banner. The hotly contested battles between the Seafarers and the Teamsters in St. Louis and other cities quickly gained national attention, with the media spotlighting them as evidence that Jimmy Hoffa's hold on membership loyalty might be slipping.[36]

Between 1962 and 1964, numerous skirmishes erupted between the Seafarers and the Teamsters over who would represent taxi drivers in St. Louis. The heated controversy embarrassed Gibbons and especially Calloway, who felt betrayed as some drivers abandoned the Teamsters in favor of the Seafarers. For Calloway, the union's decade-long attempt to upgrade the working conditions of taxi drivers, build interracial unionism, and stabilize a volatile industry represented a signal achievement. Accusing Clay of reintroducing Jim Crow unionism, Calloway bitterly denounced his rival: ". . . there will never be a more callow and irresponsible example of how a free-wheeling, self-styled 'militant' in the civil rights movement can successfully uproot a sensitive, planned program of union and employment integration." He observed in the January 31, 1964, edition of the *St. Louis Argus,* "It is interesting to note that the Yellow Cab drivers moved out of the Teamsters because of integration and the Marcella drivers moved out in search of segregation."[37]

Although his complaints about Clay's behavior were justified, Calloway glossed over several important dimensions of the taxi drivers' saga. Given the Teamsters' well-established record of raiding other unions and several NLRB rulings charging them with illegal attempts to win workers' loyalty during the decertification elections, his cry of foul was somewhat disingenuous. The Teamsters had also dismayed the black community when they resisted a request by a non-union, African-American-owned company to obtain drivers' permits left unused by white-owned companies and employ them to increase taxi service in underserved black neighborhoods. The rejection of the Teamsters by at least some black taxi drivers also suggested that William Clay's impatience with gradual change and his appeals to racial pride appeared to have triumphed over Calloway's "sensitive planned program of union and employment integration." Ultimately, the Teamsters' clashes with the Seafarers accentuated Calloway's growing political isolation and led him to seek new venues for shaping the course of black politics in St. Louis.[38]

Following the epic August 1963 March on Washington which he attended, Calloway appeared with A. Philip Randolph, Bayard Rustin, and civil rights leader John Lewis on a panel that pondered the question of "where do we go from here?" At Randolph's insistence the march had encompassed demands for both "jobs and freedom." Calloway referenced this theme in his presentation, arguing that the issue of employment held the greatest potential to unify African Americans and galvanize an interracial movement for economic justice. Seeking to regain his political footing following his clashes with William Clay, Calloway returned to a familiar arena: St. Louis's racially segmented labor market.[39]

By the early 1960s, employment opportunities for African Americans in St. Louis had worsened dramatically. Nearly two of every five workers unemployed in St. Louis were African American, even though blacks comprised only 16 percent of the city's total labor force. This circumstance was aggravated by accelerating automation that diminished the need for the unskilled and semi-skilled jobs where African Americans were compelled to cluster. Underscoring this point, William Clay issued a report early in 1963 that itemized by industry the shockingly low number of black St. Louisans employed in skilled positions. Echoing Clay's findings, Calloway warned city officials that the time for action on black employment was long overdue. As he bluntly told the head of the St. Louis Chamber of Commerce in a July 1963 letter, "You cannot appease the hunger for security and social well-being by tantalizing the victim with small tidbits and choice morsels from the table of an affluent society."[40]

Calloway chose the newly formed Negro American Labor Council (NALC) as the institutional vehicle by which he would seek to dismantle racial segmentation in St. Louis's major industries. Established in 1960 by A. Philip Randolph, the NALC pressed the AFL-CIO to end discriminatory practices within its own ranks and mobilized black trade unionists for concerted action against racial inequality at the community level. Somewhat hyperbolically, Calloway hailed a November 1961 gathering of the NALC as "perhaps the most important national meeting of Negro labor during the past half century." His exultation about the NALC reflected multiple considerations. It allowed him to strike back at an AFL-CIO hierarchy that had expelled his own union on corruption charges but refused to take similar action against unions that practiced racial separatism. And through an organization of black trade unionists, he could function from a cohesive operational base in his renewed effort to address the employment crisis facing the African American community.[41]

As president of the St. Louis NALC chapter, Calloway led local efforts in 1963 and 1964 to create voluntary "Fair Share of Jobs Covenants" as part of a national NALC campaign to increase African American employment in major private sector industries. The idea of negotiating "covenants" with employers appealed to Calloway, given its quasi-contractual overtones that resembled collective bargaining. Reminiscent of the NAACP Jobs Opportunity Council efforts several years earlier, the Fair Share of Jobs campaign revived the idea of creating a community bargaining table with some of St. Louis's most prominent employers, including telephone giant Southwestern Bell, the city's leading soft drink bottlers, and Lever Brothers, an international producer of soaps and detergents. Acknowledging black impatience over job segregation, Calloway promised to employ "militant, nonviolent mass pressure" to prompt "an aggressive but orderly transition to full and fair share employment." He also aimed to confront employers with a joint Negro-labor presence that would persuade them to participate in tripartite arrangements to open up more jobs for black St. Louisans while not upsetting traditional contractual arrangements. As he explained in a June 26, 1963, news release, "The creation of strong lines of communication among employers, unions, and the Negro community has been an integral part of NALC's program here."[42]

In the summer of 1963, Calloway blasted St. Louis employers for their "selective tokenism" in hiring African Americans, singling out Southwestern Bell's management for special criticism. His hope for labor support went unrealized, however, when the Communications Workers of America (CWA), the union that represented workers at Southwestern Bell, offered only tepid support for the campaign's demands. Calloway publicly called on CWA president Joseph Beirne to press the company to place black workers in skilled positions, expressing dismay that a "liberal" union like CWA appeared willing to condone Southwestern Bell's tokenism. After threatening picket lines and a consumer boycott, Calloway and Ted McNeal, who served as lead negotiators for NALC, canceled further direct action after receiving assurances that the company would begin to institute fairer employment practices. Although Calloway acknowledged the gap between official pronouncements and actual change on the shop floor, he told a packed July 19, 1963, NALC meeting that "we can now communicate instead of demonstrate," and hailed the prospect of continuing dialogue with top Southwestern Bell management.[43]

The soft drink industry, where Calloway had earlier worked to obtain jobs for African Americans as driver-salesmen, became the NALC's next target. The industry had an abysmal hiring record, employing only fifteen black driver-salesmen out of a total of 259 and placing no African Americans in clerical positions. Regarding employment practices in St. Louis's dairies, soda bottlers, and breweries, William Clay concluded, "Circumstantial evidence seems to be sufficient to convict both management and labor of economic murder of the Negro in the liquid refreshment business." Clay's charge of union complicity embarrassed Calloway and led him to seek a deal with the city's soft drink bottlers that would validate his strategy of joint Negro-labor mobilization to increase black employment. After three months of negotiations, he and Ted McNeal, along with Local 688 and the city's beverage firms, agreed on what Calloway called a "unique Voluntary Fair Employment Covenant." Covering eight companies and akin to a multi-employer union contract, the three-year agreement promised to review all management policies regarding hiring, training, upgrading, and promotion. However, some employers balked, claiming that the AFL-CIO union representing some bottling employees was not on board, while others feared that civil rights organizations that were not signatories might attempt to undermine the agreement. After the industry-wide pact fell through, Calloway was forced to seek individual agreements with employers, an arrangement that fell well short of the binding covenants he had hoped to fashion.[44]

In another anti-discrimination foray, Calloway allied himself with the NAACP in an effort to create a Fair Share of Jobs Covenant with Lever Brothers. Officially launched in December 1963, the campaign sought a national agreement to raise black employment at the company, whose hiring record at its St. Louis County plant (seven African Americans out of over 350 total employees) underscored Lever's racial exclusivity. The company agreed to increase black employment in St. Louis to twenty-two workers but balked at establishing a national policy to integrate its ranks. This blatant tokenism angered Calloway, who in April 1964 rejected the company's offer, charging that "to approach this problem of equal employment opportunity in such a massive national firm from a piecemeal local isolated point of view . . . can only contribute to continuing economic irritation within the Negro community." Increasingly frustrated by the intransigence of employers, Calloway adopted a more militant approach. Along with the NAACP, he announced plans to promote "selective buying campaigns" in a ten-state area, an action that prompted the company's personnel director to complain to national NAACP executive director Roy Wilkins. More symbolically, in a successor publication to *New Citizen* called *Truth*, Calloway captioned a photograph of a May 1964 NAACP-Lever Brothers' meeting as "Confrontation: NAACP Rejects Contained Approach to Job Problem." Ironically, the "confrontation" pictured Calloway and other NAACP leaders meeting with Lever officials in a corporate boardroom, an image that only reinforced criticism of his tactical approach.[45]

Calloway did not confine his campaign for tripartite covenants to the private sector. In the summer of 1963, he actively lobbied Raymond Tucker to bring together leaders from the business, labor, and black communities to address the city's employment crisis. Calloway joined other participants in describing the mood of black St. Louisans as "explosive" and implored Tucker to bring to the table "those who run the community economically." Given this mood, he hoped that the business leaders would view black employment as "a cold self-interest economic problem" that required their immediate attention. Tucker did establish the St. Louis Commission on Equal Employment Opportunity in July 1963, and Calloway hailed it as a promising move toward genuine "communication and partnership" between business, labor, and African American leaders. In the fall of 1963, facing more aggressive black protest, Tucker announced a nine-point program for fair employment. However, the reaction of Donald Danforth, a leading member of Civic Progress and one of the city's most influential businessmen, illuminated the attitude of "those who ran the community economically" and suggested that Calloway had underestimated the persuasiveness of "cold self-interest": "The 9 points may go a little further than many businessmen would have been willing to go a few years ago . . . but it should be remembered they do not go as far as many Negroes think they should."[46]

Meanwhile, the mainstream white union movement in St. Louis rejected Calloway's overtures to support the quest for workplace desegregation. Stung by his public criticism of the Communications Workers during the Southwestern Bell campaign, the St. Louis Labor Council denounced the "self-appointed Negro

Labor Council that seeks to inject itself into the collective bargaining process." The labor council went on to allege that "the absence of common courtesies in its failure or refusal to recognize collective bargaining can only add confusion to a serious and vexing problem."[47]

Calloway's preference for top-down agreements devoid of popular involvement prompted harsh criticism from some African American critics, including sardonic cartoons in the black press suggesting that he and Ted McNeal had been bought off by "Bell payola." By the middle of 1964, it was clear that Calloway's vision of a "new formula that removes government as a horizontal force and brings the three primary forces (African Americans, labor, and management) into direct and continuing communication" had failed to energize blacks, win over white-led unions, or convince management that it had vital interests in pursuing a racially integrated workplace. And in contrast to the working-class citizenship that had animated his strategy as St. Louis NAACP president, Calloway's connections to a mass constituency had grown attenuated, increasingly leaving him a general without an army. Indeed, the *St. Louis Defender* bluntly concluded that the Southwestern Bell campaign "ended the reign of gladiator Ernest Calloway as king-maker and string puller in the Sepia community."[48]

Discouraged by these setbacks, Calloway began to question the fair employment approach that had long guided African American attempts to open up racially restricted labor markets. In an October 1963 speech, he observed that in an economy where technological change was rapidly eliminating semi-skilled and unskilled jobs, the "FEPC approach" was using "salve to cure a cancer," only resulting in "the distribution of the restricted number of meaningful jobs available." Recognizing the limits of local efforts, Calloway asserted that the African American employment crisis could only be addressed by aggressive federal intervention. Specifically, he recommended that the creation of a massive public works program, the establishment of a "Division of Technological Change" in the Department of Labor to study the effects of automation, and a full-scale effort to make the shorter work week a "civil rights demand." However, with the Teamsters' pariah status impeding his access to the political circles capable of advancing such reforms, Calloway had limited ability to move this ambitious agenda.[49]

Calloway's growing marginalization within the black freedom struggle became even more pronounced during a seminal event in St. Louis's civil rights history: a community-wide uprising against the employment policies of the Jefferson Bank and Trust Company. This fierce confrontation, which began in August 1963, stemmed from St. Louis CORE's efforts to open jobs to African Americans. Spurred by what historian Clarence Lang has called a "subculture of young dissidents," CORE began to adopt more militant tactics in pressuring St. Louis's employers. In 1963, it turned its focus to St. Louis's banks, which employed almost no blacks in white-collar positions despite benefiting from black support for bond issues that enriched their coffers. Jefferson Bank became CORE's primary target for a variety of reasons: it had numerous black customers, had previously employed black tellers, and summarily rejected CORE's demands while other local banks at least took modest steps to integrate their ranks.[50]

Determined to resist CORE's demands, Jefferson Bank's management obtained a restraining order barring "disruption" of its business. Just days after the March on Washington, a small group of young demonstrators entered the bank, prompting Judge Michael Scott to find nineteen CORE activists in contempt of court. In a move reminiscent of the naked collusion between the state and corporate interests that accompanied late nineteenth- and early twentieth-century labor conflicts, Judge Scott appointed Jefferson Bank's chief counsel, who was also the son-in-law of the bank president, to prosecute the demonstrators. After Scott sentenced the activists to fines and substantial jail terms, tensions quickly escalated. Among whites, a phalanx of political, business, civic, and media support united in defense of Jefferson Bank, denouncing CORE's violation of St. Louis's gradualist political culture that had spared the city from the racial confrontations erupting in less "enlightened" southern communities. In response, much of the black community rallied behind CORE and the jailed activists.[51]

Concerned about jeopardizing the relationships they had cultivated with the white establishment and uncomfortable with CORE's demand that the bank fulfill a job quota, organizations such as the NAACP and the Urban League publicly criticized the demonstrators' tactics. In a series of public remarks issued in October 1963, Calloway joined these critics. His qualms reflected a deep sense of personal and political disappointment that had been festering for several years. At the panel he had participated in following the March on Washington less than two months earlier, Calloway had hailed a "new sense of inter-organizational unity" and a "simple but magnificent lesson in unity of purpose" that were welcome developments after "too much organizational blood-letting and throat-cutting" in recent years. The interracial character of the march also buoyed Calloway, who saw it as an important counterweight to "the emergence of an aggressive black chauvinism" that in his view threatened to alienate vital white liberal and trade union allies. However, this spirit of organizational unity and interracial amity had evaporated in the intense polarization unleashed by the Jefferson Bank hostilities.[52]

Although he condemned Jefferson Bank as "a callous financial pariah in the St. Louis community," Calloway sharply questioned CORE's strategy. Smarting from the criticism he had received, Calloway denounced "the new young school of thought" and its "new mood of intransigence" which sought "unconditional surrender" from Jefferson Bank rather than accepting specific and limited gains. By demanding unconditional surrender, CORE had relinquished its opportunity to act "as a watchdog in the implementation of this broad employment compact." However, Calloway's attempt to adapt collective bargaining precepts to the struggle for racial justice misread the emotional temperature of the black community and the unwillingness of younger activists to take direction from their generational elders.[53]

In spite of these misgivings, Calloway declared that "the community must close ranks behind these sincere young people" and present an "object lesson in solidarity in the face of massive predatory power." In addition to pledging money to help pay court fines, he called on the city to withdraw its funds from Jefferson Bank. Calloway's pledge of support, however, failed to appease many elements in the black community, which had intensified its support for the demonstrators in response to the white power structure's implacable resistance. Noting the alliance that had formed between professionals, clergy, political leaders, and the black working class, CORE activist Gene Tournour recalled, "I think that's where Calloway missed the boat, these weren't really average neighborhood people.... It [the Jefferson Bank protest] really touched a deep nerve that I don't think anyone really predicted."[54]

An even more telling albeit implicit critique of Calloway's position on Jefferson Bank came from within his own ranks. In a piece titled "Negroes Won't Wait for 'Gift' of Rights" published in the July 5, 1963, issue of the *Missouri Teamster*, Harold Gibbons acknowledged what Calloway had underestimated: a new sense of urgency in the fight for racial justice: "Today, the White man's old counsel of gradualism stands exposed as a fraud." Presciently, Gibbons recognized that the Jefferson Bank confrontation represented a tectonic shift in the culture of race relations in St. Louis, challenging the standing of both the city's power elite and its labor liberals.[55]

After months of social strife, Jefferson Bank finally relented in March 1964 and hired African Americans, an action which other banks soon followed. For those who had participated in this epic struggle, their involvement became an eternal badge of honor. As Jake McCarthy observed, leaders like William Clay had enhanced their credentials in a fight that "has become a political gravy train in the Negro community." By not boarding this "train," Ernest Calloway suffered a blow to his stature from which he never fully recovered. In the aftermath of Jefferson Bank, Gene Tournour recalled that the "'Young Turks' would always want to totally minimize him, which was not a fair thing."[56]

Bloodied but unbowed, Calloway began to look for new ways to reassert himself in St. Louis's black freedom struggle. He found a ready ally in Harold Gibbons, who joined his old comrade in launching a bold initiative to re-establish the Teamsters' place at the forefront of social insurgency. This effort, which Calloway described as "a trade union oriented war on the slums," represented a renewed attempt to make total person unionism relevant by establishing a community bargaining table where the Teamsters would again occupy prominent seats.

CHAPTER 10

"A Trade Union Oriented War on the Slums"

On October 29, 1969, a press conference was held at city hall in St. Louis to announce the end of a nine-month-long rent strike by public housing tenants. The protracted strike had become what one prominent businessman described as a "damn explosive situation," threatening to plunge St. Louis into the social turmoil experienced in many other urban communities during the 1960s. The press conference brought together a set of strange bedfellows—striking public housing tenants, grassroots community activists, members of Civic Progress, religious and political leaders—unaccustomed to sharing a public platform. At the center of these proceedings stood Harold Gibbons, who at the request of St. Louis Mayor A.J. Cervantes had played an instrumental role in negotiating an end to the conflict. In addition to outlining the settlement of the strike, Gibbons announced the formation of the St. Louis Civic Alliance for Housing, a new entity that would help administer the city's public housing. Hailed by all sides for helping to avert potential civil disorder, Gibbons savored his transition from pariah to statesman and relished the opportunity to lead the kind of public-private partnership that he and Ernest Calloway had long sought to create in St. Louis. The establishment of the Civic Alliance for Housing vindicated Gibbons and Calloway's new foray into community action that they had unveiled several years earlier, allowing them to rejuvenate their vision of working-class citizenship, align themselves with the insurgent spirit of the 1960s, and counteract the deterioration of their adopted city.[1]

* * *

Before launching their new community initiative, Calloway and Gibbons each had an electoral experience—one actual, one contemplated, one countering an insurgency, the other attempting to mount one—that clarified their personal options and freed them to collaborate on their last major political project. Although Calloway had invested most of his political energy in the Negro American Labor Council, he retained his ties to the St. Louis NAACP. He continued to serve as vice president and advised branch president Evelyn Roberts, who had succeeded Margaret Bush Wilson as the organization's top official. In December 1964, Roberts's bid for re-election, along with that of Calloway, provoked spirited opposition from a slate headed by Pearlie Evans, a social worker and NAACP officer with connections to CORE, William Clay, and the Jefferson Bank protests. Evans was joined by Margaret Bush Wilson, who charged that under Roberts's leadership, the branch had "drifted aimlessly," lost its "rapport with [the] Negro community," and grown too dependent on downtown business interests for financial support. Repeating the familiar charge that Calloway was acting as a behind-the-scenes manipulator, Evans questioned Roberts's political independence, alleging that she had "permitted Teamster Ernest Calloway to speak for her" rather than exercising strong leadership in her own right.[2]

Beyond the questions raised about Roberts's leadership and Calloway's role, the NAACP election exacerbated fissures among African American leaders that had widened during the Jefferson Bank demonstrations and now threatened to rupture St. Louis's most venerable civil rights organization. These fault lines reflected long-festering class divisions, a growing impetus for African Americans to play a more assertive role in ward politics, and a continuing generational battle for organizational control of the black freedom struggle. Pearlie Evans's support among public housing tenants especially unsettled the NAACP's middle-class professional base, leading some opponents to disparage her as the "slum social worker bringing in her slum scum to the NAACP." Calloway echoed these concerns more obliquely, alluding to "the large group of public housing citizens" that had joined the branch just prior to the election. Without offering any evidence, he also resorted to red-baiting, seeking to discredit his opponents by claiming that "some Communists" had been present at the pre-election gathering. The election reflected heated political competition among African American leaders, with Margaret Bush Wilson and William Clay seeking to supplant incumbent black Democratic committee persons supported by Calloway and his allies. Moreover, the contest assumed a generational dimension, with Evans attracting support from younger activists eager to defy elder statesmen like Calloway and connect the NAACP with the militant mood that had marked the Jefferson Bank protests.[3]

In Calloway's view the opposition to Roberts and him amounted to a coalition of expediency animated by the insurgents' desire to take over the "one community organization they could not influence" and involve the NAACP more explicitly in partisan politics. After Evans narrowly won the election and Calloway tied with his opponent, she alleged multiple irregularities in the voting process, prompting Calloway and Roberts to issue their own complaints about the conduct of the election. After several recounts, threats of lawsuits, and continuing allegations of election fraud, the national NAACP declared Roberts and Calloway the winners. For Calloway, however, the victory proved pyrrhic. His refusal to abide by the initial election result led many of his opponents to conclude that his need to retain organizational control transcended his commitment to democracy. His charge that his rivals wanted to submerge the NAACP in the morass of partisan politics also lacked credence, given his own connections to Jack Dwyer and his extensive public activity on behalf of Raymond Tucker's unsuccessful campaign to gain re-election. In the aftermath of the divisive 1964 election, the NAACP failed to recapture the stature it had attained less than a decade earlier under Calloway's leadership, with more militant, nationalist voices drowning out the gradual, integrationist approach of older civil rights organizations. As a leader with a dwindling flock of followers, Calloway drifted even farther to the margins of civil rights politics in St. Louis following the NAACP election fracas.[4]

A year later, in the summer of 1966, Harold Gibbons faced his own electoral quandary. In 1964, after years of relentless pursuit by the Justice Department, Jimmy Hoffa's string of acquittals ended when in separate cases he was found guilty of jury tampering, conspiracy, and mail fraud. Although Gibbons authored an executive board resolution that supported Hoffa remaining as Teamsters' president during the appeals process, he also sensed a political opening. Publicly declaring he would not run unless the position was vacant, he quietly began to solicit support for a presidential bid. Gibbons's platform, which he titled "Shared Responsibility and Joint Leadership," explicitly criticized Hoffa's administration of the union and offered multiple recommendations to transform the Teamsters' organizational culture. While acknowledging that the "growing complexities of ... economic society" required "strong central organization," Gibbons concluded that under Hoffa, this imperative had morphed into "one-man rule" and proposed a series of steps to create a "more democratic union." Under what he described as a new system based on "shared responsibility," Gibbons aimed to encourage greater involvement in decision-making by allowing "every local union and every officer at the joint council, area conference, and trade divisions level" to assume an "important role in determining the policies of this International Union."[5]

Gibbons's plan allocated additional resources for organizing, with a particular focus on recruiting public employees and white-collar workers. Extending an olive branch that was anathema to Hoffa, he declared his willingness to re-affiliate with the AFL-CIO and develop mutual assistance pacts with other unions. Not surprisingly, Gibbons's platform also included the establishment of a "long overdue" national education program, the "expansion" and "improvement" of political action under DRIVE, and creation of a national community services department "to develop liaisons with organizations and groups whose aim is to build a better life for all the people." The thrust of Gibbons's proposals underscored that although he had submerged his commitment to a participatory, socially oriented unionism during his association with Hoffa, he intended to reassert these convictions as the new Teamsters' president. Of course, whether this ambitious agenda could pass muster within the confines of the Teamsters' quasi-feudal, mob-influenced culture remained uncertain. Still, Gibbons found support for his proposed run, including praise from the leader of a New Jersey local who welcomed Gibbons's "democratic manner" and declared that "the time is long past for the big muscle boys and dictators in our union."[6]

When the Supreme Court agreed to hear his appeal of the jury tampering conviction, the embattled Hoffa seized this reprieve to consolidate his hold on the union presidency. He undercut Gibbons by creating a new position of general vice-president whose occupant would automatically become president in the event the incumbent could no longer serve. Then, in a move he later characterized as one of his "worst mistakes," Hoffa tapped Frank Fitzsimmons, a lackluster Detroit Teamster whose primary virtue was his fealty to the Teamsters' president, to assume the new position. Fearing Gibbons would chafe at serving in a caretaker's role, Hoffa calculated that through the more pliant Fitzsimmons, he could continue to run the union from prison and resume the presidency once he gained parole. Bitterly disappointed, Gibbons contemplated opposing Fitzsimmons at the union's upcoming convention but ultimately backed away, deterred by the delegates' deference to Hoffa and the prospect that he would relinquish his vice-president's position should his challenge fail. Hoffa attempted to soften the blow by appointing Gibbons acting director of the powerful Central Conference of Teamsters following the Supreme Court's rejection of his appeal and director of the union's airlines, sports, and paper divisions. However, these consolation prizes did little to assuage Gibbons's profound sense of disappointment and rejection. Although he remained involved in national union affairs, he shifted most of his creative energy to St. Louis as his social laboratory for extending the reach of total person unionism.[7]

In numerous public talks and articles during the mid-1960s, Gibbons and Calloway reflected on the union movement's shortcomings as they contemplated their next moves. Their analysis showed a keen awareness of what a coterie of activists and intellectuals described as the "Triple Revolution": automation's transformative impact on production and employment, the advent of new forms of weaponry that threatened human survival, and "a universal demand for full human rights" exemplified by the civil rights movement. Gibbons and Calloway suggested that this phenomenon presented an unprecedented set of challenges requiring the union movement to reorient itself in fundamental ways.[8]

Both men, who had hailed collective bargaining as a "passport to human dignity and functional freedom" just a decade earlier, now acknowledged its inadequacies. Calloway lamented that "the modern collective bargaining agreement [had become] a wordy document of intellectual stress and strain smothered in a dead language that no one understands," a result he attributed to labor's growing reliance on legalistic mechanisms in the wake of Taft-Hartley and Landrum-Griffin. Nostalgically, Calloway recalled the simpler documents of his early CIO years when "the language of the contract smelled of sweat, tears, and hope from the workbench." However, neither he nor Gibbons expected those days to return.

The ebullient faith they had previously expressed in the expansive possibilities of collective bargaining had now been replaced by a rueful recognition of its limitations.[9]

In the arenas of organizing and political action, Gibbons and Calloway questioned existing union practice. They concluded that unions had reached a "stagnant plateau" in recruitment, marked by an inability to access the growing white collar and service sectors that had sprung up as unskilled and semi-skilled jobs were being automated out of existence. They repeated their long-standing accusation that labor's approach to political action remained anchored in a narrow "reward your friends and punish your enemies" paradigm rather than pursuing "aggressive independent political action" and the pursuit of broader social goals. Perhaps most importantly, they deplored labor's lack of "moral stamina" and the prospect of its "becoming just another institution in society" by virtue of forgetting its past struggles and traditions. As Gibbons told the March 15, 1965, St. Louis Conference on Race and Religion, labor's emphasis on material gains had led it to "neglect a deeper and more abiding concern about the spiritual and moral values of this society we live in."[10]

To counteract labor's accelerating decline and diminished vitality, Gibbons advocated outreach to the unemployed and the growing white collar and service sectors, along with the mobilization of a broad political coalition to support the black freedom struggle, revitalize the city, and address the job displacement unleashed by automation. However, given the difficulties Calloway had experienced in navigating the turbulence of racial politics in St. Louis and the distrust many political insurgents displayed toward the union movement and especially the Teamsters, he and Gibbons faced formidable barriers in their quest to create a coalition of conscience. Moreover, Gibbons and Calloway's prescriptions about political action remained vague. Beyond advocating a more independent, class-oriented stance for labor, they offered few specifics on what form this type of politics should assume.[11]

In their initial search for a vehicle to reinvigorate Local 688's civic involvement, Gibbons and Calloway returned to an idea that had long intrigued them: the creation of union-management civic partnerships to jump-start St. Louis's revitalization. Both remained convinced that any viable effort to stem urban deterioration required substantial infusions of private capital to augment limited resources dispensed by the state. By the mid-1960s, Gibbons and Calloway reintroduced the notion of the community bargaining table armed with fresh evidence of their expertise and reliability as civic partners. The successful completion of the first Council Plaza complex won widespread community acclaim, firmly establishing Local 688's commitment to socially responsible urban revitalization. Gibbons and Calloway also pointed to the union's support for bond issues aimed at civic improvement, its extensive fundraising on behalf of local charities, and its overall leadership in promoting the "general welfare and prosperity of the community."[12]

Gibbons had also upgraded the Teamsters' image in St. Louis with his work on behalf of local charities, using entertainment extravaganzas as a fundraising vehicle. Beginning with a 1955 benefit for the Polio Foundation that raised $10,000, his shows became more elaborate and lucrative, drawing on his celebrity connections to bring nationally recognized entertainers to St. Louis. His crowning achievement occurred at a June 1965 benefit for Dismas House, a renowned St. Louis program begun by a local Jesuit priest that helped rehabilitate convicted felons. After opening remarks by Gibbons, "Tonight" show host Johnny Carson emceed the event before a packed house at St. Louis's storied Kiel Auditorium Opera House, with accompanying transmissions to theaters across the nation. Gibbons convinced his friend Frank Sinatra to headline the show, which also featured performances by fellow Rat Pack members Dean Martin and Sammy Davis, Jr. Beyond the star power he attracted, the money he raised, and the public relations value of his charitable work, Gibbons took considerable pride in coordinating these events himself rather than hiring a promoter, yet another example of his relentless desire to demonstrate working-class prowess in an arena typically dominated by business professionals.[13]

Seeking to capitalize on this newfound respectability, Gibbons turned to Calloway for strategic advice. In a September 1966 memo, Calloway outlined several possible arenas for labor-management cooperation: attracting new industry and investment, spurring greater city-county coordination, reducing poverty, and improving race relations. A month later, Calloway warned that if business, labor, and civil rights leaders could not overcome St. Louis's historic inertia and come together to address these structural challenges, the city was on a "collision course with urban dry-rot." Yet in spite of Calloway's warning and Gibbons's concerted public campaign to create a formal labor-management civic partnership, they found no takers. Most of the city's business elite distrusted Gibbons's ultimate intentions and remained as eager to retain management "rights" in the social sphere as they had been on the shop floor. Equally important, Gibbons and Calloway lacked the leverage they had been poised to exercise following the defeat of charter reform. Without Local 688 applying concerted pressure from below, St. Louis's power brokers lacked the incentive to enter a compact with the Teamsters and accept seats at the community bargaining table.[14]

In 1967, after failing to win business support for a civic partnership, Gibbons and Calloway created their own vehicle to promote urban revitalization: a nonprofit foundation called America 2000. America 2000 was to be funded by employer contributions and serve as a private, non-profit instrument that in Gibbons's words would "fill the gap between what the federal government is doing [to counter poverty and rebuild cities] and what private industry is capable of producing." Drawing on the Teamsters' earlier success, Gibbons and Calloway looked to the arena of housing and urban redevelopment where they hoped to replicate the Council Plaza concept on a grander scale. Underscoring their commitment to uplift all segments of the working class, he and Calloway indicated that America 2000 would also reach out to the "forgotten American who is over-income for federal subsidies and just under-income for the projects developed by private capital." They also sought to revive the insurgent spirit of the community stewards program, declaring their willingness to aid the hard-core unemployed and other workers displaced by automation by "represent[ing] them in organized fashion as to what demands can be made on [the] city, government, etc."[15]

Steeped in the protocols of St. Louis's cautious political culture, the city bureaucracy responded unenthusiastically to Gibbons and Calloway's entreaties. Robert Jones, director of the City Planning Commission on which Calloway served, rejected America 2000's initial requests to help craft St. Louis's Community Renewal program. In spite of support from Reverend Lucius Cervantes, the mayor's brother and trusted adviser in developing city social welfare policy, Jones's view prevailed. America 2000's ambitious proposal to redevelop a broad swath of St. Louis's deteriorating riverfront met a similar fate. The city's rejection of America 2000's plan made one thing unmistakably clear. Like other members of St. Louis's power elite, city officials were prepared to disregard Local 688's demonstrated public housing expertise rather than approve an arrangement with the Teamsters that might limit their authority to determine urban redevelopment policy.[16]

While Gibbons and he experienced frustration in their efforts to win support for high-level civic partnerships, Calloway began to conceptualize a grassroots effort to attack urban decline that would reinsert total person unionism into Local 688's political practice. In numerous *Missouri Teamster* columns and in a series of public addresses, Calloway painstakingly documented how the continuing deterioration of St. Louis's social, economic, and civic infrastructure was degrading African American lives. In keeping with his commitment to address the class and racial fault lines that made the city a "prime victim of [an] America in deep transition," Calloway chaired the child welfare advisory committee of the state welfare office, served on the City Plan Commission of St. Louis, and was a board member of the local Human Development Corporation (HDC), the principal entity responsible for overseeing the Johnson administration's War on Poverty in St. Louis. Lacking a secure leadership perch in a civil rights organization given the atrophy of the NALC and the NAACP, he used involvement in these public entities as new operational bases from which to articulate his prescriptions for urban revitalization.[17]

Initially, Calloway had been attracted to the War on Poverty's encouragement of "maximum feasible participation" by poor people in determining its policies. However, he quickly became disillusioned, charging that the program had been "diverted from the "ferment of social change" into "a self-help exercise" that aimed to 'contain the 'poor' . . . without disturbing traditional economic and political balances in the urban complex." Rejecting what he regarded as the implicit condescension of the culture of poverty argument that had become voguish in many policy circles, Calloway remained an unrepentant economic structuralist, insisting "there is nothing like sufficient income in our competitive society to improve motivation, work habits, [and] the desire to upgrade one's education and productive potential." Coupled with this critique, Calloway bemoaned the latest incarnation of ward politics in St. Louis, charging that a "new succession of white overlords and city political machines" had co-opted the transformational possibilities of black electoral power by providing limited patronage benefits while doing little to alter the economic foundations of racial inequality. And as a committed interracialist, Calloway was particularly troubled by the politics of new local organizations such as the Black Liberators and the Zulu 1200's, whose separatist orientation and revolutionary rhetoric were antithetical to the trade union pragmatism and democratic socialism that remained his political compasses.[18]

Calloway's denunciations of "poverty professionals," black politicians, and Black Power advocates signaled his desire to find political space for the voices of African American trade unionists. To create this space, Calloway returned to the more secure footing of his base in Local 688, whose African American membership now constituted nearly 25 percent of the union's total membership. He proposed to take "trade union principles to the community at large" by launching what he called "a trade union oriented war on the slums." Calloway's war on poverty sought to meld the discipline and strategic acumen of black trade unionists with the energy and passion of local insurgents to help focus their protest and meet "the essential needs of the great mass of dispossessed, stakeless Negroes." Over the course of 1965 and 1966, he developed a proposal to address deteriorating conditions in Tandy, a largely African American neighborhood in north St. Louis with some 30,000 residents, 4,300 dilapidated dwellings, and 6,450 homes in need of repair. If these conditions were left unaddressed, Calloway feared that Tandy might be consumed by civil disorder. Although the Tandy project explicitly aimed to strike at the structures that maintained racial inequality and white privilege, Calloway made it his business to explain to the union's white members, many of whom had migrated to the suburbs, why a trade union oriented war on the slums was in their interest. At a March 1966 stewards council meeting, he argued that all members of Local 688 had a stake in Tandy's revitalization, asserting that ". . . the only way to keep our city and suburbs safe and decent for people to live in is to start at the root of the problem and 688 plans to work in this area."[19]

Nearly 500 African-American members of Local 688, including Calloway, lived in Tandy or adjacent neighborhoods, providing the union with an indigenous base for establishing what came to be known as the Tandy Area Council (TAC). Reviving the notions of working-class citizenship that had animated the community stewards program a decade earlier, Calloway explained that "the social notion [of the Tandy Area Council] is to relate the articulate group-interest thrust the Negro trade unionist has obtained during the eight hour period where he works to the sixteen hour period in the community where he lives." Acknowledging that TAC's support for grassroots agitation would inevitably assume political overtones, Calloway insisted that it forego the temptation to become involved in the machinations of ward politics and instead be guided by the priorities identified by community residents. More broadly, Calloway and Gibbons believed that TAC would revive Local 688's social standing by fostering "the kind of union activity which built labor's reputation as the defender of all working people in the community as well as on the job."[20]

In launching Tandy, Gibbons and Calloway decided to tap new sources of leadership to find activists who would have credibility in the community and revive working-class citizenship in Local 688. Jim Pace, who in 1966 became Local 688's director of community organizing and political education, was an ordained Methodist minister who had spent nearly a decade working in rural community development in Bolivia. Gibbons hired Mike Ryan, an adult educator and anti-poverty worker, to help fashion an educational program to support the project. Recognizing the need for African Americans to play a prominent role in shaping Tandy, the union selected two respected black staff members, Claude Brown and Levi Sanford, both of whom became vitally involved in its operation.[21]

Gibbons and Calloway also recruited some talented rank-and-file members who proved especially adept at helping TAC gain community acceptance. Frank Boykin and Leroy Graham, African-American Local 688 members who worked at United Parcel Service and Royal Crown Cola, respectively, had close ties to black youth in housing projects and street-level activists that in an increasingly polarized racial environment would have been difficult for Tandy's white staff to cultivate. TAC also benefited from the union's association with a prominent local activist named Ivory Perry, whom Mike Ryan had worked with during his tenure at the city's anti-poverty program. At a time when many civil rights activists and community insurgents were shunning contact with institutions they perceived as dominated by whites, Perry's involvement paid immediate dividends for Local 688's new initiative. "Perry is such a respected man among the Negro poor," Pace explained, "that just to have him allied and associated with TAC helps us. [He is] a very good man to have on our side."[22]

Similar to the approach taken at the inception of the community stewards program, Local 688 activists canvassed the Tandy neighborhood to solicit grievances from local residents. As Jim Pace later recalled, he gave Gibbons "a dose of Saul Alinsky" in positioning Tandy as "a hard-hitting organization geared to confrontation." By confronting the problems Tandy residents faced as "both citizens and consumers," TAC aimed "to combat the powerful organizations and forces pressing down upon us" by providing "a voice to the voiceless" and "add[ing] power to voices before unheard." Over the next two years, TAC sustained this commitment, aligning itself with local insurgents, confronting unresponsive authorities, and developing bargaining relationships where Local 688 organizers could employ their expertise and flex their political muscle.[23]

Richard Baron, a lawyer who worked closely with Gibbons during the public housing tenants' rent strike, described Tandy as "just an extension of the same things he had been concerned about for his entire career, an effort to really try to get the disenfranchised organized." After surveys found that grocery stores charged Tandy residents higher prices than those paid by consumers in affluent white suburbs, the organization picketed local supermarkets and obtained price reductions. Through the community connections of Frank Boykin and Leroy Graham, Tandy became intimately involved with the emerging welfare rights movement. Boykin and Graham used their trade union experience to confront state welfare officials and negotiate agreements that won higher payments, lowered food stamp prices, and forced the state to inform welfare recipients of their rights. As evidence of their success, the League for Adequate Welfare designated Tandy as its representative in dealing with local welfare officials, granting Local 688 the kind of bargaining status that it hoped to transfer from the shop floor to the community.[24]

Tandy also mobilized the neighborhood on the basis of racial oppression, lobbying the city to hire more African-American firefighters, pressing to get African-American history taught more effectively in the schools, and challenging the police force's treatment of black citizens. Bringing trade union heft to the community bargaining table, in the spring of 1968, Mike Ryan and other TAC members joined with the Black United Front, a loose alliance of militant freedom struggle activists, to present Mayor A.J. Cervantes with demands to open city employment to blacks. These activities helped to establish TAC's credibility in the neighborhood, supporting Calloway's conviction that "the community level, like the local union level, demands practical 'bread and butter' progress." With protest and politics now closely linked, Tandy leaders saw each specific community victory paving the way for a sharper assault on the structural economic conditions most responsible for racial and social inequality.[25]

TAC's war on the slums gained additional momentum following the convergence of two events: the formation of the Alliance for Labor Action (ALA) in July 1968 and subsequent efforts to support the growing movement for tenants' rights. The ALA resulted from a shotgun wedding between the Teamsters and the United Auto Workers (UAW). Seeking greater respectability in the wake of Jimmy Hoffa's imprisonment and continuing charges of mob domination, Teamsters' leader Frank Fitzsimmons agreed to an alliance with Walter Reuther, the peripatetic UAW president who had left the AFL-CIO to protest what he regarded as the federation's inertia. ALA sought to combine the resources of two of the nation's largest unions in an ambitious crusade to pursue new organizing drives, attack urban blight, and align labor with the working poor and the unemployed.

Although many in the UAW hierarchy doubted Fitzsimmons's intentions, they were heartened when Harold Gibbons assumed a major role in launching the new alliance. Gibbons and Reuther had long admired each other and welcomed the prospect of collaborating to make their unions more relevant social actors.[26]

When Reuther died in a 1970 plane crash, the project lost its principal champion within the UAW, and most Teamsters' affiliates refused to participate in a program whose social vision they did not share. However, in St. Louis, activists from the UAW and the Teamsters forged a close working relationship that extended Tandy's outreach to local insurgencies. Talented UAW activists such as Leonard Robinson, who led a black caucus at the St. Louis Ford plant, and Jerry Tucker, a white union leader in a carburetor factory located in the Tandy neighborhood, eagerly embraced ALA. Describing Gibbons as a "very progressive unionist," Robinson recalled that "many of us thought of him as an auto worker." Tucker described the Reuther-Gibbons collaboration as a "brief, shining moment" in which ALA pumped considerable resources into St. Louis and made the community bargaining table an operative concept, especially in the contentious arena of landlord-tenant relations.[27]

With support from the ALA and TAC, tenants pressed landlords to repair their apartments, lobbied city officials to punish delinquent landlords, and sought to condemn buildings they deemed unfit for habitation. Leonard Robinson mobilized support from the Association of Black Collegians, a militant group of community college students who staffed picket lines and served as the shock troops for pressuring landlords and city authorities to upgrade housing conditions. TAC unabashedly attempted to legitimize tenant activism by describing it in trade union terms: "If workingmen have been able to fight the boss on the job by having a strong union, why can't the same be done against the 'boss' landlord?" Indeed, in what organizers described as "the first attempt to establish formal bargaining rights between tenants and private housing in the history of St. Louis private housing," TAC sought to gain recognition as the official "bargaining agent" for fifty tenants. TAC went even further in its efforts to gain acceptance for the community bargaining table by attempting to negotiate a "Wagner Act" with landlords that would govern their relations with tenants. Spurred by visible UAW-Teamster collaboration, the ALA and TAC attained a level of legitimacy in St. Louis that often eluded unions entering the crucible of inner city politics during the late 1960s.[28]

TAC and Local 688 gained additional credibility with African American insurgents in the fall of 1968 when Harold Gibbons responded forcefully to allegations that St. Louis police had assaulted leaders of the militant Black Liberators' group whom they held in custody. At a September 15, 1968, rally, Gibbons made clear that his early CIO experience remained deeply etched in his memory: "We in the labor movement have experienced the police club through the years, and I was beaten in the streets of Chicago and Louisville in the 30s and 40s." Openly linking Teamster power to supporting the citizenship rights of black insurgents, Gibbons challenged the city's political establishment to take control of the police and establish a civilian review board. As one of the few St. Louis labor leaders to speak out against police attacks on black insurgents, Gibbons's bold public pronouncements boosted the union's image in the black community and helped attract broader support for the Tandy Area Council's initiatives.[29]

Amid TAC's gaining social traction, Calloway launched a new effort to regain his personal standing as the preeminent leader of black St. Louisans: a bid for an area congressional seat in 1968. When the white incumbent congressman decided to step down after the Missouri legislature reapportioned the district to encompass a black majority, a crowded field of contenders emerged. Calloway's decision to make his first run for public office reflected multiple, overlapping motives. In collaboration with his wife Deverne, he had led the Committee on Fair Representation that devised the reapportionment plan and undoubtedly felt some measure of entitlement to the new congressional seat. In declaring his candidacy, Calloway offered another rationale for entering the race: his concern for the "self-defeating trend to write the American city off as a force for creative urban living and endeavor." He also could not resist the opportunity for a return match with his old rival William Clay, who had announced his candidacy prior to Calloway. Not surprisingly, the campaign rhetoric between Calloway and Clay quickly became superheated. Clay repeated his familiar charges of Teamsters' hypocrisy on racial matters and accused Gibbons of ordering Calloway to remain in the race in a "deliberate attempt to split the black vote" among several African Americans vying for the congressional seat. Calloway responded with equal vitriol, describing himself in one campaign ad as "The Man the Political Uncle Toms Must Destroy. Because He Walks Alone in Freedom and Self-Respect With No White Politician's Collar Around His Neck."[30]

Although both Calloway and Clay ran on similar left-liberal Democratic platforms, there were important distinctions in the arguments they made to voters. Calloway proposed a massive public works program to attack hard-core unemployment, the creation of neighborhood development corporations that encouraged maximum participation of the poor, and the pursuit of integrated tax policies to ensure a fairer distribution of resources. With his customary flair, Clay called for a sharp hike in the minimum wage, a thirty-five hour work week, and lowering the eligibility age for receiving full Social Security benefits. While Clay's proposals and his rhetoric appealed directly to the black poor and working class, Calloway took a more interracial approach with his emphasis on public works and structural changes in tax policy, along with his mobilization of a committee "to develop a large vote of whites" to support his candidacy.[31]

Clay undermined Calloway's campaign through his superior precinct-level organization and his adroit maneuvering within the corridors of St. Louis ward politics. After efforts by black community leaders to unify behind a single African American candidate succeeding in winnowing the field, Clay persuaded several black committeemen to rescind their previous support for Calloway. The most telling blow came at the hands of what Calloway called the "Syrian-Steamfitter factor," the alliance of ethnic ward leaders and the politically powerful Steamfitters Union. After reading press reports in which Harold Gibbons had predicted an easy win for Calloway, Lawrence Callanan, the hyper-competitive Steamfitters' leader with whom Gibbons enjoyed a civil but fierce rivalry, made his union's ample campaign treasury available to William Clay. This move torpedoed Calloway's candidacy. Spurred by his superior campaign organization, his charisma on the stump, and the infusion of Steamfitters' cash, Clay crushed Calloway in the August 1968 primary by a 4 to 1 margin. He then cruised to a general election victory to become St. Louis's first African American congressman and the black community's undisputed political leader.[32]

Although Calloway avoided public reflection on his defeat, Jake McCarthy later observed that William Clay's effort to "label ... Calloway an Uncle Tom" wounded him deeply and "damn near killed him." For Calloway, Clay's decisive victory represented the triumph of ward parochialism, the repudiation of an interracial, class-oriented approach to civil rights politics, and his inability to shake the impression that he was subservient to the Teamsters and Harold Gibbons. The ineluctable power of the ward political system and William Clay's more accurate feel for the pulse of the black community trumped Calloway's policy-oriented prescriptions for African American progress. The loss also marked an irrevocable setback in Calloway's personal quest to re-emerge as a recognized leader of the black freedom struggle in St. Louis.[33]

Early in 1969, however, Calloway rebounded from his disappointment when he, Harold Gibbons, and TAC became involved in a local struggle that gained national attention: a contentious rent strike staged by the city's public housing tenants. The rent strike was precipitated by a convergence of events. Initially, St. Louis's public housing had consisted of low-rise, relatively small units. However, pressure to contain costs while locating black St. Louisans displaced by urban renewal in segregated spaces led to the creation of much larger high-rise apartments, typically in areas distant from vital institutions and services. The most prominent of these were the massive Pruitt and Igoe complexes, located just northwest of downtown St. Louis in the bulldozed Mill Creek area. With the burden of covering operating costs left to local treasuries, the St. Louis Housing Authority (SLHA) had to rely on rental income to fund the maintenance of public housing which, due to shoddy construction, quickly began to deteriorate. At the same time the statutory requirement that 20 percent of adjusted income for tenants had to go to toward rent prompted better paid residents to depart. As strike leader Jean King later observed, public housing had now become "last resort housing for the poorest of the poor, not a community."[34]

When a beleaguered housing authority sought to raise rents, tenants launched a strike in February 1969 to protest its action. Although tenants in privately owned housing had frequently withheld rent to protest their landlords' inattention, St.

Louis's rent strikers gained the distinction of waging the first public housing rent strike in U.S. history. The strikers possessed several vital assets that sustained them in their lengthy fight. They had a cohort of capable leaders with deep roots in St. Louis's black freedom movement. The strikers also benefitted from the strategic acumen of Richard Baron, a young Legal Aid attorney who stymied the housing authority's efforts to evict tenants for non-payment of rent. Although most of the city's African American political leaders (recently elected Congressman William Clay was a notable exception) and mainstream civil rights organizations maintained their distance from this unpredictable group of activists, Black Power groups strongly supported the strikers, and the respected community organizer Ivory Perry mobilized direct action events on their behalf. The strikers also attracted sympathy from church and community leaders disturbed by the deplorable conditions in public housing and the city's desultory response to the tenants' demands.[35]

Angered by what one analyst called the "listless temporizing" of political leaders and buoyed by the public support they were receiving, the tenants expanded their initial demands for a rollback in rent increases to include a comprehensive restructuring of public housing. As the strike continued into the summer, city leaders began to fear the outbreak of violence. Rising public anxiety and vacillating political leadership created a vacuum that presented Gibbons, Calloway, and Local 688 an opportunity to assist what Calloway described as "a sophisticated confrontation with national policy" that could replace the paternalism of antipoverty "pacification bureaucrats" with the "creative self-determinism" of genuine grassroots leadership.[36]

As the rent strike unfolded, the Teamsters developed strong connections to the tenants through Tandy Area Council organizers Frank Boykin and Leroy Graham. Early on, Boykin championed the idea that tenants should have seats on the Housing Authority's board of commissioners, underscoring TAC's commitment to promote effective social citizenship for the disenfranchised. Local 688 also provided the strikers with funding and meeting facilities, and Jake McCarthy called for "community-wide action" to settle the conflict at a heated June 9, 1969, public meeting attended by Mayor Cervantes. Two days later, this encounter prompted the besieged mayor to seek Gibbons's involvement, requesting that the Teamster leader chair a committee to raise private funds to help subsidize rent payments. Cervantes, who as owner of a local taxi company had long dealt with Gibbons at the bargaining table, looked to the one-time social pariah to help rescue the city from a situation that threatened to spiral out of control.[37]

Gibbons initially rejected Cervantes's invitation. He recognized that private funds would be insufficient to address the gravity of the problem and remained unconvinced that the mayor grasped the strikers' demand to be taken seriously as functional citizens. However, after rent strike leaders approached Gibbons in August 1969 and explained their vision for a strong tenant role in public housing management, he warmed to the idea of becoming involved. Local 688's record on civil rights, the activities of TAC, and his understanding of the alienation of poor people made Gibbons one of the few white community leaders that the tenants could trust. As strike leader Jean King explained to her constituents, "[Gibbons believes] housing projects must be made into communities that people will want to live in and be a part of.... Nothing is going to take place in public housing through Mr. Gibbons that the *striking* tenants do not want. If you know anything at all about Mr. Gibbons, you know he *will* get the job done."[38]

Gibbons and Calloway now began to see the rent strike as a defining event for their trade union oriented war on the slums, enabling them to erect a community bargaining table where disenfranchised citizens occupied ringside seats. Gibbons's hand was strengthened by strong support from the Department of Housing and Urban Development (HUD), which in 1967 had lent Local 688 money to help build its second Council Plaza complex. George Romney, a former Michigan governor who had become HUD secretary in the Nixon administration, had praised Council Plaza during his 1968 presidential campaign and recalled the Teamsters' housing expertise as the rent strike controversy reached HUD's doorstep. Dissatisfied with the SLHA's performance, HUD sent a special panel to St. Louis in July 1969 to assess the city's public housing program. In a July 31, 1969, letter to Mayor Cervantes, HUD official Edgar Ewing reported, "The Special Panel is impressed with the expertise which has been shown in the discussions held with representatives of the Teamsters Union" and asked that "full consideration be given to the possibility that the management and operation of the total housing program be turned over to the Teamsters Union." Emboldened by this endorsement, Gibbons insisted on and received the mayor's approval to negotiate as he saw fit. He then began the arduous task of uniting top business and community leaders behind a proposed settlement that would create a civic partnership to oversee public housing in St. Louis and grant tenants a substantive voice in managing their complexes.[39]

As Gibbons became publicly involved in attempting to settle the strike, he and Calloway sought to convince Local 688's rank and file that the rent strike represented a natural extension of the union's historic commitments to working-class citizenship and total person unionism. Likening the struggles of the rent strikers to those of labor a generation earlier, they declared their willingness to use "the power principles of trade unionism on a community instead of a shop basis" to "help the poor win justice, dignity, and security through [the] power of organization." They also attempted to persuade white Local 688 members, half of whom now lived in suburbs outside of St. Louis, that it was in their interest to support striking black tenants in the inner city. "The present condition of public housing is a cancerous sore threatening the health of all of St. Louis," they asserted, declaring that failure to "insure that our community is a decent, safe city for all" would eventually undermine the quality of life for Local 688's white members who still worked in the inner city while living in suburban enclaves. However, Gibbons and Calloway's extended defense of their actions suggested a growing recognition that their actions might not be fully supported by white members disturbed by civil unrest and fearful that the union's war on the slums strayed from protecting their vital interests.[40]

On October 10, 1969, Gibbons convened an extraordinary meeting that brought together top members of the city's business elite, striking tenants, civic leaders, and community activists. August Busch, Jr., a prominent beer magnate with deep connections to neighborhood life, blessed Gibbons's effort by obtaining financial commitments from Civic Progress members to launch the new initiative. Critical support also came from Father Kirk Walsh, a special consultant to HUD who attended the meeting as Secretary Romney's personal representative. Walsh confirmed Gibbons's assertion that HUD was prepared to withdraw funding from St. Louis unless the combatants settled the strike and approved the proposed coalition for housing. Sensing the opportunity to maximize pressure on the state to assume greater responsibility for housing the poor, Gibbons emphasized that a major task of the new organization would be to lobby for adequate state and federal funding for public housing: "It is ridiculous to think that a problem as large as this can be corrected through private financing." He also insisted on the need for tenant participation in the management of public housing, declaring ". . . there cannot be any solution to the low-cost housing problem on anything like a permanent basis unless we get the deepest kind of involvement among the tenants . . . the concept of the tenant being involved is basic to all our thinking."[41]

To achieve this aim, Gibbons demanded that his proposed organization, the St. Louis Civic Alliance for Housing, be granted authority to manage the city's public housing projects, with tenants comprising one-third of the alliance's board of directors. Eventually, tenants would assume primary responsibility for managing public housing in an arrangement Gibbons proclaimed would be "funded and staffed unlike any other real estate management corporation this world has ever seen." Some business leaders expressed their distrust of Gibbons's motives, and a wary Mayor Cervantes briefly postponed signing the strike settlement agreement for fear of ceding too much power to the Teamsters. However, as Richard Baron recalled, Civic Progress leaders and the mayor swallowed their reservations because ". . . this guy was willing to step in and fill the void and as long as they didn't have riots and as long as the guy was on some kind of positive track . . . they were only too happy to cede that authority to Harold."[42]

Supported by this sentiment, the city and the rent strikers reached an agreement on October 29, 1969, that not only rolled back rents but also handed over administration of public housing to a business-labor-community partnership. An October 31, 1969, editorial on a local television station affirmed the community's gratitude: "The city owes its thanks to [Harold Gibbons]. While he may not be loved by all, no one denies he gets results." A jubilant Ernest Calloway described the settlement more poetically, praising what he called "a revolution of people over things" that reminded civic and political elites of the "living, breathing, pulsating people with dreams and tears and hopes who occupied the thousands of units of public housing in St. Louis." For Calloway, this "small October revolution" represented a rare opportunity for poor people to gain recognition as legitimate social actors capable of helping to manage a major public institution.[43]

For the next two years, the Civic Alliance administered public housing in St. Louis. In keeping with his commitment to demonstrate the social and administrative capabilities of working-class organizations, Gibbons tapped his talented Local 688 staff to run the daily operations of the Civic Alliance. Terry McCormack, a housing specialist and close Gibbons aide, oversaw day-to-day operations with assistance from Teamsters' staffers, including Ernest Calloway, who authored the "social goals" for the new organization. Frank Boykin, the gifted Tandy Area Council organizer, became chair of the St. Louis Housing Authority's new board of directors, and fellow TAC organizer Leroy Graham assumed responsibility as a top manager at the Pruitt-Igoe complex. By April 1970, HUD Secretary Romney was praising the Civic Alliance for installing "new competent management" and helping stabilize a dysfunctional system. The alliance improved the physical face of public housing by obtaining much needed modernization funds from HUD and lowered maintenance costs through agreements with building trades unions. Aided by grants from the Justice Department and the Ford Foundation, the alliance also took steps to improve security in public housing and begin training tenant managers to run their facilities.[44]

Yet in attempting to introduce trade union concepts into tenant participation and management, Local 688 organizers encountered considerable resistance. With the support of the Teamsters, tenant leaders hoped to form associations comprised of members whose dues would subsidize the hiring of full-time staff not beholden to existing political interests. Many tenants, however, balked at joining the associations, citing the lack of change in their living conditions and concern that some of the former rent strike leaders were not behaving responsibly in their new managerial roles. As Elmer Hammond, head of the Pruitt-Igoe Community Corporation, complained to Mayor Cervantes, by attempting to "unionize the tenants . . . the Teamsters are pushing around us residents and want to make us an arm of their already powerful organization."[45]

For some tenants, the attempt to transplant the union concept of dues confirmed their suspicions that the Teamsters intended to develop their own political machine and assert control over public housing. Here was an instance where trade union principles did not prove readily adaptable to the community sphere; indeed, the Civic Alliance was forced to abandon its plans for tenant associations funded by dues-paying members. Moreover, preparing tenants to manage their own affairs proved far more challenging than Gibbons and Calloway had imagined. Although Gibbons's housing team made progress in improving conditions at most of the city's projects, they were unable to stabilize the severely depleted Pruitt-Igoe complex, which in spite of their best efforts remained unfit for habitation. These circumstances prompted the Teamsters to offer a redevelopment proposal for Pruit-Igoe that took their "sophisticated confrontation with national policy" to a new level of boldness and urgency.

Through his post on the St. Louis City Plan Commission, Calloway had continued to articulate a comprehensive, socially oriented approach to urban revitalization, noting that St. Louis's declining population offered new opportunities for creative land use planning and utilization of open space. To implement these policies, he proposed a new "Municipal Land Reclamation Authority" charged with acquiring tax-delinquent property on which new housing would be built. Included in this proposal was a plan the Teamsters had developed in early 1971 to raze Pruitt-Igoe and replace it with affordable, low-rise townhouses and garden apartments. In contacts with HUD, Gibbons believed he had reached an agreement that would provide federal support for this visionary plan.[46]

However, the agreement with HUD collapsed when national and local political forces converged to undermine the proposed project. Backing away from HUD's aggressive efforts to counteract residential segregation, which ran counter to his political strategy of outreach to the white working class and southerners, President Richard Nixon signaled his willingness to freeze federal funding for subsidized housing. Locally, Leonore Sullivan, a powerful south St. Louis congresswoman with a largely white ethnic constituency, had soured on public housing, and also threatened to slash agency funding. Succumbing to these pressures, George Romney reneged on the deal he had reached with Gibbons and the Civic Alliance. Instead, to the profound dismay of Gibbons, his housing team, and their supporters, he set in motion a process that eventually led to the demolition of Pruitt-Igoe. Having lost its funding sources, the St. Louis Civic Alliance for Housing disbanded in May 1972, ending Gibbons and Calloway's brief triumph in establishing a community bargaining table that had granted insurgents and unionists substantial decision-making authority. HUD approved a dramatic series of implosions that razed the entire Pruitt-Igoe complex, leaving behind a graphic image of destruction that remained fixed in public consciousness as an enduring symbol of governmental failure and urban decline.[47]

The historian Nelson Lichtenstein has observed that the 1960s were a "liberal hour but not for organized labor." Either threatened by disruptive social protest or seen as too close to the political establishment to gain acceptance as an ally, the union movement was largely unable to tap into the insurgent spirit of the period. Yet for a fleeting moment in St. Louis, Gibbons and Calloway's trade union oriented war on the slums transcended these obstacles, uniting laborites and black freedom insurgents, addressing the structural underpinnings of urban decline, and helping the disenfranchised gain an unprecedented level of social respect and decision-making authority.[48]

This success, however, came at a price. The union's prolonged role in the rent strike and its administration of the Civic Alliance for Housing drew some of the Tandy Area Council's most talented activists away from community organizing and agitation; they were replaced by other Local 688 members who were more service oriented and lacked the confrontational instincts that had earned TAC community credibility. Nonetheless, TAC's expansive concept of the union's social role had convinced at least some of its staff that the project remained indispensable to the union's future and the community's well-being. In a July 1972 letter outlining his ambitions for TAC, organizer Frank Boykin insisted it continue to establish relations with "legions of unorganized citizens." Seeking to capitalize on the union's successes during the rent strike, he declared that "public housing tenants all across the country must be made to realize that organized labor was born of a similar struggle for the right of having a voice in the determination of its own life and welfare." "Bridging this gap," Boykin asserted, "[and] pointing out the commonality of organized labor and the millions of natural allies of labor should be the main business of the Tandy Area Council."[49]

Boykin's passionate defense of Tandy and his insistence that Local 688 rededicate itself to aligning the union movement with the disenfranchised clearly reflected the strategic approach that Gibbons and Calloway had long advocated as essential to labor's resurgence. However, as they sought new directions for total person unionism and their trade union oriented war on the slums, they faced an unanticipated firestorm: fierce political attacks from both the left and the right that forestalled their ambitious plans and prematurely ended their careers.

CHAPTER 11

"Fuck Him, He Wasn't With Us"

In a four-part series that appeared in the May 11–14, 1969, editions of the *St. Louis Post-Dispatch*, journalist Sally Bixby Defty reviewed Harold Gibbons's career, tracing his evolution from reviled "Teamster boss" to his respectability as the "new Gibbons." Although largely favorable, Defty's portrait of the fifty-nine-year-old labor leader included extensive references to earlier controversies and discussion of Gibbons's increasingly contentious relationship with the St. Louis AFL-CIO Labor Council, which had voted to double its per capita tax to resist Local 688's raids upon its affiliates. As council leader and longtime Gibbons antagonist Oscar Ehrhardt explained, "Harold Gibbons has his idea of trade unionism and we have ours."[1]

Defty also pointed out the irony of Gibbons's demand that unions "shed the business orientation that has infiltrated the labor movement" in the form of "big salaries, good living, and fat expense accounts" by reporting on his own use of union funds to sustain an unapologetic zest for the nightlife and cultivate his friendships with Hollywood celebrities such as Frank Sinatra, whose portrait hung over Gibbons's dinner table in his Council Plaza apartment. Defty's final installment concluded on a poignant note with her observation that Gibbons and his wife, Ann, had long lived apart and hinted at a nagging loneliness in spite of his whirlwind of activity. Summarizing his own view on the vast social distance he had traveled from his coal patch upbringing and the turbulence of his early days in St. Louis, a bemused yet obviously pleased Harold Gibbons observed, "I'm getting suspicious of myself; the doors are so wide open for me now."[2]

However, at a December 1972 White House meeting just three and one-half years later, President Richard Nixon and his special counsel, Charles Colson, reveled over how the social and political doors that had previously swung wide for Harold Gibbons now were being slammed shut. Recalling a conversation he had had with Teamsters president Frank Fitzsimmons, Nixon chortled to Colson, "Between you and me, you know what he really said about this fellow Gibbons. 'What happened to Gibbons? Fuck him, he wasn't with us.'" This sharp reversal of fortunes preceded a convergence of events that thrust Gibbons into the maelstrom of national politics and led to his estrangement from the Teamsters' hierarchy. These rifts also played out among Local 688's membership in St. Louis, abetting the palace coup that ousted Gibbons in the summer of 1973, terminated his political partnership with Ernest Calloway, and signaled the demise of their quest for total person unionism.[3]

* * *

By end of the 1960s, Ernest Calloway, now sixty years old, gradually began to pull away from direct involvement in civil rights activism and union affairs. In 1969, he accepted a part-time teaching post at St. Louis University as a step toward official retirement. Nonetheless, he offered social commentary in the *Missouri Teamster*, spoke at numerous educational and political functions, and continued to provide strategic advice supporting Harold Gibbons's efforts to rejuvenate Local 688.

Although Gibbons and Calloway spent considerable energy during the 1960s pursuing their trade union oriented war on the slums and attempting to establish labor-management civic partnerships, they did not relent in their commitment to expanding the union's ranks. As Gibbons noted, countering job losses caused by automation alone required that Local 688 organize 1,000 workers annually "just to stand still." Although Local 688's membership reached 12,000 by the late 1960s, much of this growth had come from raiding other unions rather than new organizing. In two major organizing initiatives during this period, the St. Louis Teamsters faced powerful resistance that underscored the obduracy of one old rival and the rise of new forms of corporate organization equally determined to circumscribe union growth.[4]

Local 688's inability to organize Famous-Barr, the "gilded sweatshop" that had successfully resisted unionization during World War II, had long rankled Gibbons, who doubtless saw the company's non-union status as an intolerable symbol of the containment of Teamster power in St. Louis. In 1965, Gibbons pledged an "all-out" effort to organize retail workers at Famous-Barr (the union represented some of the store's nonretail employees). Although he had previously made no explicit gender-based appeals in organizing campaigns, Gibbons now acknowledged that women had increasingly assumed the status of breadwinner in their families. This assertion attempted to counter Famous-Barr's argument that its female employees were primarily working for "pin money," thereby justifying their low pay. Still, Gibbons explained seeking higher pay for women in class rather than gender terms, linking it to the maintenance of the community wage standard that had been one of Local 688's most illustrious achievements. As he declared in announcing the organizing drive at Famous-Barr, "We can no longer afford to ignore the fact that low wages in the retail industry in St. Louis help to hold down the standards of living for everyone."[5]

Like Gibbons, the male Teamsters' organizers who directed the Famous-Barr effort did little to incorporate the concerns of an emerging women's movement in their outreach to a largely female workforce. Facing fierce opposition from management, the union lost a June 1966 representation election at Famous-Barr. Whether or not a campaign featuring more female organizing staff and an explicit appeal to women workers would have blunted Famous-Barr's well-cultivated community image and its willingness to commit unfair labor practices is uncertain. Nonetheless, the failure to organize such a prominent target represented an embarrassing setback for Gibbons and Calloway on their home turf and illustrated the growing difficulties the Teamsters faced in organizing a labor force increasingly populated by pink-collar workers.[6]

Concurrently, another hotly contested organizing effort highlighted the challenges posed by new forms of corporate organization, the changing occupational composition of Local 688, and a growing sense of distance between the union's leadership and its rank-and-file members. By the late 1960s, the percentage of Local 688 members employed in its previous stronghold of distribution and warehousing had dipped to 25 percent, while its membership in manufacturing and related industries had risen to 42 percent. Reflecting this development, in July 1967, Local 688 organized workers at a local plant owned by Abex Corporation, a manufacturer of metal products with facilities across the United States and overseas. After efforts to negotiate a first contract stalled, Gibbons and other 688 leaders launched a recognition strike in December 1967. In asking Local 688 members to show solidarity with Abex workers by supporting an assessment to augment the union's strike fund, Gibbons cited two concerns. Following the union's defeat at Famous-Barr, he feared that failure to win the Abex strike would lead "employers all over St. Louis [to] feel that our local is an 'easy touch.'" Gibbons also suggested that the global expansion of capital threatened to breach the walls of security he and Ernest Calloway had labored to erect, explaining that "the gains made in collective bargaining can be knocked out because everything you touch in the industry scene today is part and parcel of a large corporation."[7]

In spite of Gibbons's pleas, membership support for the assessment fell short of his expectations. Although the rank-and-file ultimately agreed to back the Abex strikers, Local 688 president John Naber reported hearing complaints that the union was neglecting shop-floor concerns in favor of its community activities. After Gibbons gained support from a British union to pressure Abex at its European facilities, Local 688 reached a settlement following an eleven-week strike. Nonetheless, the increasing willingness of multinational conglomerates to resist organization and the growing reluctance of Local 688 members to engage in acts of solidarity foreshadowed an increasing gap between leaders and the led. This gap widened with the emergence of sharp divisions over two of the late 1960s' most heated conflicts: the ongoing quest for racial justice and the Vietnam War.[8]

In part, these divisions reflected larger social trends. By late 1967, only 44 percent of Local 688's members lived in the city of St. Louis, with the rest having relocated to area suburbs. As Robert Zieger has observed, "the teeming neighborhoods of the vast industrial cities, with their union halls, saloons, social clubs, and traditions of solidarity and cultural cohesion, [now] gave way to new, transient, fragmented patterns of life." Moreover, as the older generation of union pioneers steeped in the traditions of shop-floor struggle and labor solidarity began to retire, Gibbons and Calloway faced a new membership. Sixty percent of these new members had less than four years of tenure within Local 688. Telltale signs of growing distance between this changing membership and its leaders became increasingly apparent throughout the late 1960s. In February 1968, community action director Jim Pace reported that only 45 percent of Local 688 members were registered to vote. Other signs of member apathy included limited interest in Local 688's educational offerings and poor attendance at meetings seeking to revive the community stewards program. This unmistakable evidence of member disengagement suggested that Gibbons and Calloway's notion of active working-class citizenship had atrophied, failing to connect meaningfully with the union's changing membership.[9]

Even more troubling for Gibbons and Calloway was a poll taken during the 1968 presidential race showing that a majority of Local 688 members favored the candidacy of former Alabama Governor George Wallace. In Local 688 and throughout the union movement, Wallace's racially charged populist rhetoric resonated with many white union members increasingly disenchanted with federal intervention aimed at addressing racial injustice. In a September 1968 article in the *Missouri Teamster*, Calloway advised union leaders to take Wallace's appeal seriously, arguing that his populist suspicion of power and monopoly, however racially tinged, was rooted in a venerable American distrust of centralized government and intrusive bureaucracy. A month later, however, he offered a nightmare scenario of a Wallace presidency that led to the declaration of martial law and the appointment of Nazis, anti-Semites, and Ku Klux Klan leaders to cabinet positions. This polemic provoked nearly 100 Local 688 members to sign a petition denouncing Calloway's reverie and demanding "a voice in the endorsement of candidates chosen by the union to represent us." After Gibbons launched an intensive educational effort, the union succeeded in convincing a majority of members to shift their allegiance from Wallace to Democratic presidential nominee Hubert Humphrey. Nonetheless, Calloway and Gibbons failed to appreciate that support for Wallace represented just one manifestation of a broader rank-and-file estrangement from the interracial unionism that they regarded as a fundamental obligation of working-class citizenship.[10]

Throughout 1968, open resistance to Gibbons and Calloway's racial liberalism erupted within Local 688. Although Gibbons's September 1968 denunciation of police brutality against the Black Liberators had reinforced his credibility within St. Louis's African American community, it led Robert Frazer, a white Local 688 member at Brown Shoe, to launch a petition drive condemning his action. Frazer claimed that 75 percent of Local 688's members opposed Gibbons's speaking out against the police. Although this claim was exaggerated, a press report citing 4,000 signatures on an anti-Gibbons petition attested to the depth of the white rank-and-file membership's outrage over its leader's public rebuke of local law enforcement and his apparent empathy for black protestors.[11]

Racial tensions also emerged in St. Louis neighborhoods, a familiar battleground in a city with a long tradition of restrictive housing policies. In August and September of 1968, Jim Pace pleaded with Local 688 members living in Normandy, an inner-ring white neighborhood in suburban St. Louis County where realtors were openly encouraging white flight, not to "panic sell" in response. Personally urging the 800 Local 688 members in Normandy to resist the block-busting tactics of "unscrupulous realtors," Pace invoked Franklin Roosevelt's famous line of reassurance: "Keep cool: the only thing you have to fear is fear itself in protecting your real estate investment." The urgency of Pace's plea underscored his concern that the continuing flight of white members to the suburbs represented a surrender to racial fear and a rejection of Local 688's deepening commitment to address the structural components of racial injustice.[12]

Perhaps the most dramatic evidence of member estrangement from total person unionism emerged in an extraordinary series of shop steward meetings that occurred in August 1969. Under the supervision of Mike Ryan, Local 688 staff representatives met with 260 stewards to seek their advice on "how to improve the union." The barrage of criticism at these meetings revealed that many of the union's secondary leaders had come to identify themselves more as dues-paying consumers of services rather than as socially engaged citizens. In their view Gibbons and Calloway's focus on "the other sixteen hours" had led them to neglect the interests of the rank-and-file. Some complained that the Labor Health Institute treated them like "charity patients" rather than recognizing their status as self-reliant wage-earners. Others charged that "political action has led them [union leaders] astray from bread and butter issues" and insisted that the union "take care of our own before worrying about others like the 'grape strikers,'" a reference to Local 688's strong support for the United Farm Workers. Several attendees at the August 1969 meetings urged a cessation of new organizing until servicing was improved and implored Gibbons to "hire more staff to demonstrate that we are still a first class union." In addition, staffer Levi Sanford reported that some stewards at his meeting, apparently seeking a return to union domination of the shop floor, wanted "inspirational speeches from Gibbons, wildcat strikes, [and] bosses living in terror of the business agent or the union."[13]

The accusation that the union had failed to fulfill its shop-floor obligations signified the culmination of fears previously expressed by Gibbons and Calloway.

They acknowledged that Teamster moves toward centralized bargaining, diminished roles for local union leaders, and greater reliance on union staff dampened the participatory spirit that had animated effective working-class citizenship. Some stewards complained that the stewards council functioned as a rubber stamp for already determined policies, and Gibbons and other Local 688 leaders made them feel disempowered. As the report from an August 16, 1969, stewards meeting recounted, "At the present time people feel they will be shouted down by the experts on the stage." For a union that had prided itself on creating working-class citizens confident enough to take on "experts" at both the workplace and community bargaining tables, Local 688 now seemed afflicted by the rank-and-file marginalization prevalent within Teamsters culture.[14]

Although Mike Ryan characterized much of the criticism as coming from "bitchers and parasites," he conceded that the stewards' meetings had raised "complex questions and bitter feelings" that warranted consideration. Rather than regarding themselves as working-class citizens, many white Local 688 members now appeared to identify themselves as taxpayers and homeowners who were defending their precarious security against incursion by social intruders. As Ryan explained in a September 4, 1969, memo, "The white membership feels that all of the taxes are caused by the 'niggers' and Gibbons is a bastard for helping because this causes their taxes to be increased. The black membership feels that inflation and taxes are caused by whites who want to take away the gains that blacks have made in the last few years." In response to this polarization, Ryan recommended that the union undertake a "crusade" for fair tax policies and cuts in military spending which he asserted would "continue and fulfill our commitment to the principles of trade unionism and our ideals of striving for justice with equality for all." Although Gibbons did not directly respond to Ryan's proposal, he did note that "it is probably fair to say that the white worker in America today fears social change" and especially "the threat of the black worker."[15]

The complaints of Local 688's white members reflected a broader discontent that surfaced within some segments of the working class in the late 1960s and early 1970s. Facing enhanced competition from abroad and diminished profits, many employers assumed harder stances at the bargaining table and renewed efforts to enforce greater discipline on the shop floor. Inspired by the spirit of social protest, dissident movements began to appear in numerous unions, with the Teamsters emerging as a particular hotbed of disgruntlement. Although often limited in their ability to influence national union policy, rank-and-file Teamsters had a long history of exercising shop-floor control by regulating the pace of work and setting their own production standards. Imbued with this tradition, they resented managerial intrusion on these hard-won prerogatives.[16]

In 1970, defying union general vice president Frank Fitzsimmons, members of Teamsters Local 600 in St. Louis launched a wildcat strike after the expiration of the national trucking agreement, and many remained off the job after the union reached a tentative agreement they deemed unsatisfactory. During that same year within Local 688, a vocal group of dissidents organized Rank and File Teamsters (RAFT) in response to what they regarded as the union's lackluster leadership. As RAFT leader Ron Gushleff recalled, the dissidents were "angry and dissatisfied with our Local IBT leaders and . . . the conciliatory attitude [they exhibited toward] rank-and-file grievances." Accusing their leadership of complacency and inattentiveness, RAFT alleged that "union leaders with their mohair carpeted offices, their expense accounts, their air-conditioned LTDs, and their fat salaries have forgotten what it's like to carry your lunch or what it's like to have a supervisor on your back all day."[17]

Elaborating on their belief that Local 688 leaders had neglected the shop floor, RAFT charged that "Harold Gibbons and the kind of union thinking he represents have been inadequate in meeting the needs of the workers in the shop concerning such issues as job security, speedups, safety, racism, abuse by supervisors, and inadequate, lengthy, and cumbersome grievance procedures." The problem had grown especially acute at United Parcel Service (UPS), where management's use of monitoring techniques and its insistence on raising production standards created enormous stress among its workers. The situation worsened after a 1970 contract agreement that shifted grievance adjudication from the local union to an area-wide committee, leading to a grievance backlog. After management discharged two stewards for leading a wildcat strike to protest company stonewalling, a Local 688 investigatory committee issued an extraordinary internal rebuke. The committee concluded that a "maximum effort was not made at United Parcel Service to protect the interests of the members of Local 688" and urged that "fraternization between Local 688 staff and UPS management must cease." Supported by local student radicals and others on the political left, RAFT members also protested the exclusion of local unionists from contract negotiations, questioned Gibbons's receipt of salaries from multiple sources, insisted that business agents be elected rather than appointed, and sought more input into the union's expenditures on charitable and community activities.[18]

Several years earlier, Ernest Calloway had observed that "some unions have become impersonal economic institutions many significant steps removed from the sweat and heart-beat of the rank and file worker." Indeed, Tandy Area Council staffers Claude Brown and Jim Pace recalled Calloway expressing concern that Local 688's business agents had paid insufficient attention to shop-floor matters. In a September 1968 *Missouri Teamster* column, Calloway also noted a pronounced attitudinal shift symbolized by members referring to "the union" instead of "our union" when they spoke about their organization. Yet beyond expressing nostalgia for "the good old days" . . . when the language of the contract "smelled of sweat, tears, and hope from the workbench rather than . . . the store-bought mouthings of the college-trained personnel complex," Calloway offered no alternative strategy to address RAFT's complaints.[19]

For his part, Harold Gibbons bluntly informed RAFT that "we are not going to put up with this disruption, and the rank and filers will not let this disruption continue, they should get up and defend their union and I want them to put an end to this kind of child's play." Dismissing allegations that his union-funded life style and hobnobbing with corporate leaders had caused him to lose touch with the shop floor, Gibbons allowed Local 688 staff to isolate and discredit the dissidents. After so many years within a Teamsters' culture driven by the necessity for order and discipline, Gibbons was unprepared to grant an internal insurgency the legitimacy he conferred on other social rebels taking on entrenched establishments. Moreover, he proved unwilling to take the political risk of tampering with entrenched structures of centralized authority or to reorient a union staff steeped in traditional business unionism.[20]

However, in contrast to other labor liberals threatened by rank-and-file insurgencies, Gibbons did not rely solely on a strategy of repression or cooptation to subdue his critics. In an effort to address the resentment of white rank and filers attracted to conservative political appeals, he attempted to involve them in a more engaged use of their "other sixteen hours." In the fall of 1968, the union's twenty-first annual citywide shop conference approved a resolution to launch a community action effort in south St. Louis after white Local 688 members asserted that "we want a Tandy project we can work in." Based in Carondelet, an increasingly depressed working-class neighborhood populated by second- and third-generation ethnics and a small African American community, the Carondelet Area Council (CAC) sought to emulate the Tandy project by organizing around issues such as recreational opportunities for youth, reduced utility rates for senior citizens, greater food stamp assistance for low-income residents, and expanded child care programs. Local 688 community organizers found that many Carondelet residents eligible for welfare benefits or food stamps were not receiving them and lobbied to secure a Head Start program for a neighborhood served only by a local church's limited resources. In December 1972, Mike Ryan reported to Gibbons a small but visible victory for the Carondelet effort, securing federal revenue sharing funds to build a skating rink after an eighteen-month fight. In a neighborhood lacking adequate recreational facilities for its youth, this achievement demonstrated the political possibilities of engaged citizenship under the union's aegis.[21]

However, the Teamsters found Carondelet less fertile territory for cultivating the practice of working-class citizenship and total person unionism. An already existing group, the Carondelet Community Betterment Association, noted neighborhood suspicion of Local 688's motives, although it also reported that the goal of the proposed Carondelet Area Council was neither "labor" nor "political" but an effort "to improve the community." Some of this suspicion may have been rooted in a defensive form of citizen engagement marked by the 1971 emergence of the Citizen's Council, a "white racist group" that was stirring opposition to public housing. Given the Teamsters' well-known support for African American aspirations, this assertion of homeowner politics perhaps inhibited the CAC's effort to establish roots in the community. Recruiting volunteers and generating involvement from Local 688 members proved more challenging in Carondelet than in Tandy, forcing the project to rely on program staff rather than rank and filers living in the neighborhood. The waning commitment of white members to remain in the city also may have hampered the efforts of Gibbons and Calloway to extend the Tandy project to a white working-class neighborhood. As UAW community activist Jerry Tucker recalled, many white workers in south St. Louis appeared more interested in escaping to the suburbs than remaining in Carondelet and assisting in its improvement.[22]

Recognizing this residential shift, Gibbons and Calloway sought to extend the union's community organizing efforts to the suburbs. As historian Becky Nicolaides has observed, the suburban white working-class tended to embrace the values of "self-help, individualism, Americanism, homeowner rights, [and] a distaste for activist government," sentiments inimical to the cosmopolitan ideals that guided total person unionism. By supporting efforts of white working-class suburbanites to gain a voice in decisions that affected their quality of life, Gibbons and Calloway hoped to channel their activism away from the politics of racial exclusion toward a focus on community improvement. Accordingly, in the Normandy area where Jim Pace had urged the community's Teamster members not to succumb to racially inspired appeals to sell their homes, Local 688 supported legal action by residents opposing a zoning permit for a fast food restaurant that threatened to disrupt neighborhood stability.[23]

In suburban Jefferson County just south of St. Louis, Glen Wright, a 688 member, chaired "Citizens for Better Government," a group that challenged a zoning report as emanating from an "expert who doesn't live here ... [and] tries to change our living habits rather than adapt itself to the way we prefer to live." After Jefferson County authorities ruled that local officials should permit residents a voice in modifying proposed zoning changes, Jim Pace exulted that zoning policy would be made "in accord with the wishes of residents and not just the dictates of experts." Local 688 activists in Jefferson County also supported a merger of two school districts to boost educational funding and favored uniting the St. Louis County community of Velda Village with an adjoining unincorporated area to generate greater "resource[s] for community improvement." These expansions of civic action to the suburbs offered broadly conceived initiatives for community betterment as an alternative to the politics of racial resentment and taxpayer outrage that appealed to at least some of Local 688's migrating white members.[24]

In addition to its suburban organizing and attempts to rejuvenate working-class citizenship among Local 688 members, the Teamsters returned to yet another unrealized initiative launched by the community stewards a decade earlier. Linking up with the emerging environmental and occupational safety movements, they rallied workers at St. Joseph Lead, a Jefferson County smelting plant whose emissions threatened the health of community residents and Local 688 members working in the plant. Union education director Mike Ryan recruited workers to testify at an October 1969 United States Senate subcommittee hearing on air and water pollution. Citing numerous cases of lead poisoning among workers in the plant, Milton Barlow, who worked at St. Joseph Lead, asserted, "Workers' health—community health play second fiddle to increased production and higher profits." Margaret Blackshere, a Madison, IL, schoolteacher and wife of a Local 688 leader, lamented that pollution from Illinois factories had caused her son's asthma and called for stronger penalties against polluters. UPS worker and south St. Louis resident Richard King wondered, ". . . as a taxpayer, as a voter, [and] as a union man" why the company and the government were not taking steps to reduce pollution. King's linkage of the often insular identity of taxpayer with the broader civic obligations implicit in voting and the social solidarity embodied in trade unionism demonstrated the potential for working-class citizenship to align itself with the environmental movement and extend Gibbons and Calloway's concept of the community bargaining table into a new social arena.[25]

Beyond seeking to activate disaffected white rank and filers, Gibbons and Calloway attempted to address the spirit if not the substance of the issues raised by RAFT through a series of initiatives undertaken in 1971 and 1972. They sponsored conferences aimed specifically at the union's young, black, and female members during this period and began paying particular attention to women's concerns. From his days with the red caps and especially in his NAACP work, Calloway had recognized the political potential of women and supported their ascension to leadership roles. Notably, he had not undertaken similar efforts within the Teamsters, perhaps in deference to the union's male-breadwinner-oriented culture. Similarly, Harold Gibbons had consistently consigned Local 688's female membership, nearly one-third of its total in the late 1960s, to a subordinate role within the union. Now, in response to the increasingly vocal claims of women for workplace equality, Gibbons looked to place the resources and moral authority of the union behind yet another 1960s social movement. In 1970, at the urging of Mike Ryan, Local 688's annual conference approved resolutions opposing sex discrimination, supporting women's rights, and promising more aggressive contract enforcement on these issues. At a February 1972 women's conference, participants voted in favor of making abortion legal. And in a renewed effort to make the collective bargaining process an agent for social change beyond the traditional arenas of wages and benefits, Gibbons pledged to support enhanced child care options in future union bargaining demands.[26]

Gibbons also began to consider new organizing and political initiatives proposed by his St. Louis staff in his emerging quest to jump-start Local 688's revitalization. Staff member Murray Hines urged him to form a special local or branch for "little people" working at "the small companies that cannot afford our entire fringe package.... These are traditionally the people who have supported each move forward of Local 688," Hines argued, seeking to rekindle the union's earlier commitments to uplift low-wage workers and acknowledging that area and regional agreements failed to accommodate the needs of smaller employers.[27]

In an August 1969 memo supporting the thrust of Hines's proposal, union staffer Ernie Neidel cited two several developments key to the union's future prospects. Predicting that employment growth would likely occur in industries and occupations that had been minimally penetrated by Local 688, Neidel also noted the rise of a new generation of workers that "finds meaning through face-to-face encounters, small groups, and not large pep rally type assemblies and impersonal direction." Neidel then posed a pointed question: "Will 688 have the agility to respond to the predicted work force change and anticipate it beforehand... in its structure, policy, and interaction between its leadership and membership?"[28]

Although Gibbons acknowledged the concerns raised by Hines and Neidel and formed a new local union to take in workers at smaller businesses, his embryonic efforts to create a program for union revitalization failed to materialize. Between 1969 and 1972, he became embroiled in a series of controversies within the national Teamsters hierarchy that led to his ultimate fall from power. Gibbons had long made no secret of his disdain for Teamsters' general vice president Frank Fitzsimmons, and his anger escalated as Fitzsimmons began to reject the caretaker role envisioned for him by Jimmy Hoffa. To solidify his grip on power, Fitzsimmons ceded considerable authority to other Teamsters leaders and allowed mob elements even greater influence over the investment of union pension funds than Hoffa had deemed permissible. Although Fitzsimmons tried to polish his image as a progressive leader by launching the Alliance for Labor Action and gave Gibbons a substantive role in this enterprise, he limited his potential rival's involvement in other areas of union decision-making to neutralize a potential source of opposition.[29]

At the Teamsters convention in July 1971, Gibbons considered challenging Fitzsimmons, who prepared to claim the union presidency following Hoffa's resignation as Teamsters' president a month earlier. However, Gibbons again determined that he lacked sufficient support to defeat Fitzsimmons, remaining for many Teamsters' leaders a CIO man whose social vision they rejected. Fitzsimmons helped Gibbons make his final decision by offering him the chairmanship of the powerful Central Conference, elevating the St. Louis Teamster to a position that might offer him future leverage for his suppressed ambitions. However, the Gibbons-Fitzsimmons détente proved short-lived. The tensions between the two men gathered intensity as Gibbons became an increasingly vocal opponent of the United States' involvement in Vietnam, whereas Fitzsimmons drew closer to the Nixon administration and supported its war policy.[30]

Although both Gibbons and Calloway remained ardent anti-communists, their socialist upbringing and sensibilities deterred them from an automatic embrace of

Cold War foreign policy. Instead, they repeatedly questioned an American foreign policy that in the name of suppressing communism often condoned authoritarian regimes, used covert operations to undermine elected governments, and jeopardized the lives of workers to defend its interests. Gibbons's son, Larry, recalled that his father saw war as a "particular evil of capitalism." Moreover, Gibbons and Calloway were both troubled by the American labor movement's often uncritical support for the Cold War, which in their view betrayed democratic principles and compromised labor's political independence.[31]

In articles written for the *Missouri Teamster* in 1967 and 1968, Calloway charged that American foreign policy, especially in Vietnam, mistook nationalism for communism and resisted self-determination in the Third World in violation of the United States' professed democratic commitments. Gibbons echoed Calloway's concerns, juxtaposing his "progressivism" against the AFL-CIO's unwavering support for a reflexive, aggressive anti-communism. Gibbons, reveling in the public attention he received as an anti-war Teamster while other labor liberals such as Walter Reuther responded more cautiously, was a featured speaker at the massive Vietnam Moratorium rally in November 1969. Coming at the same time he was helping settle the rent strike in St. Louis, Gibbons embraced the roles of both insider and insurgent in his ongoing effort to align unions with social protest and upstage Frank Fitzsimmons as the Teamsters' most visible leader.[32]

In condemning the Vietnam War, Gibbons's rhetoric assumed an impassioned tone. As he explained in his November 15, 1969, moratorium speech, "We are destroying America's image among the black, brown, and yellow people of the world. We are aligned with the most reactionary government in the world. And we are in a war that cannot be won." He also highlighted the class dimensions of the war, noting that "working Americans have borne the brunt of this mistake" by suffering a disproportionate share of its casualties. Gibbons implored the union movement to make class an integral part of the anti-war critique, asserting that "the peace movement is somehow unable to reflect fully all our concerns."[33]

Gibbons's fiery anti-war rhetoric, accompanied by numerous editorials and articles in the *Missouri Teamster*, attracted support from some members and bitter reaction from others. Nonetheless, he refused to equivocate, underscoring his opposition to the war in speeches before Local 688's stewards council and encouraging the union's educational programs to seek to move members from "hawk to dove." Perhaps unknown to most of Local 688's members, Gibbons's anti-war commitments contained a personal dimension that reflected the deep fault lines the war had etched across America. His older son served with a helicopter unit in Vietnam while his younger son went to Canada for several years after being drafted, later sought conscientious objector status, and ultimately enlisted on returning to be closer to his gravely ill mother in St. Louis. When Gibbons told the parents of a Teamster member who was missing in action in Vietnam that "for the past eight years I have spent time, energy, money, and effort to convince our government to get out of this stupid war," his declaration reflected a solemn personal recognition of the conflict's devastating effect on many American families.[34]

In the wake of the Nixon administration's disclosure of secret peace talks with North Vietnam early in 1972, Gibbons accelerated his anti-war activities. In late March 1972, he joined the first trade union delegation to North Vietnam, spending a hectic eight days traveling throughout the country, interacting with an array of officials, and briefly encountering two American prisoners of war. At the end of the trip, Gibbons and his delegation met with Le Duc Tho, the chief North Vietnamese negotiator conducting secret talks with the Nixon administration. The Vietnamese leader encouraged the group to convey the National Liberation Front's proposed settlement terms to national security advisor Henry Kissinger. Following his return to the United States in late March 1972, Gibbons basked in the public limelight, briefing Kissinger, appearing before an executive session of the Senate Foreign Relations Committee, being interviewed on NBC's "Today" show, and speaking to the Democratic Party's pre-convention platform committee. He climaxed his whirlwind of activity by joining a May 1972 federal district court suit charging the U.S. government with failing to obey the Mansfield Amendment's call to withdraw troops and hosting a June 1972 St. Louis gathering of Labor for Peace. Gibbons chaired this widely publicized founding conference of anti-war unionists, which was attended by over 600 delegates representing thirty different unions.[35]

Gibbons's bold pronouncements and high-profile anti-war activities enraged Frank Fitzsimmons. After his brief flirtation with labor liberalism through the Alliance for Labor Action, Fitzsimmons succumbed to the blandishments of the Nixon administration, which had developed an elaborate political strategy to attract working-class support by tapping the cultural backlash against 1960s social movements. Seen by Nixon and his chief strategist, special counsel Charles Colson, as the entrée to a substantial bloc of working-class voters, Fitzsimmons became one of Nixon's closest labor supporters. The new alliance immediately paid political dividends for Fitzsimmons when Richard Nixon commuted Jimmy Hoffa's prison sentence but imposed terms that made it nearly impossible for him to regain the Teamsters presidency. Reflecting his loyalty to Nixon, Fitzsimmons disavowed Labor for Peace, declaring that union leaders should leave diplomacy up to the Nixon administration. The antagonism between Fitzsimmons and Gibbons peaked in the summer of 1972, when Charles Colson sought to engineer a major political coup: obtaining the Teamsters' endorsement of Nixon's re-election bid.[36]

Through a complicated set of overlapping circumstances, Harold Gibbons became deeply ensnarled in the Nixon administration's war policy and its machinations to gain the Teamsters' endorsement. He had his own high-level connection to the administration through Henry Kissinger, with whom he had developed a warm relationship during visits to Harvard when Kissinger had been a professor there. Apparently seeing no contradiction between his identities as war critic and establishment habitué, Gibbons continued to excoriate the administration's war policy while maintaining close contact with Kissinger, one of its principal architects. For his part, Kissinger seemed to hold genuine affection for Gibbons, but his solicitous treatment of the Teamsters leader also served an ulterior motive. As he explained to White House counsel John Dean, "I have been at the President's request buttering up this fellow Gibbons. . . ." At the same time, the Nixon White House accompanied Kissinger's stroking of Gibbons with some behind-the-scenes hardball. As Charles Colson told Dean in a June 12, 1972, memo, "I have received a well-informed tip that there are income tax discrepancies involving the returns of Harold J. Gibbons, a vice president of the teamsters union in St. Louis . . . Gibbons, you should know, is an all out enemy, a McGovernite, ardently anti-Nixon."[37]

Just prior to the Teamsters' executive board's July 1972 meeting to approve the Nixon endorsement, Harold Gibbons launched a backdoor maneuver aimed at undercutting Fitzsimmons, boosting Jimmy Hoffa's political fortunes, and enhancing his stature as an anti-war leader. In association with William Taub, a shadowy figure who claimed to have direct connections to the North Vietnamese, Gibbons concocted what Colson and Kissinger respectively described as a "weird" and "cockeyed" scheme to have Jimmy Hoffa travel to Vietnam and negotiate for the release of American POWs. In return for what would be a political coup for an administration under growing pressure to bring the POWs home, Nixon would pardon Hoffa and pave the way for his resumption of the Teamster presidency. Charles Colson, whose elaborate wooing of Fitzsimmons was threatened by Gibbons's ploy, angrily reported that his last-minute maneuvering had made Fitzsimmons "paranoid" and "very skittish" in the hours before he was to deliver the Teamsters' endorsement to Richard Nixon.[38]

Several days before the vote, Colson predicted a unanimous endorsement of the president, telling Kissinger that ". . . Mr. Fitzsimmons explained to Mr. Gibbons last night that in the Teamsters' organization anyone who was opposed to the President will be asked to consider early retirement." Fully aware of the potential consequences of defying Fitzsimmons's threat, Gibbons cast the sole executive board vote against the Nixon endorsement at its July 15, 1972, meeting. Several years later, Gibbons portrayed his decision as a matter of personal rectitude, telling colleagues, ". . . at least I can look at myself in the mirror but you guys can't if you endorse that crook." Occurring well after the Watergate affair revelations that forced Nixon to resign in 1974, this rationale obscured the broader dimensions of Gibbons's momentous decision. Forced to choose between his insider and insurgent identities, he chose the latter, unable to support a man whose war policies and labor record ran counter to the principles that had guided him throughout his career. And in denying Fitzsimmons a unanimous vote, Gibbons asserted that in spite of the many compromises he had made as a Teamster, he neither had been tamed nor housebroken.[39]

Frank Fitzsimmons wasted little time making good on his threat of retribution. In December 1972, just after Nixon's re-election, he invoked his broad presidential powers to remove Gibbons from his Central Conference chairmanship and his leadership of the union's warehouse division. Determined to punish Gibbons for his heresy and signal that he would brook no challenge to his authority, Fitzsimmons capitalized on the discontent of Local 688's business agents. A segment of the union's staff had grown disenchanted with Gibbons's leadership, resenting his frequent absences from St. Louis, the imperious rule of Richard Kavner, the longtime Gibbons loyalist who administered Local 688 on his behalf, and the continuing devotion of resources to community-oriented activities. As Jerry Tucker later recalled, he could "feel a different atmosphere when he walked into the business agents' room" at Local 688, suggesting that a parallel, more traditional union culture now coexisted uneasily with the total person unionism espoused by Gibbons and Calloway. Gibbons's designation of Ron Borges, the research director for the Central Conference, as his heir apparent, irritated many business agents, who viewed him as an "ambitious yes-man" whose main qualification was his loyalty and subservience to Gibbons. Also, Gibbons's feud with Fitzsimmons further damaged his reputation in St. Louis. According to RAFT leader Ronald Gushleff, dissidents from both the left and the right believed that Gibbons had fallen "out of favor at the I.B.T. national level and was isolated from any major Union policy decisions," thereby limiting St. Louis's influence and robbing it of the attention demanded by a restive rank and file.[40]

Another catalyst for the simmering discontent of Local 688's dissident staff ultimately provided the official pretext for Gibbons's ouster: his support for establishing Local 102, a unit for workers in marginalized shops that could not afford Local 688's benefits package. This "catch-all" local reflected Gibbons's willingness to experiment with a new organizational structure that would allow Local 688 to incorporate more low-wage workers into its ranks. In creating this new local, Gibbons and Richard Kavner failed to apply for an official Teamsters' charter, perhaps fearing that Frank Fitzsimmons would reject this departure from customary union practice. Indeed, many Local 688 business agents complained that employers were increasingly balking at accepting Local 688's standard benefits package in negotiations, asking why they could not get the "relief" provided other employers housed under Local 102. With clear evidence of "wrongdoing" now before him, Fitzsimmons agreed to support the dissident business agents if they filed charges against Gibbons, threatening to place Local 688 under trusteeship if he resisted. Squeezed by Fitzsimmons and his local opponents, a stunned Gibbons quickly realized that his position was untenable. On May 23, 1973, at age sixty-three and after three decades as St. Louis's preeminent union leader, Gibbons resigned his posts at Joint Council 13 and Local 688. The twenty-year quest for total person unionism that he and Ernest Calloway had pursued in St. Louis was over.[41]

Deposed from his citadel in St. Louis and cast aside by the international union, Harold Gibbons spent the last decade of his life along the political margins. The loss in salary incurred by relinquishing his St. Louis positions forced him to curtail the extensive travel and generous lifestyle that had been vital sources of social status and personal pleasure. He also had to fend off a tax audit launched by the Nixon administration in retaliation for his refusal to support the Teamsters' endorsement. In 1974, he suffered another serious blow when his wife Ann, with whom he retained a close bond in spite of their long estrangement, died after an extended illness.

Angling for a political comeback, Gibbons supported the paroled Jimmy Hoffa's incipient campaign to regain the Teamsters' presidency. Hoffa's effort ended with his unsolved disappearance in 1975, a stark reminder of the subterranean forces that had become more influential within the Teamsters under Frank Fitzsimmons's leadership. Gibbons apparently contemplated opposing Fitzsimmons at the union's 1976 convention but again backed away, dissuaded by his lack of sufficient support and fears that mob elements would not countenance his candidacy. His decision was sealed by Fitzsimmons's offer to "rehabilitate" Gibbons in return for his support. At the behest of Ray Schoessling, the union's secretary-treasurer, Gibbons received an important assignment, negotiating a truce with the United Farm Workers (UFW), whom west coast Teamsters had been undercutting in collusion with California growers. The Teamsters' strong-arm tactics had generated negative publicity, damaging Fitzsimmons's efforts to improve the union's image. As a longtime supporter of the UFW and its iconic leader Cesar Chavez, Gibbons had assisted the union's grape and lettuce boycotts in St. Louis and was perhaps the only Teamsters' official with sufficient credibility to play the role of peacemaker.[42]

However, under instructions to broker a deal that would allow the Teamsters to gain greater jurisdiction over farm workers, Gibbons had limited options to offer the UFW, and his efforts proved unavailing. In 1977, he married Toni Stein, a St. Louis restaurateur, and began to spend more time at his new home in Palm Springs, CA, closer to the celebrity culture that had long captivated him. Rumors occasionally surfaced linking him to possible runs for Congress, mayor of St. Louis, and the Teamsters' presidency, none of which materialized. Perhaps his most public appearance was as the subject of the last chapter in journalist Steven Brill's 1978 book, *The Teamsters*. Gibbons spoke at length to Brill in making his case against Fitzsimmons, defending his alliance with Jimmy Hoffa, and trumpeting his own credentials as a progressive unionist. Although Brill chided Gibbons for his failure to stem corruption in the union and questioned his high-flying life style on the union's tab, he praised Gibbons's social commitment, his effectiveness as a trade unionist, and his refusal to participate personally in the pension fund chicanery that aided the union's organized crime patrons. Gibbons had to be pleased that Brill depicted him as a man "who could have been the most important labor leader of his time," although this description was a painful reminder of the many compromises he had made and his inability to move the Teamsters in a more visionary direction. Emblematic of his political exile within the Teamsters and his need to assume a larger public role, Gibbons sought, unsuccessfully, to be named director of the Federal Mediation and Conciliation Service following Ronald Reagan's election to the presidency in 1980. His quest for a new political niche ended abruptly on November 18, 1982. Returning to California from St. Louis, Gibbons suffered a ruptured abdominal aneurism at the Los Angeles airport and died at the age of 72.[43]

The *New York Times*' obituary, headlined "H.J. Gibbons, Once Viewed as Hoffa's Heir," observed that in spite of his many achievements, Gibbons had never fully escaped the shadow of his patron. More charitably, the *St. Louis Labor Tribune*, a local labor newspaper, hailed his pursuit of total person unionism, noting "his proclivity to reach out to other segments of society" and "his interests [that] went far beyond the parochial." In an attempt to have the final word, Gibbons stipulated in his will that he wanted his old comrade, Ernest Calloway, to deliver his eulogy. However, in a cruel twist of fate, Calloway could not fulfill his friend's request, having suffered a stroke a year earlier that left him unable to speak.[44]

In contrast to Harold Gibbons, Ernest Calloway found multiple outlets for political expression during the last decade of his career, assuming the role of respected community elder. After initially teaching part-time in St. Louis University's urban affairs program, he became a full-time professor from 1973 to 1977, charming students with his wit and erudition. Student reaction to a November 1974 talk he gave at Washington University titled "Labor Unions and the City" attested to his mesmerizing effect on the young. One attendee exulted, "Go on Pops. Go on, you crazy motherfucker, do it you old warrior, do it to death, and I'm sure you will." Others described him as "captivating," "excellent," "fantastic," and "walking history."[45]

Calloway also wrote prolifically and made numerous public appearances, sounding familiar themes about the deterioration of the city, the inadequacy of black political leadership, and the need for the trade union movement to reinvent itself. Ever cognizant of the complicated nexus of race and class in the urban crucible, he continued to bemoan the cumulative effects of deindustrialization, disinvestment, and redlining in St. Louis. As an alternative to focusing on downtown development instead of the city's neighborhoods, Calloway called for an urban strategy that would build on St. Louis's strong health care and educational sectors and reposition it as a service-oriented economy. He also persisted in his lifelong commitment to working-class citizenship. In his capacity as president of the north St. Louis-based Congress of Neighborhood Organizations, Calloway supported an ordinance requiring city agencies to meet and consult with community groups before implementing their development plans. Describing the proposed ordinance as "our neighborhood Declaration of Independence," he reiterated his aversion for the constricted vision of ward politics: "It would appear that neighborhoods and neighborhood organizations are better suited at working in concert with a common purpose than many of our ward political organizations."[46]

Throughout the 1970s, Calloway painstakingly documented the decline of civic participation within the African American community, citing lagging voter registration and what he called the propensity of black leadership for "suffocating in its own little ward turfs and self-interest penny-ante games." Arguing that African Americans needed to focus on the structural economic underpinnings of racial oppression, he again urged the community to adopt a broader perspective: "Black collective self-interest in the past has been to try to halt racism, but now it should be more sophisticated in terms of social goals." Although his suggestions gained limited traction among most black politicians in St. Louis, Calloway spotlighted the complex challenges of post-civil-rights politics. He also anticipated the rise of a new generation of African American political leaders more open to his advocacy of interracial politics and comprehensive strategies for urban revitalization.[47]

Calloway accompanied his concerns about the state of black politics in St. Louis with a series of prophetic reflections about the increasing debility of the union movement. Noting the rise of the global multinational corporation, he warned in a February 1976 *Missouri Teamster* article that unions faced a "new economic ball game." Calloway averred, "If the environment of democracy is polluted by omnipotent private power and decision, the trade union movement is destroyed. Consequently, it is much later for U.S. unionism that one would think." Several months later, in a widely syndicated article, he chided the labor movement for not responding aggressively to these developments, denounced a protectionist approach as unworkable, and urged unions to build global alliances capable of bargaining with corporations no longer constrained by national boundaries.[48]

After suffering a stroke in 1981, Calloway remained infirmed until his death on December 31, 1989, a day short of what would have been his eighty-first birthday. His wife Deverne, who herself had suffered a stroke after years as his caregiver, died four years later, leaving St. Louis without the couple who for nearly three decades had been an integral force in the city's black freedom struggle and post–World War II politics. The *St. Louis Post-Dispatch* praised him as a man who had "labored for the underdog" and declared that "St. Louis is better for his efforts." His old foe William Clay offered "an ode to my friend" in *Congressional Record*, saluting his rival as "a rugged fighter for social justice who used facts for ammunition." One of the most incisive reflections on Calloway's legacy came from *Post-Dispatch* columnist William Woo. Noting Calloway's many social roles—"scholar and teacher, civil rights leader, astute political adviser, writer,"—Woo concluded that another of his identities ranked as first among equals: "But I suspect that when he came to Heaven's door, all that was written on the calling card in his hand was the words, 'Ernest Calloway, Trade Unionist.'"[49]

Certainly, Calloway would not have rejected Woo's epitaph. However, one can imagine him explaining at "Heaven's door" that trade unionism was the starting point and effective citizenship the ultimate destination. Presumably Harold Gibbons would have joined him, continuing a conversation that these coal miners' sons had begun in a Chicago bar four decades earlier on how they could "extend the trade union apparatus into the primary mainstreams of American life."

EPILOGUE

Just before his retirement from teaching at St. Louis University, Ernest Calloway offered several extended reflections on the concept of total person unionism. In a May 1976 talk before a student audience, Calloway observed, "If there has been one weak strain running through the history of U.S. unionism, it is in the accepted definition of a union member." Throughout his long career, Calloway resisted the tendency to define union members in what he described as "one-dimensional, fragmented terms." As he noted in a "biographical sketch" he wrote in 1976, "the union member was also a live, breathing social being with a great number of complex problems in his social environment. He worked eight hours a day on the job, but lived, breathed, loved, dreamed, prayed, and hoped sixteen hours a day."[1]

Determined to help union members realize the full potential of their "other sixteen hours," Ernest Calloway and Harold Gibbons attempted to enhance the quality of their lives and the well-being of their communities. This commitment led them to create or inspire an impressive list of institutions—a metropolitan sewer district, a bi-state public transit agency, a community college system, housing for senior citizens—that demonstrably improved the lives of both union members and St. Louis's broader working class. They also played a crucial role in enabling African Americans to uproot St. Louis's entrenched culture of racial hegemony, and help the city avert the civil disorder that permanently scarred many other urban communities during the 1960s. Although Gibbons and Calloway fell short in their ultimate quest to rejuvenate the post-industrial city, their efforts to introduce "trade union principles in the community at large" made discernible progress in chipping away at racial and class disparities in St. Louis.[2]

Testimony to the continuing influence of Gibbons and Calloway also lies in the careers of people they inspired. Richard Baron, the legal aid lawyer who became attached to Gibbons during the St. Louis rent strike, has become one of the nation's most prominent developers of low- and moderate-income urban housing. Baron employs a "total person" approach that draws on many of the concepts developed during the Civic Alliance for Housing's administration of public housing in St. Louis. Jean King, the most visible tenant leader during the strike, subsequently dedicated herself to the cause of tenant management and is the subject of an inspiring new film that describes her collaborative work with Richard Baron in promoting urban revitalization. The career of Clint Zweifel, a rising star in

Missouri politics, is a more recent manifestation of the Gibbons-Calloway tradition. Just re-elected in 2012 to a second term as Missouri state treasurer, Zweifel previously held Calloway's post as research and education director of Local 688 and highlighted this connection during his initial campaign. Zweifel's commitment to a vigorous role for government echoes Gibbons and Calloway's belief that social well-being depends on the ability of public institutions to provide sufficient infrastructure to sustain the quality of community life.[3]

The fate of Council Plaza, however, serves as a sobering reminder that visionary social experimentation is not easily sustained. Gibbons's successors showed little interest in Council Plaza, canceling expansion plans and selling the complex to new managers. Belated recognition of Council Plaza's integral role in helping revive St. Louis's deteriorating inner core came three decades later in 2007 when the Missouri Department of Natural Resources gained approval to place it on the National Register of Historic Places as a project of "exceptional significance" that provided "inestimable value to the community." This recognition, however, was bittersweet. As a woman whose grandparents resided in Council Plaza noted in a 2011 Facebook posting, "Difficult to find a residence that respects the people who live there the way the Teamsters did their retirees. It didn't do nearly as well after it sold."[4]

Like Council Plaza, Gibbons and Calloway's beloved union movement has not fared well in the decades following their deaths. Regrettably, many of their warnings about the precarious status of trade unions have proved strikingly prophetic. Pummeled by the converging forces of globalization, technological change, employer resistance to new organizing, and political efforts to undermine collective bargaining, the percentage of the U.S. labor force that belongs to unions recently fell to a ninety-seven-year low. Income inequality and the mal-distribution of wealth have reached record levels, a reality brilliantly dramatized by the Occupy Wall Street movement. With the bargaining power of workers sharply diminished and the forces of capital enjoying virtual free rein, social observers are increasingly questioning the union movement's relevance in a twenty-first century global economy.[5]

The Teamsters' experience over the past thirty years starkly illustrates the searing impact of these developments. The Carter administration's deregulation of the trucking industry in 1980 unleashed fierce nonunion competition that gutted the underpinnings of Teamster power. Jimmy Hoffa's successors—Frank Fitzsimmons, Roy Williams, and Jackie Presser—had no strategic answers to counter this assault, and their acquiescence to increased influence by organized crime figures damaged the union's already shaky legitimacy. This debility spawned several reform movements within the rank-and-file, most notably Teamsters for a Democratic Union (TDU), which galvanized opposition to concessionary contracts and inept leadership.[6]

Pressure from these movements prompted the federal government to monitor the election of national officers, and in 1991, reformer Ron Carey became Teamsters' president. Reminiscent of Harold Gibbons's "Shared Responsibility and Joint Leadership" platform, Carey's agenda, which included a renewed commitment to organizing and forging closer ties with other unions and community groups, culminated in the Teamsters' 1997 strike against United Parcel Service, one of the most significant labor victories in a generation. However, facing a challenge from James P. Hoffa, the son of the former Teamsters' president, Carey became embroiled in election irregularities and was expelled by a court-appointed review board in 1998. Although the Hoffa name may have inspired the rank-and-file to believe that a return to the union's glory days was eminent, the Teamsters have been unable to rebound under the younger Hoffa's leadership. Once an emblem of raw working-class power, the Teamster brand has lost its luster, no longer possessing the ability to disrupt the economy, intimidate economic and political decision makers, or command public attention.

Gibbons and Calloway's experience offers some valuable insights for a union movement whose relevance is being questioned. As far back as the 1960s, they lamented the stagnation of union organizing amid structural changes in the economy that were diluting labor's strength. Indeed, the implosion of private sector union membership that has ensued over the last four decades arguably represents the labor movement's most urgent and formidable challenge. This development has been exacerbated by conscious efforts to pit private and public sector workers against each other, thereby threatening to derail worker solidarity and dismantle the public employee unions that currently represent labor's most vital source of strength.

Just as Gibbons and Calloway thought creatively about how the Teamsters could exercise decisive economic leverage, the union movement will need to develop strategies that respond to a service-oriented economy that is aggressively eliminating mid-level jobs and treating most workers as contingent or disposable. In response to this disturbing development, some unions are actively assisting independent, alternative forms of organization seeking to rally workers in the service sector. Similar to the support that Gibbons and Calloway lent social insurgents during their trade union oriented war on the slums, the AFL-CIO opened the proceedings of its 2013 convention to numerous groups from outside the official union movement, including immigrants, day laborers, and domestic workers. Many top labor leaders now agree on the need to build a broadly based working-class movement committed to new forms of organizing and representation. Bringing these initiatives up to a visible public scale and winning victories that illustrate the efficacy of collective action should become a top labor priority. There have also been promising efforts to extend this worksite organizing into community campaigns that address the needs of workers as "whole persons," an approach that the Service Employees International Union and others have employed with some success over the last decade. Undoubtedly, Gibbons and Calloway would have lauded such efforts while wondering why it has taken so long for the union movement to heed the warnings they issued four decades earlier.[7]

Any chance for reviving private sector unionism will also require a concurrent political effort. Facing resistance in organizing and at the bargaining table, unions have increasingly turned to politics. However, in spite of growing worker involvement, increased technological sophistication, and electoral success, labor's political participation too often remains episodic, defensive, and limited in the scope of its demands. Here is where the democratic, civic spirit that animated the community stewards program might be usefully employed. While unions by no means should eschew electoral politics or party involvement, a strategy that emphasizes active, engaged citizenship and makes family and community security a defining theme will ultimately be needed to help re-establish labor's social relevance.

Gibbons and Calloway's concept of treating workers as total persons might find new political resonance in tackling the work-family divide that has arisen as dual earner families have become a social norm. In spite of much rhetoric about the "family friendly workplace," neither public nor private institutions have provided adequate support for families seeking to balance the competing demands of work and family life. Moreover, the supports that do exist are far less available to working-class families, who are often left to fend for themselves. A labor-inspired effort (one could see Gibbons and Calloway calling it a "crusade") around work-family issues could offer new avenues to create community and even national bargaining tables where engaged worker-citizens and their allies press for policies that address their needs as total persons. Moreover, such an effort would have a powerful unifying effect, benefitting all workers and nurturing the cross-class alliances essential to building a broader social movement. The successes of several efforts to enact paid sick leave at the local level attest to the political potential of these initiatives.

There are also several sobering aspects of Gibbons and Calloway's careers that deserve attention. For all the attractiveness of total person unionism as both a philosophy and a strategy, its successes were short-lived. Although part of the blame rested on the diversion of Gibbons's attention to national Teamsters politics, total person unionism faced a deeper set of challenges. In spite of Gibbons and Calloway's best efforts, many of their members continued to distinguish between the politics of work and the politics of community, favoring the worksite over the community bargaining table as the venue where their vital interests were most likely to be addressed. For contemporary unions that are cultivating community allies and building relationships with workers outside their official ranks, Gibbons and Calloway's experience sounds a cautionary note. As they painfully discovered, a focus on "the other sixteen hours" of workers' lives cannot ignore the equally critical eight hours that workers spend on the job. The workplace setting still remains the primary lens through which many workers view the world, and unions must be careful to ensure that their community efforts do not detract from their ability to defend job-related interests.

Gibbons's decision to make the community rather than the union the principal arena where members could practice democracy also had serious consequences for total person unionism. As Local 688 became more enmeshed in the dominant Teamsters culture, the democratic spirit that had previously guided the union yielded to centralized authority, a muted rank-and-file voice in shaping union policy, and limited tolerance for dissent. Gibbons and Calloway's pursuit of high-level civic partnerships also left little space for direct worker involvement. And in their questionable behavior during the Joint Council 13 and St. Louis NAACP elections, Gibbons and Calloway's willingness to sidestep democratic procedures sullied their credentials as exponents of working-class citizenship. Arguably, Gibbons and Calloway were at their best when leading campaigns where empowered workers demanded that power brokers treat seriously their claims as citizens. When they strayed from democratic principles and lost their connection to engaged workers making such claims, their efforts faltered, drained of the participatory spirit, social drama, and civic education that characterized their most successful efforts to find seats for worker-citizens at the community bargaining table.

The reach of total person unionism also remained limited, both within St. Louis and elsewhere. Gibbons foreclosed some of these possibilities during the sectarian bloodletting of the 1940s and 1950s. Although his resolute anti-communism reflected deeply held principles, it also led him to deny political legitimacy to even those elements on the non-communist left who remained willing to work with the CP. This decision had lasting consequences, leaving many other left-liberal unions suspicious of Gibbons's motives and making unified labor action in St. Louis much harder to obtain. Local 688's go-it-alone approach further hampered its ability to attract a broader set of local allies, and the Teamsters' expulsion from the AFL-CIO diminished Gibbons and Calloway's ability to present their ideas on a broader stage. The lost potential of Gibbons and Calloway's political exile was underscored by the brief success of the Alliance for Labor Action and Gibbons's important role in leading labor opposition to the Vietnam War, both of which illustrated the political possibilities of Teamsters' residence within the house of labor. The implications of Gibbons and Calloway's experience for contemporary unions, especially those seeking to advance visionary policies, are clear. Although the barriers to greater cooperation and coordination are longstanding and cannot be wished away, a besieged union movement can ill afford the luxury of disunity and needs to model the practice of solidarity that it preaches as its core value.

Gibbons and Calloway's most powerful legacy, however, was their insistence on the essential linkages between work, citizenship, and democracy. Justifying these linkages when a critic questioned Local 688's development of a school desegregation plan, Gibbons explained that "by its very nature democracy cannot become an exclusive club of exclusive people with exclusive privileges." Accordingly, he insisted, the union's "citizen-members" had a fundamental obligation to support racial equality to maintain a fully functioning democracy.[8]

In light of the controversy surrounding the death of Michael Brown, a young African American killed in August 2014 by a white police officer in the St. Louis suburb of Ferguson, Gibbons's reference to racial equality as a fundamental labor obligation has particular resonance. Gibbons and Calloway would have both recognized and lamented the continuing patterns of residential segregation, political disenfranchisement, and deep suspicion between African Americans and the police that fueled the outpouring of anger and recrimination following Brown's killing. They surely would have applauded AFL-CIO president Richard Trumka's September 2014 appeal for the union movement to "draw the line" against the militarization of the police and the disproportionate incarceration of people of color while supporting his call to fight racism by building "larger working-class political alliances." Delivered before a union audience in St. Louis, the AFL-CIO president's remarks echoed similar declarations made by Harold Gibbons in 1968 after police officers assaulted members of the Black Liberators at a local precinct house. Trumka's impassioned plea to confront racism within the house of labor and fight for racial justice reflected a degree of political courage rare among contemporary labor leaders. It is the kind of courage that Gibbons and Calloway displayed in their best moments and represents a part of their legacy that remains especially relevant for our times.[9]

In a September 1955 letter responding to a *St. Louis Post-Dispatch* reader's complaint that the community stewards were functioning as an unnecessary "intermediary" between citizens and government, Harold Gibbons affirmed the necessity for engaged working-class citizenship: "The working man, the average citizen is apt to be bewildered by the many pressure groups, apt to feel helpless and ultimately to become complacent or cynical about his own role in a democracy." Far from being an intermediary," Gibbons asserted, "the union's role is to encourage our working members to use their rights as citizens in a democracy."[10]

Gibbons's observation assumes special meaning in light of Ernest Calloway's prophetic prediction that "new economic concentrations of power . . . seriously undermine social and democratic institutions by establishing the supremacy of private decision-making." In this context their abiding faith that ordinary people could use their experiences as workers to enhance their roles as citizens offers hope, in Calloway's words, not only for extending "democratic unionism" but also for reviving "democracy itself."[11]

NOTES

Abbreviations

AD-UIC	Annetta M. Dieckmann Papers. Richard J. Daley Library Special Collections and University Archives, University of Illinois at Chicago
AJC-WU	A.J. Cervantes Collection. Manuscripts Division, Olin Library, Washington University, St. Louis
ALES-CU	American Labor Education Service Records. Kheel Center for Labor-Management Documentation and Archives, Cornell University
APR-LC	A. Philip Randolph Papers, Library of Congress, Washington, D.C.
BCLP-UMSL	Black Community Leaders Project. Western Historical Manuscripts Collection, University of Missouri at St. Louis
Dagen-UMSL	Irvin and Margaret Dagen History of St. Louis CORE Collection. WHMC-UMSL
EC	Ernest Calloway
EC-FBI	Ernest Calloway Federal Bureau of Investigation Records
EC-SLU	Ernest Calloway Manuscript Collection. Special Collections: Archives and Manuscripts, Saint Louis University Libraries
EC-UMSL	Ernest Calloway Collection. Western Historical Manuscripts Collection, Thomas Jefferson Library, University of Missouri at St. Louis. Collection comprised of three segments, No. 11, No. 540, and No. 550
FR-UMSL	Freedom of Residence, Greater St. Louis Committee Records. Western Historical Manuscripts Collection, University of Missouri at St. Louis
FTA-CUA	Congress of Industrial Organizations. National and International Union Files, Food, Tobacco, and Allied Workers Union of America, Catholic University of America Archives
HJG	Harold J. Gibbons
HJG-Blount	Elzie F. (Red) Smith, interview with Dale F. Blount, March 5, 1997. Oral Histories with Teamsters. Southern Illinois University Edwardsville
HJG-FBI	Harold J. Gibbons Federal Bureau of Investigation Records
HJG-SIUE	Harold J. Gibbons Collection. Louisa H. Bowen University Archives and Special Collections, Lovejoy Library, Southern Illinois University Edwardsville
HK-DNSA	Henry Kissinger Telephone Conversations. Digital National Security Archive

HUD-NA	Department of Housing and Urban Development General Records. Region VII, Kansas City, National Archives, College Park, Maryland
JC 13-SIUE	Teamsters Joint Council 13 Collection. University Archives and Special Collections, Southern Illinois University at Edwardsville
JLC-NYU	Jewish Labor Committee Records. Tamiment Library, Robert F. Wagner Labor Archives, New York University
Keiser-UIS	John Keiser Collection. Brookens Library Archives and Special Collections, University of Illinois at Springfield
KT-UMSL	Ernest Calloway Writings, compiled by Kenn Thomas. University of Missouri at St. Louis
LP-UMSL	Labor for Peace Records. Western Historical Manuscripts Collection, University of Missouri at St. Louis
LEV-UMSL	Lift Every Voice and Sing Oral History Project. University of Missouri at St. Louis
LWV-UMSL	League of Women Voters Records. Western Historical Manuscripts Collection, University of Missouri at St. Louis
MCF-UMSL	Metropolitan Church Federation Records. Western Historical Manuscripts Collection, University of Missouri at St. Louis
MLW	*Midwest Labor World*
NAACP-LC	National Association for the Advancement of Colored People Records. Manuscript Division, Library of Congress, Washington, D.C.
NUL-LC	National Urban League Records. Library of Congress, Washington, D.C.
RWDSU-CUA	Congress of Industrial Organizations. National and International Unions, Retail, Wholesale, Department Store Union, Catholic University of America Archives
Senate-NA	Senate Select Committee on Improper Activities in the Labor or Management Field, 1957–1960 Records. National Archives, Washington, D.C.
Sentner-WU	William Sentner Collection, Department of Special Collections, Olin Library, Washington University, St. Louis
SLGD	*St. Louis Globe-Democrat*
SLPD	*St. Louis Post-Dispatch*
Sverdrup-WU	Leif Sverdrup Papers, Manuscripts Division, Olin Library, Washington University, St. Louis
Teamsters-GWU	Teamsters Archives. Labor History Research Center, George Washington University
Tucker-WU	Raymond R. Tucker Files, City of St. Louis, Office of the Mayor, 1953–1965. Department of Special Collections, Olin Library, Washington University, St. Louis
UTSE-CIO	United Transport Service Employees, Congress of Industrial Organizations. Also referred to as United Transport Service Employees of America
UTSEA-CUA	Congress of Industrial Organizations. National and International Union Files, United Transport Service Employees of America
Wheeler-UMSL	Henry Winfield Wheeler Papers, Western Historical Manuscripts Collection, University of Missouri at St. Louis

Introduction

1. "New Affluence, Unity for Labor," *Life*, Vol. 38, No. 24, December 12, 1955, 28, 33.
2. "Officers' Report, Local No. 688, to the Ninth Annual Citywide Shop Conference, January 20, 1952," Affiliated Bodies Series, Local #688, St. Louis, Missouri, 1952, Teamsters-GWU.
3. Brill, *The Teamsters*, 397.
4. Burnside, "Calloway at 73."
5. Ernest Calloway "Biographical Sketch," Box 50, File 3, HJG-SIUE.
6. Vasquez interview.

Chapter 1. Coming Up the Hard Way

1. Defty, "Teamster Boss," Ernest Calloway (hereafter EC), "Union Philosophy as Related to Economic Structure," August 12, 1965, Box 1, File 5, No. 11, EC-UMSL.
2. McCarthy, "Portrait of Gibbons," Box 1, File 16, JC 13-SIUE; Jake McCarthy to H.J. Gibbons, August 22, 1967, Box 5, File 24; Ernest Calloway, "Biographical Sketch," Box 50, File 31, HJG-SIUE; Vasquez interview; de Somer interview; EC, "How We Came to Appalachia and the Ky. Cumberlands in 1913," *St. Louis American*, February 19, 1981.
3. Dublin and Licht, *Face of Decline*, 10, 25; Blatz, *Democratic Miners*, 9, 12, 27; "Summary of Anthracite Accidents," www.dep.state.pa/us/dep/deputate/minres/bmr/annualreport, accessed December 25, 2008; Miller and Sharpless, *Kingdom of Coal*, 63.
4. Blatz, *Democratic Miners*, 64, 142–52, 259; Miller and Sharpless, *Kingdom of Coal*, 258–59, 286.
5. EC, "How We Came to Appalachia"; Corbin, *Life, Work, and Rebellion*, 8; Trotter, Jr., *Coal, Class, and Color*, 12–13, 19; Lewis, *Black Coal Miners in America*, 132.
6. Lewis, *Black Coal Miners*, 126, 130, 138, 144–46; Trotter, *Coal, Class, and Color*, 21.
7. Corbin, *Life, Work, and Rebellion*, 8, 14–18; Miller and Sharpless, *Kingdom of Coal*; 150–51, 275–83.
8. Corbin, *Life, Work, and Rebellion*, 27–28, 32–33; Lewis, *Black Coal Miners*, 133–40; Trotter, *Coal, Class, and Color*, 53.
9. Corbin, *Life, Work, and Rebellion*, 90–95; EC, "How We Came to Appalachia."
10. EC, "How We Came to Appalachia"; "Kentucky Coal Heritage," www.coaleducation.org, accessed January 16, 2009; Lewis, *Black Coal Miners*, 126–27, 147–48; Jenkins Area Jaycees, "The History of Jenkins, Kentucky," 1973.
11. EC, "How We Came to Appalachia."
12. McCarthy, "Portrait of Gibbons"; "Hal Gibbons: Teamster," Teamsters Local 20 (Toledo, Ohio), *Union Leader World*, 9, No. 10, n.d., Box 5, File 3, JC 13-SIUE; Defty, "Teamster Boss."
13. Dublin and Licht, *The Face of Decline*, 49; Defty, "Teamster Boss"; *Union Leader World*, "Hal Gibbons: Teamster"; Vasquez interview.
14. "Teamsters' Gibbons: His Tough Climb Up," *New York Herald Tribune*, August 15, 1964; "Hal Gibbons: Teamster."
15. EC, "Negro in Kentucky Coal Fields"; "Lonely Colossus of U.S. Labour"; and "Melange."
16. Patrick Gibbons interview; McCarthy, "Portrait of Gibbons"; Burnside, "Socialist Teamster."

17. EC, "Union Philosophy."
18. EC, "New Challenges to American Labor," Labor and International Affairs Forum, Brainerd, Minnesota, October 2, 1964, Box 7, File 234, No. 540, EC-UMSL; "Harlem Summer, 1925"; EC interview with Robert Davis.
19. EC (editor), "Ten Years of Trade Union Democracy in Action," Teamsters Local 688 Tenth Anniversary Report, 1951, Box 42, File 41, HJG-SIUE; "Mine Union Shows Way"; "Lonely Colossus."
20. Patrick Gibbons interview; "Testimony of Harold J. Gibbons," Hearings Before the Select Committee on Improper Activities in the Labor or Management Field, Eighty-Fifth Congress, Second Session, Part 39, September 2, 1958, 14559 (hereafter HJG Testimony); McCarthy, "Portrait of Gibbons"; "Harold J. Gibbons," FBI File SL 92-441, August 7, 1959; Ball, "Case History."
21. McCarthy, "Before It Was Fashionable"; "The Ernest Calloway Story, 1934–1972," Box 7, File 540, No 540, EC-UMSL.
22. EC, "Union Philosophy"; "Harlem Summer, 1925"; Clark, "Local Labor Pioneer"; Senator T. D. McNeal, "Who Is Ernest Calloway, Candidate?" *TRUTH*, Vol. 2, no. 2, June 8, 1968, Box 23, File 1, HJG-SIUE; EC interview with Robert Davis.

Chapter 2. "Apostles of a New Order"

1. Brill, *The Teamsters*, 354; EC, "To Sleep, Perchance to Dream."
2. Newell, *Chicago and the Labor Movement*, 9–11, 15–24; Cohen, *Making A New Deal*; 7, 12–13, 42–49; Drake and Cayton, *Black Metropolis*, 5–8; Lyons, *Teachers and Reform*, 5–8, 24–25; Fraser, *Labor Will Rule*, 57–60.
3. McCarthy, "Portrait of Gibbons"; Brill, *The Teamsters*, 353; HJG Statement Before Subcommittee on Unemployment and the Impact of Automation, House Committee on Education and Labor, April 12, 1961, Box 5, File 3, HJG-SIUE.
4. "Annetta M. Dieckmann, Biographical Sketch" in finding guide to Dieckmann Collection; untitled reflection on the "YWCA and Citizenship," Box 6, File 65, AD-UIC; Kweder, "Annetta Dieckmann," 220–21; Annetta M. Dieckmann, "Education for Citizenship," *Women's Press*, November 1950; Lillian Herstein interview by Elizabeth Balanoff, "Oral History Project in Labor History," Roosevelt University, October 26, 1970, 34, 38, 40, and May 7, 1971, 248–50, 261, 270–74; Balanoff, "Lillian Herstein," 387–90; Lyons, "Lillian Herstein," 585–86; Annetta M. Dieckmann to Harold J. Gibbons, October 19, 1937, Box 1, File 1, JC 13-SIUE.
5. "Harold Gibbons," *St. Louis Globe-Democrat* (hereafter *SLGD*), November 19, 1982; McCarthy, "Portrait of Gibbons"; Brill, *The Teamsters*, 354; Ball, "Case History of a Labor Union"; Burnside, "Socialist Teamster."
6. "Harold Joseph Gibbons," FBI File No. 124-4416, August 1950; Biles, *Crusading Liberal*, 15–20, 24.
7. Joyce L. Kornbluh, "New Deal Teacher-Training Centers, 1934–1935," www.distance.syr.edu/ kornbluh.htlml, accessed February 6, 2009.
8. HJG Testimony, 14561; McCarthy, "Portrait of Gibbons"; Herstein interview, 260.
9. HJG, "Youth Week Speech," n.d., 1934, Box 5, File 3, HJG-SIUE.
10. McCarthy, "Portrait of Gibbons"; EC, "Norman Thomas."
11. McCarthy, "Portrait of Gibbons." On references to Gibbons's Socialist past, see "Emphasis, " HJG interview with Chet Huntley on NBC television, March 30, 1965, Box 1, File

5, Keiser-UIS; Transcript, "The Barry Gray Show," April 28, 1964, Box 6, File 5, JC 13-SIUE; Burnside, "Socialist Teamster."

12. Calloway interview with Robert Davis; Burnside, "Calloway at 73."

13. "To Sleep, Perchance to Dream"; Davis interview; Sanford, "Calloway in Earnest."

14. EC, "To Sleep, Perchance to Dream"; Calloway interview with Davis.

15. EC, "Who Am I?"

16. McCarthy, "Before It Was Fashionable"; Sanford, "Calloway in Earnest"; EC, "The Night They Lynched Jimmie Madison," Box 51, File 605, No. 540, EC-UMSL.

17. Davis interview; Cawthra, "Ernest Calloway."

18. EC, "Negro in the Kentucky Coal Fields"; and "A Labor Study (South)."

19. Ibid.

20. Parris and Brooks, *Blacks in the City*, 250–54; Zieger, *For Jobs and Freedom*, 108; EC "Biographical Sketch," 1976, Box 50, File 31, HJG-SIUE.

21. Jonathan D. Bloom, "Workers Education and Adult Education," www.distance.syr.edu/bloom/html, accessed February 10, 2009; and "Brookwood Labor College," 71–80; Howlett, *Brookwood Labor College*, 207–10.

22. EC, "Brookwood Labor College"; "Forty Years of Unionism"; "Making of Professional Agitator"; "The Ernest Calloway Story, 1934–1972," Box 7, File 231, No. 540, EC-UMSL; Senator T.D. McNeal, "Who Is Ernest Calloway, Candidate?" *TRUTH*, Vol. 2, No. 2, June 8, 1968, Box 23, File 1, HJG-SIUE; Howlett, *Brookwood Labor College*, 68–75; EC interview with Richard Resh, July 31, 1970, BCLP-UMSL; "The Labor Movement: A Re-Examination, A Conference in Honor of David J. Saposs," Industrial Relations Institute, University of Wisconsin, 1967, 156–57.

23. EC, "The CIO and the Negro," *Opportunity*, Vol. XIV, No. 11, November 1936, 326–30. For Saposs's views, see David J. Saposs, "The Labor Movement: A Look Backward and Forward," in "The Labor Movement: A Re-Examination," 73–78; and *Left-Wing Unionism*.

24. EC, "Workers Education"; "Jobless Meeting"; "1936 Marks Turning Point in Human Needs Approach"; "Early Attempt"; Solomon, *Cry Was Unity*, 291–92, 301–7.

25. EC, "Sectarian Tradition"; *Cry Was Unity*, 81–88; Draper, *American Communism*, 345–56; Painter, *Hosea Hudson*, 16–17.

26. EC, "Sectarian Tradition," and "Race and Culture," KT-UMSL.

27. On Jay Lovestone, see Draper, *American Communism*, 272–78; Buhle, "Thin Red Line"; Lichtenstein, *Most Dangerous Man*, 114–15; Morgan, *A Covert Life*, 87–94.

28. Morgan, *Covert Life*, 124–25.

Chapter 3. Able and Militant Fighters for Workers

1. EC, "New CIO Leader."

2. Richard Wright, quoted in St. Clair Drake and Horace R. Cayton, xvii.

3. McCarthy, "Portrait of Gibbons"; Eaton, *American Federation of Teachers*, 79; Murphy, *Blackboard Unions*, 135, 148, 162.

4. Report of the Proceedings of the Twentieth Annual Convention of the American Federation of Teachers, August 17–21, 1936, 25, 27, 87.

5. "Notes on Anti-Communist Activities of Harold J. Gibbons," Box 53, File 628, No. 540, EC-UMSL; "An Election Statement of the Progressive Group of Local #346," June 23, 1936, Box 1, File 1, JC 13-SIUE; Eaton, *American Federation of Teachers*, 80; Cayton, *Long Old Road*, 237–39.

6. "Election Statement of Progressive Group."

7. McCarthy, "Portrait of Gibbons"; "Anti-Communist Activities of Harold J. Gibbons"; Biles, *Crusading Liberal*, 14.

8. HJG to All Locals of the American Federation of Teachers, January 7, 1937, Box 1, File 1, JC 13-SIUE; Newell, *Chicago and the Labor Movement*, 107–9.

9. McCarthy, "Portrait of Gibbons"; *Midwest Taxi Drivers Organizer*, Vol. 1, No. 4, April 18, 1937, Box 1, File 1, JC 13-SIUE; Burnside, "Socialist Teamster."

10. Newell, *Chicago and the Labor Movement*, 224; "Adult Teachers' Union Ousted from A.F. of L for CIO Link," n.d., 1937, Box 1, File 1, JC 13-SIUE; Eaton, *American Federation of Teachers*, 81.

11. McCarthy, "Portrait of Gibbons"; Brill, *The Teamsters*, 355; HJG Testimony, 14559–60, 14562.

12. "CIO Forces Weaker as Laundry and Cleaning Operations Are Increased," *The News-Gazette* (Champaign, Illinois), October 23, 1937; McCarthy, "Portrait of Gibbons"; "U.S. Marshal Arrests Four at Bike-Web," n.d. 1937, Box 1, File 1, JC 13-SIUE; Brill, *The Teamsters*, 355.

13. Daniel, *Culture of Misfortune*, 61–70; Fraser, *Labor Will Rule*, 40–41, 378–82, 385.

14. McCarthy, "Portrait of Gibbons"; Burnside, "Socialist Teamster"; International Brotherhood of Teamsters Biography of HJG, Box 1, File 5, Keiser-UIS; FBI, NY HJG File No. 124-2880, August 25, 1950.

15. Rose, "Teamsters New Boss?"; Fraser, *Labor Will Rule*, 321.

16. Vasquez interview; Brill, *The Teamsters*, 355.

17. EC, "Story of Red Cap Union."

18. Arnesen, *Brotherhoods of Color*," 152–55; and "Willard Townsend," 151; EC, "New CIO Leader"; Drake and Cayton, *Black Metropolis*, 237–39; EC, "Story of Red Cap Union"; and "The Red Caps' Struggle"; Townsend interview.

19. Arnesen, *Brotherhoods of Color*, 155, 157–58; EC, "Story of the Red Cap Union"; "The Red Caps' Struggle"; and "Birth of a Union," *Convention Journal*, UTSE-CIO, July 14, 1943; Drake and Cayton, *Black Metropolis*, 242.

20. Townsend interview; EC, "Story of Red Cap Union"; "Red Caps' Struggle"; Arnesen, *Brotherhoods of Color*, 161–64.

21. Drake and Cayton, *Black Metropolis*, 240–41; Arnesen, *Brotherhoods of Color*, 161–62; and "Willard Townsend," 152–53; EC, "Story of Red Cap Union."

22. Townsend interview.

23. Arnesen, *Brotherhoods of Color*, 168; EC, "A Plain Talk with the Red Caps of America," September 10, 1937; "Conference of Red Caps Proceedings," January 1938, Box 14, APR-LC; Cayton, "UTSEA in Action."

24. EC, "Story of the Red Cap Union"; and "Red Caps Victorious"; Arnesen, *Brotherhoods of Color*, 168–70; and "International Brotherhood of Red Caps-UTSEA," *Encyclopedia of U.S. Labor and Working-Class History*, Vol. 1, A-F Index, edited by Eric Arnesen, (New York: Routledge, 2007), 666; "Conference of Red Caps Proceedings," APR-LC.

25. EC, "Birth of a Union"; Arnesen, *Brotherhoods of Color*, 171–73.

26. EC, "Building Your Union."

27. EC, "Women, Home, and Union"; "Martha Calloway Appointed National Director," *Bags and Baggage*, June 1942.

28. EC, "Women, Home, and Union"; Lewis, *In Their Own Interests*, 5–6, 128–31. On women's auxiliaries, see Chateauvert, *Marching Together*, xi–xiii, 74–75, 97, 140; and Cobble, *Other Women's Movement*; 23–25, 149.

29. EC, "Requiem for Compassionate Spirit"; Meier and Rudwick, *CORE*; 4–14; "Ernest Calloway," FBI File 100-11057, May 2, 1949; Knupfer, *Chicago Black Renaissance*, 40–44.

30. EC, "Requiem;" HJG FBI File 100–11057, May 2, 1949; "U.S. Commonwealth Party Formed by Chicago," n.d., Box 53, File 630, No. 540, EC-UMSL; EC, "Labor Building"; Drake and Cayton, *Black Metropolis*, 354–55; Biles: *Big City Mayor*, 13–20; Grimshaw, *Bitter Fruit*, 48.

31. Drake and Cayton, *Black Metropolis*, 376–77; Grimshaw, *Bitter Fruit*, 48; Floyd, "Calloway Wants a Revolution"; Biles, *Big City Mayor*, 97–100; Nordin, *New Deal's Black Congressman*; 114, 117; EC, "Requiem for Compassionate Spirit."

32. EC, "Negro Labor."

33. Drake and Cayton, *Black Metropolis*, 379–85; Knupfer, *Chicago Black Renaissance*, 1–6; EC, "Forty Years of Unionism"; Burgess, "Unusual Husband-Wife Team."

34. "Professor H.H. Sutton, Veteran Educator, Visits Chicago," May 31, 1941; "Hold Rites for Former Philander Smith Educator," July 28, 1945; "Diana Marries," January 31, 1942; "Martha Briggs Sutton Leaves for Barber-Scotia," October 10, 1936; "Gifted Soprano," May 22, 1937, all in *Chicago Defender*; "Martha Calloway Appointed National Director."

Chapter 4. "A Bunch of Fellows Who Have Taken the Declaration of Independence Seriously"

1. Walter J. Sheridan to Robert F. Kennedy, August 19, 1959, Vol. 86, 18–5, Hoffa Serials, 3893–3950, Senate-NA; Rose, *Union Solidarity*, 16–17; EC, "10 Years of Trade Union Democracy in Action," Box 42, File 41, HJG-SIUE; "The Nature of Power and Its Roots in a Community," Center of Community Studies, University of Missouri, March 19, 1968, Box 7, File 236, No. 540, EC-UMSL; "Summary of the Report of the St. Louis Labor Education Project," Box 34, File 16, ALES-CU; Primm, *Lion of the Valley*, 437–38; Feurer, *Radical Unionism in the Midwest*, 3–7, 16–17; Gordon, *Mapping Decline*, 13.

2. Ball, "Case History of a Labor Union"; McCarthy, "Portrait of Gibbons"; "Meet Your Union," Box 40, File 1, HJG-SIUE; Milton Zatinsky, "Let's Look at Our Union: Its Aims, Activities, and Accomplishments," October 1, 1945, Educational Department, St. Louis Joint Council URWDSEA, Pamphlet Collection, Duke University Library; Smith interview, 5, 7, 11–12, HJG-Blount; Wolff, *Improving Warehouse Productivity*, 8; Nelson, *Shifting Fortunes*, 8–10.

3. Ball, "Case History," 18–22; EC, "10 Years of Trade Union Democracy," 11; Smith interview, 3–6, 11–12.

4. Smith, "Experiment in Trade Union Democracy," 30; Ball, "Case History," 24–28; EC, "10 Years of Trade Union Democracy," 12; McCarthy, "Portrait of Gibbons"; Opler, *For All White-Collar Workers*, 88–91, 108; Phillips, *Renegade Union*, 39.

5. *St. Louis Organizer*, Vol. 1, No. 4, December 15, 1941, Box 5, File 3, JC 13-SIUE; "Pentland: Senator with a Perfect Record," *Midwest Labor World* (hereafter *MLW*), February 1, 1956; "10 Years of Trade Union Democracy," 14, 17, 38; Vasquez interview.

6. Harry Cashion, Edward P. Englart, and Leo M. England to Allen Haywood, March 21, 1940, Series I, Box 9, File 17; "In the Matter of Jurisdiction of the International Longshoremen's and Warehousemen's Union Before the Committee on Appeals of the Congress of Industrial Organizations, Meeting of December 18, 1940, Series I, Box 4, File 15, RWDSU-CUA; Zieger, *The CIO*, 73, 396.

7. "Bridges Invades St. Louis," *St. Louis Organizer*, Vol. 1, No. 2, September 15, 1941; "Hal Gibbons, Teamster," *Union Labor World*, Vol. 9, No. 10, IBT Local 20, Box 5, File 3, JC 13-SIUE.

8. McCarthy, "Portrait of Gibbons," 5–6; Ball, "Case History," 33–34, 41–42; Samuel Wolchok to Affiliated Locals, August 15, 1942, Series 1, Box 9, File 19, RWDSU-CUA.

9. Zieger, *The CIO*, 142–46; Lichtenstein, *Labor's War at Home*, 78–82; Levenstein, *Communism, Anti-Communism, and the CIO*, 170–80; Isserman, *Which Side Were You On?* 134–41.

10. Ball, "Case History,"102–3, 135, 139; "How to Decrease Strikes," March 22, 1944, and "Withdraw No-Strike Pledge," *MLW*, April 26, 1944; Defty, "Gibbons Kept Cool."

11. "CIO Political Action," August 25, 1943; "Betwixt the Cup and the Lip," November 8, 1944, *MLW*.

12. Gruenberg interview; HJG FBI File 92-4241, July 6, 1959. On charges that Gibbons was affiliated with the SWP, see Feurer, *Radical Unionism in the Midwest*, 196–97. The Trotskyist position on labor's role during World War II is vigorously conveyed in Preis, *Labor's Giant Step*.

13. EC, "10 Years of Trade Union Democracy," 20–21; Ball, "Case History," 50–90; *May Department Stores Company v. NLRB*, 326 U.S. Supreme Court, October 12, 1945.

14. Feurer, *Radical Unionism in the Midwest*, 122–23, 133, 163–76; Isserman, *Which Side Were You On?* 132–34; "Notes on Anti-Communist Activities of Harold J. Gibbons," Box 53, File 678, No. 540, EC-UMSL; Ball, "Case History," 110–17; "CIO Political Action," *MLW*, August 25, 1943; "Two Units Quit Council Over Communists," *SLGD*, August 28, 1943.

15. Ball, "Case History," 120, 151; "Resolution, St. Louis Labor Council, URWDSEA," *MLW*, January 26, 1944; Lichtenstein, *Labor's War at Home*, 182–85; Feurer, *Radical Unionism in the Midwest*, 196–97; Lens, *Unrepentant Radical*, 110–11, and *Left, Right, and Center*, 132–33; Opler, *For All White-Collar Workers*, 136–42; Phillips, *Renegade Union*, 84–87; Zieger, *The CIO*, 172; Preis, *Labor's Giant Step*, 217–22.

16. Vasquez interview.

17. Isserman, *Which Side Were You On?* 136–41; Zieger, *The CIO*, 253–56, 140–46; Lens, *Left, Right, and Center*, 394–98; Feurer, *Radical Unionism in the Midwest*, 196–97; "CIO Political Action."

18. Brody, "Uses of Power I," 192–93; Ball, "Case History," 169–71; and "Union History," 1950, Box 40, File 11, HJG-SIUE; EC, "Ten Years of Trade Union Democracy," 26; Hepner, "Union's Health Institute"; Klein, *For All These Rights*, 177–89.

19. Franz Goldmann, M.D., and Evarts A Graham, M.D., "The Quality of Medical Care Provided at the Labor Health Institute, St. Louis, Missouri," 1954, Box 1, File 5, Keiser-UIS; EC, "10 Years of Trade Union Democracy," 25; Ball, "Case History," 172; "Statement of Harold Gibbons," Hearings Before the Committee on Interstate and Foreign Commerce, House of Representatives, Eighty-Third Congress, Second Session on Available Health Plans and Group Insurance Programs, January 27, 1954, 2140–41; "Teamsters Local 688's 'Labor Health Institute' Lauded by Post-Dispatch," *St. Louis Labor Tribune*, January 19, 1950.

20. Goldmann and Graham, "Quality of Medical Care"; Baron interview; Gruenberg interview; Klein, *For All These Rights*, 187–90.

21. "LHI Report, 1950;" Hepner, "CIO Union's Health Institute."

22. "Planning for an Integrated School System in St. Louis," Committee on Democratic Rights of Members, Warehouse and Distribution Workers Local 688, December 15, 1951,

Box 41, File 7, HJG-SIUE; Heathcott, "Black Archipelago," 709–20; Kersten, *Race, Jobs, and the War*, 112–15; Adams, "Fighting for Democracy."

23. "St. Louis CIO in Action," April 1946, Jt. Council 13-SIUE; Unsigned editorial, *MLW*, August 23, 1944, quoted in Ball, "Case History"; Address of H.J. Gibbons, National Conference on Fair Employment Practices, United Auto Workers, CIO, July 27, 1945, Box 5, File 3, JC 13-SIUE; Rose, *Union Solidarity*, 25–26; "Wolchok to Affiliated Locals," August 15, 1942; Ball, "Case History of a Union," 162, 192–95. On the CIO and race, see Zieger, *For Jobs and Freedom*, 152–60.

24. McCarthy, "Portrait of Gibbons."

25. Stanford, *If We Must Die*, 142; Wynn, *Afro-American and Second World War*, 22–23.

26. Wynn, *Afro-American and Second World War*, 25; "Conscientious Objectors," *Chicago Defender*, January 18, 1941. Calloway outlined his position in several places. See EC, "Why I Cannot Serve"; "Why I Cannot Serve in a Jim Crow Army," December 23, 1940, Box 1, File 11, EC No. 11, EC-UMSL; and a retrospective reflection in "Jim Crow Army."

27. EC, "Why I Cannot Serve"; "Won't Serve in U.S. Army, Cites Bias," *Chicago Defender*, January 11, 1941; "Calloway Elected to Governing Board of Anti-War Congress," *Bags and Baggage*, June 1941.

28. Stanford, *If We Must Die*, 146; Wynn, *Afro-Americans and Second World War*, 29; Blum, *V Was for Victory*, 181–85, 1989; White to Calloway, January 10, 1941; EC to Walter White, January 28, 1941; "To Thurgood Marshall from Andy," Group II, Box B, File 148, Selective Service, NAACP-LC; "Jim Crow Army"; EC Chicago FBI File 100-11057, April 10, 1943.

29. EC, "Jim Crow Army"; and "The Red Caps' Struggle." For suggestions of tension between Calloway and Willard Townsend, see Mama to Well Papa, My Love, December 26, 1948, Box 2, File 50, No. 540, EC-UMSL; and John L. Yancey to Ernest, October 8, 1949, Box 1, File 1, No. 550, EC-UMSL.

30. EC, quoted in Arnesen, *Brotherhoods of Color*, 179; "Comments of GEB on Strike Vote," *Bags and Baggage*, August 1941.

31. Calloway FBI File No. 100–11057; "Street Car Jobs," *Chicago Defender*, August 28, 1943; Gellman, "'Carthage Must Be Destroyed,'" 109–12; EC Biographical Sketch-1976, Box 50, File 31, HJG-SIUE; EC interview with Dr. Richard Resh, BCLP-UMSL.

32. Resh interview. An extensive review of the rationale for anti-communism among African American unionists can be found in Arnesen, "No 'Graver Danger.'"

33. EC Biographical Sketch; EC, "Forty Years of Unionism"; "Negro Labor in 1942"; Negro Press"; and "Public Housing"; Sugrue, *Origins of the Urban Crisis*, 30.

34. "Hold Rites for Chicago Columnist," *The Afro-American*, October 19, 1946.

35. Deverne Calloway interview, BCLP-UMS; Clark, "Deverne Calloway."

36. Ibid.

37. "Laborite Wins Year at Oxford," *Chicago Defender*, July 18, 1948; "CIO Leader Gets Oxford Scholarship," *Chicago Daily News*, July 15, 1948; Cole, *Short History*, 1948.

38. EC to Darling, October 7, 1948; EC to Sweetheart, November 26, 1948, Box 2, File 50, No. 540, EC-UMSL. On Ben Roberts, see "The Author," in Roberts, *Trade Unions in a Free Society*.

39. EC to Sweetheart, November 26, 1948.

40. EC, "Trade Unions and the State," October 11, 1948; "A Critical Analysis of British Trade Union Structure," October 18, 1948, Box 3, File 60, No. 540, EC-UMSL.

41. EC, "American Politics," n.d., 1948, EC Writings, KT-UMSL; and "Goals of U.S. Unionism Today"; EC to Lester Granger, February 26, 1949, Box 8, File 238, No. 540, EC-UMSL.

42. EC, "Goals of U.S. Unionism."

43. Mama to Well Papa, My Love, December 26, 1948; Deverne to Calloway, July 15, 1949, Box 2, File 50, No. 540, EC-UMSL.

44. EC to Deverne, n.d., 1949; "An Ode to the Left Bank of Paris," n.d., Box 2, File 50, No. 540, EC-UMSL; EC, "Women of Belhaven."

45. Zieger, *The CIO*, 153, 282–83; Korstad, *Civil Rights Unionism*; Willard S. Townsend to Allan S. Haywood, January 8, 1951 and January 7, 1953, Series 1, Box 20, File 20, UTSEA-CUA; C.W. Fowler to Allan S. Haywood, March 28, 1947; and Donald Henderson to Allan Haywood, August 18, 1947, Series 1, Box 3, File 5, CIO National and International Union Files, Food, Tobacco, and Allied Workers Union of America, FTA-CUA; Martin, "UTSEA Prexy."

46. EC, "Women of Belhaven;" John L. Yancey to Ernest, October 8, 1949; and October 25, 1949, Box 1, File 1, No. 550, EC-UMSL.

47. EC, "Race and Culture Behind the Iron Curtain," June 3, 1949, KT-UMSL; Townsend, "British Labor Begins Move"; "Ode to the Left Bank of Paris."

48. John L. Yancey to Ernest, October 3, 1949, Box 1, File 1; EC Radio Statement, October 16, 1949, Box 4, File 35, No. 550, EC-UMSL; Korstad, *Civil Rights Unionism*, 407; Zieger, *The CIO*, 283.

49. EC to Willard S. Townsend, "Confidential Report on the Reynolds Campaign," March 15, 1950, Box 4, File 35, No. 550, EC-UMSL; Korstad, *Civil Rights Unionism*, 398.

50. EC, "General Recommendations," Box 4, File 35, No. 550, EC-UMSL; Willard S. Townsend to R.J. Thomas, January 5, 1951, Series I, Box 20, File 20, UTSEA-CUA. Years later, Calloway remained troubled by the Reynolds campaign. Although he expressed no regret for his role, his comments reflected a lingering suspicion that he and the UTSEA had been used as pawns by the CIO leadership for its own purposes. For more details, see Resh interview.

Chapter 5. "The Most Powerful Union in America"

1. "Allan S. Haywood," HJG FBI File 124-4416, September 27, 1950; Herling, "Hoffa Heir Apparent."

2. EC, "Biographical Sketch," Box 50, File 31, HJG-SIUE.

3. EC, "Pioneers in Race Relations"; Ames, Rich, Pace, and Gruenberg interviews; Rich interview, Dagen-UMSL; Ball, "Case History," 480.

4. Smith, "Experiment in Trade Union Democracy," 91.

5. Smith, "Experiment in Trade Union Democracy," 92–93; McCarthy, "Portrait of Gibbons"; Lichtenstein, *State of the Union*, 102–3.

6. EC, "10 Years of Trade Union Democracy in Action," Box 42, File 41, HJG-SIUE; Smith, "Experiment in Trade Union Democracy," 89–90; Ball, "Case History," 243; McCarthy, "Portrait of Gibbons."

7. On Taft-Hartley's impact, see Zieger, *The CIO*, 246–47; Lichtenstein, *State of the Union*, 114–18; and Nelson, *Shifting Fortunes*, 138–39.

8. "To Our Employees," August 16, 1948, Box 45, File 27; "Memorandum of J.H. Grady Company," Case No. 14-RC-400, Box 45, File 25; "Re: No. 14, CA-121, J.H. Grady

Notes to Chapter 5

Manufacturing Company," Box 45, File 28, HJG-SIUE; Ball, "Case History," 432; EC, "Ten Years of Union Democracy," 30–31; Smith, "Experiment in Union Democracy," 112.

9. "Teamsters Local No. 688 Picketing of J.H. Grady Company Challenges Firm's Attempt to Run Open Shop," February 2, 1949; "Anti-Labor Madison Act, Taft-Hartley Law Hurt AFL Teamsters 688 Members' Strike; Local Seeks Help of Other Unions," May 11, 1949, both in *St. Louis Labor Tribune*; Ball, "Case History," 438–44; Smith, "Experiment in Union Democracy," 115–24; EC, "Ten Years of Union Democracy, 30–31."

10. Harry V. Ball, Jr., "Union History," 1950, Box 40, File 11, HJG-SIUE, 12; and "Case History," 500; Smith, "Experiment in Union Democracy," 125; Zieger, *The CIO*, 248–49.

11. Opler, *For All White-Collar Workers*, 153–54; Phillips, *Renegade Union*, 84–88, 100–113; "Charges Against Samuel Wolchok," filed by Irving Abramson and Joseph G. Kane, October 27, 1947, Series I, Box 10, File 3, RWDSU-CUA; Ball, "Case History," 295.

12. Lou Berra to Samuel Wolchok, October 13, 1947, Series I, Box 2, File 7; To the Members of the International Executive Board of the Retail, Wholesale Department Union, CIO, n.d., 1947; Irving Abramson to Philip Murray, November 20, 1947, Series I, Box 10 File 4, both in RWDSU-CUA; Ball, "Case History," 301, 337–39.

13. United Distribution Workers Stewards Council Minutes, January 25, 1949, Box 34, File 20, ALES-CU; Ball, "Case History," 350, 413–18; Farabee interview, HJG-Blount; Lens, *Unrepentant Radical*, 146–47; EC, "Ten Years of Union Democracy," 33; and H.J. Gibbons To Friends of the United Distribution Workers Union and Its Personnel, January 27, 1949, in "Ten Years of Union Democracy," 66; Biographical Sketch and Achievement Dossier of Harold J. Gibbons, December 1980, Box 1, File 2, HJG-SIUE; Kirsten, *Stores and Unions*, 91; HJG Testimony, 14564.

14. Russell, *Out of the Jungle*, 59, 74–76, 109; Witwer, *Corruption and Reform*, 17–18, 78–79; Garnel, *Rise of Teamster Power*, 37–38; James and James, *Hoffa and the Teamsters*, 78–80; Jacobs, "World of Jimmy Hoffa (I)," 8.

15. Nelson, *Shifting Fortunes*, 125–26; Witwer, *Corruption and Reform*, 70–73, 132–37; Russell, *Out of the Jungle*, 40, 58; James and James, *Hoffa and the Teamsters*, 92–101; Garnel, *Teamster Power*, 107–16.

16. Sloane, *Hoffa*, 28–31; Garnel, *Teamster Power*, 74–76; Jacobs, "World of Jimmy Hoffa (I)," 7–8, 14–15; Witwer, *Corruption and Reform*, 146–48; Russell, *Out of the Jungle*, 60, 121–28; Lichtenstein, *State of the Union*, 145–46.

17. Farabee interview, HJG-Blount; "Educational Contact," January 26, 1949, Box 33, File 16, ALES-CU; H.J. Gibbons To Friends of the United Distribution Workers Union.

18. Ames interview; EC, "Ten Years of Union Democracy," 15; Burnside, "Socialist Teamster"; HJG FBI File No. 100-339783, May 25, 1960; Smith, "Experiment in Union Democracy," 135–36; James, "Gibbons' Red Front"; Blair, "AFL Teamsters Raid CIO"; "A Profile of Harold Gibbons: Hoffa's Left Hand," *New Republic*, September 9, 1957.

19. Ball, "Case History," 418–19; EC, "Ten Years of Union Democracy," 15, 33; H.J. Gibbons To Friends of the Distribution Workers. Further details on the merger are found in HJG Testimony, 14563–70, and Testimony of Lawrence J. Camie, Hearings Before the Select Committee on Improper Activities in the Labor or Management Field, Eighty-Fifth Congress, Second Session, Part 38, August 26, 1958, 14237–47 (hereafter Camie Testimony).

20. "Union Contact" (Oscar Ehrhardt interview) reported by Mrs. Marie Alger, January 10, 1950, Box 33, File 16, ALES-CU; Blair, "AFL Teamsters Raid CIO."

21. "AFL Unions Start to Organize Large Department Stores Here," April 20, 1949; and "Teamsters No. 688 Department Store Drive Ahead of Schedule," May 4, 1949; both in *SL Labor Tribune*; Rose, *Union Solidarity*, 28; Ball, "Case History," 453, 464.

Notes to Chapter 5

22. Dave Beck to Daniel J. Tobin, May 9, 1949; Dave Beck to Sir and Brother, October 12, 1949, Affiliated Bodies Series, Local #688, St. Louis, Missouri, Teamsters-GWU; "Union Contact," April 20, 1949; "Personal Contact," both reported by Annetta Dieckmann, June 29, 1949, Box 33, File 16, ALES-CU; Ball, "Case History," 464–66.

23. William R. James, "Exposing the Communist Conspiracy"; Ames interview; Ball, "Case History," 468; "Personal Contact," reported by Annetta Dieckmann, June 29, 1949; John F. English to Harold J. Gibbons, August 2, 1949; Harold Gibbons to John F. English, October 27, 1949, Affiliated Bodies Series, Local #688, St. Louis, Missouri, Teamsters-GWU.

24. Ball, "Case History," 481; McCarthy, "Portrait of Gibbons"; Rose, *Union Solidarity*, vii–ix, 29. The quote on "wage and union consciousness" is found in "Preliminary Notes: Outline of Organizational Policy for Warehouse Operations," n.d., Box 33, File 1, HJG-SIUE.

25. "Summary of St. Louis Labor Education Project," Box 34, File 16; "Educational Activity," January 22, 1950, Box 33, File 16; HJG to Eleanor Coit, June 11, 1946, and Eleanor Coit to HJG, July 1, 1946; Annetta Dieckmann to EC, September 13, 1949, Box 33, File 17; Annetta Dieckmann to Theodore Kaprola, October 24, 1949, Box 34, File 18, ALES-CU.

26. Annetta Dieckmann to HJG, December 22, 1949; Annetta Dieckmann to Wayne Terry, December 22, 1949; Wayne Terry to Miss Dieckmann, February 13, 1950; Educational Activity, reported by Annetta Dieckmann, January 24, 1950; Personal Contact [HJG], reported by Annetta Dieckmann, February 25, 1950; Educational Activity, February 6, 1950; Box 33, File 16; Annetta Dieckmann to Paul Crouse, February 27, 1950, Box 34, File 18, ALES-CU.

27. Dieckmann, "Union Makes Use," 343; Rose, *Union Solidarity*, 109–15, 121–22, 138–39, 191; St. Louis CORE Report, June 10, 1952; and George Schermer, "The Fairgrounds Park Incident," conducted for St. Louis Council on Human Relations, July 27, 1949, Box 1, File 3, Dagen-UMSL; Loomis interview, Sentner-WU.

28. Personal Contact, January 4, 1949; Union Contact, January 18, 1950; Educational Activity reported by Annetta Dieckmann, January 19, 1950, Box 33, File 16, ALES-CU; Rose, *Union Solidarity*, 134–35, 167. Several years later, Dieckmann was still pressing Gibbons about what the union was doing to encourage female leadership, apparently with limited success. See Annetta Dieckmann to Harold Gibbons, January 31, 1955, Box 49, File 574, No. 540, EC-UMSL.

29. Rose, *Union Solidarity*, 68–69, 184–85; Educational Activity, reported by Annetta Dieckmann, January 19, 1950, Box 33, File 16, ALES-CU; Purcell, *Blue Collar Man*.

30. Educational Activity, January 19, 1950.

31. Ball, "Union History 1950," 12, 15–19.

32. Union Contact, October 19, 1949; Educational Activity reported by Annetta Dieckmann, January 22, 1950; Personal Contact (HJG) reported by Annetta Dieckmann, February 25, 1950, Box 33, File 16; Annetta Dieckmann to Harry V. Ball, Jr., February 21, 1950, Box 34, File 28, ALES-CU.

33. Ball, "Case History," 387; EC, "Ten Years of Union Democracy," 29; "Union Members to Meet as Crews, Board Decides," *MLW*, July 9, 1947; Lens, *Left, Right, and Center*, 417; "Meet Your Union," n.d., 1949, Box 40, File 1, HJG-SIUE; Dieckmann to Ball, February 21, 1950.

34. Burnside, "Socialist Teamster."

35. Ryan interview; Pace interview; Ames interview; "Gibbons Announces Three Staff Changes for Local," April 12, 1950; "New Staff Assignments Announced by Gibbons," July

11, 1951; "Local's Administration Overhauled; Prepare for Taft, War, or Depression," July 9, 1952; "Calloway Given Organizing Post," September 15, 1958, all in *MLW*; HJG to Lou Berra et al., June 27, 1951; HJG Memo, September 15, 1958, Box 5, File 40, No. 550, EC-UMSL.

36. Wilson interview with author; EC, "Harold Gibbons Story;" Brill, *The Teamsters*, 352; Oldham interview; Seay interview; Larry Gibbons interview; Patrick Gibbons interview; Vasquez interview.

37. Stein, *Triumph of Tradition*, 22–31, 45–46, 79–84; Clay, *Political Voice at Grassroots*, 88–89; Salisbury, "St. Louis Politics," 330; Vasquez interview; Rose, *Union Solidarity*, 84; EC, "Requiem for Political Myth."

38. Lubell, *The Future of American Politics*, 207–8; Sugrue, *Origins of the Urban Crisis*, 80–84; Lichtenstein, *Most Dangerous Man*, 307–8; "688 Re-states Its Position on Elections," in EC, "Ten Years of Union Democracy," 55.

39. "Minutes of the Stewards Meeting of the United Distribution Workers," April 27, 1948, Box 34, File 20, ALES-CU.

40. "Reaching the Voter: The 1956 Pentland Campaign," Report to the 11th Annual City-Wide Shop Conference, Teamsters Local 688, January 27, 1957, Box 4, 1957, IBT, Jewish Labor Committee Anti-Discrimination File, JLC-NYU; Wilson, "Between the Lines"; Conn, "Union in St. Louis"; Ames interview; Transcript of HJG speech at Westminster College, Box 1, File 1, Keiser-UIS; Ball, "Case History," 406; "Gibbons: ADA and Labor Leader"; "688 Expands Its Political 'Know-How,'" in EC, "Ten Years of Democracy," 54.

41. Personal Contact, reported by Annetta Dieckmann, February 1950, Box 34, File 26, ALES-CU; Ames interview.

42. "Planning for an Integrated School System in St. Louis," December 12, 1951, Prepared and Presented By the Committee on Democratic Rights of Members, Local 688, Box 41, File 7, HJG-SIUE; HJG, "Why the Union Is Concerned"; Oldham interview, August 12, 1995, Dagen-UMSL; Ames interview; Valien, *St. Louis Story*; EC Biographical Sketch.

Chapter 6. *"Those Fellows Back There Actually Hate You"*

1. Kelliher, "Meet Harold Gibbons."

2. Exhibit No. 50, "Gangland Murders in St. Louis and East St. Louis Areas," Hearings Before the Special Committee to Investigate Organized Crime in Interstate Commerce, United States Senate, Part 4-A, 812–17; Witwer, *Corruption and Reform*, 78–79; Bell, "The Racket-Ridden Longshoremen," in Bell, *End of Ideology*, 173–74; Walsh, "Mob Likes Legitimate Business."

3. HJG Testimony, 14646; HJG FBI File SL 92–441, July 6, 1959; Burnside, "Socialist Teamster"; Brill, *The Teamsters*, 365; Smith, "Experiment in Trade Union Democracy," 210.

4. "Teamsters Local Acts to Rid Union of Gangsters," March 19, 1953; "Teamsters Drop Two Ex-Convicts from Council Pay," March 30, 1953, *SLPD*; Hearings Before the Special Committee to Investigate Organized Crime in Interstate Commerce, United States Senate, 1950–1951, Exhibit No. 52, 819–20; Testimony of Thomas L. Moran, Committee on Improper Activities in Labor or Management Field, 14258–59 (hereafter Moran Testimony); and Report of SA (special agent), HJG FBI File 92-441, August 7, 1959.

5. Jacobs, "The World of Jimmy Hoffa (II)," 20; HJG Testimony, 14647; Moran Testimony, 14259, 14263; James W. Connor to Senator McClellan, March 25, 1957, Vol. 18–23, St. Louis Area, Through Serial 149, Senate-NA; Testimony of Capt. John Dougherty, Committee

on Improper Activities in Labor or Management Field, 14011, 14015 (hereafter Dougherty Testimony); Burnside, "Socialist Teamster"; Ames interview; Witwer, *Corruption and Reform*, 173–74; McCarthy, "Portrait of Gibbons"; HJG FBI File WFO 92-365 (Washington Field Office), Harold J. Gibbons, July 31, 1959; and HJG FBI File 92-44, Report of SA, August 7, 1959. John Dougherty's name is spelled "Doherty" in St. Louis press accounts.

6. Brill, *The Teamsters*, 365; Smith, "Experiment in Democracy," 211, 213; Martin, *Jimmy Hoffa's Hot*, 83–84; Burnside, "Socialist Teamster"; "Hoffa's Left Hand." On Hoffa's relationship with organized crime, see Sloane, *Hoffa*, 31–34, 45–47; Witwer, *Corruption and Reform*, 168–70; James and James, *Hoffa and the Teamsters*, 80–85; Russell, *Out of the Jungle*, 88–90.

7. Ames interview; "Gangsters Grab at City Locals on Teamsters Union Under Inquiry," *SLPD*, March 6, 1953; "AFL International Union Opens Drive to Completely Organize Teamsters' Jurisdiction in St. Louis Area," *SL Labor Tribune*, March 12, 1953; "Fists Fly During Amalgamation of Teamster Unions," *SLGD*, March 17, 1953; Brill, *The Teamsters*, 365; HJG Testimony, 1467–68; "Teamsters Local Acts to Rid Union of Gangsters," March 19, 1953, *SLPD*.

8. James and James, *Hoffa and the Teamsters*, 66.

9. On Robert Bernard "Barney" Baker, see Burnside, "Socialist Teamster"; Brill, *The Teamsters*, 366–67; Testimony of Robert Bernard Baker, Committee on Improper Activities in Labor or Management Field, 14060–70; Dougherty testimony, 14009–10; Sloane, *Hoffa*, 117–19.

10. Walsh, "Debt and a Threat"; Brill, *The Teamsters*, 236–37; Witwer, *Corruption and Reform*, 178–79.

11. Larry Gibbons interview; Witwer, *Corruption and Reform*, 173–76; James and James, *Hoffa and the Teamsters*, 256, 269, 274; Brill, *The Teamsters*, 367, 370–71; Allan May, "The St. Louis Family," Chapter 7, accessed at www.trutv.com/library/crime/gangsters, January 5, 2013; Jake McCarthy, "Investigator with a Jimmy Hoffa Fixation," review of Walter Sheridan's *The Fall and Rise of Jimmy Hoffa*," January 28, 1972, found in Box 4, File 11, JC 13-SIUE. Further confirmation of the mob's continuing role in the St. Louis Teamsters came nearly a decade after Gibbons had relinquished power when Local 682 leader Nino Parrino reportedly was in line to become boss of the St. Louis mob.

12. HJG Testimony, Part 39, September 2, 1958, 14648; Burnside, "Socialist Teamster"; McCarthy, "Portrait of Gibbons"; "In Defense of Teamsters Local 688," Box 40, File 25, HJG-SIUE; Riesel, "Big Blow"; "Memorandum," April 16, 1953, HJG FBI File No. 92-933.

13. "Union Story Not Told in 682 Strike," July 1, 1953; "Research Helps," September 1, 1953; "Local 688 Stewards Council Proceeding for May 1955," June 1, 1955; all in *MLW*; McCarthy, "Portrait of Gibbons."

14. Statement of Teamsters Joint Council No. 13, Joseph McCann, July 20, 1953; "Statement of Teamsters Local 682 to Mayor Raymond R. Tucker," July 15, 1953; "Memorandum in Support of Ready Mix Material Dealers' Proposal," n.d., July 1953; all in Box 49, File 573, No. 540, EC-UMSL.

15. Woods, "Losses Pile Up"; "Statement by Mayor Tucker," July 17, 1953, Box 5, File, 1, JC 13-SIUE; "Tucker Appeals Again to Public to Help Settle Trucker Strike," July 19, 1953; "'Non-Stop' Sessions Open in Mayor's Office to Settle AFL Construction Drivers Strike Now 45 Days Long," June 25, 1953; "Union Offers to Negotiate Publicly or Over TV to End Materials Strike," July 23, 1953; both in *St. Louis Labor Tribune*.

16. "Building Truck Drivers Reject Any Arbitration to Settle Strike," August 4, 1953; "Wives of Jobless Take Woes to Mayor in Crusade to End Truck Walkout," August 5, 1953;

"Parent Trucker Union Enters Strike Here to Seek Accord," August 6, 1953; "Truck Strike Settled, Union Accepts Terms Ending 13-Week Walkout," August 12, 1953, all in *SLPD*; "12 Week AFL Building Materials Strike Ends: Men Return to Work Immediately," *St. Louis Labor Tribune*, August 13, 1953; Kelliher, "Meet Harold Gibbons."

17. "AFL Teamsters Local 682 to Initiate Full Scale Organizing Drive of Materials, Coal, and Ice Drivers in 5 Missouri Counties," *St. Louis Labor Tribune*, January 14, 1954.

18. Brown, *Race, Money, and Welfare State*, 99–100, 138–40, 163–68; Lichtenstein, *State of the Union*, 261, 284; Brody, "Uses of Power I," 173–75.

19. "Preliminary Notes: Outline of Organizational Policy for Warehouse Operations," Box 33, File 1, HJG-SIUE.

20. EC, "The Nature and Structure of the Collective Bargaining Agreement," Box 50, File 30, HJG-SIUE; Metzgar, *Striking Steel*.

21. "In Defense of St. Louis Teamsters Local 688," Box 40, File 25, HJG-SIUE.

22. "Right to Strike for Job Security Proposed in New Grievance Clause," *MLW*, June 11, 1952; "Brown Shoe Signs 5-Year Pact Guaranteeing 2,000 Hours of Work Annually," *St. Louis Labor Tribune*, January 22, 1953; "Anti-Recession Contract," 130; "Guaranteed Wage Covers 65 Companies," *MLW*, December 15, 1953; "Quotes from Officers' Report," January 31, 1954, Box 1, File 7, Keiser-UIS.

23. Ball, "Case History," 192–99; "Taxicab Service Halted; Protest Against Police," *SLPD*, July 25, 1953; Daniel Murphy to Thomas E. Flynn, September 18, 1945; Unnamed person "acting for President Daniel Tobin" to J. Lampe, Secretary-Treasurer, Joint Council 13, March 29, 1946; Affiliated Bodies Series, Local #688, St. Louis, Missouri, Teamsters-GWU.

24. Hodges, *Taxi!* 3–9, 48–53, 76, 102.

25. "First LHI and Vacation Gains Won in Taxi Unit from New Firm . . . Supreme," July 12, 1950; "Cab Drivers Win 7-Week B & W Strike," December 1, 1953; "Injunction Is Used in Cab Strike," December 15, 1953; "Local 688 Taxicab Unit Wins Health and Welfare Clause for First Time," January 1, 1955, all in *MLW*; "Taxicab Service Halted, Protest Against Police," *SLPD*, July 25, 1953.

26. "Taxicab Service Halted"; "Police Brutally Beat Member of Local 688," *MLW*, August 1, 1953; "Yellow Cab Drivers Start Back to Work," December 3, 1953; "Harold Gibbons Arrested on Cab Violence Charge," December 6, 1953; "Cab Apparently Stolen as Part of Driver Strike," December 7, 1953; "3 Cabs Fired On After One Firm's Men Quit Union," November 2, 1954, all in *SLPD*; SAC to Director, November 24, 1954, SL 122-84, HJG FBI Files; "Kavner Case Dismissal Called Big Victory for Entire Labor Movement," *MLW*, December 1, 1954.

27. C.E. Framenta to HJG, March 3, 1954, Box 1, File 2, JC 13-SIUE; "Notice to All Employees," Chase Candy Company, January 1, 1954; "To All Employees at St. Louis, Subject: Plans for St. Louis Operation," Warner-Hudnut closing," March 3, 1954; Julius Warner to HJG, April 3, 1954; W.H. Armstrong to HJG, April 30, 1954; all in Box 5, File 1, JC 13-SIUE.

28. "AFL Teamsters Local 688 Members Give Up $830,000 in Benefits to Help Firm," *St. Louis Labor Tribune*, December 2, 1954; Annual Report, National Warehouse Division, 1954–1955, Box 33, File 2; National Policy Committee, Warehouse Division, Minutes, February 10–11, 1955, Box 62, File 2, both in HJG-SIUE. For the union's defense see HJG to S.B. Armstrong, March 31, 1954, Box 45, File 36, HJG-SIUE; "'Facts': Driving Business Out of Town," *MLW*, July 1, 1954; and "In Defense of St. Louis Teamsters Local 688," Box 40, File 25, HJG-SIUE.

29. "AFL's Leo Havey Indicted on US Racket Charge," December 18, 1953; Carl L. Baldwin, "Bricklayers Use Political Power to Curb Shift to Other Material," December 29, 1953;

"Builders, Union Men 'At Mercy' of Labor Czars, Grand Jury Says," July 22, 1954; all in *SLPD*.

30. "'Menace' of Local 688 Discussed in Certain Business Circles in 1953," June 1, 1954; "What's the Matter with St. Louis," April 1, 1954, both in *MLW*; Defty, "Gibbons Kept Cool"; William W. Crowdus to Warren Olney III, May 28, 1953; Office Memorandum, From SAC (Special Agent in Charge), St. Louis (92-46), to Director, FBI, June 2, 1953; Memorandum, April 16, 1953 (unattributed); Warren Olney III to United States Attorney, St. Louis, Missouri, August 25, 1953, HJG FBI File, 92-933.

31. Interview Between Sergeant X of the St. Louis Police Force and Dr. Y., Tuesday, March 9, 1954, Box 5, File 40, No. 550, EC-UMSL.

32. SAC (Special Agent in Charge) to Director, March 1, 1953, SL 92-46; "Basis for Investigation," December 18, 1953; "Harold J. Gibbons"; St. Louis (Milnes) to Director, FBI, February 17, 1954; Mr. Evans to Mr. Rosen, March 5, 1954; Winterrowd to FBI Director, March 5, 1954; J.E. Milnes to FBI Director, March 7, 1954; Mr. Winterrowd to Mr. Rosen, March 7, 1954; E.H. Winterrowd to Mr. Rosen, March 17, 1954; J.E. Milnes to Honorable Harry Richards, March 19, 1954; Harold Joseph Gibbons, St. Louis Labor Health Institute, March 31, 1954; Milnes to FBI Director, May 21, 1954, HJG FBI File, 92-933; "Text of Report By Federal Grand Jury on Labor Rackets Here. Panel 'Astonished' at Loose Handling of Union Funds; Hints State Action in Order," June 9, 1954, Box 40, File 25, HJG-SIUE. On Max Goldschein, see "Max Goldschein, 89, Ex-Prosecutor for U.S.," *New York Times*, November 23, 1988; Winterrowd to FBI Director, March 4, 1954; SAC to Communications Section, March 12, 1954; and Mr. Winterrowd to Mr. Rosen, March 7, 1954, HJG FBI File 92-933.

33. Report, HJG, Local 688, June 24, 1954; Milnes to Director, November 4 and November 9, 1954; Report, November 19, 1954, HJG FBI File 92-933; Report, February 2, 1955, SL 122-84; Warren Olney III to Director, FBI, October 18, 1955; HJG FBI File 100-339783; St. Louis Case Synopsis, Vol. 9, 18–214, IBT, St. Louis, Serial 428–481, Senate-NA; Daniel Bell, "Labor Notes," (regarding 1954 *Fortune* article), Box 2, File 6, HJG to Victor Riesel, May 31, 1954, Box 2, File 34, HJG-SIUE; "In Defense of St. Louis Teamsters Local 688"; November 1954 Stewards Minutes, Box 40, File 23, HJG-SIUE; "U.S. Court Punished Refusal to Open Books," *SLPD*, February 18, 1954; "Gibbons Speech," February 15, 1955; and "Black Holds Berra Term Too Severe," May 15, 1956, both in *MLW*.

34. James, "Exposing the Communist Conspiracy"; "Gibbons' Red Front;" and "Gibbons Admits Red Front Membership"; Paul H. Douglas to HJG, May 13, 1954; HJG to Victor Riesel, May 5, 1954, Box 2, File 5, HJG-SIUE; "In Defense of St. Louis Teamsters Local 688," "Bill Sentner's Newsletter," No. 8, March 12, 1954; and Pete Saffo to HJG, February 22, 1954, Box 53, File 628, No 540, EC-UMSL; Pencak, *For God and Country*, 228–34, 318–32; Feurer, *Radical Unionism in the Midwest*, 97, 108–9.

35. "In Defense of Local 688," "A Resolution of Faith in St. Louis Teamsters Local 688 Leadership," Box 40, File 26, HJG-SIUE.

36. "In Defense of Local 688"; "Resolution of Faith"; and November 1954 Stewards Minutes.

37. EC, "1954: The Year of the Wolf Pack," January 15, 1955, Box 7, File 234, No. 540, EC-UMSL.

38. Alvaine Hamilton to H.J. Gibbons, March 9, 1954; C.M. Mulqueeny to HJG, August 5, 1954; Box 49, File 575, No. 540, EC-UMSL; Dan Bell to HJG, May 5, 1954, Box 2, File 6; HJG to Victor Riesel, May 5, 1954, Box 2, File 5, and May 31, 1954, Box 2, File 24, HJG-SIUE.

Chapter 7. "The Other Sixteen Hours"

1. Officers' Report, Local No. 688, to the Ninth Annual Citywide Shop Conference, January 20, 1952, Affiliated Bodies Series, Local #688, St. Louis, Missouri, 1952, Teamsters-GWU; "The Wide View and the Narrow View," Report of the Committee on Continuing Education to the Teamster City-wide Educational Conference, January 31, 1954, Box 50, File 4, HJG-SIUE.

2. Sallie Heller to Ernest Calloway, June 7, 1954, Box 49, File 579, No. 540, EC-UMSL.

3. "Unions in the Community," Local 688 Notes, Staff Orientation, 1953, Box 40, File 24, HJG-SIUE.

4. On St. Louis's political culture, see Stein, *Triumph of Tradition*, xvii, xxi, 3–7; Gordon, *Mapping Decline*, 40–41; Salisbury, "St. Louis Politics," 329–32; Banfield, *Big City Politics*, 124; "The City-County-Problem in St. Louis," Digest of Remarks Made By Dr. Paul Steinbicker before the St. Louis Chapter, Public Relations Society of America, December 8, 1955, Series 1, Box 7, Tucker-WU; Jones, *Fragmented by Design*, 4–14; EC, "Requiem for Political Myth."

5. HJG, "Labor's Task in the Precinct," 21.

6. HJG, "Labor's Task in the Precinct," 21–22; Conn, "Union in St. Louis," 9; "Transcript of Harold Gibbons Talk at Westminster," January 21, 1965, Box 1, File 5, Keiser-UIS.

7. On the work-community divide, see Katznelson, *City Trenches*, 6–19; Nicolaides, *My Blue Heaven*, 254; McGreevy, *Parish Boundaries*, 4; Sugrue, *Origins of the Urban Crisis*, 84; "New Shop Stewards Training Course: The Political and Community Action Program of Teamsters Local 688," May 4, 1955, Box 8, File 240, No. 540, EC-UMSL.

8. Annetta M. Dieckmann, "Report of the St. Louis Education Project, 1948–1950," Box 5, File 3, AD-UIC; "Experts' Blueprint," 65; Gordon, *Mapping Decline*, 22–23; Heathcott and Murphy, "Corridors of Flight," January 2005.

9. "Minutes, Community Meetings," November 1954, Box 40, File 23, HJG-SIUE; "Political and Community Action Program"; Pells, *Liberal Mind*, 182–97, 253–61.

10. "Gibbons Talk at Westminster"; McCarthy, "Portrait of Gibbons"; "The Wide View and the Narrow View"; Banfield, *Big City Politics*, 128.

11. "Community Action No. 8"; Teamsters Local 688, "The People Must Act: A Report to the Community Stewards Assembly," n.d., both in Box 41, File 36, HJG-SIUE; "Community Meetings: A New Approach to Political Action," Box 48, File 567, No. 540, EC-UMSL; "How 'Community Action' Succeeds," 11.

12. "Community Meetings Are Popular—Bus Fares and Service Lead Complaints," November 14, 1951; "Transportation Problem First Tackled By Local," December 12, 1951; both in *MLW*.

13. "Community Action, No. 8"; Discussion Guide for Staff Members, Staff Meetings, March 1952, Box 40, File 23, HJG-SIUE; "Up to the People," August 16, 1952; "Union to Oppose Proposal for Metropolitan Transit District," November 17, 1954; and "District Plan Indorsed by CIO Council," January 14, 1955, all in *SLPD*.

14. "County Chamber of Commerce Board Indorses Sewer Proposal," *SLPD*, December 3, 1953; "How 'Community Action' Succeeds," 8–9; "A St. Louis Union: Its Members and Its Community," March 8, 1954; and "Facts About the Metropolitan St. Lewis Sewer District Plan"; both in Series 1, Box 11, Tucker-WU; Brill, *The Teamsters*, 357; Gordon, *Mapping Decline*, 46–47; Schandt, Steinbicker, and Wendel, *Metropolitan Reform*, 2–6; Steinbicker, "City-County Problem"; "Community Action," September 30, 1954; "A St. Louis Union: Its

Members and Its Community"; Primm, *Lion of the Valley*, 477; Kaiser, "St. Louis Sewer District," 1247–48; Bollens, *Exploring the Metropolitan Community*, 50.

15. "Community Man," March 1, 1955; "Judge's Liver," January 1, 1957; "Hunger of Jobless Union Members Sparked Drive," March 15, 1958; "Zagri Appointed as Director of Public Relations," June 1, 1958; all in *MLW*; McCarthy, "For Sid Zagri."

16. Sid Zagri to staff, n.d., Box 41, File 36; "Committee Action Progress Report to Be Used in Community Meetings"; Minutes, Community Meetings, November 1956, March 1957, Box 40, File 23, HJG-SIUE; Kelliher, "Meet Harold Gibbons."

17. Gilbert, *Cycle of Outrage*, 74–78.

18. Sid Zagri to staff; "October Stewards' Council Proceedings," November 1, 1955; "Goof Ball Letter Interests Parents," September 15, 1955; "Members Say Delinquency Big Problem," November 15, 1955; "688 Spokesman Calls for Attack on Juvenile Crime Causes," July 15, 1956; "Back Youth Plans," September 15, 1956; all in *MLW*. Robert E. Weber, Jr., letter to the editor, *SLGD*, September 5, 1955.

19. Brill, *The Teamsters*, 357; "Community Meetings Are Popular—Bus Fares and Service Lead Complaints," November 14, 1951, *MLW*; Conn, "Union in St. Louis." On women connecting workplace, family, and community, see Faue, *Community of Suffering*, 15–18, 108–25; and Hyman, "Labor Organizing and Female Institution Building," 22–38. For a contrary view, see Durr, *Behind the Backlash*, 77–78.

20. "Lifeline of the Union," December 1, 1954; "Baby-Sitters at Community Open House," May 1, 1955; "Home Meeting Given Tryout," April 1, 1957; "Assembly Elects First Officers," October 1, 1958; all in *MLW*; Gray, *Report on Politics in Saint Louis*, Part V, 10.

21. Primm, *Lion of the Valley*, 459; Gordon, *Mapping Decline*, 71–83; "Reports from Local 688's Neighborhood Meetings," *MLW*, November 1, 1954.

22. "Additional Police Assigned to Igoe, Pruitt Housing Sites," August 10, 1955; "Obstacles Cited to Enforcing Housing Rules," November 2, 1955; "Tenants Protest Higher Public Housing Rates," November 9, 1956; all in *SLGD*.

23. Zagri, "Labor's Stake"; Primm, *Lion of the Valley*, 460–63; "Additional Police Assigned to Igoe, Pruitt Housing Sites"; "Obstacles Cited to Enforcing Housing Rules"; "Tenants Protest Higher Public Housing Rates"; Sid Zagri to staff.

24. "Statement by Mayor Tucker," July 17, 1953, Box 5, File 1, JC 13-SIUE; Robert E. Smith to Sidney Zagri, November 2, 1955, Mayoral Files, Series 1, Box 15, Labor Organizations, Other Matters, Tucker-WU.

25. "The People Must Act"; "How 'Community Action' Succeeds," 7; "St. Louis Rat Probe Draws Fire," February 28, 1955; "Teamsters' Official Says City Still Does Nothing About Rats," June 15, 1955; "Teamsters' Union Shows Vigorous Interest in Controlling City's Rats," n.d., 1955; all in *St. Louis Argus*; "Rat Control Report Is Scheduled Today," February 18, 1955, Box 6, File 3, JC-13-SIUE; "Protection Money," March 1, 1955, *MLW*.

26. C.M. Copley, Jr. to J. Earl Smith, March 5, 1955; C.M. Copley, Jr. to Honorable Raymond B. Tucker, August 11, 1955; Raymond Tucker to Jack Brune, April 5, 1956; Thomas J. Neenan, Charles J. Dolan to J. Edward Smith, May 22, 1956; Raymond Tucker to Edward A. Pollack, August 30, 1956; Series 1, Box 27, Tucker-WU; "Action for Rat Control," March 15, 1955; and "Red Faces," May 1, 1955, both in *MLW*.

27. Harold J. Gibbons to Raymond Tucker, August 10, 1955; Mayor to Harold J. Gibbons, August 11, 1955; Series 1, Box 27, Tucker-WU.

28. J. Earl Smith to Mrs. Edward J. Brumgard (confidential), September 12, 1955; "The Health Division's Proposed New Rat Ordinance," Statement, J. Earl Smith, January 23, 1957;

"A Statement Made Before the Public Welfare Committee of the Board of Aldermen on Board Bill #55 (Rat Control Ordinance)," February 22, 1957; Harold J. Gibbons to Raymond Tucker, February 5, 1957; Mayor to Harold J. Gibbons, February 7, 1957; Russell Letner to J. Earl Smith, February 15, 1957; all in Series 1, Box 27, Tucker-WU; "Rat Control Victory Won By Members Who Kept the Issue Alive," *MLW*, March 15, 1957.

29. "Teamsters Local 688 Agenda Guide," March 1957, Box 40, File 23, HJG-SIUE; "The People Must Act"; "Rat Control Victory Won by Members."

30. "Survey Made on Free City College Idea," December 15, 1954; "Free College Plan Endorsed by AFL Trades," February 15, 1955; both in *MLW*; "Bond Group to Consider 4-Year City College," March 29, 1955; "Union Leaders Urge Free City College," April 9, 1955; both in *SLGD*; "How 'Community Action' Succeeds," 11.

31. Goluboff, *Lost Promise of Civil Rights*, 181–222; "Calloway Heads NAACP Campaign," *MLW*, March 11, 1951; "Officers Report to the General Membership of the St. Louis NAACP, for the Year Ending December 31, 1956," Group III, Box C77, St. Louis, Missouri, 1956, NAACP-LC.

32. EC, "Full Negro-White Partnership"; "St. Louis Black Renaissance"; and "Passing of 'Delivered' Vote"; Lang, *Grassroots at the Gateway*, 24–25, 100; Stein, *Triumph of Tradition*, 22–24; Freeman, *Song of Faith and Hope*, 45–47; Clay, *Voice at the Grassroots*, 40–42.

33. Henry Winfield Wheeler to EC, October 28, 1953, Box 45, File 500, No. 540; Note by EC, October 1955, Box 1, File 10, No. 11, EC-UMSL; Henry W. Wheeler to Gloster Current, October 26, 1953, Box 122, File I, Henry Winfield Wheeler Papers, Wheeler-UMSL; "Wheeler Reinstated by NAACP: No Dishonesty in Funds Found," *St. Louis American*, November 5, 1953; Lang, *Grassroots at the Gateway*, 100–101; Freeman, *Song of Faith and Hope*, 49.

34. "The NAACP Election," December 3, 1955; and "Calloway-Draper: A Teams," December 9, 1955; both in *St. Louis Argus*; Lang, *Grassroots at the Gateway*, 100–101; EC, "Planning for a New Offensive on the Local Civil Rights Front," January 3, 1956, Box 1, File 4, No. 11, EC-UMSL.

35. EC, "On the Democratic Party of St. Louis and the Aspirations of the Negro Community," June 19, 1956, Box 8, File 238, No. 540, EC-UMSL; President's Report to Executive Committee, July 30, 1956, Group III, Box C77, St. Louis, Missouri, 1956, NAACP-LC.

36. EC to Gloster Current, February 2, 1956, Group III, Box C77, St. Louis, Missouri, 1956, NAACP-LC.

37. "Officers Report to the General Membership of the St. Louis NAACP, for the Year Ending December 31, 1956," Group III, Box C77, St. Louis, Missouri, 1956; "Membership Campaign, St. Louis, Missouri, 1957–1960," Group III, Box C288; "St. Louis NAACP Charts Special Program to Reduce Job Bias," August 29, 1957, Labor, Missouri, 1956–1965, Group III, Box A188; NAACP-LC; "Trade Union Workshop Formed by Local NAACP," Vol. 1, No. 8, *St. Louis NAACP Citizen*, Box 23, File 330, No. 540, EC-UMSL; M. Leo Bohanon to EC, June 30, 1954, Box 49, File 575, No. 540; "NAACP Board Elects Heads of Committees," *SL Argus*, January 11, 1957; Lang, *Grassroots at the Gateway*, 103–4; Margaret Bush Wilson interview with Doris Wesley, LEV-UMSL; "In the People's Court of the City of St. Louis, State of Missouri," Box 46, File 520, No. 540, EC-UMSL.

38. Henry, "Race, Power, and the Building Trades," 90–101; Herbert Hill to Leonard Woodcock, June 3, 1956, Group II, Box A188, Labor, Missouri, 1956–1965, NAACP-LC; EC interview in Gray, *Report on Politics in Saint Louis*, Part V, 4–6; "Officers Report to General Membership," December 31, 1956; EC, "Union Philosophy as Related to the Economic Structure," August 12, 1965, Box 1, File 5, No. 11, EC-UMSL.

39. EC, "Approaching the Problems of Community Organization in the Fight Against Poverty," May 15, 1965, Box 1, File 5, No. 11, EC-UMSL; "Negroes Must Eat Too! The A & P Story"; Gloster Current, "Negro in the North, Report from Branches," Branches, April 1958, Group III, Box 239; "St. Louis NAACP Charts Special Program," NAACP-LC; MacLean, *Freedom Is Not* Enough, 5–7.

40. "An Open Letter from the NAACP President to All Business Firms Drawing Trade from the Negro Community," May 14, 1956, Group III, Box C77, St. Louis, MO, 1956, NAACP-LC.

41. "President's Report to Executive Committee," July 30, 1956; "President's Report for June and July 1956," July 30, 1956; "Officers Report to the General Membership of the St. Louis NAACP, for the Year Ending December 31, 1956"; Group III, Box C77, St. Louis, MO, 1956, NAACP-LC.

42. "The Story of the 12 Day 'Rump' Taxicab Strike in St. Louis, MO, Against the Employment of Negro Drivers As Seen Through Newspaper Headlines and Quotations," Group III, Box A188, Labor, Missouri, 1956–1965, NAACP-LC. See also "Testimony of Harold Donald Cortor," "Investigation of Improper Activities in the Labor or Management Field," Part 38, 14387–88; "History of Wild Cat Strike, August 1956," Vol. 12, 18–214, IBT, St. Louis, 613–80; and "Teamsters Local #405—Taxicab Drivers," Vol. 13, 18–214, IBT, St. Louis, 661–770, Senate-NA; "Ace Cab Company to Hire Ten Drivers," August 17, 1956; "The Taxi Drivers' Strike," August 31, 1956; "Wildcat Taxi Strike Made Way for New Progress Era," September 7, 1956; all in *St. Louis Argus*.

43. "Rump Taxicab Strike Backfires on Drivers," August 24, 1956; "Rump Taxi Strike Falls Flat on Its Biased Face," August 31, 1956, *St. Louis Argus*; "The Story of the 12 Day 'Rump' Strike"; HJG Testimony, 14600–14604; "History of Wildcat Strike."

44. "The Taxi Drivers' Strike"; "Story of the 12 Day 'Rump' Strike." For statements supporting the union's stance, see "Story of the 12 Day 'Rump' Strike"; and Allen Hackett to Public Service Commission, March 13, 1957, Box 7, File 211, MCF-UMSL.

45. "Statement Issued By The Metropolitan Church Federation of St. Louis," in "Story of the 12 Day 'Rump' Strike."

46. "Story of the 12 Day 'Rump' Strike."

Chapter 8. "A Hell of a Whipping"

1. Trask, "New Charter Defeated," and "Charter Foes Criticize Tucker"; both in *SLPD*; Civic Progress Minutes, December 26, 1957, Series 5, Box 1,Tucker-WU; "St. Louis Gets Experts' Blueprint for Areawide City-County Rule," *Business Week*, August 24, 1957, 68.

2. On Civic Progress, see Mayor to Powell B. McHaney, January 8, 1954; Harry B. Wilson to Raymond R. Tucker, May 23, 1958; Harry B. Wilson to George J. Ringrose, November 27, 1959; Series 5, Box 1, Tucker-WU; Primm, *Lion of the Valley*, 465–66; Stein, *Triumph of Tradition*, 93; Lang, "Civil Rights versus 'Civic Progress,'" 617–21.

3. "What's the Matter with St. Louis?" *MLW*, April 1, 1954; EC, "Some Significant Weaknesses in the Proposed St. Louis Earnings Tax," TV Statement, KETC, September 23, 1954, Box 1, File 4, EC No. 11, EC-UMSL; "Pentland Charges Mayor with Earnings Tax Double-Cross"; "Community Action," No. 4, May 1, 1952, Box 95, File 1218, LWV-UMSL.

4. "Stewards to Fight Unfair Bond Finance," March 1, 1953; "Mayor Addresses Local 688 Community Stewards," June 15, 1955, *MLW*.

5. Zagri, "Your Community and Mine"; Primm, *Lion of the Valley*, 466–67; Lang, *Grassroots at the Gateway*, 106–7; Heathcott and Murphy, "Corridors of Flight," 181.

6. Stein, *Triumph of Tradition*, 98–99; Salisbury, "St. Louis Politics," 332; Lang, "Civil Rights versus 'Civic Progress,'" 619–21; Citizens Charter Committee Statement by Mayor Raymond R. Tucker, August 3, 1957, Series 1, Box 5, Tucker-WU; League of Women Voters Committee Meeting, June 19, 1957, Box 70, File 889, LWV-UMSL.

7. EC, "In Defense of Grass Roots Legislative Representation," February 2, 1957; "Why We Are in Opposition to the Proposed New City Charter," July 30, 1957; Box 1 File 4, No. 11, EC-UMSL.

8. "Why We Are in Opposition"; "NAACP Citizen Groups Formed in Nine Wards to Work Against Charter," July 8, 1957, Group III, Box C77, St. Louis, Missouri, 1957, NAACP-LC; "A Bad Charter," n.d.; "To Members of Civic Progress, Inc. from Fleishman-Hillard," September 25, 1957, Series 1, Box 4, Tucker-WU; Lang, "Civil Rights versus 'Civic Progress,'" 623–24.

9. Zagri, "'Slick' Public Relations Job"; Bick, Jr., "Thoughts on the Charter." For a photo of Calloway and Zagri conferring, see *SLGD*, p. 10A, June 24, 1957, found in Group III, Box C77, St. Louis, Missouri, 1957, NAACP-LC.

10. "Proponent Says Charter Will Aid Efficiency," *SLPD*, July 6, 1957.

11. Lang, "Civil Rights versus 'Civic Progress,'" 623–28, and *Grassroots at the Gateway*, 109–11; EC, "St. Louis Black Renaissance"; "Who's Really Running the Show?" undated cartoon in Box 8, File 239, No 540, EC-UMSL; "Speakers Clash During NAACP Charter Meeting" and "Mr. Calloway and the NAACP," July 5, 1957; both in *St. Louis Argus*.

12. "Unionist Says New Charter Would Make Mayor a 'King,'" *SLPD*, June 19, 1957; Citizens Committee Against the Charter: "Charter Facts," Box 6, File 7, JC 13-SIUE; "New Charter May Burden Small Firms," *Wellston Journal*, Vol. 44, No. 29, August 17, 1957. Leaflets opposing the charter change can be found in Group III, Box C77, NAACP-LC. See also "A Bad Charter."

13. Civic Progress Minutes, December 26, 1957, Series 5, Box 1, Tucker-WU; Schandt, Steinbicker, and Wendel, *Metropolitan Reform in St. Louis*, 63–64; Gray, *Report on Politics in Saint Louis*, Part III, 9–17; Stein, *Triumph of Tradition*, 98–99, 106–7; Lang, "Civil Rights versus 'Civic Progress,'" 629.

14. Kelliher, "Meet Harold Gibbons"; Trask, "New Charter Defeated"; Salisbury, "St. Louis Politics," 332; Hahn, "Giant Get-out-Vote Setup"; Spreche, "St. Louis Teamsters Union Experiments," and "AFL-CIO, Unlike Teamsters' Setup."

15. "Labor's New Look," *E. St. Louis Journal*, November 24, 1957; Civic Progress Minutes, December 26, 1957, February 27, 1958, and May 22, 1958, Series 5, Box 1, Tucker-WU.

16. "Landslide Defeat for Charter May Result in Real Civic Cooperation," *MLW*, October 1, 1957; Zagri, "Charter Defeat."

17. "Sewer District Comes Under Fire," *SLGD*, September 25, 1957; HJG Release, December 13, 1957, Box 2, File 18, JC 13-SIUE; "Steward Council Proceedings," *MLW*, March 1, 1958.

18. News release, January 9, 1958, Box 2, File 18, JC 13-SIUE; "School Merger Would Create More Problems, Economist Says," June 13, 1958, and "Teamsters Will Open Community Action Program," *SLGD*, April 28, 1958; "Petitions Filed in County for Freeholders," *SLPD*, March 26, 1958; Civic Progress Minutes, February 27, 1958, and May 22, 1958, Series 5, Box 1, Tucker-WU; "'Groups of Seven' Organized as Grassroots for Assembly," March 1,

1958; "County Area 'Crawls with Grievances,'" April 1, 1958; "New Faces in Neighborhood Local Action Work," May 1, 1958; "History Made as Community Assembly Opens," June 15, 1958; "Odor Control," August 1, 1958; "Area Wide Attack on Pollution Urged," October 16, 1958; "First Goals in Air Pollution Project Reached," November 1, 1958; "City Dads Given Smelly Facts on Pollution of Air," November 15, 1958, all in *MLW*.

19. EC, "St. Louis Black Political Renaissance"; Wilson interview with author.

20. "NAACP and Chain Store Reach Understanding on Employment Policies," January 20, 1958, Group II, Box C77, St. Louis, MO, 1957; "Negroes Must Eat Too! The A & P Story," in Gloster Current, "Negro in the North," Report from Branches, April 1958, Group III, Box 239, NAACP- LC; EC, "St. Louis Black Renaissance"; Lang, *Grassroots at the Gateway*, 112–13.

21. Wilson interview with author; EC, "St. Louis Black Renaissance"; "Negro in the North"; "St. Louis NAACP Begins Efforts to Stop Public Utilities Job Bias," April 17, 1958, Group III, Box A188, Labor, Missouri, 1956–1965; "Release," May 14, 1958, Group III, Box C77, St. Louis, Missouri, January-June 1958, NAACP-LC; Lang, *Grassroots at the Gateway*, 112–13.

22. EC, "On Famous-Barr Department Store: The Value of the Disciplined Consumer Dollar in the Fight for Jobs," Box 8, File 239, No. 540, EC-UMSL; EC, "St. Louis Black Renaissance"; Lang, *Grassroots at the Gateway*, 114–15.

23. EC, "St. Louis Black Renaissance"; Wilson interview with author; EC, "The Ultimate Conquest of Negro Economic Inequality: An Expansion of Remarks Before the St. Louis Chapter of the Frontiers International, October 10, 1963," Box 2, File 2, FR-UMSL; EC, "Seeking to Heal Some Differences Between the St. Louis NAACP and the *St. Louis Argus*," September 19, 1958, Box 8, File 238, No. 540, EC-UMSL.

24. Press release, August 9, 1956, Box 2, File 8, JC 13-SIUE; Jacobs, "World of Jimmy Hoffa (II)," 36; Sloane, *Hoffa*, 67; Romer, *International Brotherhood of Teamsters*, 38.

25. Kennedy, *Enemy Within*, 4–16; Russell, *Out of the Jungle*, 182–85; Baltakis, "Agendas of Investigation," 37–38, 159; Witwer, *Corruption and Reform*, 157–59; Sloane, *Hoffa*, 159; Mollenhoff, *Tentacles of Power*, 145; Schlesinger, Jr., *Kennedy and His Times*, 143.

26. Witwer, *Corruption and Reform*, 160; Romer, *International Brotherhood of Teamsters*, 36; Sloane, *Hoffa*, 51–52; Baltakis, "Agendas of Investigation," 90–94, 105, 129–30; "Statement by Harold J. Gibbons on his activities within the International Brotherhood of Teamsters," Box 2, File 18, JC 13-SIUE.

27. Baltakis, "Agendas of Investigation," 129–30, 150–71; Sloane, *Hoffa*, 72–103; Witwer, *Corruption and Reform*, 159–60, 163–65, 176–78; Brill, *The Teamsters*, 201–5; "Full Cooperation in Jimmy Hoffa Defense Voted By Stewards," April 1, 1957, *MLW*; "John Herling's Labor Letter," August 31, 1957.

28. Sloane, *Hoffa*, 99–103; Goulden, *Meany*, 244–52.

29. "A Profile of Harold Gibbons: Hoffa's Left Hand," *New Republic*, September 9, 1957; McCormick, "Hoffa's Gem Smooth Prince"; Judy, "Teamsters' No. 1 Egghead."

30. Martin, *Jimmy Hoffa's Hot*, 82–83; Kempton, "Prince Hal at the Tavern."

31. EC to Richard Kavner and HJG, November 21, 1957, Box 5, File 2, HJG-SIUE.

32. EC to Richard Kavner and HJG; Witwer, *Corruption and Reform*, 181.

33. Membership of Joint Council 13, Box 3, File 1, JC 13-SIUE; Sloane, *Hoffa*, 108; "Hoffa's Left Hand," 8–9; Irwin Langenbacher to Robert F. Kennedy, August 1, 1958, Vol. 12, 18–214, IBT-SL, 613–80, Senate-NA.

34. "Gibbons Facing Revolt, Rival Teamsters Union Files Slate," December 12, 1957; Ted Schafers, "Walla Has Made Rapid Rise in Union," January 5, 1958, *SLGD*.

35. Joint Council 13 Minutes, March 11, 1957, Box 49, File 2, HJG-SIUE; "Testimony of Elmer E. Walla," Committee on Improper Activities in the Labor or Management Field, Part 38, 14512–13 (hereafter Walla Testimony); "Testimony of Robert F. Lewis," Committee on Improper Activities in the Labor or Management Field, Part 38, 14502; "HJG Testimony," 14666–69; "Hoffa Supports Gibbons Slate in Vote Here," August 31, 1957; "Gibbons Calls Election Fight 'Internal Affair,'" December 17, 1957; *SLGD*.

36. Ted Schafers, "Walla Group Claims Gibbons Stalls for Time," *SLGD*, January 1, 1958; "Says Unionist Got $5387 Fee to Get Evidence Against Gibbons," January 3, 1958; "Gibbons Denies Backer Acted Against Him," *SLPD*, January 9, 1958; "Tell Us More, Mr. Bender," Joint Council 13 advertisement in *SLGD*, January 13, 1958; "Gibbons Wins, But Insurgents Elect Three in Teamsters Vote," *SLPD*, January 16, 1958; Cartoon, January 20, 1958, Box 6, File 3, JC 13-SIUE; "HJG Testimony," 14680–81; Walla Testimony, 14513–14; "Senate Group Is Considering Investigation of Teamsters Vote," *SLPD*, January 18, 1958.

37. James W. Connor to Senator McClellan, March 25, 1957, Vol. 18–23, St. Louis Area, Through Serial 149, Senate-NA.

38. Irwin Langenbacher to Robert F. Kennedy, November 19, 1957, Vol. 1, 18–24, IBT-St. Louis, Serial 1–34, and February 17, 1958, Vol. 3, 18–214, Serial 88–133, 1958; Connor to Senator McClellan, March 25, 1957, Senate-NA; "Statement of Senator John L. McClellan Relative to the Activities of Harold J. Gibbons," September 11, 1958, Box 1, File 15, JC 13-SIUE; "Testimony of Thomas L. Moran," Committee on Improper Activities in the Labor or Management Field, Part 38, 1428 (hereafter "Moran Testimony"); "Statement by Harold J. Gibbons on his activities within the International Brotherhood of Teamsters," January 18, 1958, Box 2, File 18, JC 13-SIUE; Kennedy, *Enemy Within*, 91–92, 324–25; "HJG Testimony," 14690–96.

39. "Moran Testimony," 14254–66; "Testimony of James Ford," 14272–79; "Testimony of Oldron A. Mitchell," 14279–86, 14288–96; "Testimony of Harold Sparks," 14306–16; "Testimony of Brian A. Foster," 14365–78; all in Part 38, Committee on Improper Activities in the Labor or Management Field; "Testimony of Robert Bernard Baker," Part 37, Committee on Improper Activities in the Labor or Management Field, 14059–81; Kennedy, *Enemy Within*, 135–36.

40. HJG, "Speech Before Brookings Institution," n.d., Box 5, File 54, HJG-SIUE; Defty, "Gibbons Kept Cool"; Martin, *Jimmy Hoffa's Hot*, 84; Jacobs, "Extracurricular Activities," 72; "HJG Testimony," 14650–55, 14568–70, 14582–83, 14598–14604, 14617, 14628, 14642, 14668–81.

41. "HJG Testimony," 14593–95, 14663; Ives, "School of Industrial and Labor Relations,"

42. The only senators present during Gibbons's testimony were Ives and McClellan, with the bulk of the questioning conducted by committee counsel Kennedy and committee chair McClellan.

42. McClellan, *Crime Without Punishment*, 10; "Proposed Findings, International Brotherhood of Teamsters, James R. Hoffa," Vol. 85, 18–5, Hoffa, Serials 3345–3892, Senate-NA.

43. "HJG Testimony," 14573, 14586, 14590, 14593, 14595.

44. Jacobs, "Extracurricular Activities," 71–72, 86–87; "Labor: Hard-Boiled Egghead," *Time*, September 15, 1958; HJG to Francis Heisler, May 5, 1959, Box 35, File 3, HJG-SIUE; Bell, "Capitalism of the Proletariat," 222–23.

45. "Zagri Takes Teamsters Public Relations Post," *SLPD,* May 28, 1958; "Trainee Program is Suspended," January 1, 1959; "Home Stewards' Responsibility Bigger," February 1959; "Stewards Council Proceedings," October 1959; "It Started Here Ten Years Ago," November 1961; all in *MLW.*

46. Witwer, *Corruption and Reform,* 205–10; Lee, *Eisenhower and Landrum-Griffin,* 81–82, 156.

47. Lee, *Eisenhower and Landrum-Griffin,* 118–19; Romer, *International Brotherhood of Teamsters,* 76–77; "The Congress: The Persuader," *Time,* July 27, 1959.

48. "Memorandum for Limited Release," August 4, 1959, Box 4, File 33, No. 550, EC-UMSL.

49. Poston, "How Hoffa Is Fighting"; "Says Teamsters Would Control Negro Voters," Vol. 48, No. 15, n.d., Box 2, File 17, No. 11, EC-UMSL.

50. EC to Adam Clayton Powell, August 8, 1954; "Why We Support an Anti-Discrimination Amendment of the Landrum-Griffin Bill," August 14, 1959; Box 1, File 4, No 11, EC-UMSL.

51. EC, "Why We Support an Anti-Discrimination Amendment."

Chapter 9. *"A Planned Social Revolution"*

1. "Emphasis," Chet Huntley interview with HJG, March 30, 1965, Box 1, File 3, JC 13-SIUE.

2. Students for a Democratic Society, "The Port Huron Statement," in Miller, *Democracy Is in the Streets,* 331.

3. O'Brien, "Hoffa Team Moves Into Washington"; Romer, *International Brotherhood of Teamsters,* 66–67, 74; Sloane, *Hoffa,* 143–44; Vasquez interview.

4. "U.S. Jury Issues Indictments for Political Action," February 1960; "Political Cards Okayed," November 1960; "Local 405 Fined in Political Case," April 1961, all in *MLW*; "Newspaper Denounces Persecution," *The International Teamster,* Vol. 56, No. 11, November 1959.

5. O'Brien, "Senate Witness" and "Gibbons Says He Can't Remember"; Woods, "Gibbons Hid High Officers' Forgery"; Witwer, *Corruption and Reform,* 218–33.

6. Widick, *Labor Today,* 100, 162; HJG Speech to Western Conference of Teamsters, Los Angeles, California, July 23, 1963, Box 5, File 12, HJG-SIUE.

7. Brill, *The Teamsters,* 372; EC, "Hymn to a Gentle Soul"; Albrecht interview; Garrow, *Bearing the Cross,* 536; Russell, *Out of The Jungle,* 121–28. King delayed a meeting to gain the Hoffa contribution after the FBI leaked information to the press about the proposed arrangement.

8. "Phone Call to Sidney Zagri," April 8, 1965, Box 1, File 1, Keiser-UIS; Romer, *International Brotherhood of Teamsters,* 74–79; James and James, *Hoffa and the Teamsters,* 38–39; Bernstein interview.

9. James and James, *Hoffa and the Teamsters,* 38–40; Romer, *International Brotherhood of Teamsters,* 81–82; "Officers' Report to the 18th Convention Details Teamsters' Progress," *International Teamster,* Vol. 58, No. 8, August 1961, 59; Bernstein interview.

10. James and James, *Hoffa and the Teamsters,* 135–36; HJG Address Before Industrial Relations Division, American Bakers Association, October 15, 1962, Box 5, File 8; "Material from Abram Weiss for HJG talk at Johnson and Johnson, October 13, 1963, Box 5, File 14, HJG-SIUE; "To Work Toward National Agreement," *International Teamster,* May 1962, 6.

11. Romer, *International Brotherhood of Teamsters*, 84, 86; HJG Speech to Western Conference of Teamsters, Los Angeles, California, July 23, 1963, Box 5, File 12; "Needed: A Revolution in Labor," Box 5, File 62, HJG-SIUE; "The Teamster Structure," Box 1, File 7, Keiser-UIS.

12. Bernstein interview; Vasquez interview; Patrick Gibbons interview; Defty, "Emergence of 'New Gibbons'"; Lens, *Unrepentant Radical*, 146.

13. McCarthy, "Portrait of Gibbons"; News, U.S. Department of Labor, Office of Information, Week of December 8, 1972, Box 4, File 11, JC 13-SIUE; Baron, "Top Teamster Hits Back."

14. Baron, "Top Teamster Hits Back"; McCarthy, "Portrait of Gibbons"; Kempton, "Hoffa the Pure"; Brill, *The Teamsters*, 374; Sloane, *Hoffa*, 279; "John Fitzgerald Kennedy," *Missouri Teamster*, November 1963.

15. Raskin, "Hoffa Facing Palace Revolt."

16. McCarthy, "Portrait of Gibbons"; Brill, *The Teamsters*, 374; Sloane, *Hoffa*, 280; James and James, *Hoffa and the Teamsters*, 59–60; "Steinberg Resigns as Aide to Hoffa," *Toledo Blade*, December 6, 1963; "Transcript of Gibbons' Interview on Resignation Report," December 20, 1963; and "Gibbons Resigns National Teamster Position," January 3, 1964; both in *Missouri Teamster*.

17. Rabbi Bertram Klausner to EC, May 15, 1959, Box 1, File 5, No. 11, EC-UMSL; Wolensky, Wolensky, and Wolensky, *Fighting for the Union Label*, 123; Parmet, *Master of Seventh Avenue*, 110; Teamsters Local 688, "Health and Medical Camp"; Teamsters Local 688, "Away from the Crowded City: A New Concept in Health Care for Union Members"; Box 23, File 4, HJG-SIUE; Albrecht and Vasquez interviews.

18. EC, "In Support of the Mill Creek Massive Slum Clearance Program," March 17, 1958, Box 1, File 4, No. 11, EC-UMSL; Heathcott and Murphy, "Corridors of Flight," 159–63; Gordon, *Mapping Decline*, 99, 168; National Register of Historic Places Registration Form, Council Plaza, submitted by Missouri Department of Natural Resources, January 16, 2007; EC, "Mill Creek Negroes Fleeced."

19. Press Release, September 5, 1963, Box 14, File 1; Council House Reports No. 2, May 1963, Box 23, File 22; Council Plaza Draft Brochure, Box 23, File 16, HJG-SIUE; Defty, "Teamster Boss."

20. Gross, "New Way of Life" and "Adventure in Retirement Living"; HJG Address to Harvard Trade Union Program: "Society's Needs Demand New Cooperative Spirit," *Missouri Teamster*, March 10, 1970.

21. Arthur E. Klein to Richard Kavner, September 7, 1965, Arthur E. Klein to William Douthit, Pearlie Evans, and Ruth Porter, September 7, 1965, Box 23, File 17, HJG-SIUE.

22. "Preliminary Observations on the Educational Program of Teamsters #688, September 1964"; "Further Observations on the Education Program of Teamsters #688," November 1964, Box 5, File 60; AD-UIC.

23. "Local 688 Health and Medical Camp Report," September 1966, Box 22, File 6, HJG-SIUE.

24. EC, "Why We Must Elect Rev. John J. Hicks to School Board," March 31, 1959, Box 1, File 4, No. 11, EC-UMSL; "Hicks Becomes the First Negro Elected to Education Board," *St. Louis NAACP Citizen*, June 1959; Lang, *Grassroots at the Gateway*, 119; Clay, *Bill Clay*, 47–48.

25. EC, "St. Louis Black Renaissance"; Lang, *Grassroots at the Gateway*, 120; Stein, *Triumph of Tradition*, 121–22.

26. "Manager," *MLW*, December 1960; Clay, *Political Voice*, 81–83.

27. Margaret Bush Wilson interview with author; EC, "Full Negro-White Political Partnership," *Citizen Crusader*, Vol. 1, No. 8, February 24, 1961, Box 19, File 305, No. 540, EC-UMSL.

28. EC, "Victory Gives St. Louis Six Negro Aldermen," *St. Louis NAACP Citizen*, June 1959; "Politics in the St. Louis Negro Community," September 30, 1961, Box 21, File 320; "100,000 Negro Voters Make Up Political Power Corridor," *New Citizen*, June 22, 1962, Box 22, File 323, No. 540, EC-UMSL; EC, "St. Louis Black Renaissance;" Stein, *Triumph of Tradition*, 22–23; Gray, *Report on Politics in Saint Louis*, Part II, 27.

29. EC, "The Antioch Conference: A Quick Look at the Recent 'Summit' Meeting," *New Citizen*, Vol. 1, No. 32, October 13, 1961, Box 21, File 320, No. 540, EC-UMSL; EC, "Politics in the St. Louis Negro Community"; EC, "Time of the St. Louis Black Renaissance."

30. Deverne Calloway interview; EC, "Jack Dwyer."

31. R.R. Tucker to EC, January 24, 1962; David R. Calhoun, Jr. to EC, January 25, 1962; C.L. Farris to EC, January 30, 1962; Dave Calhoun to EC, March 29, 1962; Box 1, File 2, No. 11, EC-UMSL.

32. "Report of President," March 26, 1956, Group III, Box C77, St. Louis, Missouri, 1956, NAACP-LC; author's interview with William Clay, January 7, 2009; Clay, *Bill Clay*, 75.

33. Rustin, "From Protest to Politics," 111–22; EC, "The Negro Revolution in St. Louis," *Truth*, Vol. 1, No. 3, May 1964, Box 23, File 331, No. 540, EC-UMSL; EC, "The March on Washington: Where Do We Go From Here," August 28, 1963; EC, "Some Working Lessons from the CORE-Jefferson Bank Controversy," October 27, 1963; both in Box 8, File 238, No. 540, EC-UMSL; EC, "The Nature of Power."

34. Clay, *Bill Clay*, 54–57, 59–60; author's interview with William Clay; Clay interview, Clay-MSRC; Stein, *Triumph of Tradition*, 132–33.

35. Author's interview with William Clay; author's interview with Charles Oldham; Tournour interview; Lang, *Grassroots at the Gateway*, 121; Miller, "Jack Dwyer, White Boss"; "Where Do We Go for Leadership in the 26th Ward? A Review of the Serious Political Climate in the 26th Ward," n.d., Box 8, File 243; EC, "Enter Emperor Clay—The King of I Am," *Truth*, Vol. 1, No. 2, March-April 1964, and Vol. 1, No. 6, August 1, 1964, Box 23, File 331, No. 540, EC-UMSL.

36. Author's interview with William Clay; Romer, *International Brotherhood of Teamsters*, 137; "Labor: Fires in the Backyard," August 25, 1961; and "Labor: Breaking Out in Boils," September 15, 1961; both in *Time*.

37. Lonesome, "Controversy Swirls"; "Teamsters Calloway Raps Clay for His Role in Taxicab Vote," *St. Louis Argus*, January 31, 1964.

38. "500 Ask for Cabs," June 7, 1963; "The Case for More Cabs," June 7, 1963; EC, "Attempt to Create a 'Jim Crow' Union of Taxi Drivers," January 23, 1964, *St. Louis Argus*; "Alderman Clay Soundly Defeated in Century Electric Vote," *Truth*, Vol. 1, No. 3, May 1964, Box 23, File 331, No. 540, EC-UMSL.

39. "March on Washington," August 28, 1963.

40. "Memorandum on Civil Rights in the AFL-CIO," Submitted to AFL-CIO Executive Council by A. Philip Randolph, June 25–30, 1961; Report by Frank Campbell, Industrial Secretary of St. Louis Urban League, "Negro American Labor Council," Group III, Box A178, NAACP-LC; Frank Campbell to M. Leo Bohanon, January 16, 1962, and March 13, 1962, Series II, Box 19, St. Louis, 1962, Part II, NUL-LC; Clay, "Anatomy of an Economic

Murder"; "Calloway Hits Selective Tokenism in Employment; Calls Upon Industry to Re-evaluate Its Practices," *St. Louis Argus*, July 5, 1963.

41. On the NALC, see Pfeffer, *A. Philip Randolph*, 210–14; Zieger, *For Jobs and Freedom*, 170–71; Newman, "Negro American Labor Council," 15–20, 62–63; and EC, "Era of 'Patroonism.'"

42. Lang, *Grassroots at the Gateway*, 135; "Labor Council Establishes Block Groups for Crusade," *St. Louis Argus*, July 5, 1963; NALC News Release, June 26, 1963, Box 2, File 14, No. 11, EC-UMSL.

43. NALC Press Releases, July 5, 12, and 19, 1963, Box 2, File 14, No. 11, EC-UMSL; "Council Calls Off Pickets, Tells of Gains," *St. Louis Argus*, July 19, 1963; "The Business Community and Selective Tokenism in Negro Employment"; EC to Aloys P. Kaufman, n.d., 1963, Box 8, File 238, No. 540, EC-UMSL; Lang, *Grassroots at the Gateway*, 136.

44. Clay, "Anatomy of an Economic Murder"; "Summary of Exploratory Meeting With Beverage Industry Employers on Matter of Fair Share Employment Covenants," September 25, 1963; "Summary of Meeting Between Beverage Industry, Unions, and NALC," October 4, 1963; G. Newton Cox to EC, October 25, 1963; Edward J. Fitzgerald to EC, October 29, 1963; A.F. Overbeck to EC, November 4, 1963, Box 2, File 14, No. 11, EC-UMSL; News Release, October 6, 1963, Box 1, File 2, No. 11, EC-UMSL.

45. Lang, *Grassroots at the Gateway*, 13; "Metropolitan St. Louis NAACP's Project on Fair Employment at the Lever Bros. Plant Locates in the St. Louis Area," April 7, 1964, Group II, Box C416, Missouri, 1956–1965; Humphrey Sullivan to Roy Wilkins, July 31, 1964, Group III, Box A188, Labor, Missouri, 1956–1965, both in NAACP-LC; *Truth*, Vol. 1, No. 3, May 1964, Box 23, File 33, No. 540, EC-UMSL; "The Lever Brothers Campaign: Its Background and Thrust," April 25, 1964, NAACP Flyers and Reports, Box 1, File 10, No. 11, EC-UMSL; "NAACP Rejects Lever Brothers Job Offer," April 24, 1964, SL Council on Human Relations, Series III, Box 13, Tucker-WU.

46. "Posing a New Municipal Approach to Negro Employment Problem," Meeting with Mayor, June 6, 1963; Memorandum on Meeting in Mayor's Office at 3:00 pm on June 6, 1963; Equal Employment Opportunity, St. Louis Commission on Equal Employment Opportunity, November 2, 1963, Box 8, File 238, No. 540, EC-UMSL; Civic Progress Minutes, October 28, 1963; "To: The Mayor of St. Louis, Honorable R.R. Tucker," n.d., SL Council on Human Relations, both in Series III, Box 13, Tucker-WU.

47. Lang, *Grassroots at the Gateway*, 137.

48. "Negro Job Holders Up at Southwestern Bell," May 7, 1965, Group III, Box A188, Labor, Missouri, 1956–1965, NAACP-LC; "Labor Council Cracks Phone Company Craft Groups" and "A Huge Breakthrough," August 9, 1963, both in *St. Louis Argus*; Lang, *Grassroots at the Gateway*, 137; Minutes, St. Louis Labor Council, July 16, 1963, Box 4, File 36, No. 11, EC-UMSL; EC, "The Ultimate Conquest of Negro Economic Inequality," October 10, 1963, published by the St. Louis Division of the NALC, January 15, 1964, Box 2, File 72, FR-UMSL.

49. EC, "Ultimate Conquest of Negro Inequality."

50. Author's interview with Margaret Bush Wilson; Oldham interview; Tournour interview; Seay interview; Lang, *Grassroots at the Gateway*, 160–62; Clay, Sr., *Jefferson Bank Confrontation*; Lipsitz, *Life in the Struggle*, 75–76.

51. Clay, *Jefferson Bank*, 34–38, 45–49; Lang, *Grassroots at the Gateway*, 162–65; McCarthy, "Negro Revolution Comes Home."

52. EC, "The March on Washington: Where Do We Go From Here?" August 18, 1963, Box 1, File 4, No. 11, EC-UMSL.

53. "Labor Leader Takes a Look at Bank Controversy," October 11, 1963, and "Groups React to Jailing of CORE Leaders," November 1, 1963, both in *St. Louis Argus*; EC, "Some Working Lessons from the CORE-Jefferson Bank Controversy," October 27, 1963, Box 1, File 4, No. 11, EC-UMSL

54. "Some Working Lessons"; Tournour interview.

55. HJG, "Negroes Won't Wait"; McCarthy, "Negro Revolution Comes Home," and "Story That Will Never End"; "Injunctions New and Old," November 1, 1963; all in *Missouri Teamster*.

56. Tournour interview.

Chapter 10. *"A Trade Union Oriented War on the Slums"*

1. L.J. Sverdrup to Buck (W.R. Person), October 23, 1969, Box 78, Sverdrup-WU.

2. Leonard Carter to Roy Wilkins and Gloster Current, "Special Report on the St. Louis Branch Administration," October 4, 1963; Evelyn Roberts to Roy Wilkins, November 3, 1963; EC, "A Proposal for the Assumption of Greater Responsibility on the Part of the Executive Committee of the St. Louis NAACP," November 26, 1963, St. Louis, October-December, 1963, Group III, C78; "Elect Pearlie Evans"; St. Louis Election Dispute, December 23, 1964–March 20, 1965, Group III, C302, all in NAACP-LC; Chait, "NAACP Leadership Ineffectual Here."

3. Leonard H. Carter to Roy Wilkins, March 31, 1964, Group III, Box C80, Missouri State Conference, 1964, NAACP-LC; Braithwaite, "Politicians Lead NAACP Plan"; EC, "How to Succeed in the NAACP Without Really Trying," n.d., Box 46, File 525, No. 540, EC-UMSL; Jackson, "Struggle for Control of St. Louis NAACP"; Evans interview by Doris Wesley, LEV-UMSL.

4. "How to Succeed in the NAACP"; Gloster Current to Pearlie Evans, December 4, 1964; Deverne Calloway to Gloster Current, December 14, 1964; Margaret Bush Wilson to Roy Wilkins and Gloster Current, December 16, 1964; EC to Judge Herbert T. Delaney, January 14, 1965; Box 46, File 525, No. 540, EC-UMSL; Margaret Bush Wilson to Stephen Gill Spottswood, February 2, 1965, Group III, Box C302, St. Louis Election Dispute, December 23, 1964–March 20, 1965, NAACP-LC; "Miss Roberts Ruled Winner of Contested NAACP Election," *SLPD*, January 4, 1965; Clay, *Bill Clay*, 131–33; author's interviews with Pearlie Evans and Margaret Bush Wilson.

5. Sloane, *Hoffa*, 310–11; "Won't Take Away Hoffa's Right to Appeal: Gibbons," *Missouri Teamster*, September 14, 1964; HJG interview with *SLPD* reporter Kenneth Jacobson, August 23, 1964, Box 1, File 7, Keiser-UIS; "Campaign Check List," October 5, 1965, Box 3, File 2; "Platform, (Revised January 9, 1966)," Box 3, File 5, HJG-SIUE.

6. Platform, January 9, 1966; Martin J. Carroll to HJG, n.d., Box 3, File 6, HJG-SIUE.

7. "Gibbons Gives Positions on National Question," December 17, 1965, and "Hoffa Names Gibbons to Directorship of Central Conference," *Missouri Teamster*, March 17, 1967; Sloane, *Hoffa*, 315–18; Brill, *The Teamsters*, 375–76; Gilbride, "Hoffa Riding High"; "Don't Rock the Boat, Hoffa Tells Teamsters Vice-President," *The Evening News* (Sault Ste. Marie, Michigan), July 5, 1966; "Hoffa Moves to Hold Power," (Hopkinsville) *Kentucky New Era*, June 8, 1966; Hoffa, *Hoffa: The Real Story*, 13–14; "Harold Gibbons," *SLGD*, November 19, 1982; Bernstein interview; Crancer interview; Larry Gibbons interview.

8. For representative critiques of labor in the 1960s, see Jacobs, *Old Before Its Time*, 256–93; Swados, "Over the Top or Over the Hill," 69–92; Bell, "Capitalism of the Proletariat," 218–26; Widick, *Labor Today*; "The Port Huron Statement," in Miller, *Democracy Is in the Streets*, 343–44. Walter Reuther's critique is found in Boyle, *Heyday of American Liberalism*, 154–69.

9. "Stewards Council Proceedings," *MLW*, May 1963; HJG, "Collective Bargaining in Perspective"; EC, "New Challenges to American Labor," October 2, 1964, Speech Before Labor and International Affairs Forum, Brainerd, Minnesota, Box 7, File 234, No. 540, EC-UMSL, and "Whatever Happened to Simple Union Contracts?" For analysis of collective bargaining and shop-floor relations in the post–World War II era, see Lichtenstein, *State of the Union*, 122–32; Jacobs, *Old Before Its Time*; Brody, "Workplace Contractualism," 223–45.

10. "HJG Remarks," later reprinted as "Old Challenges and New Horizons for US Unionism," December 25, 1962, Box 5, File 11; HJG Speech before St. Louis Conference on Race and Religion," March 15, 1965; and "A New Society Through New Alliances," Box 5, File 63, HJG-SIUE; EC, "New Challenges to American Labor"; "Shadows without Substance"; and "Stagnant Plateau of Membership Growth"; Defty, "'New Gibbons.'"

11. Bell, "Capitalism of the Proletariat," 225; "The Teamster Structure," Box 1, File 7, Keiser-UIS.

12. "Proposed Outline: Labor and Business in St. Louis"; "Speech Outline for Young Lawyers' Association Talk," October 14, 1966, Box 5, File 16, HJG-SIUE; "Mr. Hoffa and Mr. Gibbons," July 1, 1966, *SLGD*; EC, "Feeding and Care of a Slum"; "Gibbons, Persons Agree: Labor Not the Issue," *Missouri Teamster*, November 11, 1966.

13. Press Release, September 11, 1964; Press Release, October 12, 1964; Lou Berra to HJG et al., October 27, 1964, Box 10, File 1; Dismas Clark Foundation Newsletter, July 1965, Box 10, File 3, HJG-SIUE; "First Charity Show Netted Just $10,000," *Missouri Teamster*, February 14, 1967.

14. "Municipal Mediation Plans," Institute of Industrial and Labor Relations Bulletin, University of Illinois, 1, No. 5, October 1946, www.ideals.illinois.edu/bitstream/municipalmediati15univ.pdf, accessed December 26, 2011; Joann Herbst to EC, August 29, 1966; EC to HJG, "Memorandum on Creating Greater Communication Between Labor and Management in St. Louis Area," September 29, 1966, Box 5, File 40, No. 550, EC-UMSL; HJG on Dick Amberg, *SLGD* publisher, Box 2, File 12, HJG-SIUE; "Report of the Labor Climate Subcommittee of the Metropolitan St. Louis Labor-Management Committee," November 18, 1964, Series III, Box 24; "Labor-Management," Tucker-WU; "Gibbons Calls for Management, Labor to Build Bridges Between Differences," *Missouri Teamster*, October 22, 1965.

15. "Gibbons Proposes 16 Million Development in West End," *Missouri Teamster*, January 7, 1966; Stewards Council Minutes, March 15, 1967, Box 41, File 16, HJG-SIUE; "Some Preliminary Notes on the Creation of a Non-Profit Foundation to Promote New Creative Horizons in Urban Living," "Draft: 'The Foundation,'" America 2000; Minutes, September 1, 1967, America 2000; Minutes of Board of Trustees Meeting, November 27, 1967; all in Box 4, File 29, No. 550, EC-UMSL.

16. Robert T. Jones to Alfonso J. Cervantes, March 14, 1967; Lucius F. Cervantes to Jake McCarthy, March 15, 1967; Minutes, America 2000, September 1, 1967; Stanley M. Rosenblum to Arthur E. Klein, December 8, 1972, Box 4, File 29, No. 550, EC-UMSL; "Plan Group Picks River City Development," *Missouri Teamster*, May 3, 1968; HJG

Graduation Address, Harvard Trade Union Program, May 6, 1971, Box 5, File 42, HJG-SIUE.

17. EC, "Old, New Inequities"; "Statement of Ernest Calloway in Declaring His Candidacy in the First Congressional District of Missouri," Box 23, File 1, HJG-SIUE.

18. EC, "Approaching the Problems of Community Organization"; "Urban Slums and Self-Hood Revolution"; "Conspiracy Against the Poor"; "City Could Become a Riot Leader"; Jackson, "The State, the Movement, and the Urban Poor," 424–29. For the full range of Calloway's thinking on race, poverty, and urban decline, see "The Urban Trap." On St. Louis civil rights politics during this period, see Lang, *Grassroots at the Gateway*, 184–85, 193–95, 202–12; Jolley, *Black Liberation in the Midwest*, 71–78; Clay, *Bill Clay*, 131–35, 143–48; EC, "McNeal and Missouri Politics"; Lipsitz, *Life in the Struggle*, 118–32.

19. EC, "Negro Middle Class Is Problem"; "Local 688 Launches New Community Organizing Project in Greater Tandy Area on the North Side," *Missouri Teamster*, December 8, 1967; Stewards Council Meeting Minutes, March 16, 1966, Box 41, File 16; EC to Richard Kavner, September 27, 1966, Box 43, File 20, HJG-SIUE; "Voice to the Voiceless: Report of Tandy Area Council," n.d., 1969, Box 3, File 6, JC 13-SIUE; "The Tandy Community," Box 4, File 32, No. 550, EC-UMSL.

20. EC, "A Trade Union Oriented War"; "Voice to the Voiceless"; Boyle, *Heyday of American Liberalism,* 213–16; Murphy, "Developing Communities," 28–37.

21. Ryan interview; Brown interview; Sanford interview; Pace interview; John P. Nichols to HJG, July 14, 1966, Box 43, File 15; "Proposed Local 688 Education Program," Box 43, File 38, HJG-SIUE.

22. Pace interview; Ryan interview; Tucker interview; Jim Pace to HJG, September 4, 1968; Jim Pace to Richard Kavner, January 8, 1969; both in Box 37, File 16, HJG-SIUE, "Area Residents Responding Well to 688 Tandy Project," *Missouri Teamster*, December 22, 1967; Levy, *The New Left and Labor*; 72–83.

23. Pace interview; "Outline of Proposals for a Permanent Community Action Program in Greater Tandy Area," "Outline for Development of Program in Tandy Area," May 18, 1966, Box 1, File 12, No. 550, EC-UMSL; Pace, Boykin, Bryson to HJG, Kavner, Nabcr, n.d, Box 3, File 9, JC 13-SIUE; Tandy Area Council Minutes, November 16, 1967, Box 37, File 16, HJG-SIUE; Pace to Kavner, January 8, 1969.

24. Baron interview; Frank Boykin to Harold J. Gibbons et al., n.d., Box 43, File 37; Stewards Council Meeting Minutes, February 21, 1968, Box 41, File 17, HJG-SIUE; Pace interview; "Voice to the Voiceless," "Tandy Area Food Stores Drop Prices," February 16, 1968, "Teamsters Offer Support to Poor People's Movement," May 17, 1968, both in *Missouri Teamster*; "Carter, Protestors to Meet," *SLPD*, December 2, 1969.

25. "Tandy Area Council Confrontation Activities," n.d., Box 3, File 9, JC 13-SIUE.

26. Boyle, *Heyday of American Liberalism*, 246–48; Lichtenstein, *Most Dangerous Man*; 430–33; Devinatz, "To Find Answers," 69–87; "Alliance for Labor Action," July 23, 1968, Box 2, File 15, HJG-SIUE.

27. Tucker interview; Robinson interview.

28. Tucker interview; Robinson interview; Riddell, "Blacks Using Labor Tactics"; Stewards Council Minutes, February 18, 1970, Box 41, File 18; Tandy Council Report, n.d.; Mike Ryan to HJG, January 27, 1971, Box 43, File 15; Community/Political Action Department Report, January 1, 1971–May 1, 1971, Box 43, File 16; Tandy Area Council Minutes, n.d, Box 37, File 16, HJG-SIUE; Lichtenstein, *State of the Union*, 187; Boyle, *Heyday of American Liberalism*, 215–16.

29. "Proposed Outline for Speech on Police Brutality," September 15, 1968, Box 5, File 32, HJG-SIUE; "U.S. to Investigate Police," *SLPD*, September 16, 1968; Lang, *Grassroots at the Gateway*, 218–20. The Gibbons St. Louis Argus quote is found in Jolley, *Black Liberation in the Midwest*, 167.

30. EC, "Realigned First Congressional District"; Kneeland, "Districting Bill Is Passed"; "Vote Your Conscience," Box 1, File 14, No. 540, EC-UMSL; "Statement of Ernest Calloway in Declaring His Candidacy for Congress in the First Congressional District of Missouri," March 15, 1968; "A Testament of Faith and Concern," *Truth*, June 8, 1968, Vol. 2, No. 2, Box 23, File 1, HJG-SIUE; "A Political Conversation," *St. Louis Sentinel*, July 6, 1968; Clay, *Bill Clay*, 156–57, 159–60; author's interview with William Clay.

31. Clay, *Bill Clay*, 160; "31 Are Candidates for Congressional Seats in Five Area Districts," *SLPD*, January 28, 1968; Press Release, July 12, 1968, Box 3, File 1, JC 13-SIUE; "Calloway Gears Campaign for Congress to Grassroots Needs," *Truth*, June 8, 1968, Vol. 2, No. 2, Box 23, File 1, HJG-SIUE.

32. Calloway to Harold J. Gibbons, July 1, 1968, Box 23, File 1, HJG-SIUE; Clay, *Just Permanent Interests*, 115; Clay, *Bill Clay*, 163–66; Flach, "Teamsters, Steamfitters at Odds"; Clay interview with author; EC, "Can Black St. Louisans Support Black Candidates?"; Lang, *Grassroots at the Gateway*, 206.

33. McCarthy, "Before It Was Fashionable."

34. Fleishman, "Not Without Honor," 4–5; Baron, "Community Organizations"; Baron interview; Gordon, *Mapping Decline*, 98–99; Lipsitz, *Life in the Struggle*, 147–48; HJG Press Statement on Pruitt-Igoe, April 23, 1966, Box 1, File 6, JC 13-SIUE; Meehan, *Quality of Federal Policymaking*, 62–75; Cervantes, *Mr. Mayor*, 48–50; Lang, *Grassroots at the Gateway*, 213; "General Information Regarding Public Housing and the Current Rent Strike," n.d, Box 14, File 474, MCF-UMSL; A.J. Cervantes Statement to Community Leaders, June 6, 1969, Series 2, Box 49, AJC-WU; St. Louis Housing Authority, Final Environmental Impact Statement, Pruitt Homes and Igoe Apartment Housing Complex, Report Number HUD-R07-EIS-07F, September 1974, HUD-NA. Jean King is quoted in the 2012 documentary film "Envisioning Home: The Jean King and Richard Baron Story."

35. Sugrue, *Sweet Land of Liberty*, 408; Lang, *Grassroots at the Gateway*, 213–14; Lipsitz, *Life in the Struggle*, 148–52; Fleishman, "Not Without Honor," 11–13; Coburn, "All Systems Fail"; Baron Interview.

36. Coburn, "All Systems Fail"; Baron interview; Fleishman, "Not Without Honor," 21, 31, 33–36; "General Information Regarding Public Housing and the Current Rent Strike"; Minutes, Dialogue Committee of Civic Progress, March 14, 1969, Civic Progress, General Correspondence, Box 78, Sverdrup-WU; Dave Meeker to Mayor Cervantes, April 23, 1969, "Rent Strike Meeting, May 15, 1969, "City-Wide Rent Strike Committee Demands," Series 2, Box 49, AJC-WU; EC, "Creative Self-Determinism."

37. Cervantes, *Mr. Mayor*, 51, 57; T.P. Costello to David Meeker, October 16, 1969, Box 52; "Minutes, Meeting with Rent Strikers, June 9, 1969"; A.J. Cervantes to Harold J. Gibbons, June 11, 1969, Box 49, AJC-WU; Baron interview; Brown interview; Fleishman, "Not Without Honor," 20; Jake McCarthy to I. Jean King, April 24, 1969, Box 35, File 2; I. Jean King to Jake McCarthy, April 10, 1969, May 7, 1969, Box 34, File 35, HJG-SIUE.

38. Fleishman, "Not Without Honor," 51–52; Jean King to "All Residents of Peabody-Darst Webbe Residents, Striking and Non-Striking," August 29, 1969, Box 49, AJC-WU; I. Jean King to Jake McCarthy, April 10, 1969, May 7, 1969, Box 34, File 35, HJG-SIUE.

39. "Romney Praises Council House During Visit Here," *Missouri Teamster*, September 22, 1967; *HUD News*, April 4, 1967, Box 23, File 19, HJG-SIUE; Edgar M. Ewing to A.J. Cervantes, July 31, 1969; Dave Meeker to Mayor, October 10, 1969; Lawrence M. Cox to Stuart Symington, October 15, 1969, Box 49, AJC-WU; Baron interview; HJG Graduation Address.

40. "The Rent Strike is Trade Unionism," n.d., Box 43, File 34; Stewards Council Minutes, September 17, 1969, Box 44, File 11, HJG-SIUE; HJG, "Poor Must Find Dignity, Security."

41. "Convening of the Coalition," October 10, 1969, Background Document, Box 52, AJC-WU.

42. Cervantes, *Mr. Mayor*, 59–60; Fleishman, "Not Without Honor," 71–72; Baron interview.

43. KMOX TV Editorial, October 31, 1969, Box 78, Sverdrup-WU; EC, "Small October Revolution"; "Evolution of New Housing Concept."

44. Arthur E. Klein to HJG, December 8, 1969; Maurice A. Chambers to Members of Civic Progress, Inc., December 1, 1969, Box 78, Sverdrup-WU; "Civic Alliance Instrumental in $250,000 to Public Housing," August 27, 1970, "Housing Authority Gets $5,100,000," April 30, 1971, both in *Missouri Teamster*; "St. Louis Housing Authority," September 28, 1970, Box 3, File 2, JC 13-SIUE; "St. Louis Civic Alliance for Housing Newsletters," December 22, 1970, April 20, 1971, and May 21, 1971, Box 80, File 3, HJG-SIUE; Meehan, *Quality of Federal Policymaking*, 99; "Romney Reports Getting Tough with Cervantes," *SLPD*, April 30, 1970.

45. Joyce Weaver to HJG, March 12, 1970, Box 80, File 1; Civic Alliance Executive Committee Minutes, January 29, 1971; Richard D. Baron to Terence K. McCormack, January 26, 1971, Box 80, File 3, HJG-SIUE; Statement made by Mrs. Ann Pickett and Callie Mae Johnston, April 27, 1970, Box 49; Elmer Hammond to A.J. Cervantes, March 5, 1970; A.J. Cervantes to HJG, May 7, 1970, Box 52, AJC-WU; Elmer N. Hammond to George Romney, November 11, 1970, Box 90, NN3-209-94-001, HUD-NA.

46. EC, "Building a Balanced City"; "Capitalizing a Loss," *SLPD* editorial, September 23, 1970; Baron interview; Baron, "Community Organizations."

47. Baron interview; "Will Poor Get to Live in Townhouses?" *Tuscaloosa* (Alabama) *News*, May 24, 1971; Bonastia, *Knocking on the Door*, 108–13, 134–43; Cervantes, *Mr. Mayor*, 62–63; "St. Louis Civic Alliance for Housing Newsletter," July 23, 1971, Box 80, File 3, HJG-SIUE; "Civic Alliance Here Is Disbanded," *SLPD*, March 15, 1972; McCarthy, "Next Time Too Late," "Tenant Management Corporations in St. Louis Public Housing: The Status After Two Years," Center for Urban Programs, St. Louis University, 1975; Lipsitz, *Life in the Struggle*, 164–65; Heathcott and Murphy, "Corridors of Flight," 181.

48. "Tenant Organization Convenes," *Missouri Teamster*, October 1969.

49. Frank Boykin to Harold J. Gibbons et al., July 6, 1972, Box 43, File 37, HJG-SIUE.

Chapter 11. "Fuck Him, He Wasn't With Us"

1. Defty, "New Gibbons."
2. Defty, "Teamster Boss," "Gibbons Kept Cool," "New Gibbons," "Hoffa-Gibbons Split."
3. Nixon Tapes, December 15, 1972, Conversation 34-92 with Charles W. Colson, accessed at www.youtube.com/watch?v=-iBXz007wbA, July 6, 2012.
4. Television Panel on Automation, KMOX TV, Box 5, File 63, HJG-SIUE.
5. Press Release on Famous-Barr, n.d., Box 3, File 1, JC 13-SIUE.

6. Stewards Council Minutes, June 15, 1966, Box 41, File 16; Ed Brown to HJG, April 5, 1968, and Richard Kavner to HJG, May 20, 1968, Box 26, File 3, HJG-SIUE; Howe, *Pink Collar Workers*, 95–102.

7. Ernie Neidel to All 688 Staff, August 21, 1969, Box 44, File 11; Minutes of January Meeting of Education Committee, November 3, 1967, Box 22, File 4, HJG-SIUE.

8. London Trip, HJG, March 11, 1968, Box 29, File 2; Stewards Council Minutes, February 21, March 20, April 17, 1968, Box 41, File 17, HJG-SIUE.

9. Minutes, Stewards Council Meeting, August 10, 1967, Box 41, File 16; Minutes, Stewards Council Meeting, February 21, 1968, Box 44, File 11; Jim Pace to HJG et al., August 20, 1968, Box 43, File 15; Stewards Council Minutes, October 16, 1968, Box 41, File 17; all in HJG-SIUE; "A Voice to the Voiceless," Box 3, File 6, JC 13-SIUE.

10. Poll of Local 688 members on 1968 presidential race, Box 41, File 38, HJG-SIUE; EC, "Troubled Times for U.S. Unionism," and "For Whom the Bell Tolls"; Boyle, *Heyday of American Liberalism*, 253–56; Cowie, *Stayin' Alive*, 129–34; Pace interview.

11. Note on Frazer petition on Black Liberators, September 24, 1968, Box 2, File 12, HJG-SIUE; "Teamsters for Police Review," *SLPD*, September 30, 1968.

12. Gordon, *Mapping Decline*, 25, 102–4; Jim Pace to Brother 688er, August 28, 1968; Jim Pace to HJG, September 4, 1968, Box 37, File 16; "Does Integrated Housing Lower Property Values?" Box 43, File 15, n.d., HJG-SIUE.

13. John Cooney's Shop Stewards, August 5, 1969; Otto Sanders' Shop Stewards, August 6, 1969; Levi Sanford's Shop Stewards, August 7, 1969; Joe Galli's Stewards Meeting, August 18, 1969; Roger Jackson's and Roger Whitby's Stewards, August 27, 1969, Box 44, File 11, HJG-SIUE.

14. Murray Hines' Stewards Meeting, August 16, 1969, Box 44, File 11, HJG-SIUE; EC, "Simple Union Contracts."

15. Mike Ryan to H.J. Gibbons and Dick Kavner, September 4, 1969, Box 44, File 11; Stewards Council Minutes, November 5, 1969, Box 41, File 16, HJG-SIUE; Ryan interview.

16. La Botz, "Tumultuous Teamsters," 204–8.

17. Ronald Gushleff, email correspondence with author, April 8, 2012; "Rank and File Forms RAFT," "On the Line," Issue No. 5, Box 3, File 7, JC 13-SIUE.

18. Ronald Gushleff to author; La Botz, "Tumultuous Teamsters," 207; Minutes, Stewards Council, September 16, 1970, Box 41, File 18; Minutes, Community Action Committee, September 2, 1971, Box 43, File 16; *On the Line*, Issue No. 5; "RAFT—Test Yourself"; "Is Ron Borges An Expert?"; "RAFT: Vote Against Local 688 Dues Increase," n.d., 1970; Box 43, File 37, HJG-SIUE; Rank and File Majority Report-Stewards Council, September 15, 1971; George Lipsitz to HJG, August 28, 1971, Box 3, File 7, JC 13-SIUE; Lipsitz, "Beyond the Fringe Benefits," 33–37, and "Harold and Me," 151–53.

19. Brown interview; Pace interview; EC, "Simple Union Contracts," "Troubled Times for U.S. Unionism."

20. Ronald Gushleff to author; Stewards Council Minutes, n.d., Box 41, File 19; HJG to Ronald M. Gushleff, May 31, 1972, Box 43, File 37, HJG-SIUE.

21. Harris, *History of Carondelet*; Boyle, *Heyday of American Liberalism*, 253; EC, "St. Louis Black Politics Today"; Pace interview; Resolutions Committee Report, 21st Citywide Shop Conference, "Our Changing World," September 21, 1968, Box 43, File 12; Community Action Committee Minutes, May 14, 1970; "Present Activities of Carondelet Area Council," October 30, 1970, Box 43, File 15; Mike Ryan to HJG, January 27, 1971; Report,

Community/Political Action Department, January 1, 1971-August 1, 1971, Box 43, File 16, HJG-SIUE; Mike Ryan to HJG, December 7, 1972; "Will You Become Involved?" *St. Louis Neighborhood News*, April 9, 1970, Box 3, File 7, JC 13-SIUE.

22. Report, Community/Political Action Department; "Will You Become Involved?"; Community Action Committee Minutes, June 11, 1970; Mike Ryan to HJG, January 27, 1971, Box 43, File 15, HJG-SIUE; Tucker interview, May 30, 2002.

23. Nicolaides, *My Blue Heaven*, 276; "Teamsters Back Beverly Hills Drive-in Protest," and "Teamsters Join in Fight for Normandy Annexation;" both in *Missouri Teamster*, December 20, 1968.

24. "Community Action-Political Education Report," n.d., 1969; Jim Pace to HJG, Richard Kavner, and John Naber, October 24, 1969; December 17, 1969; Community Action Committee Minutes, October 9, 1969; "Let the People Speak," n.d, 1969; "Facts You Should Know to Unite Velda Village and Adjoining Unincorporated Area"; all in Box 43, File 15, HJG-SIUE.

25. Ryan interview; "Testimony of Teamsters Local 688 members to U.S. Senate Air and Water Pollution Subcommittee," October 27, 1969; Box 43 File 15, HJG-SIUE.

26. HJG to all Female Members, n.d., Box 3, File 2, JC 13-SIUE; Mike Ryan to HJG, Richard Kavner, John Naber, Ernie Neidel, Local 688 Staff, October 28, 1970, Box 43, File 16, HJG-SIUE; Timnick, "Give Women a Say."

27. Murray Hines, "A Concept in Unionism," n.d., 1969, Box 43, File 34, HJG-SIUE.

28. Ernie Neidel to All 688 Staff, August 21, 1969, Box 44, File 11; Report of Resolutions Committee, 23rd Citywide Conference, Local 688, September 24, 1972, Box 43, File 14, HJG-SIUE.

29. Wehling, "Key Incidents in Fall of Gibbons"; Brill, *The Teamsters*, 377–78; Sloane, *Hoffa*, 339–41; Salpukis, "Teamsters Elect Fitzsimmons"; Patrick Gibbons interview.

30. Brill, *The Teamsters*, 378; Thomas MaQuire and Thomas O'Malley to HJG, n.d., 1971, Box 27, File 15, HJG-SIUE. According to Brill's sources, Gibbons also may have feared retribution from mob elements if his bid proved successful.

31. Ryan interview; Larry Gibbons interview.

32. EC, "Arts of Corruption" and "The Trauma of Asia in American Politics"; Defty, "Hoffa-Gibbons Split"; Levy, *New Left and Labor*, 55–56; Boyle, *Heyday of American Liberalism*, 235–40, 247–50; Lichtenstein, *Most Dangerous Man*, 420; Wehrle, *Between a River and a Mountain*, 138–42.

33. HJG Vietnam Moratorium Speech, November 15, 1969, Box 5, File 38; HJG to Mr. and Mrs. Frank Repinski, n.d., Box 1, File 30, HJG-SIUE; HJG Opening Remarks, Labor for Peace Conference, Box 1, File 1, LP-UMSL; McCarthy, "Hanoi Doubts US Desires Peace"; Livingston et al., "Labor Mission to Hanoi," 520–22.

34. Ryan interview; Patrick Gibbons interview; Larry Gibbons interview; Fred J. Wheeler to Editor, *Missouri Teamster*, March 1, 1968; Education Department Monthly Report, July 1969, Box 22, File 6, HJG-SIUE.

35. Statement of Evelyn F. Grubb, National Coordinator, National League of Families of American Prisoners and Missing in Southeast Asia, Box 1, File 4; "Gibbons and Commoner Join Suit Against War," May 13, 1972, Box 1, File 5, LP-UMSL; Weiss, "Trade Union Parley"; "An Interview with Harold Gibbons," "Today Show," March 30, 1972, Box 1, File 30, HJG-SIUE.

36. Cowie, *Stayin' Alive*, 154–55; "Fitzsimmons Disclaims Teamster Support for Splinter Peace Groups," May 19, 1972, Box 1, File 4, LP-UMSL; Murdock, "Labor for Peace."

37. Larry Gibbons interview; HJG to Doctor Henry A. Kissinger, January 17, 1969, Box 35, File 2; HJG to Henry Kissinger, October 5, 1971, Box 35, File 9, HJG-SIUE; TELECON, Harold Gibbons/Mr. Kissinger, June 29, 1972; Kissinger Telephone Conversations, KA08281; TELECON/San Clemente, John Dean/Kissinger, July 13, 1972, HK-DNSA; "First Colson Memo to Dean," June 12, 1972, accessed at www.colorado.edu/AmStudies/lewis/film/enemies.htm, July 4, 2012.

38. Graham, "Officials Chagrined By Hoffa's 'Lawyer,'" and "Hoffa 'Lawyer'"; Hershberger, *Traveling to Vietnam*, 213–14.

39. TELECON/San Clemente, Chuck Colson/Kissinger, July 13, 1972, HK-DNSA; Brill, *The Teamsters*, 381; Salpukis, "Teamster Aide Expects Ouster."

40. Blount interview with Ernest Neidel, HJG-Blount-SIUE; Gushleff e-mail to author; "Is Ron Borges An Expert"; Wehling, "Key Incidents"; McCarthy, "Behind the Gibbons Ouster."

41. Wehling, "Key Incidents"; McCarthy, "Behind the Gibbons Ouster"; Brill, *The Teamsters*, 382.

42. Brill, *The Teamsters*, 382–89; McCarthy, "Fitz's Teamsters," *SLPD*, June 16, 1976; Ray Schoessling to Edwin D. Dorsey, January 28, 1975; Ray Schoessling to HJG, February 7, 1975, Box 65, File 3, HJG-SIUE.

43. Brill, *The Teamsters*, 391–92; "Harold Gibbons Dies; Was Teamster Leader," *SLPD*, November 18, 1982; "Gibbons Is Seeking Post in Reagan Administration," *SLGD*, January 15, 1981; Ledbetter, "H.J. Gibbons Dies."

44. Ledbetter, "H.J. Gibbons Dies"; "Our Viewpoint: Harold J. Gibbons, 1919–1982," *St. Louis Labor Tribune*, November 25, 1982; Burnside, "Calloway at 73"; Vasquez interview.

45. HJG to EC, June 28, 1969, Box 35, File 3, HJG-SIUE; Student Evaluations of Washington University talk, "Labor Unions and the City," November 21, 1974, in "News Clippings: A Social and Political Journey in St. Louis, Deverne and Ernest Calloway, Part 2, 1970–1978," EC-SLU; Freeman Bosley, "The History Makers," accessed at www.thehistorymakers.com/biography/freeman-bosley-4 July 30, 2012.

46. Norfolk, "Urban Strategist"; EC, "Strategies for Containment," "Coalition Opposes Team IV Plan," *St. Louis Urban League Bulletin*, August 1975; Harmon, "Citizen Participation Bill to Be Considered"; EC, "Promise of Jim Conway."

47. EC, "St. Louis Black Politics Today," "A Political Comment," "One Man's Thoughts," "Political Ku Kluxism"; Norfolk, "Urban Strategist"; Stein, *Triumph of Tradition*, 182.

48. EC, Speech Before National Convention of the National Alliance of Postal and Federal Employees, August 16, 1976, Box 7, File 234, No. 540, EC-UMSL; EC, "New Economic Ball Game"; "Professor, Former Labor Leader Says Global Unions Necessary," *Arkansas Gazette*, January 18, 1976.

49. Cawthra, "Ernest Calloway"; "E. Calloway Dies," *SLPD*, January 4, 1990; "Ernest Calloway Labored for the Underdog," *SLPD*, January 6, 1990; Poor, "Calloway Eulogized as Champion"; Woo, "Epitaph for a Trade Unionist."

Epilogue

1. EC, "The Failure of the U.S. Trade Union Movement," May 3, 1976, Box 7, File 236, No. 540, EC-UMSL; EC, "Biographical Sketch," 1976, Box 50, File 3, HJG-SIUE.

2. "Local 688 Launches New Community Organizing Project in Greater Tandy Area on North Side," *Missouri Teamster*, December 8, 1967.

3. King, "Teamster Clint Zweifel Enters Final Drive."

4. Ronald F. Gamache and Edwin D. Dorsey to Alvin Baron, October 1, 1973, Box 13, File 14, HJG-SIUE; Jake McCarthy, "The New Teamster Faces," *SLPD*, November 28, 1973; National Register of Historic Places Registration Form, submitted by Missouri Department of Natural Resources, January 16, 2007, www.dnr.mo.gov/shpo/nps-nr/06000217.pdf, accessed September 8, 2012; "Council Plaza: Exceptionally Significant," *Modern St. L.*, www.modern-stl.com/council-plaza-exceptionally-significant, accessed February 2, 2013.

5. Greenhouse, "Share of the Workforce Falls."

6. Belzer, *Sweatshops on Wheels*; Salvatore, "Teamster Democracy."

7. On "whole person unionism," see McAlevey, "It Takes a Community."

8. "School Segregation," Box 1, File 12, HJG-SIUE.

9. Trumka, "At Missouri AFL-CIO Convention," September 15, 2014; Rothstein, "The Making of Ferguson"; Lang, "On Ferguson, Missouri."

10. HJG to editor, *SLPD*, September 24, 1955.

11. EC, "Unions in a New Economic Ball Game," *Missouri Teamster*, February 16, 1975, and "Failure of Trade Union Movement."

BIBLIOGRAPHY

Manuscripts and Archives

American Labor Education Service Records. Kheel Center for Labor-Management Documentation and Archives, Cornell University.
Ernest Calloway Collection. Western Historical Manuscripts Collection, Thomas Jefferson Library, University of Missouri at St. Louis. Collection comprised of three segments, No. 11, No. 540, and No. 550.
Ernest Calloway Federal Bureau of Investigation Records.
Ernest Calloway Manuscript Collection. Special Collections: Archives and Manuscripts, Saint Louis University Libraries.
Ernest Calloway Writings, compiled by Kenn Thomas.
A.J. Cervantes Collection. Manuscripts Division, Olin Library, Washington University, St. Louis.
Congress of Industrial Organizations. National and International Union Files, Food, Tobacco, and Allied Workers Union of America, Catholic University of America Archives.
Congress of Industrial Organizations. National and International Union Files, United Transport Service Employees of America.
Congress of Industrial Organizations. National and International Unions, Retail, Wholesale, Department Store Union, Catholic University of America Archives.
Department of Housing and Urban Development General Records. Region VII, Kansas City, National Archives, College Park, Maryland.
Annetta M. Dieckmann Papers. Richard J. Daley Library, Special Collections and University Archives, University of Illinois at Chicago.
Freedom of Residence, Greater St. Louis Committee Records. Western Historical Manuscripts Collection, University of Missouri at St. Louis.
Harold J. Gibbons Collection. Louisa H. Bowen University Archives and Special Collections, Lovejoy Library, Southern Illinois University at Edwardsville.
Harold J. Gibbons Federal Bureau of Investigation Records.
Jewish Labor Committee Records. Tamiment Library, Robert F. Wagner Labor Archives, New York University.
John Keiser Collection. Brookens Library Archives and Special Collections, University of Illinois at Springfield.
Henry Kissinger Telephone Conversations. Digital National Security Archive.
Labor for Peace Records. Western Historical Manuscripts Collection, University of Missouri at St. Louis.
League of Women Voters Records. Western Historical Manuscripts Collection, University of Missouri at St. Louis.

Metropolitan Church Federation Records, Western Historical Manuscripts Collection, University of Missouri at St. Louis.
National Association for the Advancement of Colored People Records. Manuscript Division, Library of Congress.
National Urban League Records. Library of Congress, Washington, D.C.
Senate Select Committee on Improper Activities in the Labor or Management Field, 1957–1960 Records. National Archives, Washington, D.C.
Leif Sverdrup Papers, Manuscripts Division, Olin Library, Washington University, St. Louis.
Teamsters Archives. Labor History Research Center, George Washington University.
Teamsters Joint Council 13 Collection. University Archives and Special Collections, Southern Illinois University at Edwardsville.
Raymond R. Tucker Files, City of St. Louis, Office of the Mayor, 1953–1965. Department of Special Collections, Olin Library, Washington University, St. Louis.
Henry Winfield Wheeler Papers, Western Historical Manuscripts Collection, University of Missouri at St. Louis.

Books and Articles in Books

Arnesen, Eric. *Brotherhoods of Color: Black Railroad Workers and the Struggle for Equality*. Cambridge: Harvard University Press, 2001.
———. "International Brotherhood of Red Caps-UTSEA." In *Encyclopedia of U.S. Labor and Working-Class History*. Vol. 2, G-N Index, Edited by Eric Arnesen. New York: Routledge, 2007.
———. "Willard Townsend." In *Portraits of African American Life Since 1865*. Edited by Nina Mjagkij. Wilmington, DE: Scholarly Resources, 2003.
Balanoff, Elizabeth. "Lillian Herstein." In *Women Building Chicago 1790–1990: A Biographical Dictionary*. Edited by Rima Lunin Schultz and Adele Hast. Bloomington: Indiana University Press, 2001.
Banfield, Edward C. *Big City Politics*. New York: Random House, 1965.
Bell, Daniel. "The Capitalism of the Proletariat: A Theory of American Trade-Unionism." In *The End of Ideology: On the Exhaustion of Political Ideologies in the Fifties*. New York: The Free Press, 1962.
Belzer, Michael H. *Sweatshops on Wheels: Winners and Losers in Trucking Deregulation*. New York: Oxford University Press, 2002.
Biles, Roger. *Big City Mayor in Depression and War: Mayor Edward J. Kelly of Chicago*. DeKalb, IL: Northern Illinois University Press, 1984.
———. *Crusading Liberal: Paul H. Douglas of Illinois*. DeKalb, IL: Northern Illinois University Press, 2002.
Blatz, Perry K. *Democratic Miners: Work and Labor Relations in the Anthracite Coal Industry. 1875–1925*. Albany: State University of New York Press, 1994.
Bloom, Jonathan D. "Brookwood Labor College." In *The Re-Education of the American Working Class*. Edited by Steven H. London, Elvira R. Tarr, and Joseph F. Wilson. Westport, CT: Greenwood Press, 1990.
Blum, John Morton. *V Was for Victory: Politics and American Culture During World War II*. New York: Harcourt, Brace, Jovanovich, 1976.

Bollens, John Constantinus. *Exploring the Metropolitan Community*. Berkeley: University of California Press, 1961.

Bonastia, Christopher. *Knocking on the Door: The Federal Government's Attempt to Desegregate the Suburbs*. Princeton: Princeton University Press, 2006.

Boyle, Kevin. *The UAW and the Heyday of American Liberalism, 1945–1968*. Ithaca: Cornell University Press, 1995.

Brill, Steven. *The Teamsters*. New York: Simon and Schuster, 1978.

Brody, David. "The Uses of Power I: Industrial Battleground." In *Workers in Industrial America: Essays on the 20th Century Struggle*. New York: Oxford University Press, 1980.

———. "The Uses of Power II: Political Action." In *Workers in Industrial America*.

———. "Workplace Contractualism: A Historical/Comparative Analysis." In *Labor's Cause: Main Themes on the History of the American Worker*. New York: Oxford University Press, 1993.

Brown, Michael K. *Race, Money, and the American Welfare State*. Ithaca: Cornell University Press, 1999.

Bussel, Robert. *From Harvard to the Ranks of Labor: Power Hapgood and the American Working Class*. University Park: Pennsylvania State University Press, 1999.

Cayton, Horace R. *Long Old Road: An Autobiography*. Seattle: University of Washington Press, 1963.

Cervantes, A.J. (with Laurence G. Blochman). *Mr. Mayor*. Los Angeles: Nash Publishing, 1974.

Chateauvert, Melinda. *Marching Together: Women of the Brotherhood of Sleeping Car Porters*. Urbana: University of Illinois Press, 1998.

Clay, Bill. *A Political Voice at the Grassroots*. St. Louis: Missouri Historical Society Press, 2004.

Clay, Sr., William L. *The Jefferson Bank Confrontation*. St. Louis: William L. Clay Research and Scholarship Foundation, 2008.

Clay, William L. *Just Permanent Interests: Black Americans in Congress, 1870–1991*. New York: Amistad Press, 1992.

Cobble, Dorothy Sue. *The Other Women's Movement: Workplace Justice and Social Rights in Modern America*. Princeton: Princeton University Press, 2004.

Cohen, Lizabeth. *Making A New Deal: Industrial Workers in Chicago, 1919–1939*. Cambridge: Cambridge University Press, 1990.

Cole, G.D.H. *A Short History of the British Working-Class Movement, 1789–1947*. London: George Allen and Unwin Ltd., 1948.

Corbin, David A. *Life, Work, and Rebellion in the Coal Fields: The Southern West Virginia Miners, 1880–1922*. Urbana: University of Illinois Press, 1981.

Cowie, Jefferson. *Stayin' Alive: The 1970s and the Last Days of the Working Class*. New York: The New Press, 2010.

Daniel, Cletus E. *Culture of Misfortune: An Interpretive History of Textile Unionism in the United States*. Ithaca: ILR Press, 2001.

Drake, St. Clair, and Horace Cayton. *Black Metropolis: A Study of Negro Life in a Northern City*. New York: Harcourt, Brace and Company, 1945.

Draper, Theodore. *American Communism and Soviet Russia: The Formative Period*. New York: Vintage Books, 1986.

Dublin, Thomas, and Walter Licht. *The Face of Decline: The Pennsylvania Anthracite Region in the Twentieth Century*. Ithaca: Cornell University Press, 2005.

Durr, Kenneth D. *Behind the Backlash: White Working-Class Politics in Baltimore, 1940–1980*. Chapel Hill: University of North Carolina Press, 2003.

Eaton, William Edward. *The American Federation of Teachers, 1916–1961*. Carbondale: Southern Illinois University Press, 1975.

Faue, Elizabeth. *Community of Suffering and Struggle: Women, Men, and the Labor Movement in Minneapolis, 1915–1945*. Chapel Hill: University of North Carolina Press, 1991.

Feurer, Rosemary. *Radical Unionism in the Midwest, 1900–1950*. Urbana: University of Illinois Press, 2006.

Fraser, Steve. *Labor Will Rule: Sidney Hillman and the Rise of American Labor*. New York: The Free Press, 1991.

Freeman, Frankie Muse, with Candace O'Connor. *A Song of Faith and Hope: The Life of Frankie Muse Freeman*. St. Louis: Missouri Historical Society Press, 2003.

Garnel, Donald. *The Rise of Teamster Power in the West*. Berkeley: University of California Press, 1972.

Garrow, David J. *Bearing the Cross: Martin Luther King, Jr. and the Southern Christian Leadership Conference*. New York: W. Morrow, 1986.

Gilbert, James. *A Cycle of Outrage: America's Reaction to the Juvenile Delinquent in the 1950s*. New York: Oxford University Press, 1986.

Goluboff, Risa L. *The Lost Promise of Civil Rights*. Cambridge (MA): Harvard University Press, 2007.

Gordon, Colin. *Mapping Decline: St. Louis and the Fate of the American City*. Philadelphia: University of Pennsylvania Press, 2008.

Goulden, Joseph C. *Meany*. New York: Atheneum, 1972.

Gray, Kenneth E. *A Report on Politics in Saint Louis*. Cambridge: Center for Urban Studies, Harvard University, 1961.

Grimshaw, William J. *Bitter Fruit: Black Politics and the Chicago Machine, 1931–1991*. Chicago: University of Chicago Press, 1992.

Harris, NiNi. *A History of Carondelet*. St. Louis: The Patrice Press, 1991.

Henry, Deborah J. "Race, Power, and the Building Trades Industry in Postwar St. Louis." In *The Other Missouri History: Populists, Prostitutes, and Regular Folk*. Edited by Thomas Morris Spencer. Columbia: University of Missouri Press, 2004.

Hershberger, Mary. *Traveling to Vietnam: American Peace Activists and the Vietnam War*. Syracuse: Syracuse University Press, 1998.

Hodges, Graham Russell Gao. *Taxi! A Social History of the New York City Cab Driver*. Baltimore: The Johns Hopkins University Press, 2007.

Hoffa, James R., as told to Oscar Fraley. *Hoffa: The Real Story*. New York: Stein and Day Publishers, 1975.

Howe, Louis Kapp. *Pink Collar Workers: Inside the World of Women's Work*. New York: G.P. Putnam's Sons, 1977.

Howlett, Charles F. *Brookwood Labor College and the Struggle for Peace and Social Justice in America*. Lewiston (NY): The Edwin Mellen Press, 1993.

Hyman, Colette A. "Labor Organizing and Female Institution Building: The Chicago Women's Trade Union League." In *Women, Work, and Protest: A Century of U.S. Women's Labor History*. Edited by Ruth Milkman. Boston: Routledge and Kegan Paul, 1985.

Isserman, Maurice. *Which Side Were You On? The American Communist Party During the Second World War*. Middletown (CT): Wesleyan University Press, 1982.

Jackson, Thomas J. "The State, the Movement, and the Urban Poor: The War on Poverty and Political Mobilization in the 1960s." In *The "Underclass" Debate: Views from History*. Edited by Michael B. Katz. Princeton: Princeton University Press, 1993.

Jacobs, Paul. *Old Before Its Time: Collective Bargaining at 28*. In *The State of the Unions*. New York: Atheneum, 1963.

———. "Extracurricular Activities of the McClellan Committee (1963)." In *The State of the Unions*. New York: Atheneum, 1963.

———. "World of Jimmy Hoffa (I)." In *The State of the Unions*. New York: Atheneum, 1963.

———. "World of Jimmy Hoffa (II)." In *The State of the Unions*. New York: Atheneum, 1963.

James, Ralph C., and Estelle Dinerstein James. *Hoffa and the Teamsters: A Study of Union Power*. Princeton: D. Van Nostrand Company, Inc., 1965.

Jolley, Kenneth S. *Black Liberation in the Midwest: The Struggle in St. Louis, Missouri, 1964–1970*. New York: Routledge, 2006.

Jones, E. Terrence. *Fragmented by Design: Why St. Louis Has So Many Governments*. St. Louis: Palmerston & Reed Pub., 2000.

Katznelson, Ira. *City Trenches: Urban Politics and the Patterning of Class in the United States*. New York: Pantheon Books, 1981.

Kennedy, Robert F. *The Enemy Within*. New York: Harper and Brothers, 1960.

Kersten, Andrew Edmund. *Race, Jobs, and the War: The FEPC in the Midwest, 1941–46*. Urbana: University of Illinois Press, 2000.

Kirsten, George G. *Stores and Unions: A Study of the Growth of Unions in Dry Goods and Department Stores*. New York: Fairchild Publications, 1950.

Klein, Jennifer. *For All These Rights: Business, Labor, and the Making of America's Public-Private Welfare State*. Princeton: Princeton University Press, 2003.

Knupfer, Anne Meis. *The Chicago Black Renaissance and Women's Activism*. Urbana: University of Illinois Press, 2006.

Korstad, Robert Rodgers. *Civil Rights Unionism: Tobacco Workers and the Struggle for Democracy in the Mid-Twentieth-South*. Chapel Hill: University of North Carolina Press, 2003.

Kweder, Melinda. "Annetta Dieckmann." In *Women Building Chicago, 1790–1990: A Biographical Dictionary*. Edited by Rina Lumin Schultz and Adele Hest. Bloomington: Indiana University Press, 2001.

La Botz, Dan. "The Tumultuous Teamsters of the 1970s," In *Rebel Rank and File: Labor Militancy and Revolt from Below During the Long 1970s*. Edited by Aaron Brenner, Robert Brenner, and Cal Winslow. London: Verso, 2010.

Lang, Clarence. *Grassroots at the Gateway: Class Politics and the Black Freedom Struggle in St. Louis, 1936–1975*. Ann Arbor: University of Michigan Press, 2009.

Lee, R. Alton. *Eisenhower and Landrum-Griffin: A Study in Labor-Management Politics*. Lexington: University Press of Kentucky, 1991.

Lens, Sidney. *Left, Right, and Center: Conflicting Forces in American Labor*. Hinsdale (IL): Henry Regnery Company, 1949.

———. *Unrepentant Radical: An American Activist's Account of Five Turbulent Decades*. Boston: Beacon Press, 1980.

Levenstein, Harvey A. *Communism, Anti-Communism, and the CIO*. Westport (CT): Greenwood Press, 1981.

Levy, Peter B. *The New Left and Labor in the 1960s*. Urbana: University of Illinois Press, 1994.

Lewis, Earl. *In Their Own Interests: Race, Class, and Power in Twentieth-Century Virginia*. Berkeley: University of California Press, 1991.

Lewis, Ronald L. *Black Coal Miners in America: Race, Class, and Community Conflict, 1780–1980*. Lexington: University Press of Kentucky, 1987.

Lichtenstein, Nelson. *Labor's War at Home: The CIO in World War II*. Cambridge: Cambridge University Press, 1982.

———. *The Most Dangerous Man in Detroit: Walter Reuther and the Fate of American Labor*. New York: Basic Books, 1995.

———. *State of the Union: A Century of American Labor*. Princeton: Princeton University Press, 2002.

Lipsitz, George. *A Life in the Struggle: Ivory Perry and the Culture of Opposition* (Revised Edition). Philadelphia: Temple University Press, 1995.

Lubell, Samuel. *The Future of American Politics, Second Edition, Revised*. Garden City (NY): Doubleday and Company, 1956.

Lyons, John F. "Lillian Herstein." In *Encyclopedia of U.S. Labor and Working-Class History, Volume I*. Edited by Eric Arnesen. New York: Routledge, 2007.

———. *Teachers and Reform: Chicago Public Education, 1929–1970*. Urbana: University of Illinois Press, 2008.

MacLean, Nancy. *Freedom Is Not Enough: The Opening of the American Workplace*. Cambridge (MA): Harvard University Press, 2006.

Martin, John Bartlow. *Jimmy Hoffa's Hot*. Greenwich (CT): Fawcett Publications, 1959.

McClellan, John L. *Crime Without Punishment*. New York: Duell, Sloan and Pearce, 1962.

McGreevy, John T. *Parish Boundaries: The Catholic Encounter with Race in the Twentieth Century Urban North*. Chicago: University of Chicago Press, 1996.

Meehan, Eugene J. *The Quality of Federal Policymaking: Programmed Failure in Public Housing*. Columbia: University of Missouri Press, 1979.

Meier, August, and Elliot Rudwick. *CORE: A Study in the Civil Rights Movement, 1942–1968*. New York: Oxford University Press, 1973.

Metzgar, Jack. *Striking Steel: Solidarity Remembered*. Philadelphia: Temple University Press, 2000.

Miller, Donald L., and Richard E. Sharpless. *The Kingdom of Coal: Work, Enterprise, and Ethnic Communities in the Mine Fields*. Philadelphia: University of Pennsylvania Press, 1985.

Miller, James. *"Democracy Is in the Streets": From Port Huron to the Siege of Chicago*. New York: Simon and Schuster, 1987.

Mjagkij, Nina (editor). *Portraits of African American Life Since 1865*. Wilmington (DE): Scholarly Resources, 2003.

Mollenhoff, Clark R. *Tentacles of Power: The Story of Jimmy Hoffa*. Cleveland: The World Publishing Company, 1965.

Morgan, Ted. *A Covert Life: Jay Lovestone, Communist, Anti-Communist, and Spymaster*. New York: Random House, 1999.

Murphy, Marjorie. *Blackboard Unions: The AFT and the NEA, 1900–1980*. Ithaca (NY): Cornell University Press, 1990.

Nelson, Daniel. *Shifting Fortunes: The Rise and Decline of American Labor, From the 1820s to the Present*. Chicago: Ivan R. Dee, 1997.

Newell, Barbara Warne. *Chicago and the Labor Movement: Metropolitan Unionism in the 1930's*. Urbana: University of Illinois Press, 1961.

Nicolaides, Becky. *My Blue Heaven, Life and Politics in the Working-Class Suburbs of Los Angeles, 1920–1965*. Chicago: University of Chicago Press, 2002.

Nordin, Dennis S. *The New Deal's Black Congressman: A Life of Arthur Wergs Mitchell*. Columbia: University of Missouri Press, 1997.

Opler, Daniel J. *For All White-Collar Workers: The Possibilities of Radicalism in New York City's Department Stores, 1934–1953*. Columbus: Ohio State University Press, 2007.

Painter, Nell Irvin. *The Narrative of Hosea Hudson: His Life as a Negro Communist in the South*. Cambridge (MA): Harvard University Press, 1979.

Parmet, Robert. *The Master of Seventh Avenue: David Dubinsky and American Labor Movement*. New York: New York University Press, 2005.

Parris, Guichard, and Lester Brooks. *Blacks in the City: A History of the National Urban League*. Boston: Little, Brown and Company, 1971.

Pells, Richard H. *The Liberal Mind in a Conservative Age: American Intellectuals in the 1940s and 1950s*. New York: Harper and Row, 1985.

Pencak, William. *For God and Country: The American Legion, 1919–1941*. Boston: Northeastern University Press, 1989.

Pfeffer, Paula F. *A. Philip Randolph, Pioneer of the Civil Rights Movement*. Baton Rouge: Louisiana State University Press, 1990.

Phillips, Lisa. *A Renegade Union: Interracial Organizing and Labor Radicalism*. Urbana: University of Illinois Press, 2013.

Preis, Art. *Labor's Giant Step: Twenty Years of the CIO*. New York: Pioneer Publishers, 1964.

Primm, James Neal. *Lion of the Valley: St. Louis, Missouri, 1764–1980, Third Edition*. Saint Louis: Missouri Historical Society Press, 1998.

Purcell, Theodore Vincent. *Blue Collar Man: Patterns of Dual Allegiance in Industry*. Cambridge (MA): Harvard University Press, 1960.

Roberts, B.C. *Trade Unions in a Free Society*. London: The Institute of Economic Affairs, published on its behalf by Hutchinson and Company, 1962.

Romer, Sam. *The International Brotherhood of Teamsters: Its Government and Structure*. New York: John Wiley and Sons, 1962.

Rose, Arnold M. *Union Solidarity: The Internal Cohesion of a Labor Union*. Minneapolis: University of Minnesota Press, 1952.

Russell, Thaddeus. *Out of the Jungle: Jimmy Hoffa and the Remaking of the American Working Class*. New York: Alfred A. Knopf, 2001.

Rustin, Bayard. "From Protest to Politics: The Future of the Civil Rights Movement." In Bayard Rustin, *Down the Line: The Collected Writings of Bayard Rustin*. Chicago: Quadrangle Books, 1971.

Saposs, David J. *Left-Wing Unionism: A Study of Radical Policies and Tactics*. New York: International Publishers, 1926.

Schandt, Henry J., Paul G. Steinbicker, and George D. Wendel. *Metropolitan Reform in St. Louis: A Case Study*. New York: Holt, Rinehart, and Winston, 1961.

Schlesinger, Jr., Arthur M. *Robert Kennedy and His Times*. Boston: Houghton Mifflin Company, 1978.

Sloane, Arthur A. *Hoffa*. Cambridge (MA): The MIT Press, 1991.

Solomon, Mark. *The Cry Was Unity: Communists and African Americans, 1917–36*. Jackson: University of Mississippi Press, 1998.

Stanford, Karin L. (editor). *If We Must Die: African American Voices on War and Peace*. Lanham (MD): Rowman and Littlefield Publishers, Inc., 2008.

Stein, Lana. *St. Louis Politics: The Triumph of Tradition*. Saint Louis: Missouri Historical Society Press, 2002.

Sugrue, Thomas J. *The Origins of the Urban Crisis: Race and Inequality in Postwar Detroit*. Princeton: Princeton University Press, 1996.

———. *Sweet Land of Liberty: The Forgotten Struggle for Civil Rights in the North*. New York: Random House, 2008.

Swados, Harvey. "The UAW-Over the Top or Over the Hill." In Swados, *A Radical at Large: American Essays*. London: Rupert Hart-Davis, 1968.

Trotter, Jr., Joe William. *Coal, Class, and Color: Blacks in Southern West Virginia, 1915–1932*. Urbana: University of Illinois Press, 1990.

Valien, Bonita H. *The St. Louis Story: A Study of Desegregation*. New York: Anti-Defamation League of B'nai B'rith, 1956.

Wehrle, Edmund F. *Between a River and a Mountain: The AFL-CIO and the Vietnam War*. Ann Arbor: The University of Michigan Press, 2005.

Widick, B.J. *Labor Today: The Triumphs and Failures of Unionism in the United States*. Boston: Houghton Mifflin, 1964.

Witwer, David. *Corruption and Reform in the Teamsters Union*. Urbana: University of Illinois Press, 2003.

Wolensky, Kenneth C., Nicole H. Wolensky, and Robert P. Wolensky. *Fighting for the Union Label : The Women's Garment Industry and the ILGWU in Pennsylvania*. University Park: Pennsylvania State University Press, 2002.

Wolff, Joel C. *Improving Warehouse Productivity*. New York: American Management Association, 1981.

Wynn, Neil. *The Afro-American and the Second World War*. New York: Holmes and Meier Publishers, 1975.

Zieger, Robert H. *The CIO: 1935–1955*. Chapel Hill: The University of North Carolina Press, 1995.

———. *For Jobs and Freedom: Race and Labor in America since 1865*. Lexington: University Press of Kentucky, 2007.

Articles

Adams, Patricia L. "Fighting for Democracy in St. Louis: Civil Rights During World War II." *Missouri Historical Review*, October 1985.

Arnesen, Eric. "No 'Graver Danger': Black Anti-Communism, the Communist Party, and the Race Question." *Labor: Studies in the Working-Class History of the Americas*, 2006.

Baldwin, Carl L. "Bricklayers Use Political Power to Curb Shift to Other Material." *St. Louis Post-Dispatch*, December 29, 1953.

Baron, Richard D. "Community Organizations: Antidote for Neighborhood Succession and Focus for Neighborhood Improvement." *Saint Louis University Law Journal*, 1978.

Baron, Sam. "A Top Teamster Hits Back at Hoffa." *Life*, July 20, 1962.

Bick, Jr., Frank. "Thoughts on the Charter." *Southside Journal*, July 24, 1957.

Blair, William M. "AFL Teamsters Raid CIO Local in St. Louis, Add 600 Members." *New York Times*, January 27, 1949.

Braithwaite, Lee. "Say Politicians Lead NAACP Plan." *St. Louis Argus*, November 13, 1964.

Buhle, Paul. "Lovestone's Thin Red Line." *The Nation*, May 24, 1999.

Burgess, Charles E. "Unusual Husband-Wife Team." *St. Louis Globe-Democrat,* April 23, 1977.
Burnside, Gordon. "Calloway at 73." *St. Louis Magazine,* March 1973.
———. "Life and Times of the Socialist Teamster." *St. Louis Weekly,* July 13, 20, 1983.
Calloway, Ernest. "Approaching the Problems of Community Organization in the Fight Against Poverty." *Missouri Teamster,* May 15, 1965.
———. "Arts of Corruption in a Free Society." *Missouri Teamster,* February 28, 1967.
———. "Brookwood Labor College Left Its Mark on U.S. Unionism." *St. Louis Labor Tribune,* September 1, 1977.
———. "Building a Balanced City." *St. Louis Sentinel,* October 19, 1970.
———. "Building Your Union." *Bags and Baggage,* January 1941.
———. "By Statistics, City Could Become a Riot Leader." *Missouri Teamster,* January 5, 1968.
———. "Can Black St. Louisans Fully Support Black Candidates for City-Wide Office?" *St. Louis American,* September 4, 1980.
———. "The CIO and the Negro." *Opportunity,* November 1936.
———. "City Needs a Full Negro-White Partnership." *Missouri Teamster,* January 19, 1968.
———. "Conspiracy Against the Poor in St. Louis." *Missouri Teamster,* October 31, 1967.
———. "Creative Self-Determinism." *St. Louis Sentinel,* August 23, 1969.
———. "The Current Stagnant Plateau of Membership Growth." *Missouri Teamster,* April 22, 1966.
———. "An Early Attempt to Join the CIO Staff." *St. Louis American,* January 12, 1981.
———. "Era of 'Patroonism' Ends as Negro Labor Meets in Chicago." *New Citizen,* November 10, 1961.
———. "The Evolution of a New Public Housing Concept." *Missouri Teamster,* October 1969.
———. "Faith and the Valiant Black Women of Belhaven, NC." *St. Louis American,* December 25, 1980.
———. "The Feeding and Care of a Slum in St. Louis." *Missouri Teamster,* October 14, 1966.
———. "Forty Years of Unionism." *St. Louis Post-Dispatch,* August 11, 1973.
———. "For Whom the Bell Tolls." *Missouri Teamster,* October 11, 1968.
———. "Harlem Summer, 1925." *St. Louis Sentinel,* October 31, 1970.
———. "How We Came to Appalachia and the Ky. Cumberlands in 1913." *St. Louis American,* February 19, 1981.
———. "Hymn to a Gentle Soul, Martin Luther King." *St. Louis Sentinel,* April 13, 1968.
———. "The Jack Dwyer Image in St. Louis Politics." *Missouri Teamster,* May 27, 1966.
———. "A Jim Crow Army." *St. Louis Sentinel,* February 6, 1971.
———. "Labor Building Its Own Political Party." *Bags and Baggage,* October 1937.
———. "Labor's Political Action: Shadows without Substance." *Missouri Teamster,* April 8, 1966.
———. "A Labor Study (South)." *Opportunity,* June 1934.
———. "The Lonely Colossus of U.S. Labour." *New Epoch,* May 1949.
———. "The Making of a Professional Agitator and Organizer in the 30s." *St. Louis American,* April 9, 1981.
———. "McNeal and Missouri Politics." *St. Louis Sentinel,* January 31, 1970.
———. "Meet a New CIO Leader." *Bags and Baggage,* July 1942.
———. "Melange, A Yultetide Reminder." *Bags and Baggage,* December 1937.
———. "Memories of a Jobless Meeting." *Missouri Teamster,* January 16, 1976.

———. "Mill Creek Negroes Fleeced, Charges Report of WECC." *New Citizen*, July 21, 1961.
———. "Mine Union Shows Way to End Harlan Terror." *Workers Age*, June 2, 1937.
———. "The Nature of Power and Its Roots in a Community." *Missouri Teamster*, June 7, 1963.
———. "The Negro in the Kentucky Coal Fields." *Opportunity*, March 1934.
———. "Negro Labor in 1942." *Chicago Defender*, July 14, 1942.
———. "Negro Middle Class Is Problem for Its Race." *Missouri Teamster*, October 22, 1965.
———. "Negro Press Is Close to People's Problems." *CIO News*, July 31, 1944.
———. "Norman Thomas—Moral Man." *St. Louis Sentinel*, December 28, 1968.
———. "Notes on The Realigned First Congressional District." *Missouri Teamster*, July 14, 1967.
———. "Old, New Inequities Institutionalize Urban Tensions." *Missouri Teamster*, April 14, 1967.
———. "One Man's Thoughts: Politics, 1980." *St. Louis American*, April 10, 1980,
———. "The Passing of the 'Delivered' Vote." *Missouri Teamster*, March 5, 1965.
———. "A Political Comment: 'Operation Self-Destruct': Uprooting a Black Political Base in North St. Louis." *St. Louis American*, March 31, 1977.
———. "Political Ku Kluxism Emerges at City Hall with Zych-Percich Axis." *St. Louis American*, August 14, 1980.
———. "The Promise of Jim Conway." *St. Louis Post-Dispatch*, April 25, 1977.
———. "Public Housing: U.S. Democracy in Action." *CIO News*, August 14, 1944.
———. "Red Caps Are Victorious in Status Fight." *Chicago Defender*, October 15, 1938.
———. "The Red Caps' Struggle for a Livelihood." *Opportunity*, June 3, 1940.
———. "Reflections: The Harold Gibbons Story." *St. Louis Sentinel*, January 10, 1970.
———. "Requiem for a Free Compassionate Spirit." *Missouri Teamster*, May 13, 1966.
———. "Requiem for a Political Myth." *Missouri Teamster*, August 18, 1972.
———. "St. Louis Black Politics Today: An Inventory and Balance Sheet." *Proud Magazine*, July 1973.
———. "The Sectarian Tradition in American Unionism." *Missouri Teamster*, November 19, 1965.
———. "Sending to Know For Whom the Bell Tolls." *Missouri Teamster*, October 11, 1968.
———. "A Small October Revolution." *St. Louis Sentinel*, November 8, 1969.
———. "Story of the Red Cap Union." *Missouri Teamster*, January 30, 1978.
———. "Strategies for Containment." *St. Louis Post-Dispatch*, September 21, 1975.
———. "Teamsters Local 688: Pioneers in Trade Union Race Relations." *New Citizen*, September 1, 7, 14, 1961.
———. "The Time of the St. Louis Black Renaissance." *St. Louis American*, June 12, 17, 19, 26, July 3, 10, 17, 1980.
———. "To Sleep, Perchance to Dream: A Ridge in Mexican Sierras." *St. Louis American*, March 26, 1981.
———. "A Trade Union Oriented War on the Slums." *Missouri Teamster*, February 1968.
———. "The Trauma of Asia in American Politics." *Missouri Teamster*, April 5, 1968.
———. "Troubled Times for U.S. Unionism." *Missouri Teamster*, September 27, 1968.
———. "Unions in a New Economic Ball Game." *Missouri Teamster*, February 16, 1975.
———. "Urban Slums and Self-Hood Revolution." *Missouri Teamster*, April 14, 1967.
———. "The Urban Trap: Race and Poverty Reprints." *Missouri Teamster*, February 1968.

———. "Whatever Happened to Simple Union Contracts?" *Missouri Teamster*, January 19, 1968.
———. "Who Am I? Whose Foot Is Up My Rump?" *St. Louis American*, April 30, 1981.
———. "Why I Cannot Serve." *Bags and Baggage*, December 22, 1940.
———. "Women, the Home, and the Union." *Bags and Baggage*, January 1940.
———. "Workers Education." *St. Louis Sentinel*, December 26, 1970.
Cawthra, Benjamin. "Ernest Calloway: Labor, Civil Rights, and Black Leadership in St. Louis." *Gateway Heritage Magazine*, Winter 2000–2001.
Cayton, Horace R. "The UTSEA in Action and Problems Facing the Freight Handlers." *Bags and Baggage*, June 1941.
Chait, Manuel. "NAACP Leadership Ineffectual Here, State Officer Charges." *St. Louis Post-Dispatch*, December 3, 1964.
Clark, E. Lamont. "Deverne Calloway: A Partner in the Struggle." n.d., *St. Louis American*, found in Box 6, File 230, No. 540, EC-UMSL.
———. "Local Labor Pioneer Revered." *St. Louis American*, August 29-September 3, 1985.
Coburn, Judith. "All Systems Fail." *The Village Voice*, September 18, 1969.
Conn, Harry. "A Union in St. Louis." *New Republic*, February 4, 1952.
Curry, Jerry. "Gibbons, Hoffa's Stand-in a Solid Teamster." *Newark Star-Ledger*, August 9, 1964.
Defty, Sally Bixby. "Emergence of the 'New Gibbons.'" *St. Louis Post-Dispatch*, May 13, 1969.
———. "Gibbons Kept Cool Under Senate Fire." *St. Louis Post-Dispatch*, May 12, 1969.
———. "Harold J. Gibbons: Teamster Boss." *St. Louis Post-Dispatch*, May 11, 1969.
———. "Hoffa-Gibbons Split: What's Ahead?" *St. Louis Post-Dispatch*, May 14, 1969.
Devinatz, Victor G. "'To Find Answers to the Urgent Problems of Our Society': The Alliance for Labor Action's Atlanta Union Organizing Offensive, 1969–1971." *Labor Studies Journal*, 31, No. 2, Summer 2006.
Dieckmann, Annetta M. "Education for Citizenship." *Women's Press*, November 1950.
———. "The Union Makes Use of the Social Scientist." *Journal of Educational Sociology*, February 1952.
Flach, Jack. "Teamsters, Steamfitters at Odds in 1st District Democratic Race." *St. Louis Globe-Democrat*, July 11, 1968.
Floyd, James. "Ernest Calloway Wants a Revolution . . . In the Attitudes of Our People." *St. Louis Globe-Democrat*, February 7, 1972.
Gellman, Erik S. "'Carthage Must Be Destroyed': Race, City Politics, and the Campaign to Integrate Chicago Transportation Work, 1929–1943." *Labor: Studies in the Working-Class History of the Americas*, Vol. 2, No. 2, 2005.
Gibbons, Harold J. "Collective Bargaining in Perspective." *Missouri Teamster*, August 2, 1963.
———. "Labor's Task in the Precinct." *New Republic*, January 5, 1953.
———. "Negroes Won't Wait for 'Gift' of Rights." *Missouri Teamster*, July 5, 1963.
———. "Poor Must Find Dignity, Security in Housing." Box 5, File 139, No. 540, EC-UMSL.
———. "Why the Union Is Concerned." *St. Louis Post-Dispatch*, February 28, 1952.
Gilbride, Neil. "Jimmy Hoffa Is Still Riding High." *Port Angeles Evening News*, February 3, 1966.
Graham, Fred P. "Hoffa 'Lawyer,' Despite Dossier, Presented Film at White House." *New York Times*, September 13, 1972.

———. "Officials Chagrined By Hoffa's 'Lawyer' in P.O.W. Incident." *New York Times*, September 12, 1972.

Greenhouse, Steven. "Share of the Workforce in a Union Falls to a 97-Year Low, 11.3%." *New York Times*, January 24, 2013.

Gross, Nell. "Adventure in Retirement Living." *St. Louis Globe-Democrat Sunday Magazine*, February 26, 1967.

———. "A New Way of Life for Senior Citizens." *St. Louis Globe-Democrat Sunday Magazine*, February 14, 1965.

Hahn, John R. "Teamsters Plan Giant Get-out-Vote Setup." *St. Louis Globe-Democrat*, December 1, 1957.

Harmon, Dennis. "Citizen Participation Bill to Be Considered by Board of Aldermen." *Southside Journal*, December 1, 1976.

Heathcott, Joseph. "Black Archipelago: Politics and Civic Life in the Jim Crow City." *Journal of Social History*, Vol. 38, No. 3, Spring 2005.

Heathcott, Joseph, and Maire Agnes Murphy. "Corridors of Flight, Zones of Renewal: Industry, Planning, and Policy in the Making of Metropolitan St. Louis, 1940–1980." *Journal of Urban History*, Vol. 31, No. 3, January 2005.

Hepner, Arthur W. "CIO Union's Health Institute an Experiment in Co-operative Insurance." *St. Louis Post-Dispatch*, July 7, 1948.

Herling, John. "Jimmy Hoffa Heir Apparent." *Washington Daily News*, December 1, 1959.

Ives, Irving M. "The New York State School of Industrial and Labor Relations—A New Venture in Education." *Journal of Educational Sociology*, September 1945.

Jackson, Robert A. "Struggle for Control of St. Louis NAACP Has Political Overtones." *St. Louis Globe-Democrat*, n.d., found in Box 46, File 525, No. 540, EC-UMSL.

James, William R. "Exposing the Communist Conspiracy in the United States." *Spotlight News*, Vol. VII, No. VI, 1954.

———. "Gibbons Admits Red Front Membership." *Spotlight News*, Vol. VIII, No. XI, 1954.

———. "Gibbons' Red Front." *Spotlight News*, Vol. VIII, No. VII, 1954.

Judy, Bernard. "Harold J. Gibbons: Teamsters' No. 1 Egghead, Public Relations Star." *Toledo Blade*, November 10, 1957.

Kaiser, Charles B. "Creation and Operation of the Metropolitan St. Louis Sewer District." *Journal (Water Pollution Control Federation)*, September 1982.

Kelliher, Con. "Meet Harold Gibbons." *St. Louis Globe-Democrat*, August 22, 1956.

Kempton, Murray. "Hoffa the Pure." *New Republic*, January 18, 1964.

———. "Prince Hal at the Tavern." *New York Post*, October 7, 1957.

Kneeland, Douglas E. "Districting Bill Is Passed in Missouri." *New York Times*, June 29, 1967.

Lang, Clarence. "Civil Rights versus 'Civic Progress': The St. Louis NAACP and the City Charter Fight, 1956–1957." *Journal of Urban History* 34.4.

———. "On Ferguson, Missouri: History, Protest, and 'Respectability,'" accessed at lawcha .org/wordpress/2014/08/17/ferguson-missouri-history-protest-respectability/, October 24, 2014.

Ledbetter, Les. "H. J. Gibbons Dies, Once Viewed as Hoffa's Heir." *New York Times*, November 19, 1972.

Lipsitz, George. "Beyond the Fringe Benefits: Rank and File Teamsters in St. Louis." *Liberation*, July/August 1973.

———. "Harold and Me: The Problem of the Progressive Union Leader." *New Politics*, Winter 1992.
Livingston, David, Harold Gibbons, and Clifton Caldwell. "Labor Mission to Hanoi." *The Nation*, April 24, 1972.
Lonesome, Buddy. "Controversy Swirls 'Round Clay's Head—Even in Jail." *St. Louis Argus*, January 31, 1964.
Martin, Louis. "UTSEA Prexy Cites Gains in Dixie Drive." *Chicago Defender*, April 2, 1949.
McAlevey, Jane. "It Takes a Community: Building Unions From the Outside In." *New Labor Forum*, Spring 2003.
McCarthy, Jake. "Before It Was Fashionable." *St. Louis Post-Dispatch*, April 9, 1973.
———. "Behind the Gibbons Ouster." *St. Louis Post-Dispatch*, May 30, 1973.
———. "Fitz's Teamsters." *St. Louis Post-Dispatch*, June 16, 1976.
———. "For Sid Zagri: An Epitaph for a Friend." *Missouri Teamster*, February 14, 1967.
———. "Gibbons: Hanoi Doubts US Desires Peace." *St. Louis Post-Dispatch*, March 28, 1972.
———. "More About the Story That Will Never End." *Missouri Teamster*, November 1, 1963.
———. "The Negro Revolution Comes Home." *Missouri Teamster*, October 18, 1963.
———. "Next Time May Be Too Late." *St. Louis Post-Dispatch*, March 20, 1972.
McCormick, Ken. "Meet Hoffa's Gem Smooth Prince." *Detroit Free Press*, October 6, 1957.
Miller, Jim. "Jack Dwyer, White Boss of All-Negro 4th Ward, Reaches Out for Control of Entire Negro Area." *St. Louis Defender*, October 1, 1963.
Murdock, Steve. "Labor for Peace: The Unions Find Consensus." *The Nation*, July 10, 1972.
Murphy, Michael J. "Developing Communities: The UAW and Community Unions in Los Angeles, 1965–1974." *Labor: Studies in the Working-Class History of the Americas* 6.4.
Norfolk, Robert L. "An Urban Strategist Views Black Dilemma in St. Louis." *St. Louis Sentinel*, August 20, 1974.
O'Brien, Edward W. "Gibbons Says He Can't Remember Statement of Police Protection." *St. Louis Globe-Democrat*, January 26, 1961.
———. "Hoffa Team Moves Into Washington." *St. Louis Globe-Democrat*, January 26, 1958.
———. "Senate Witness Hits Hoffa and Gibbons." *St. Louis Globe-Democrat*, January 25, 1961.
Poor, Tim. "Calloway Is Eulogized as Champion of Rights." *St. Louis Post-Dispatch*, January 7, 1990.
Poston, Ted. "How Hoffa Is Fighting the Labor Bill." *New York Post*, August 10, 1959.
Raskin, A.H. "Hoffa Facing Palace Revolt." *New York Times*, December 15, 1963.
Riddell, Janet. "St. Louis Blacks Using Labor Tactics." *Boston Globe*, September 7, 1970.
Riesel, Victor. "Big Blow to Organized Crime." *Chicago Herald American*, March 28, 1953.
Rose, Richard. "Teamsters New Boss?" *The Nation*, March 23, 1957.
Rothstein, Richard. "The Making of Ferguson." *American Prospect*, October 15, 2014, accessed at http://prospect.org/article/making-ferguson-how-decades-hostile-policy-created-powder-keg, October 24, 2014.
Sanford, Robert. "Calloway in Earnest." *St. Louis Post-Dispatch*, July 21, 1974.
Salisbury, Robert. "St. Louis Politics: Relationships Among Interests, Parties, and Governmental Structure." *Western Political Quarterly*, Vol. 13, No. 2, June 1960.
Salpukis, Agis. "Teamster Aide Expects Ouster." *New York Times*, December 14, 1972.
———. "Teamsters Elect Fitzsimmons to Succeed Hoffa as President." *New York Times*, July 9, 1971.

Salvatore, Nick. "Teamster Democracy: A Moment of Possibility." *New Politics*, Winter 1991.
Schafers, Ted. "Walla Group Claims Gibbons Stalls for Time." *St. Louis Globe-Democrat*, January 1, 1958.
———. "Walla Has Made Rapid Rise in Union." *St. Louis Globe-Democrat*, January 5, 1958.
Spreche, Jim. "AFL-CIO, Unlike Teamsters' Setup, Concentrates on Welfare Field." *E. St. Louis Journal*, November 24, 1957.
———. "St. Louis Teamsters Union Experiments in Grass Roots Approach to Government." *E. St. Louis Journal*, November 10, 1957.
Timnick, Lois. "Give Women a Say in Abortion, Final Teamster Demand." *St. Louis Globe-Democrat*, February 14, 1972.
Townsend, Willard. "British Labor Begins Move to Uproot Commies." *Chicago Defender*, January 8, 1949.
Trask, Herbert A. "Charter Foes Criticize Tucker for 'Misrepresentation' Charge." *St. Louis Post-Dispatch,* November 20, 1957.
———. "New Charter Defeated by Margin of 35,000 in Big Setback for Tucker." *St. Louis Post-Dispatch*, August 7, 1957.
Trumka, Richard L. "At the 2014 Missouri AFL-CIO Convention," September 15, 2014, accessed at http://www.aflcio.org/Press-Room/Speeches/At-the-2014-Missouri-AFL-CIO-Convention, October 24, 2014.
Walsh, Denny. "A Debt and a Threat Reveal Mob's Link to Unions." *St. Louis Globe-Democrat,* January 10, 1968.
———. "The Mob Likes Legitimate Business—It's a Good Front." *St. Louis Globe-Democrat,* January 16, 1968.
Wehling, Robert J. "Key Incidents Are Cited in the Fall of Gibbons." *St. Louis Post-Dispatch*, May 25, 1973.
Weiss, Lenore. "Trade Union Parley Presses for War's End." *Daily World*, June 23, 1972.
Wilson, Harry B. "Between the Lines." *St. Louis Globe-Democrat,* October 23, 1951.
Woo, William F. "An Epitaph for a Trade Unionist." *St. Louis Post-Dispatch*, January 7, 1990.
Woods, Edward F. "Losses in Building Industry Pile Up as Truck Drivers, Concrete Men Continue." *St. Louis Post-Dispatch,* July 19, 1953.
———. "Two Say Gibbons Hid High Officers' Forgery." *St. Louis Post-Dispatch,* January 25, 1961.
Zagri, Sidney. "Charter Defeat Places Labor in a New Position." *Midwest Labor World*, October 4, 1957.
———. "Labor's Stake in Good Neighborhoods." *St. Louis Argus*, November 8, 1957.
———. "'Slick' Public Relations Job Being Set Up on Charter." *North County Journal*, January 10, 1957.
———. "Your Community and Mine." *St. Louis Argus*, August 2, 1957.

Unpublished Materials

Ball, Jr., Harry Vernon. "Case History of a Labor Union: The United Distribution Workers." Masters' thesis, Washington University, 1950.
Baltakis, Anthony. "Agendas of Investigation: The McClellan Committee, 1957–1958." PhD thesis, University of Akron, 1997.

Clay, William L. "Anatomy of an Economic Murder: A Statistical Review of the Negro in the Saint Louis Employment Field." 1963, copy provided to author.
Fleishman, Joel L. "Not Without Honor: A Prophet Even in His Own Country, A Case Study of the St. Louis Public Housing Tenant Strike of 1969." 1979, Box 1, File 3, HJG-SIUE.
McCarthy, Jake. "Portrait of Gibbons." Box 1, File 16, JC 13-SIUE.
Newman, Mark J. "Black Labor in the 1960s: The Negro American Labor Council." BA thesis, Princeton University, 1976.
Smith, Lon W. "An Experiment in Trade Union Democracy: Harold Gibbons and the Formation of Teamsters Local 688, 1937–1957." PhD thesis, Illinois State University, October 1993.

Interviews

BY AUTHOR

Marcus Albrecht: October 14, 2003
Joseph Ames: November 9, 2001
Richard Baron: November 14, 2001
Jules Bernstein: telephone interview, July 15, 2011
Claude Brown: November 14, 2001
William L. Clay, Sr.: January 7, 2009
Barbara Crancer: October 13, 2004
Pearlie Evans: October 12, 2004
Frankie Freeman: September 20, 2005
Larry Gibbons: telephone interview, December 7, 2011
Patrick Gibbons: telephone interview, December 18, 2008
Gladys Gruenberg: November 13, 2001
Ronald Gushleff: email correspondence, April 8, 2012
Charles Oldham: October 7, 2004
James Pace: telephone interview, March 9, 2001
Marvin Rich: January 24, 2001
Leonard Robinson: telephone interview, April 16, 2002
Mike Ryan: November 12, 2001
Levi Sanford: November 14, 2001
Norman Seay: October 8, 2004
Kim de Somer: telephone interview, December 28, 2009
Eugene Tournour: October 30, 2001
Jerry Tucker: telephone interviews, May 21, 30, 2002
Elizabeth Vasquez: telephone interview, March 24, 2008
Margaret Bush Wilson: October 7, 2004

OTHER INTERVIEWS

Deverne Calloway interview with Irene Cortonovis, September 9, 1971. Black Community Leaders Project, Western Historical Manuscripts Collection, University of Missouri at St. Louis.

Ernest Calloway interview with Robert Davis, August 25, 1937. In Michael Ulreich, "The WPA and Labor," www.chicagoguild.org, accessed February 4, 2009.

Ernest Calloway interview with Dr. Richard Resh, July 31, 1970. Black Community Leaders Project. Western Historical Manuscript Collection, University of Missouri at St. Louis.

William L. Clay interview, November 25, 1968. Moorland-Spingarn Research Center, Howard University, Washington, D.C.

Pearlie Evans interview by Doris Wesley, May 7, 1997. "Lift Every Voice and Sing Oral History Project," University of Missouri at St. Louis.

John Farabee interview with Dale F. Blount, March 7, 1997. "Oral Histories with Teamsters," Southern Illinois University Edwardsville.

Henry Loomis interview, May 1948. Series 4, Box 1, File 14, William Sentner Collection, Department of Special Collections, Olin Library, Washington University.

Ernest Neidel interview with Dale F. Blount, February 20, 1997. "Oral Histories with Teamsters," Southern Illinois University at Edwardsville.

Charles Oldham interview, CORE Project, August 12, 1995. Irvin and Margaret Dagen Collection, WHMC-UMSL.

Marvin Rich interview, CORE Project, July 29, 1995. Irvin and Margaret Dagen Collection, WHMC-UMSL (Dagen-UMSL)

Elzie F. (Red) Smith, interview with Dale F. Blount, March 5, 1997. "Oral Histories with Teamsters," Southern Illinois University Edwardsville.

W.S. Townsend interview by Robert Davis, August 25, 1937. In Michael Ulreich, "The WPA and Labor," www.chicagoguild.org, accessed March 18, 2009.

Margaret Bush Wilson interview with Doris Wesley. "Lift Every Voice and Sing Oral History Project," University of Missouri at St. Louis.

INDEX

Page numbers in italics refer to illustrations

A & P stores, "Freedom Lines" at, 109
abbreviations, 185–86
Abex Corporation, 162
Adams, Leoulie, 93
adult education teachers, 26–27
affordable housing, 92–93
AFL (American Federation of Labor), 1, 40
AFL-CIO, 1, 111–12, 120, 135–36, 181
African Americans: on charter reform initiative, 106; CIO's commitment to, 36–37; civic participation of, 177; coal miners, 10–11, 14; at Council Plaza, 128; employment discrimination campaign, 109–10; employment strategy for, 98–99; fair employment for, 134–40, 150; military segregation, 47–48; 1933 lynching, 21; People's Forum, 35–36; political campaigns, 130; political independence for, 36; red cap unionization, 31–35; taxi drivers, 79–80, 99–100; as unionists, 22–24; as voters, 97
AFT (American Federation of Teachers) Local 346, 18, 26–27
air pollution campaign, 169, *253*
ALA (Alliance for Labor Action), 150–51, 170
Albrecht, Marcus, 127
Allen Cab, 80
Alliance for Labor Action (ALA), 150–51, 170
Amalgamated Clothing Workers, 29
America 2000, 146–47
American Commonwealth Party, 36
American Federation of Labor (AFL), 1, 140
American Federation of Teachers (AFT), 18, 26–27
American Legion citation, for Gibbons, 83
American union movement, 51–52
Ames, Joseph, 56
anthracite coal mines, 10, 13
Appalachian coal industry, 10–11
Archibald Mine, 10
Archibald Patch, PA, 9
arrests, strike, 29, 80
Association of Black Collegians, 151
auxiliaries, women's, 35
Avery, Sewell, 44

Bags and Baggage publication, 33, 49
Baker, Barney, 74, 80, 116
Baldwin-Felts agency, 12
Ball, Harry, 58, 63, 65, 71
Barlow, Milton, 169
Baron, Richard, 150, 154, 179
Baron, Sam, 126
Beck, Dave, 60, 61–62, 111
Bedford County, VA, 10
Beirne, Joseph, 136
Bell, Daniel, 84
Bender, Fred, 83
Berra, Lou, 55, 59, 82
bituminous coal mines, 10
Black Liberators, 148, 151–52
Black Renaissance, Chicago's, 37
blacks. *See* African Americans
Blackshere, Margaret, 169
Black United Front, 150
Board of Monitors, 122
Borges, Ron, 174
boycotts, ban on secondary, 58
Boykin, Frank, 149, 154, 157
Bridges, Harry, 41–42
Brill, Steven, 1–2, 175–76
British Labour Party, 51
British Trades Union Congress (TUC), 53–54
British Trades Union Congress scholarship, 50
British union movement, 51
Bronzeville, 37
Brookwood Labor College, 23–25
Brotherhood of Railway and Steamship Clerks (BRSC), 32
Browder, Earl, 24–25
Brown, Claude, 149
Brown, Earle, 1, 95
Brown, Edward, 82
Brown, Michael, 184
Brown Shoe, long-term agreements at, 78–79
BRSC (Brotherhood of Railway and Steamship Clerks), 32
Building Service Employees, organization of, 61–62
Busch Jr., August, 156
Butler Brothers, 1

Cabin Creek strikes, 12
CAC (Carondelet Area Council), 167–68
Calhoun, David, 132
Callanan, Lawrence, 68, 153
Callanan, Thomas, 68
Calloway, Deverne (née Lee), 7, 50, 52, 131–32, 177, 254
Calloway, Ernest: as campaign manager, 130; childhood, 9–10, 12, 14–15; on *CIO News* staff, 49–50; Clay rivalry with, 132–34; on communism, 24–25, 49, 53–54; for Congress, 152–53; on CORE, 138–40; death, 177; education of, 14–15, 23–25, 50–52, 53–54, *248*; on friend's lynching, 21; Gibbons with, *252*, *254*; in Harlem, 15; on Jim Crow army during World War II, 47–48; at Local 688 meeting, *249*; move to St. Louis, 66–67; newspapers started by, 130–31; overview of, 2–3, 7–8; personality, 67; physical traits, 67; Powell Amendment opposition, 119–20; as president of NAACP, 95–101, 142–43; as professor, 176; with red caps, 31–34; on total person unionism, 179; wives of, 50; on working-class citizenship, 34–35; as young adult, 20–25; Zagri with, *250*. *See also* NAACP (National Association for the Advancement of Colored People)
Calloway, Ernest (father), 9, 10, 12
Calloway, Martha Sutton, 50
Carey, Archibald, 37–38
Carey, Ron, 181
carnival workers, votes by, 114–15, 116
Carondelet Area Council (CAC), 167–68
Carondelet Community Betterment Association, 167
Carson, Johnny, 146, 252
Cayton, Horace, 33
Central States Conference, 76
Central States Pension Fund, 74
Cervantes, Alfonso (A. J.) 141,150,154
CFL (Chicago Federation of Labor), 28–29
Chambers, Jordan, 96, 131
Chapin. Arthur, 56
charter reform initiative, St. Louis, 104–10
Chicago, IL: Black Renaissance, 37; labor ethos of, 16–17; Memorial Day Massacre, 26; taxi driver strike, 28
Chicago Defender newspaper, 36
Chicago Federation of Labor (CFL), 28–29
Chicago Industrial Union Council, 49
Chicago Labor College, 18
CIO (Congress of Industrial Organizations): AFL merger with, 1; anti-FTA effort, 53; commitment to African Americans, 36–37; Committee to Abolish Racial Discrimination, 49; IUC, 44, 46; PAC, 42; St. Louis, 40
"The CIO and Negro Labor" (Calloway), 23–24

The CIO News, 49–50
Citizen Crusader newspaper, 130
Citizens Committee Against the Charter, 106–7
Citizen's Council, 167–68
"Citizens for Better Government," 168
City-Wide Shop Conference, St. Louis, 85
Civic Alliance for Housing, St. Louis, 141, 156–58
civic involvement, Local 688, 145–48
civic participation, African American decline in, 177
Civic Progress, 102–4, 105
class antagonism, 65
class vs. race, 37
Clay, William: on Calloway after his death, 177; Calloway rivalry with, 132–34; for congress, 152–53; on fair employment practices, 136; overview of, 7
coal miners, life of, 9–14
Coca Cola, driver-salesman jobs at, 99
Cohen, Raymond, 123
Cold War: foreign policy, 171; union challenges during, 53
collective bargaining process: centralization of, 124; importance of, 52; inadequacies of, 144–45; long-term agreements, 78–79, 80–81; transformational power of, 77–78
Colson, Charles, 160, 173
Commission on Equal Employment Opportunity, St. Louis, 137
Committee for Fair Representation, 152
Committee on Democratic Rights of Members, Local 688, 63, 69–70
"Committees for a Decent, Democratic Trade Union in the RWDSU," 58
Committee to Abolish Racial Discrimination, CIO, 49
Communications Workers of America (CWA), 136
communism: Calloway on, 24–25, 49, 54–55; Gibbons on, 27–28, 44–45, 171, 183
Communist Party (CP), 24–25, 43–44, 49, 53–54
"community assembly," 108–9
community bargaining table, 93, 145–46
community betterment initiatives, 168
community politics, work politics vs., 87–88
Community Renewal program, St. Louis, 147
community stewards program: demise of, 118; development of, 86; expansion of efforts, 108–9; handling grievances, 88–90; higher education campaign, 95; housing issues, 92–93; overview of, 1–2, 4–5; public transportation campaign, 89–90, *249*; quality of life campaign, 108–9; rat control campaign, 93–94; sewer district campaign, 89–90;

training for, 88; women's involvement in, 91–92
concrete drivers, Local 682, 74, 75–76
Congress of Industrial Organizations (CIO), 1
Congress of Neighborhood Organizations, 176–77
Congress of Racial Equality (CORE), 95, 110, 138–40
Connor, James W., 115
Conscientious Objectors Against Jim Crow, 47–48
Consolidation Coal Company, 12
construction drivers, Local 682, 114
construction drivers' strike, 71
construction industry, organized crime and, 71–75
CORE (Congress of Racial Equality), 95, 110, 138–40
corporate organization, 162, 177
corruption investigations, union. *See* investigations
Cortor, Donald, 99–100, 117
Council Plaza, 127–28, 180
"county group," 86
covenants, negotiation, 135–37
CP (Communist Party), 24–25, 43–44, 53–54
"crew meetings," union, 66
CWA (Communications Workers of America), 136

Danforth, Donald, 137
Davis Jr., Sammy, 146, 252
Defty, Sally Bixby, 160
delinquency, juvenile, 90–91
Democratic-Republican-Independent Voter Education (DRIVE), 124
Denham, Robert, 58
Department of Housing and Urban Development (HUD), 155
Department of Labor, Division of Technological Change, 138
"Department Store Organizing Council," 61–62
Despres, Leon, 33–34
Dieckmann, Annetta, 17, 63, 64, 65–66, 129
Dioguardia, John "Johnny Dio," 112, 116
discrimination, committee on racial, 46
Dismas House, 146
distribution workers, unrepresented, 40
"Division of Technological Change," 138
Dobbs, Farrell, 60
Dorfman, Paul "Red," 112
"Double V," 48
Douglas, Paul, 17, 33
Drake, St. Clair, 48
Draper, George, 96
DRIVE (Democratic-Republican-Independent Voter Education), 124

driver-salesman jobs, Coca Cola, 99, 136
"dual loyalty," union and company, 64
Dunne, Vincent, 60
Dwyer, John, 130

earnings tax, 103
education, workers, 18, 26–27
educational program campaign, Local 688, 129
education campaign, higher, 95
Ehrhardt, Oscar, 61, 160
elections: Clay vs. Calloway for Congress, 152–53; Deverne Calloway to legislature, 132; Hicks' school board, 130; Joint Council 13, 114–15; McNeal's senate race, 130; NAACP St. Louis presidency, 96, 142–43; Pentland's senate race, 68–69; political independence, 249
employment discrimination campaign, 109–10, 134–40, 150
environmental movements, Teamsters, 168–69
ethical practices commission, Local 688, 113
Evans, Pearlie, 142

fair employment, African Americans, 134–40
Fairgrounds Race Riot, 82
Fair Labor Standards Act (FLSA), 34
Fair Share of Jobs Covenant, 136–37
family-focused health and fitness program, 127, 129
Famous-Barr department store: employment discrimination campaign, 110; strike, 43; women's higher pay campaign, 161–62
Federal Bureau of Investigation (FBI), on Gibbons, 81
Ferguson, MO, 184
Fisher, Bernice, 56, 62
Fitzpatrick, John, 29
Fitzsimmons, Frank, 144, 150–51, 160–61, 170–74
"floor shop stewards," 128
FLSA (Fair Labor Standards Act), 34
Flynn, Thomas, 73, 76
Food, Tobacco, Agricultural, and Allied Workers Union (FTA), 53–54
Ford, James, 116
Frazer, Robert, 164
"Freedom Lines," at A & P stores, 109
FTA (Food, Tobacco, Agricultural, and Allied Workers Union), 53–54
fundraisers, Teamster, 146

gangsters, St. Louis, 71–75
gender concerns, union, 64
Gibbons, Anne (née Culter), 31, 160
Gibbons, Harold: American Legion citation, 83; arrests at strikes, 29, 80; the Calloways with, 254; Calloway with, 252; career summation, 160–61; in Chicago, 17–20; child-

hood, 9–10, 12–15; on communism, 27–28, 44–45, 171, 183; death, 176; on Dioguardia, 116; early employment, 18; education of, 14, 16–20; extravagant lifestyle of, 125, 160; fall from power, 170–76; FBI on, 81; fundraising extravaganzas, 146; on health care, 45–46; Hoffa relationship with, 6–7, 72–74, 125–27, 251; as Hoffa's executive assistant, 112–13, 125–27; idealism of, 121–22; investigations on, 81–84, 122–23; Joint Council 13 president, 113; Kissinger and, 172–73; McClellan Committee investigation, 111, 113–17; mobsters threatening, 71–75; move to St. Louis, 39–47, 247; on Nixon, 172–73; Nixon with, 254; obituary, 176; overview of, 1–3, 7–8; personality, 67; physical traits, 67; on police harassment, 151–52; political attacks on, 82–83; political philosophy, 18–19, 31; on racial justice, 46, 63–64, 123–24, 140; on RAFT, 167; raiding Retail Clerks union, 61–62; with Rat Pack, 252; rent strike negotiations, 141, 154–57; retirement, 175; on socialism, 17, 19; SWP and, 43; taxi driver strike negotiations, 28; Teamsters merger, 55, 58–61; Teamsters presidential bid for, 143–44; trade union delegation to North Vietnam, 172; at TWOC, 29–31; unionism philosophy, 31, 46–47; on union's importance, 13; on Vietnam, 171–72; on violence during strikes, 117–18; in Washington D.C., 122–26; womanizing of, 125; women's higher pay campaign, 161–62; Zagri relationship with, 124
Gibbons, Patrick (father), 9–10, 13
Glen Alden Coal Company, 10
Glimco, Joey, 111, 123
Glisper, Floyd, 93
Goldschein, Max, 81–82
government, labor support from, 85–86
Graham, Leroy, 149, 154, 157, 253
grand jury investigations, 81–84
Granger, Lester, 22–23, 24
"Great Strike" of 1902, coal miners, 11
guaranteed annual employment, 78–79
Gushleff, Ronald, 166

Hall, Paul, 133
Hall, Rothchild, 93
Hammond, Elmer, 157
Harlem, NY, 15
Harrington, Reginald, 93
Hayes, Mary, 9
Haywood, Allan, 55
HDC (Human Development Corporation), 147
"Health and Medical Camp," Local 688, 127, 129
health care program, union, 45–46
Hendricks, Herman, 80

Herling, John, 55
Herndon, Angelo, 49
Herstein, Lillian, 17, 18, 129
Hicks, John, 130
Hillman, Sidney, 30
Hines, Murray, 169
"Hiroshima Flats," 127–28
Hoffa, James P., 181
Hoffa, Jimmy: assault on Baron, 126; dealing with St. Louis mobsters, 72–74; disappearance of, 175; gala dinner honoring, 110–11; gangster connections, 111–12; Gibbons' relationship with, 125–27, 251; investigations on, 111–12, 122–23; on Kennedy family, 126; overview of, 6–7; as Teamster president, 112, 122–26, 143–44, 170
Hogan, Edward "Jellyroll," 68, 130
"hot cargo," handling, 78–79
housing: affordable, 92–93; redevelopment, 146–47; rent strike, 141; senior citizen, 127–28
HUD (Department of Housing and Urban Development), 155
Human Development Corporation (HDC), 147
Huntley, Chet, 121

IBT (International Brotherhood of Teamsters). See Teamsters
idealism, Gibbons' spirit of, 121–22
Igoe complexes, Pruitt and, 153–58
ILWU (International Longshoremen's and Warehousemen's Union), 41–42
Industrial Union Council (IUC), 44, 46
International Brotherhood of Red Caps, 32
International Brotherhood of Teamsters (IBT). See Teamsters
International Longshoremen's and Warehousemen's Union (ILWU), 41–42
International Shoe St. Louis warehouse strike, 56–57
investigations: Beck, 111; Gibbons, 81–84, 122–23; Hoffa, 111–12, 122–23; McClellan Committee, 111, 113–17; unions, 74, 81–84, 99–100, 106, 113, 115–16, 122–23
IUC (Industrial Union Council), 44, 46
Ives, Irving, 116–17

Jefferson Bank and Trust Company, 138–40
Jenkins, KY, 9, 12
J.H. Grady Company strike, 57–58
Jim Crow army, World War II, 47–48
Job Opportunities Council (JOC), 109
JOC (Job Opportunities Council), 109
Johnson, Arthur, 56
Joint Council 13, Teamsters, 113–15, 174
Jones, Robert, 147
juvenile delinquency, 90–91

Index

Karsh, Harry, 114
Kato, Yuki, 46
Kavner, Richard, 56, 59, 174
Kennedy, John F., 126
Kennedy, Robert, 111, 115–17, 122–23
Kerber, Steve, 2
King, Jean, 153, 155, 179
King, Richard, 169
King Jr., Martin Luther, 251
Kissinger, Henry, 172–73
Klein, Arthur, 128
Krueger, Maynard, 18

Labor Council, St. Louis, 137–38
"labor ethos," Chicago, 16–17
Labor Health Institute (LHI), 45–46, 56, 248
labor-management civic partnerships, 146
"Labor's Stake in Good Neighborhoods" (Zagri), 92–93
labor support, governmental, 85–86
Landrum-Griffin Act, 118–19, 120
Langenbacher, Irwin, 115
lead poisoning, 169
League for Adequate Welfare, 150
Lee, Deverne. *See* Calloway, Deverne (née Lee)
Lens, Sidney, 125
Letner, Russell, 94
Lever Brothers, 135, 136–37
Lewis, John L., 30
LHI (Labor Health Institute), 45–46, 56, 248
Lichtenstein, Nelson, 57
Liuzzo, Viola, 251
Local 22, FTA, 53–54
Local 102, Teamsters, 174
Local 346, AFT, 18, 26–27
Local 405, Teamsters, 80, 122–23
Local 600, Teamsters, 164–65
Local 682, construction drivers, 114
Local 682 concrete drivers, 74, 75–76
Local 688, Teamsters: anti-charter campaign, 104–10; assessment on, 62–65; civic involvement, 145–48; class antagonism, 65; Committee on Democratic Rights of Members, 63, 69–70; corruption in, 81–84, 113, 122–23; derailment of, 81; dual loyalty challenges, 64; educational program campaign, 129, 184; ethical practices commission, 113; go-it-alone approach, 183; health and fitness program, 127, 129; jurisdictional conflict, 60–61; juvenile delinquency committee, 90–91; long-term agreements for, 78–79, 80–81; as organization of conflict, 71; overview of, 1–2; political education committee, 68; political strategies, 87; public relations for, 84; racial attitudes, 62–63; racial justice apathy, 162–65, 167–68; shop steward meetings, 164–65; strike fund assessment, 162; voluntary social integration, 129; war on slums, 148–52; white member complaints, 164; women's involvement in, 64. *See also* community stewards program
long-term agreements, Local 688, 78–79, 80–81
Louisville Textile Company, 30
Lovestone, Jay, 25
lynching, 1933, 21

machine politics, St. Louis, 67–68
"maintenance of membership," 42
"March Forward to Legality" strategy, 34
March on Washington, D.C. (1963), 134
Martin, Dean, 146, 252
"mayor's group," 86
McCarthy, Jake, 84, 122
McClellan, John, 111
McClellan Committee, 111, 113–17
McCormack, Terry, 157
McNeal, Theodore "Ted," 109, 130, 136
"membership, maintenance of," 42
Memorial Day Massacre, 26
military segregation, 47–48
Mill Creek Valley, 127–28
miner-farmers, 10–11
mining, coal, 9–14
Mitchell, Arthur, 36
mobsters, St. Louis, 71–75
Montgomery Ward strike, 44
Moon, Henry Lee, 24
Mulhern, Bridget, 9
"Municipal Land Reclamation Authority" (Calloway), 158
Murray, Philip, 53

NAACP (National Association for the Advancement of Colored People): anti-charter campaign, 104–10; Calloway as president of St. Louis, 95–101; elections, 142–43; JOC, 109; member recruitment, 97–98; overview of, 5; Wilson as president of St. Louis, 110
National Association for the Advancement of Colored People (NAACP). *See* NAACP
National Industrial Recovery Act (NIRA), 22
National Negro Congress, 24–25
National War Labor Board (NWLB), 42
"The Nature and Structure of the Collective Bargaining Agreement" (Calloway), 77–78
Nedich, John, 62
Negro American Labor Council (NALC), 135–36, 137–38
"Negroes Won't Wait for 'Gift' of Rights" (Gibbons), 140
"The Negro in the Kentucky Fields" (Calloway), 22
"Negro Republic," 24–25
Neidel, Ernie, 170

New Citizen newspaper, 130–31
NIRA (National Industrial Recovery Act), 22
Nixon, Richard, 160, *254*
Nixon Administration, endorsement of, 172–73
Normandy, MO, 164
North Vietnam, trade union delegation in, 172
no-strike pledge, 42
NWLB (National War Labor Board), 42

occupational safety movements, Teamsters, 168–69
Opportunity journal, 22
organization, corporate, 162, 177
organized crime, St. Louis, 71–75
"other sixteen hours," background on, 85
Oxford, England, 50–52

Pace, Jim, 149, 164, 168
Paint Creek strikes, 12
"patches," 10
Pentland, Robert, 68–69, *249*
People's Forum, 35–36
Perry, Ivory, 149
Peverly, MO, 127
picket lines, Gibbons on, 29
"Planning for an Integrated School System in St. Louis," 69–70
police harassment: Black Liberators group, 151–52; taxi driver strike, 80
Political Action Committee, CIO, 42
politics: African Americans in, 36, 130; St. Louis, 67–68; Teamsters in national, 123–24; of work vs. community, 87–88
pollution campaign, air and water, 169, *253*
Port Huron Statement, Students for a Democratic Society, 121
Poston, Ted, 119
Poverty, War on, 147–48
"poverty professionals," 148
Powell, Adam Clayton, 119–20
Powell Amendment, 119–20
price controls, wartime, 56
Pruitt-Igoe complex, 153–58
public housing strike, 141, 153–59
public relations, Local 688, 84
"push button warehouse," 81

quality of life campaign, 108–9
Quill, Michael, 79

race, class vs., 37
racial discrimination, 46
racial equality: in education, 184; overview of, 6
racial justice: importance of, 46, 62–63, 123–24; union's agenda on, 69, 162–65, 167–68

racial segregation: in schools, 69–70; World War II, 47–48
RAFT (Rank and File Teamsters), 166–67
Railway Labor Act (RLA), 34
Randolph, A. Philip, 134, 135
Rank and File Teamsters (RAFT), 166–67
Raskin, A. H., 126
rat control campaign, St. Louis, 93–94
red caps, 31–35, 48–49
rent strike, public housing, 141, 153–59
Republic Steel plant, 28
"responsible unionism," 30
Retail Clerks, raid on, 61–62
Retail Wholesale and Distribution Workers Union (RWDSU), 58–59
Reuther, Walter, 150–51
Rice-Stix, 41, 80
Rich, Marvin, 56
Riesel, Victor, 74, 84
R.J. Reynolds, 53–54
RLA (Railway Labor Act), 34
Roberts, Ben, 51
Roberts, Evelyn, 142–43
Robinson, Leonard, 151
Romney, George, 155
Roosevelt administration, union movements bargain with, 42
Rose, Arnold, 62–65
Rosenblum, Frank, 29
Ruskin College in Oxford, 50–52, *248*
Rustin, Bayard, 134
RWDSU (Retail Wholesale and Distribution Workers Union), 58–59
Ryan, Mike, 67, 149, 164–65

Saffo, Pete, 55, 59, 82
Sanford, Levi, 149
Saposs, David, 23–25
Schoessling, Ray, 175
school board election, 130
school desegregation campaign, 184
School for Workers, University of Wisconsin, 17–18
Scott, Michael, 139
Seafarers' International Union, 133–34
secondary boycotts, ban on, 58
segregation, military, 47–48
Senate Rackets Committee, 111
senior citizens' housing, Mill Creek Valley, 127–28
Sentner, William, 40, 43–44, 81
service-oriented economy, union movement in, 181
sewage system problems, St. Louis, 89
Shapleigh Hardware strike, 56
Shenker, Morris, 68, 74
shop steward meetings, Local 688, 164–65

Sinatra, Frank, 125, 146, 160, 252
SLHA (St. Louis Housing Authority), 153
slums, trade union oriented war on, 148–52
slums, war on, 5–6
small companies, organizing, 169–70
Smith, Elzie "Red," 40
Smith, Gerald L.K., 63–64
social integration, voluntary, 129
socialism, Gibbons exposure to, 17, 19
Socialist Workers Party (SWP), 43
soft drink industry, 135–36
Sommer, Ada, 106
Southwestern Bell Telephone, 109–10, 135–36, 137–38
Spotlight News smear campaign, 83, 84
Steamfitters Union, 153
Steel Workers Organizing Committee (SWOC), 24
Stein, Toni, 175
Steinberg, Larry, 126
St. Joseph Lead, 169
St. Louis: charter reform initiative, 102, 104–10; Civic Alliance for Housing, 141, 156–58; Commission on Equal Employment Opportunity, 137; Community Renewal program, 147; industry, 40; Labor Council, 137–38; organized crime in, 71–75; overview of, 3–4; politics, 67–68, 86; rat control ordinance, 93–94; sewage system problems, 89; transit problems, St. Louis, 89
St. Louis Housing Authority (SLHA), 153
"St. Louis Labor Education Project," 63
St. Louis Post-Dispatch, 160
Stone, Thelma Lee, 89
strikes: arrests at, 29; Chicago taxi drivers, 28; coal mine, 11–12; construction drivers, 71; Famous-Barr department store, 43; International Shoe's at St. Louis warehouse, 56–57; J.H. Grady Company, 57–58; Local 682 concrete drivers, 75–76; Louisville Textile Company, 30; Montgomery Ward, 44; no-strike pledge, 42; public housing, 153–59; public housing rent, 141; Shapleigh Hardware, 56; taxi drivers, 79–80; taxi driver wildcat, 99–101; trucking agreement, 164–65; UPS, 166, 181; violence during, 117–18; Yellow Cab, 80
Students for a Democratic Society, 121
Sullivan, Leonore, 158
Sutton, Martha, 37–38
SWOC (Steel Workers Organizing Committee), 24
SWP (Socialist Workers Party), 43
"Syrian-Steamfitter factor," 153

Taft-Hartley Act, 57–58
Tandy Area Council (TAC), 148–52, 159
Taub, William, 173
tax, earnings, 103
taxi drivers: African American, 79–80, 99–100; jurisdictional conflict, 133–34; strikes, 79–80, 99–101; unionization of, 79–80
TDU (Teamsters for a Democratic Union), 180
teachers, adult education, 26–27
Teamsters: background on, 59–60; on corruption convictions, 123; environmental movements, 168–69; fundraising extravaganzas, 146; Gibbons' merger with, 55, 58–61; Gibbons' presidential bid for, 143–44; Joint Council 13, 113–15; membership growth, 124; mob connections, 74; national politics, 123–24; Nixon Administration, endorsement of, 173; occupational safety movements, 168–69; overview of, 3–4; RAFT, 166–67; Seafarers' jurisdictional conflict with, 133–34; UAW and, 150–51. *See also* Local 688, Teamsters
The Teamsters (Brill), 1–2, 175–76
Teamsters for a Democratic Union (TDU), 180
"Teamster Teentown" program, 91
tenant activism, 151
tenants, unionizing, 157–59
Textile Workers Organizing Committee (TWOC), 29–31
Tho, Le Duc, 172
Tobin, Daniel, 111
"To Sleep, Perchance to Dream" (Calloway), 20–21
total person unionism: challenges of, 64, 182–83; community improvement with, 168; concept of, 179; membership estrangement from, 128–29, 164–65; overview of, 5–6, 14; on retirement, 128; urban decline fixed with, 147–48. *See also* community stewards program; LHI (Labor Health Institute)
Tournour, Gene, 140
Townsend, Willard, 31, 32, 53
trade union delegation, North Vietnam, 172
transit problems, St. Louis, 89
"Triple Revolution," union movement, 144
trucking industry, deregulation of, 180
Truth newspaper, 137
TUC (British Trade Union Congress), 53–54
Tucker, Jerry, 151
Tucker, Raymond, 75–76, 93, 94, 137
TWOC (Textile Workers Organizing Committee), 29–31

UAW (United Auto Workers), 150–51
UE (United Electrical Workers), 40, 43–44
UFW (United Farm Workers), 175
UMWA (United Mine Workers of America), 11
"unionism, responsible," 30
unionism philosophy, Gibbons,' 46–47
unionizing tenants, 157–59
union-management-civic partnerships, 145

union movement: American, 51–52; British, 51; CP's involvement in St. Louis, 43–44; current state of, 180; health care program, 45–46; overview of, 4; private sector, 182; Roosevelt administration bargain with, 42; in service-oriented economy, 181; Triple Revolution, 144; weakness of, 177; wide and narrow view of mission, 85

unions: centralization of, 65; coal mine, 11, 12–13; committees, 66; corruption in, 113; corruption investigations, 74, 81–84, 99–100, 106, 113, 115–16, 122–23; crew meetings, 66; democracy of, 65–66; dual loyalty between companies and, 64; importance of, 13; maintenance of membership, 42; member definition, 179; as "miniature government," 34–35; organized crime and, 71–75; "other sixteen hours," 85; percentage of U.S. labor force in, 180; raiding other, 61–62; red caps, 31–35; for small companies, 169–70; strike fund, 162; taxi drivers, 79–80; women's involvement in, 35, 64, 161–62, 169; during World War II, 39, 42. *See also* Local 688, Teamsters; Teamsters; *specific unions*

Union Solidarity (Rose), 63
United Auto Workers (UAW), 150–51
United Electrical Workers (UE), 40, 43–44
United Farm Workers (UFW), 175
United Mine Workers of America (UMWA), 11
United Parcel Service (UPS), 166, 181
United Retail, Wholesale, and Department Store Employees of America (URWDSEA), 39, 44–45
United Transport Service Employees of America (UTSEA), 32–33, 48–49, 58
University of Wisconsin's School for Workers, 17–18
UPS (United Parcel Service), 166, 181
Urban League, 22–23
urban revitalization: America 2000, 146–47; Council Plaza, 127–28
URWDSEA (United Retail, Wholesale, and Department Store Employees of America), 39, 44–45, 58
UTSEA (United Transport Service Employees of America), 32–33, 48–49

Vietnam Moratorium rally, 171
Vinyard, Vera, 91–92
Vitale, John, 72
Voluntary Fair Employment Covenant, 136
voluntary social integration, 129
Vorse, Mary Heaton, 84

"Wagner Act," 151
Walla, Elmer "Gene," 114

Wallace, George, 163
Walsh, Kirk, 156
ward organizations, importance of, 87
warehouse division statement, 77
warehouse facilities, exodus from St. Louis, 80–81
warehouse workers, 40, 247
War on Poverty, 147–48
war on slums: overview of, 5–6; trade union oriented, 148–52
wartime price controls, protest of, 56
Washington, D.C., 122–26
water pollution campaign, 169, 253
WDL (Workers Defense League), 118
Weber, Robert, 91
welfare rights movement, 150
West Virginia, coal mining in, 10–12
Wheeler, Henry Winfield, 96
White, Walter, 48
"whole persons," workers as, 181–82
Widick, B. J., 123
widow's rows, 10
Wilson, Margaret Bush, 67, 109, 110, 142
wives, union, 35
Wolchok, Samuel, 39, 40–41, 58–59
women: auxiliaries, 35; higher pay campaign for, 161–62; union involvement by, 64, 169
"Women, the Home, and the Union" (Calloway), 35
Woo, William, 177–78
"worker-citizens," 88–89, 93. *See also* community stewards program
Workers Defense League (WDL), 118
workers education, 18
working-class citizenship, 34, 52. *See also* community stewards program; TAC (Tandy Area Council)
work politics, community politics vs., 87–88
Works Progress Administration (WPA), 18, 20, 24, 26–30, 31
World War II: Jim Crow army, 47–48; postwar price controls, 56; strikes during, 43; union strategy during, 39, 42–43
Wortman, Frank "Buster," 71–73
WPA (Works Progress Administration), 18, 20, 24, 26–30, 31
Wright, Glen, 168

Yancey, John, 31, 53
Yellow Cab strike, 80

Zagri, Sidney, 90, 106, 122–23, 124, 250
Zulu 1200's, 148
Zweifel, Clint, 179–80

ROBERT BUSSEL is a professor of history and director of the Labor Education and Research Center at the University of Oregon. He is the author of *From Harvard to the Ranks of Labor: Powers Hapgood and the American Working Class.*

THE WORKING CLASS IN AMERICAN HISTORY

Worker City, Company Town: Iron and Cotton-Worker Protest in Troy and Cohoes, New York, 1855–84   *Daniel J. Walkowitz*

Life, Work, and Rebellion in the Coal Fields: The Southern West Virginia Miners, 1880–1922   *David Alan Corbin*

Women and American Socialism, 1870–1920   *Mari Jo Buhle*

Lives of Their Own: Blacks, Italians, and Poles in Pittsburgh, 1900–1960   *John Bodnar, Roger Simon, and Michael P. Weber*

Working-Class America: Essays on Labor, Community, and American Society   *Edited by Michael H. Frisch and Daniel J. Walkowitz*

Eugene V. Debs: Citizen and Socialist   *Nick Salvatore*

American Labor and Immigration History, 1877–1920s: Recent European Research   *Edited by Dirk Hoerder*

Workingmen's Democracy: The Knights of Labor and American Politics   *Leon Fink*

The Electrical Workers: A History of Labor at General Electric and Westinghouse, 1923–60   *Ronald W. Schatz*

The Mechanics of Baltimore: Workers and Politics in the Age of Revolution, 1763–1812   *Charles G. Steffen*

The Practice of Solidarity: American Hat Finishers in the Nineteenth Century   *David Bensman*

The Labor History Reader   *Edited by Daniel J. Leab*

Solidarity and Fragmentation: Working People and Class Consciousness in Detroit, 1875–1900   *Richard Oestreicher*

Counter Cultures: Saleswomen, Managers, and Customers in American Department Stores, 1890–1940   *Susan Porter Benson*

The New England Working Class and the New Labor History   *Edited by Herbert G. Gutman and Donald H. Bell*

Labor Leaders in America   *Edited by Melvyn Dubofsky and Warren Van Tine*

Barons of Labor: The San Francisco Building Trades and Union Power in the Progressive Era   *Michael Kazin*

Gender at Work: The Dynamics of Job Segregation by Sex during World War II   *Ruth Milkman*

Once a Cigar Maker: Men, Women, and Work Culture in American Cigar Factories, 1900–1919   *Patricia A. Cooper*

A Generation of Boomers: The Pattern of Railroad Labor Conflict in Nineteenth-Century America   *Shelton Stromquist*

Work and Community in the Jungle: Chicago's Packinghouse Workers, 1894–1922   *James R. Barrett*

Workers, Managers, and Welfare Capitalism: The Shoeworkers and Tanners of Endicott Johnson, 1890–1950   *Gerald Zahavi*

Men, Women, and Work: Class, Gender, and Protest in the New England Shoe Industry, 1780–1910   *Mary Blewett*

Workers on the Waterfront: Seamen, Longshoremen, and Unionism in the 1930s   *Bruce Nelson*

German Workers in Chicago: A Documentary History of Working-Class Culture from 1850 to World War I   *Edited by Hartmut Keil and John B. Jentz*

On the Line: Essays in the History of Auto Work *Edited by Nelson Lichtenstein and Stephen Meyer III*
Labor's Flaming Youth: Telephone Operators and Worker Militancy, 1878–1923 *Stephen H. Norwood*
Another Civil War: Labor, Capital, and the State in the Anthracite Regions of Pennsylvania, 1840–68 *Grace Palladino*
Coal, Class, and Color: Blacks in Southern West Virginia, 1915–32 *Joe William Trotter Jr.*
For Democracy, Workers, and God: Labor Song-Poems and Labor Protest, 1865–95 *Clark D. Halker*
Dishing It Out: Waitresses and Their Unions in the Twentieth Century *Dorothy Sue Cobble*
The Spirit of 1848: German Immigrants, Labor Conflict, and the Coming of the Civil War *Bruce Levine*
Working Women of Collar City: Gender, Class, and Community in Troy, New York, 1864–86 *Carole Turbin*
Southern Labor and Black Civil Rights: Organizing Memphis Workers *Michael K. Honey*
Radicals of the Worst Sort: Laboring Women in Lawrence, Massachusetts, 1860–1912 *Ardis Cameron*
Producers, Proletarians, and Politicians: Workers and Party Politics in Evansville and New Albany, Indiana, 1850–87 *Lawrence M. Lipin*
The New Left and Labor in the 1960s *Peter B. Levy*
The Making of Western Labor Radicalism: Denver's Organized Workers, 1878–1905 *David Brundage*
In Search of the Working Class: Essays in American Labor History and Political Culture *Leon Fink*
Lawyers against Labor: From Individual Rights to Corporate Liberalism *Daniel R. Ernst*
"We Are All Leaders": The Alternative Unionism of the Early 1930s *Edited by Staughton Lynd*
The Female Economy: The Millinery and Dressmaking Trades, 1860–1930 *Wendy Gamber*
"Negro and White, Unite and Fight!": A Social History of Industrial Unionism in Meatpacking, 1930–90 *Roger Horowitz*
Power at Odds: The 1922 National Railroad Shopmen's Strike *Colin J. Davis*
The Common Ground of Womanhood: Class, Gender, and Working Girls' Clubs, 1884–1928 *Priscilla Murolo*
Marching Together: Women of the Brotherhood of Sleeping Car Porters *Melinda Chateauvert*
Down on the Killing Floor: Black and White Workers in Chicago's Packinghouses, 1904–54 *Rick Halpern*
Labor and Urban Politics: Class Conflict and the Origins of Modern Liberalism in Chicago, 1864–97 *Richard Schneirov*
All That Glitters: Class, Conflict, and Community in Cripple Creek *Elizabeth Jameson*
Waterfront Workers: New Perspectives on Race and Class *Edited by Calvin Winslow*

Labor Histories: Class, Politics, and the Working-Class Experience
   Edited by Eric Arnesen, Julie Greene, and Bruce Laurie
The Pullman Strike and the Crisis of the 1890s: Essays on Labor and Politics
   Edited by Richard Schneirov, Shelton Stromquist, and Nick Salvatore
AlabamaNorth: African-American Migrants, Community, and Working-Class
   Activism in Cleveland, 1914–45   *Kimberley L. Phillips*
Imagining Internationalism in American and British Labor, 1939–49   *Victor Silverman*
William Z. Foster and the Tragedy of American Radicalism   *James R. Barrett*
Colliers across the Sea: A Comparative Study of Class Formation in Scotland
   and the American Midwest, 1830–1924   *John H. M. Laslett*
"Rights, Not Roses": Unions and the Rise of Working-Class Feminism, 1945–80
   Dennis A. Deslippe
Testing the New Deal: The General Textile Strike of 1934 in the American South
   Janet Irons
Hard Work: The Making of Labor History   *Melvyn Dubofsky*
Southern Workers and the Search for Community: Spartanburg County,
   South Carolina   *G. C. Waldrep III*
We Shall Be All: A History of the Industrial Workers of the World (abridged edition)
   Melvyn Dubofsky, ed. Joseph A. McCartin
Race, Class, and Power in the Alabama Coalfields, 1908–21   *Brian Kelly*
Duquesne and the Rise of Steel Unionism   *James D. Rose*
Anaconda: Labor, Community, and Culture in Montana's Smelter City   *Laurie Mercier*
Bridgeport's Socialist New Deal, 1915–36   *Cecelia Bucki*
Indispensable Outcasts: Hobo Workers and Community in the American Midwest,
   1880–1930   *Frank Tobias Higbie*
After the Strike: A Century of Labor Struggle at Pullman   *Susan Eleanor Hirsch*
Corruption and Reform in the Teamsters Union   *David Witwer*
Waterfront Revolts: New York and London Dockworkers, 1946–61   *Colin J. Davis*
Black Workers' Struggle for Equality in Birmingham   *Horace Huntley and
   David Montgomery*
The Tribe of Black Ulysses: African American Men in the Industrial South
   William P. Jones
City of Clerks: Office and Sales Workers in Philadelphia, 1870–1920
   Jerome P. Bjelopera
Reinventing "The People": The Progressive Movement, the Class Problem,
   and the Origins of Modern Liberalism   *Shelton Stromquist*
Radical Unionism in the Midwest, 1900–1950   *Rosemary Feurer*
Gendering Labor History   *Alice Kessler-Harris*
James P. Cannon and the Origins of the American Revolutionary Left, 1890–1928
   Bryan D. Palmer
Glass Towns: Industry, Labor, and Political Economy in Appalachia, 1890–1930s
   Ken Fones-Wolf
Workers and the Wild: Conservation, Consumerism, and Labor in Oregon, 1910–30
   Lawrence M. Lipin
Wobblies on the Waterfront: Interracial Unionism in Progressive-Era Philadelphia
   Peter Cole
Red Chicago: American Communism at Its Grassroots, 1928–35   *Randi Storch*

Labor's Cold War: Local Politics in a Global Context   *Edited by Shelton Stromquist*
Bessie Abramowitz Hillman and the Making of the Amalgamated Clothing Workers
   of America   *Karen Pastorello*
The Great Strikes of 1877   *Edited by David O. Stowell*
Union-Free America: Workers and Antiunion Culture   *Lawrence Richards*
Race against Liberalism: Black Workers and the UAW in Detroit
   David M. Lewis-Colman
Teachers and Reform: Chicago Public Education, 1929–70   *John F. Lyons*
Upheaval in the Quiet Zone: 1199/SEIU and the Politics of Healthcare Unionism
   Leon Fink and Brian Greenberg
Shadow of the Racketeer: Scandal in Organized Labor   *David Witwer*
Sweet Tyranny: Migrant Labor, Industrial Agriculture, and Imperial Politics
   Kathleen Mapes
Staley: The Fight for a New American Labor Movement   *Steven K. Ashby and
   C. J. Hawking*
On the Ground: Labor Struggles in the American Airline Industry   *Liesl Miller Orenic*
NAFTA and Labor in North America   *Norman Caulfield*
Making Capitalism Safe: Work Safety and Health Regulation in America, 1880–1940
   Donald W. Rogers
Good, Reliable, White Men: Railroad Brotherhoods, 1877–1917   *Paul Michel Taillon*
Spirit of Rebellion: Labor and Religion in the New Cotton South   *Jarod Roll*
The Labor Question in America: Economic Democracy in the Gilded Age
   Rosanne Currarino
Banded Together: Economic Democratization in the Brass Valley   *Jeremy Brecher*
The Gospel of the Working Class: Labor's Southern Prophets in New Deal America
   Erik Gellman and Jarod Roll
Guest Workers and Resistance to U.S. Corporate Despotism   *Immanuel Ness*
Gleanings of Freedom: Free and Slave Labor along the Mason-Dixon Line, 1790–1860
   Max Grivno
Chicago in the Age of Capital: Class, Politics, and Democracy during the Civil War
   and Reconstruction   *John B. Jentz and Richard Schneirov*
Child Care in Black and White: Working Parents and the History of Orphanages
   Jessie B. Ramey
The Haymarket Conspiracy: Transatlantic Anarchist Networks   *Timothy Messer-Kruse*
Detroit's Cold War: The Origins of Postwar Conservatism   *Colleen Doody*
A Renegade Union: Interracial Organizing and Labor Radicalism   *Lisa Phillips*
Palomino: Clinton Jencks and Mexican-American Unionism
   in the American Southwest   *James J. Lorence*
Latin American Migrations to the U.S. Heartland: Changing Cultural Landscapes
   in Middle America   *Edited by Linda Allegro and Andrew Grant Wood*
Man of Fire: Selected Writings   *Ernesto Galarza, ed. Armando Ibarra and
   Rodolfo D. Torres*
A Contest of Ideas: Capital, Politics, and Labor   *Nelson Lichtenstein*
Making the World Safe for Workers: Labor, the Left, and Wilsonian Internationalism
   Elizabeth McKillen
The Rise of the Chicago Police Department: Class and Conflict, 1850–1894
   Sam Mitrani

Workers in Hard Times: A Long View of Economic Crises   *Edited by Leon Fink, Joseph A. McCartin, and Joan Sangster*

Redeeming Time: Protestantism and Chicago's Eight-Hour Movement, 1866–1912   *William A. Mirola*

Struggle for the Soul of the Postwar South: White Evangelical Protestants and Operation Dixie   *Elizabeth Fones-Wolf and Ken Fones-Wolf*

Free Labor: The Civil War and the Making of an American Working Class   *Mark A. Lause*

Death and Dying in the Working Class, 1865–1920   *Michael K. Rosenow*

Immigrants against the State: Yiddish and Italian Anarchism in America   *Kenyon Zimmer*

Fighting for Total Person Unionism: Harold Gibbons, Ernest Calloway, and Working-Class Citizenship   *Robert Bussel*

The University of Illinois Press
is a founding member of the
Association of American University Presses.

University of Illinois Press
1325 South Oak Street
Champaign, IL 61820-6903
www.press.uillinois.edu